A Billion Dollars a Day

A Billion Dollars a Day

The Economics and Politics of
Agricultural Subsidies

E. Wesley F. Peterson

WILEY-BLACKWELL

A John Wiley & Sons, Ltd., Publication

This edition first published 2009
© 2009 by E. Wesley F. Peterson

Blackwell Publishing was acquired by John Wiley & Sons in February 2007. Blackwell's publishing program has been merged with Wiley's global Scientific, Technical, and Medical business to form Wiley-Blackwell.

Registered Office
John Wiley & Sons Ltd, The Atrium, Southern Gate, Chichester, West Sussex, PO19 8SQ, United Kingdom

Editorial Offices
350 Main Street, Malden, MA 02148-5020, USA
9600 Garsington Road, Oxford, OX4 2DQ, UK
The Atrium, Southern Gate, Chichester, West Sussex, PO19 8SQ, UK

For details of our global editorial offices, for customer services, and for information about how to apply for permission to reuse the copyright material in this book please see our website at www.wiley.com/wiley-blackwell.

The right of E. Wesley F. Peterson to be identified as the author of this work has been asserted in accordance with the Copyright, Designs and Patents Act 1988.

Library of Congress Cataloging-in-Publication Data is available for this title

9781405185875 [hbk] / 9781405185868 [pbk]

A catalogue record for this book is available from the British Library.

Set in 10.5/12.5pt Times by SPi Publisher Services, Pondicherry, India
Printed in Singapore by Ho Printing Singapore Pte Ltd

001   2009

Contents

Preface

Food and agricultural policies have been much in the news of late. In 2008, the United States adopted controversial new farm legislation when Congress overrode a presidential veto. Global trade talks at the World Trade Organization (WTO) broke down in July 2008 after seven years of intense negotiation largely as a result of conflicts between two newly assertive developing countries (India and China) and the United States over agricultural trade policies. Rising food prices and worries about food safety generated much controversy and even led to riots and demonstrations in Haiti, Korea, Argentina and elsewhere, and popular books criticizing food systems in the United States and Europe have made the best-seller lists. The public policies that have helped to shape world and national food markets seem to be under attack from all sides even though it does not appear that there is much agreement on just what, if anything, needs to be done about them. The purpose of this book is to examine the main issues related to food and agricultural policies around the world. In particular, I attempt to shed light on a question that has become quite prominent over the past several years, namely, how food and agricultural policies in the high-income countries of North America, Europe, and the Pacific Rim affect the well-being of farmers and others living in developing countries.

To explore this and related issues, the book includes background information on the world food system and global institutions and in-depth examinations of the food and agricultural policies found in different countries. The first four chapters develop the foundation for understanding the world food system and the place in this system of international trade and national agricultural policies. The fifth chapter analyzes the food and farm policies of high-income countries belonging to the Organization for Economic Cooperation and Development (OECD) including detailed descriptions of government policy interventions and a preliminary assessment of the effects of these policies on world food markets and prices. The next four chapters focus on the origins, history, and effects of farm policies in the United States, the European Union, the Pacific Rim countries of Japan, Korea, Australia and New Zealand, and developing countries. The final chapter is a conclusion that ties together the themes developed throughout the book and assesses the implications of the analysis for the world food system.

This book is aimed at a broad audience of students, social scientists, and others interested in public policies, trade, development and agriculture. Although the reasoning and argumentation are clearly based on economic principles, I have tried to keep the discussion somewhat non-technical and accessible to readers without extensive training in economics. There are no graphs or mathematical equations and much of the theoretical background has been placed in footnotes or appendices that can generally be skimmed over lightly without losing the continuity of the arguments being made. While some of the topics addressed are unavoidably complex, I am confident that interested readers will be able to find their way through these more complicated matters regardless of their background in economic theory and principles. Because the book targets a broad global audience, I have generally chosen to use metric measurements such as hectares and metric tons although in some cases both metric and English measures are reported. I have also tried to use the more common international terms for crops such as maize (corn in the United States) or groundnuts (peanuts) and many of the statistics on agricultural spending are reported in national currencies, usually with dollar and euro exchange rates.

In writing this book, I have benefitted enormously from the sensible suggestions and comments of my friends and colleagues who have been extremely generous in helping me to sort through the various issues addressed. The following reviewers also offered useful suggestions as well as information that I had overlooked and corrections of some important details:

Jean-Paul Chavas, University of Wisconsin
Esendugue Greg Fonsah, University of Georgia
Johanna Gibson, Queen Mary University of London
Sam Goff, Texas A&M University
Michael Hammig, Professor Emeritus, Clemson University
P. Lynn Kennedy, Louisiana State University
Conrad Lyford, Texas Tech University
Robin F. Neill, Professor Emeritus, Carleton University
Jay E. Noel, California Polytechnic State University
Glenn Pederson, University of Minnesota
Rick Whitacre, Illinois State University

I have presented the main arguments in this book to university students and numerous groups in Nebraska and the reactions of these individuals have been invaluable in my effort to craft a work that translates a set of complex issues into language that can be followed by students and non-specialists. The editorial staff at Wiley-Blackwell has provided full support and excellent guidance in bringing this project to term. To all of those who have so kindly helped me in the writing of this book, I would like to express my thanks and profound appreciation. Of course, any errors or deficiencies that may remain are mine alone.

List of Abbreviations

AA	World Trade Organization Agreement on Agriculture
AAA	Agricultural Adjustment Act
ACP	African, Caribbean and Pacific Countries
AMS	Aggregate Measure of Support
ARS	Agricultural Research Service (USDA)
AWB	Australian Wheat Board
BRIC	Brazil, Russia, India and China
BSE	Bovine Spongiform Encephalopathy (mad cow disease)
CAFTA-DR	Central American Free Trade Agreement-Dominican Republic
CAP	Common Agricultural Policy
CDC	Centers for Disease Control
CGIAR	Consultative Group on International Agricultural Research
CIF	Cartage, Insurance, Freight
CIMMYT	Centro Internacional de Mejoramiento de Maíz y Trigo (International Maize and Wheat Improvement Center)
CIS	Commonwealth of Independent States (former Soviet Union)
CRP	Conservation Reserve Program
CSE	Consumer Support Estimate
DSB	Dispute Settlement Body (World Trade Organization)
EAGGF	European Agricultural Guidance and Guarantee Fund
EC	European Communities
ECLA	Economic Commission for Latin America (United Nations)
ECU	European Currency Unit
EEC	European Economic Community
EEP	Export Enhancement Program
ERS	Economic Research Service (USDA)

EU	European Union
EWG	Environmental Working Group
FAO	Food and Agriculture Organization (UN)
FAPRI	Food and Agricultural Policy Research Institute
FNS	Food and Nutrition Service
FOB	Free on Board
FTA	Free Trade Agreement
GAO	Government Accountability Office
GATT	General Agreement on Tariffs and Trade
GM	Genetically Modified
GMO	Genetically Modified Organism
GNI	Gross National Income
GSP	Generalized System of Preferences
GSSE	General Services Support Estimate
IBRD	International Bank for Reconstruction and Development (World Bank)
IFPRI	International Food Policy Research Institute
IMF	International Monetary Fund
IRRI	International Rice Research Institute
ITO	International Trade Organization
MERCOSUR/ MERCOSUL	Southern Cone Common Market (-SUL in Brazil, -SUR in other members)
MCA	Monetary Compensatory Amounts (European Union)
MMPA	Marine Mammal Protection Act
NAFTA	North American Free Trade Agreement
NGO	Non-government Organization
NTB	Non-tariff Trade Barrier
ODA	Official Development Assistance
OECD	Organization for Economic Cooperation and Development
OPEC	Organization of Petroleum Exporting Countries
PSE	Producer Support Estimate
RAN	Rainforest Action Network
SAP	Structural Adjustment Programs
SDR	Special Drawing Rights
SFP	Single Farm Payment
SPS	World Trade Organization Sanitary and Phytosanitary Agreement
TFP	Total Factor Productivity
TPA	Trade Promotion Authority
TRIM	Trade-Related Investment Measure
TRIP	Trade-Related Intellectual Property

TRQ	Tariff Rate Quota
TSE	Total Support Estimate
UN	United Nations
UNCTAD	United Nations Conference on Trade and Development
UNDP	United Nations Development Program
UR	Uruguay Round
USDA	United States Department of Agriculture
VER	Voluntary Export Restraint
vCJD	Variant Creutfeldt–Jakob Disease
WTO	World Trade Organization

Prologue

In 1996, delegates from 180 countries met at the headquarters of the United Nations' Food and Agriculture Organization (FAO) in Rome, Italy to develop a plan for cutting the incidence of hunger in half by 2015, an objective that has since become part of the United Nations' Millennium Development Goals. A bit more than five years later a follow-up meeting was held to review the progress that had been made since the first World Food Summit. Several delegates at that meeting observed that wealthy countries were spending a billion dollars a day to subsidize their farmers who then produced surpluses that were dumped on the world market depressing prices for poor farmers in developing countries (FAO, 2002). The argument that agricultural subsidies in high-income countries contribute to poverty in developing countries where the majority of the population depends on agriculture for its livelihood has since become an article of faith among many advocates for global social and economic justice (see, for example: Oxfam International, 2006; Carter, 2007; *New Statesman*, June 20, 2005). The editors of several prominent news organizations also seem to have been persuaded by this argument (see, for example: Godoy, 2008; Thakurta, 2006; *New York Times*, April 28, 2004, July 6, 2008; *Washington Post*, June 24, 2007).[1]

Some of the writers claiming that the wealthy countries spend a billion dollars a day on agricultural subsidies pointed to the OECD as the source of the

---

[1] According to its website (http://www.newstatesman.com/nsabout.htm), the *New Statesman* is a publishing organization that aims to spread socialist ideas among the "educated and influential classes." The Inter Press Service is a news agency that "raises the voices of the South and civil society" (http://www.ips.org/institutional). Oxfam International is a charitable organization based in the United Kingdom and works on development in low-income countries. Former U.S. President Jimmy Carter directs the Carter Center and received the Nobel Peace prize in 2002.

monetary figure being used. The OECD is an international organization that coordinates discussions among 30 high-income countries located in Europe, North America, and the Pacific Rim on a variety of topics including both agriculture and development. OECD staff members collect, interpret, and present data on agricultural policy in the member countries in an annual report entitled *Producer and Consumer Support Estimates*. The statistical information in this report is available in an online database and includes measures of a wide variety of government support programs related to food and agriculture (OECD, 2008c). The summary statistic in these reports is the "total support estimate" which is made up of direct support for agricultural producers, more general support for the agricultural sector such as research or infrastructure development, and consumer support such as the U.S. food stamp program. From 2000 to 2002, the aggregate total support estimate for all 30 OECD countries averaged about $313 billion a year and has been close to or exceeded $365 billion (a billion dollars a day) several times. The preliminary estimate for 2007 was precisely $365 billion down from a high of $381 billion in 2004 (OECD, 2008c).

Most popular critics of agricultural subsidies do not go into great detail on the particular types of government intervention that are of concern. My background as an agricultural economist gives me reasons to be receptive to the argument that farm subsidies in high-income countries distort prices and reduce global well-being. Economists and agricultural economists have conducted many studies of agricultural policies finding almost without exception that the overall impacts of these policies are just about as bad as suggested by the critics. When I teach courses on international trade, I spend a fair amount of time demonstrating that trade barriers lower world welfare and generally reduce national income in both importing and exporting countries. But are the classic barriers to trade such as tariffs on agricultural imports considered to be farm subsidies? What about other forms of agricultural support such as direct government payments to farmers or government-funded agricultural research? What exactly are these farm subsidies that are supposed to be having such dramatic negative impacts on developing countries? It turns out that the OECD database includes a wealth of detail on agricultural policies making it an invaluable resource for identifying and defining the various types of intervention in food and agricultural markets practiced by national governments. One of the purposes of this book is to use the information in the OECD database to clarify the nature of these policy interventions.

But there are broader questions about agricultural subsidies that are also of great interest. Do the farm subsidies, whatever they are, really harm farmers in developing countries? Could they also harm particular groups of farmers in high-income countries as well? What about consumers in both high- and low-income countries? Are there justifications for these policies in relation to the world's needs for food or as ways to preserve family farms? Is a billion dollars a day a lot of money in a world economy approaching $55 trillion? Who would benefit if the farm subsidies were eliminated and who would be harmed? How big are the actual benefits and costs of these policies? If the policies are costly and harmful, why do the governments of high-income countries seem incapable of getting rid of them? Do all OECD countries subsidize their farmers? Are there any harmful policies in developing countries themselves or are the detrimental policies all found in high-income countries? What exactly would a set of beneficial public policies related to food and agriculture look like? These are the kinds of questions I have set out to address in this book.

When I began this project, there was little on the horizon to foreshadow the storm that would hit world commodity markets in late 2007 and 2008. Between 2005 and mid-2008, world food prices increased 80 percent in terms of U.S. dollars, according to the International Monetary Fund (IMF) food price index (IMF, 2008). Measured in terms of Special Drawing Rights (SDR),[2] the increase was almost 65 percent, a reflection of the relative weakness of the U.S. dollar at that time. Increases in the prices of food and other commodities provoked much comment and led to demonstrations and riots in several countries. A 2008 World Food Program (WFP) report noted that higher food prices threatened the long-term goal of international food security and had already led to reductions in the availability of food for use in the organization's programs (WFP, 2008b). In 2008, the FAO launched an "Initiative on Soaring Food Prices" to assist food-insecure countries in dealing with the food crisis (FAO, 2008b). Although these food price increases were impressive, they were not without precedent. In fact, world food prices increased about 141 percent over a similar four-year period from 1971 to 1974 and then continued to rise more gradually until 1980 when they began to fall as farm output increased in response to the favorable prices (IMF, 1996).

The main motivation for writing this book is to work out the implications of farm policies in high-income countries, including their price-depressing effects, for world agricultural markets. It may seem odd to worry about this topic at a time when food and other commodity prices have risen dramatically. Past episodes of rising food prices, however, have usually stimulated greater output with the result that prices eventually return to more normal levels. This

---

[2] SDRs, sometimes referred to as "paper gold," are a special reserve asset created by the IMF in 1969 as a supplement to gold and the major reserve currencies used to settle international transactions. The value of the SDR is based on the values of the U.S. dollar, the euro, the Japanese yen, and the British pound sterling (see the glossary at www.imf.org).

is precisely what happened following the commodity price booms of the 1970s and 1990s.[3] There is no guarantee, of course, that events will follow the historic pattern this time around. An editorial in *The Economist* (December 8, 2007) claimed that the world has reached the end of the era of cheap food. But if this claim is incorrect, as I suspect it is, surpluses in the high-income countries will eventually reappear and the problem of price-depressing agricultural subsidies will be as salient as ever. In fact, after peaking in June 2008, food prices fell about 27 percent on the IMF food price index by October and the decline appeared set to continue as the year ended. Falling commodity prices in the second half of 2008 were caused by declines in demand as a result of the worldwide financial crisis and recession rather than by increased farm output. As a result, economic recovery may well lead to rising demand in coming years that could set off a new round of food price increases. But even if food prices eventually start to rise again, there are good reasons to question the need for and benefits of the agricultural subsidies currently employed by governments in high-income countries. In particular, the distorted prices resulting from these policies disguise true market conditions and lead to costly inefficiencies.

Moreover, the effects of past agricultural policies in both high- and low-income countries are relevant to an understanding of the root causes of the 2007–8 food price increases. These policies have resulted in lower producer prices in developing countries, reducing the returns to agricultural innovation and contributing to increased poverty among the millions of poor farmers in low-income countries. Because the policies slow agricultural development, low-income countries become more dependent on food imports and more vulnerable to economic disruption when food prices rise. The implications of these policies for economic growth and development are an important issue in debates about agricultural trade and national food and agricultural policies whether prices decline in the future or not.

Still, it may be useful to comment on the causes of the 2007–8 food price increases as they relate to the agricultural policies that are the primary focus of this book. The most common explanations for these events drew attention to both supply shortfalls and demand increases. On the supply side, bad weather in some of the major agricultural exporting countries such as Australia

---

[3]   The substantial commodity price increases between 1970 and 1974 gave rise to increased agricultural production which eventually led to price declines. In 1986, food prices were 32 percent lower than the level reached in 1974. Between 1986 and 1996, the food price index rose by about 50 percent setting off another round of increased production followed by the inevitable fall in prices. By 1999, the food price index had declined about 29 percent relative to 1995.

and Thailand may have reduced the amounts of food available (FAO, 2008d). In addition, rising petroleum prices increased the cost of transporting food and this added cost was passed along to consumers. Much of the fertilizer used around the world is derived from petroleum and as petroleum prices rose the cost of fertilizer increased, less was used and growth in crop yields may have faltered. Because petroleum and its derivatives are important inputs for agricultural production, increases in their prices are factored into the cost of food production and these rising costs eventually lead to higher food prices. Note also that when the prices of one commodity increase, farmers devote more land to its production and less to alternative crops. This shift in land use results in lowered supplies of the other crops and increases in their prices. Competition among alternative crops for land and other resources is one reason why agricultural commodity prices all tend to rise at the same time. Rising agricultural prices also lead to increases in land values. Johnson (2008) reported that farmland values in Nebraska (USA) rose 23 percent over the 12-month period ending in March 2008, the largest one-year increase ever recorded.

On the demand side, many pointed to the impressive income growth in several Asian countries, notably China, India, Malaysia, and Indonesia. As incomes grow, people may not consume a great deal more food but they are likely to change the kinds of food they purchase. For example, consumption of livestock products usually increases as incomes grow and the production of more livestock products requires grain and other feedstuffs that, if consumed directly, would feed a lot more human beings than they do when processed through animals. The idea that increased demand in developing countries caused the run-up in food prices was criticized by many in India who felt that their prosperity was being blamed for high food prices when, in fact, they suggested, price increases were more closely related to over-consumption and waste in the United States and other Western countries (Timmons, 2008). It should also be noted that China and India had experienced strong economic growth for many years suggesting that other factors may have been behind the relatively sudden increase in food prices. On the other hand, the FAO (2008d) pointed out that in previous years, some of the increased consumption had been covered by drawing on grain stocks. By 2008, however, these stocks were much lower than normal so they could not be relied upon to augment market supplies. As a result, the full effects of growing consumption in Asia were reflected in the prices.

Another source of increased demand was the greater use of agricultural products such as maize, sugar cane, and palm oil in the production of biofuels. According to World Bank analysts, world maize production increased by 51 million metric tons between 2004 and 2007 while the use of maize in ethanol production in the United States rose 50 million metric tons. There was an additional increase over the same period in consumption of maize for other purposes of about 33 million metric tons that was covered by a draw-down of global maize stocks of some 30 million metric tons (World Bank, 2008d). Martin (2008) reports estimates suggesting that growing biofuel production was responsible for between 10 and 30 percent of the increase in commodity prices. Perrin (2008) found that ethanol production may have accounted for 30 to 40 percent of the increase in grain prices between January 2006 and December 2007. Because grain makes up a relatively small part of total food consumption in high-income countries, the impact of maize ethanol on their food prices was somewhat limited. On the other hand, in low-income countries where grains and oilseeds are major sources of calories, the diversion of agricultural commodities from the food chain to the biofuels industries may have had much more serious consequences for food prices (Perrin, 2008).

It is worth pointing out that biofuel production depends on government support which should also be thought of as a kind of farm subsidy. Steenblik (2007) estimated that subsidies for biofuels in Australia, Canada, the EU, Switzerland, and the United States amounted to $11 billion in 2006. Historically, ethanol and biodiesel would not have been used for fuel without the subsidies although increased petroleum prices and technological advances in biofuel production may make these alternative fuels somewhat more viable. Even with high petroleum prices, there may still be problems with ethanol made from maize. A recent study at MIT found that it takes about as much energy to produce a liter of maize ethanol as is obtained from burning it, although other types of biofuel may make more sense (Stauffer, 2007). Other sources indicate that the energy balance (amount of energy provided by a fuel relative to the amount needed to produce it) is 1.5 for maize ethanol produced in the United States compared to 8.2 for ethanol made from sugar cane in Brazil (Preto, 2008). Some of the countries with generous biofuel subsidies have begun to reconsider the advisability of these policies in light of food price increases and the environmental impact of expanded production of biofuel feed stocks (Rosenthal, 2008). The use of palm oil for biodiesel production in Europe has grown substantially leading to forest clearing and habitat destruction in Malaysia and Indonesia in order to plant more oil palms (Koh and Wilcove, 2008).

Other reasons advanced to explain the food price increases include speculation by traders on commodity markets. This explanation almost certainly gets the causation backwards by suggesting that events on financial markets can give rise to actual shortages of real goods. After all, commodity futures traders trade pieces of paper representing bushels of wheat not actual bushels of wheat. Food price increases were also attributed to the falling value of the U.S. dollar. The weak dollar would add to the food price inflation within the

United States and any countries that peg their currencies to the U.S. dollar but would not really explain the general increase in commodity prices as measured, for example, in SDRs or other national currencies. A final explanation points to the reaction of the governments in several important agricultural exporters to the initial rise in food prices. In an effort to mitigate domestic price increases, many of these countries began to restrict exports and these restrictions further reduced world supplies adding to the upward pressure on world food prices. Bradsher and Martin (2008) reported that 29 food-exporting countries introduced limits or bans on exports in 2008.

It will probably be some time before economists will be able to accurately assess the relative importance of all these various explanations for the 2007–8 food price increases. But the agricultural subsidies that are the subject of this book have clearly played a role in these events. In the past, many developing countries implemented policies aimed at keeping food prices low as a way to avoid consumer unrest in urban areas. Such policies have often been bolstered by the provision of low-cost food from high-income countries either through subsidies that lead to increased agricultural output subsequently diverted to world markets or, more directly, through food aid. While low food prices may have benefitted urban consumers, they undermined efforts to modernize traditional agricultural sectors in developing countries. Some of the cheap-food policies in developing countries were modified as part of the structural adjustment programs introduced in the 1980s in response to debt and other financial problems. These policy reforms would have done more for growth and development in low-income countries, however, if they had been complemented by other policies targeting the creation of market institutions and infrastructure as well as development of the large agricultural sectors in these countries. Paarlberg (2008) notes that after 1980, the United States reduced the share of its relatively modest foreign aid budget devoted to agricultural development from 25 percent to only 1 percent in 2007 while the share of World Bank lending that was devoted to agriculture fell from 30 percent to 8 percent. Funding for international agricultural research has also declined over the last three decades.

The preceding discussion will be viewed by some as seriously off the mark. Zepp-LaRouche (2008), for example, argues that pretty much all the ills of the world, including rising food prices, have been caused by "… the obvious bankruptcy of murderous free trade." It has been argued that structural adjustment programs with their emphasis on trade liberalization, currency devaluation, and other macroeconomic policy reforms have destroyed vibrant agricultural systems in low-income countries that have now become dependent on cheap food provided by subsidized farmers in high-income countries. These perspectives cannot be dismissed out of hand but most of the discussion in this book will be based on an alternative vision of how the world economic system works, a vision grounded in contemporary theoretical and empirical economic analysis. Economists and other social scientists have produced an extensive literature related to the issues addressed in this book and I will draw on that body of work to examine the questions raised earlier. No original empirical analysis has been done but I have made extensive use of the abundant analytical results from the modeling work of others to shed light on the effects of the various policies investigated. I have also relied on economic data published by governments and international organizations to provide both historical background and quantitative assessments of the policies implemented by OECD and developing countries.

The data that will be used most extensively to describe agricultural policies are those reported by the OECD in the producer and consumer support estimates. In July 2008, that data set was updated to include preliminary results for 2007 as well as some adjustments in the data recorded for earlier years. I have chosen to use the preliminary 2007 data in many of the descriptive tables even though it is possible that these preliminary estimates will later be modified. For the most part, the final data will probably not differ significantly from the early estimates. I have endeavored throughout to present the most recent statistical evidence available. It is unfortunately true, however, that data only become available after the fact and their shelf-life is not very long. As a result, some of the numbers reported in the tables may seem a little out of date. In many cases, this will not matter much. For example, statistical data are used to describe food production and consumption in various regions of the world in Chapter 3. The production and consumption patterns shown in the statistical tables may change gradually over time but the overall image presented in the tables is unlikely to be altered substantially over the next several years. In other cases, data that will be published in the future may confirm or disconfirm some of the conjectures I make in the book. The European Union adopted a new policy orientation in 2003 that could result in a very different picture of farm support in that region. Preliminary indications of that new direction are visible in the 2007 data but it is too soon to tell if the new policy orientation will be sustained. I have tried to indicate throughout the text where special considerations related to the data should be kept in mind in interpreting the information presented. In Chapter 1, we begin with a detailed examination of the particular issues that are the focus of the book.

1

Introduction: The Problem of Agricultural Subsidies

Benin

In February of 1968, along with about 25 other young Americans, I arrived in Cotonou, Dahomey, a West African country that subsequently changed its name to Benin. We were there to begin our tours of duty as Peace Corps Volunteers working on various agricultural, educational, and public health programs. I was assigned to the village of Golo Djigbe in the southern part of the country where I worked on a project to introduce low-cost grain storage systems. Maize is the staple crop along much of the West African coast where there is abundant rainfall distributed over two separate seasons so that farmers are able to grow two crops a year. Maize is often grown in conjunction with another staple food, cassava (a starchy tuber also known as manioc, tapioca or, in Latin America, yucca). Farmers typically practice slash-and-burn agriculture which involves cultivation of the same plots for several years without extensive use of fertilizer. When the soil nutrients are exhausted on a particular plot, it is abandoned to natural fallow, a new plot is cleared and the vegetation is burned off. It can take as long as 10 or more years before the soil in the original plot is naturally rejuvenated so that the field can be brought back into cultivation. Most of the food produced is consumed by members of the household itself rather than sold on the market. Because of the humid climate, farmers lose substantial amounts of maize to moisture damage and insects during storage and it was that problem that I and some of my Peace Corps colleagues spent the next several years trying to solve.

Other volunteers were assigned to different projects in the drier regions of Benin where crops such as sorghum, millet, and peanuts were more common than maize. In many of these regions, cotton was becoming an important cash crop. Data on Benin's average annual exports are shown in Table 1.1 for the periods 1968–70 and 2002–4. During the earlier period, palm oil and other

Table 1.1   Average annual merchandise exports from Benin, 1968–70 and 2002–4 (millions of current US dollars and percentages)

	Total exports, 1968–70 in million $	% total exports, 1968–70	% agricultural exports 1968–70	Total exports, 2002–4 in million $	% total exports, 2002–4	% agricultural exports 2002–4
Total merchandise exports	54.8	100.0	–	514.0	100.0	–
Total agricultural exports	22.9	41.8	100.0	223.3	43.4	100.0
Palm and palm kernel products	11.1	20.3	48.5	15.4	3.0	6.7
Cotton and cotton products	4.1	7.5	18.0	166.8	32.5	74.7
Cashew nuts	–	–	–	21.4	4.1	9.6
Karite (sheanuts)	0.7	1.2	2.8	3.5	0.7	1.6
Peanut products	1.0	1.9	4.5	–	–	–

Sources: Food and Agriculture Organization (FAO) at www.faostat.fao.org (FAOSTAT, statistical databases); World Bank (*World Tables*, 1989–90 Edition, Johns Hopkins University Press, Baltimore, 1990); World Trade Organization (WTO, 2007) at www.wto.org; and author's calculations.

products from the oil palm constituted the main export crops. Oil palms are grown in the more humid regions of West Africa where they are a source of products that can be sold for cash and exported as well as used domestically. Palm oil is the basis for the local cuisine in much of southern Benin. Oil palms produce large bunches of small, hard kernels that are like miniature coconuts encased in an oily pulp. The pulp can be pressed for oil (palm oil) as can the kernels (palm kernel oil). Palm oil and palm kernel oil are saturated which limited their use in processed foods until recently when food manufacturers recognized that palm oil could be a relatively healthy alternative to ingredients containing trans fats (partially hydrogenated vegetable oils, for example). Palm kernel oil is used mainly to manufacture soap. In fact, Palmolive soap took its name from the fact that it was originally made from palm and olive oils (About Business and Finance, http://inventors.about.com/library/inventors/blsoap.htm). In recent years, demand for palm oil has increased both as a replacement for trans fats in processed foods and as a source of oil for biodiesel fuel (Bradsher, 2008). In its unrefined form, palm oil is fairly nutritious containing beta-carotene and vitamin E. The sap from oil palms can be tapped and fermented to make palm wine which is drunk directly or distilled to make stronger alcoholic beverages. The Nigerian writer Amos Tutuola tells a fantastic story involving palm wine in his extraordinary novel, *The Palm-Wine Drinkard and his Dead Palm-Wine Tapster in the Dead's Town.*[1]

Over the last three decades, oil palm products have been replaced by cotton as Benin's major export crop as shown in Table 1.1. It appears that cotton currently accounts for about a third of Benin's exports, although other sources suggest the proportion is somewhat higher. According to the World Trade Organization (WTO, 1998), 36 percent of Benin's exports in 1996 were re-exports, that is goods destined for other countries that transited through the major port in Cotonou. Using the WTO data for 1996, cotton lint and seed accounted for almost 85 percent of exports of goods produced within Benin and 54 percent of all exports, including re-exports. Any of these estimates of the importance of cotton exports supports the conclusion that cotton has become a key element in Benin's economy. It turns out that similar changes have occurred in other African countries, including Chad, Burkina Faso, and Mali. In 2003, the government of Benin teamed up with the governments of these three countries to submit a proposal for a special initiative on cotton to the Director-General of the WTO (WTO, 2008b). The four African countries pointed to the harm to their cotton industries they believe has been caused by cotton subsidies in the United States and Europe and called for elimination of these subsidies.

The cultivation of cotton in West Africa has a relatively long history. Bassett traces the development of cotton in the region of Korogho in northern Côte d'Ivoire noting that there were thriving indigenous industries devoted to growing and weaving cotton prior to the arrival of French colonialists. According to Bassett (2001), local traders competed vigorously with French colonial officials for the raw cotton destined for both local and European textile industries. Following the Second World War, a French company, the Compagnie française pour le développement des fibres textiles (CFDT), jointly owned by the French government and private French commercial

---

[1] The central figure in the novel is a young aristocrat who spends his time drinking palm wine brought to him by a servant hired by his father for the specific task of tapping the oil palms and keeping his master constantly supplied with palm wine. One day, the tapster falls from the tree and dies. The young man then sets off to the land of the dead to find his tapster and bring him back to continue supplying him his palm wine. The main part of the story concerns the adventures the young man has in the land of the dead including encounters with all kinds of ghosts and incredible creatures.

interests, began actively promoting new cotton varieties and cultivation techniques in Africa (Bassett, p. 176).[2] With the help of the colonial governments in French West Africa and French Equatorial Africa, the CFDT was able to establish vertically integrated monopolies that controlled the supply and distribution of seed and other inputs, the ginning (separating the cotton fibers from the seeds) and commercialization of harvested cotton, and research on new varieties and technologies in most of the French colonies in Africa (Bassett, p. 176).

In 1958, French President Charles de Gaulle organized a referendum in France's African colonies on the question of independence. The French government was proposing that the colonies maintain an association with France until 1960 when they would be granted full independence. Guinea was the only colony to vote for immediate independence, angering the French who withdrew support for the newly independent country (World Bank, 2008a). Benin, along with seven other former French colonies in West Africa, duly achieved independence in 1960. As was the case in several of the new countries, a state-owned cotton monopoly was eventually established in Benin. The Société nationale pour la promotion agricole (SONAPRA) maintained the vertically integrated structure that had been developed by the CFDT prior to independence. On some accounts, the national cotton monopolies were often quite effective at expanding production and this was certainly the case in Benin where cotton production has increased from an average of 3,400 metric tons per year in the 1960s to more than 150,000 metric tons per year since 2000 (World Bank, 2002 and FAOSTAT).

The first decade of Benin's independence was characterized by extreme political instability:

> During the nine years between 1963 and 1972 there were six military coups d'état in Dahomey. Prior to this, during the six years between 1957 and 1963, there had been nine different civilian governments, each the result of civilian seizure of power in the form of elections or coalitions (Ronen, 1975, p. 187).

One reason for this political turmoil was the fact that the Beninese had shown themselves to be particularly adept at colonial administration and had been posted by the French colonial authorities throughout West Africa. With

---

[2] In 2001, the CFDT was renamed DAGRIS (Développement des Agro-industries du Sud). The French government no longer participates in the company which continues to trade cotton and oilseeds. See http://www.dagris.fr/ http://r0.unctad.org/infocomm/anglais/cotton/companies. htm.

independence, the Beninese bureaucrats were replaced by citizens of the new countries and forced to return to Benin which wound up with large numbers of unemployed civil servants. Another reason was the significant regional and ethnic division in this small country. Benin has a surface area about the same as that of Pennsylvania but with more than 20 ethnic groups speaking different, although sometimes related, languages (Ronen, p. 5). Substantial linguistic and cultural differences prevailed between the northern and southern parts of the country and there were historic inter-ethnic animosities due to centuries of war and the participation of certain ethnic groups in the European slave trade.[3] Citizens of the new country had little reason to view themselves as participants in a common national project.

At independence, three aspirants to national leadership had emerged each with a base in a particular region of the country. Hubert Maga from the north, Sourou Migan Apithy from the area around the capital of Porto Novo in Southeastern Benin, and Justin Ahomadegbe from the dominant southern ethnic group, the Fon, each took a turn as president of the country in the aftermath of successive coups, finally joining together in a Presidential Council in 1970.[4] This arrangement, which specified that each would serve successive two-year terms as head of the Council, lasted through the first rotation when Ahomadegbe succeeded Maga as Council head in May 1972 (Ronen). Shortly thereafter, a new political figure, army Major Mathieu Kérékou, emerged to stage another coup d'état and put an end to the political instability that had come to characterize the country. Kérékou was to remain in power for the next 17 years, a truly remarkable accomplishment in a country that had previously changed governments almost every other year.

In 1974, Kérékou ushered in a shift in economic policy and, in 1975, a change in the country's name to the République Populaire du Bénin or People's Republic of Benin (Westebbe, 1994, p. 82). The Marxist–Leninist policy orientation initiated at this time meant state control of most economic activity including state-owned sugar and cement complexes, public monopolies for export products, and state farms (Westebbe, p. 82). It also meant the termination of the Peace Corps' grain storage program on which I had worked in line with a common worry in socialist states about hoarding in the countryside. Socialist

---

[3]   The southern coast of West Africa was traditionally divided into sections corresponding to major commodity exports—ivory, gold, and slaves—along the different parts of the coast. Today, the country of Côte d'Ivoire (Ivory Coast) retains one of these names while the British colony known as the Gold Coast is part of the nation of Ghana. Because of the large number of slaves taken from Togo and Benin, that stretch of coastline was known as the slave coast.

[4]   In addition to several interim governments led by military officers, another civilian leader, Emile Zinsou, held the presidency from 1968 to 1969 (Ronen, p. 249).

development strategies were quite common during the 1970s and 1980s throughout Africa, Asia, and Latin America. In addition to state-owned enterprises, such strategies usually included overvalued exchange rates, expansionary monetary policies, protectionist trade policies, and large government bureaucracies. These policies invariably led to debt problems and balance of payments crises. Since independence, Benin has been a member of the West African Economic and Monetary Union (UEMOA).[5] This monetary union has a common currency, the CFA franc,[6] backed by the French Treasury. As a result, Benin's currency was less overvalued and inflationary monetary policies were less prevalent than was the case in many other developing countries. In other respects, however, Benin's economic policies were fairly typical.

Benin is a poor country with per capita income of about $570 in 2007 (World Bank 2008b) and per capita income growth rates less than 1 percent per year prior to 1990 (UNDP, 2008). Its rank on the UNDP Human Development Index for 2007 was 163 out of 177 countries. Benin experienced fairly strong economic growth in the 1970s as a result of investment in new industries (sugar and cement), high commodity prices, foreign borrowing (the 1970s were characterized by very low real interest rates), and development of Benin's re-exportation activities (Westebbe, p. 84). The transit trade was encouraged by the petroleum boom in Nigeria and the discovery and commercialization of uranium in landlocked Niger to the north. Economic prosperity was short-lived, however, as international inflation rates subsided, commodity prices stagnated, and interest rates began to rise. As the economic crisis became more severe, the Kérékou government encountered increasing difficulty in paying its employees. In 1989, the government agreed to economic policy reforms in return for financial support from the World Bank and

---

[5] Originally, the Union monétaire ouest-africaine, UMOA, it became the Union économique et monétaire ouest-africaine, UEMOA, in 1994 (www.izf.net/IZF/FicheIdentite/UEMOA.htm).

[6] The initials "CFA" originally stood for Colonies françaises d'Afrique. Following independence, its meaning was changed to Communauté financière d'Afrique. From 1960 until 1994, the CFA franc had a fixed exchange rate with the French franc of 50 CFA francs equal to one French franc. In 1994, the CFA franc was devalued to 100 CFA francs equal to one French franc. In 1999, the euro was introduced as the common currency among some members of the European Union (EU). The French franc disappeared at that time but France and the EU continue to guarantee the CFA franc used in West Africa as well as the CFA franc in circulation in six Central African countries (Gabon, Equatorial Guinea, Central African Republic, Chad, Cameroon, and Republic of Congo). The CFA franc is now in a fixed parity with the euro based on the euro/French franc conversion rate at the time the euro was introduced. This works out as 665.957 CFA francs to the euro (http://www.un.org/ecosocdev/geninfo/afrec/ subjindx/ 124euro3.htm).

the International Monetary Fund (IMF). Westebbe argues that these reforms undermined the ability of politicians in Benin to enrich themselves at the expense of the general public leading to political reforms and democratic elections in 1991. In the 1991 elections, Kérékou was defeated by Nicephore Soglo but was returned to office in 1996 and again in 2001. Yayi Boni, was elected president in 2006 (Infoplease).

Western Agricultural Subsidies

At independence, most African states were led by nationalist politicians who had spent many years working for independence and were democratically elected. In some cases, the regimes became authoritarian and nepotism and corruption were common. Disillusion with the initial wave of democratically elected, civilian governments gave rise to military takeovers and by the 1970s many African states were headed by military dictators or one-party governments. Financial crises in the 1980s and the discrediting of socialist development models following the collapse of the Soviet Union led to widespread rejection of the authoritarian, one-party states and military dictatorships in Africa. Widner (1994) notes that about half the countries in sub-Saharan Africa moved toward multi-party democracies in the period 1989–92. Benin was one of the first sub-Saharan African countries to make this transition and has been one of the more successful of the new African democracies having held a series of free and fair elections that led to peaceful changes in the elected leaders. The government of Benin has abandoned its Marxist–Leninist approach to development, embracing democratic politics and free-market economics. Major reforms are underway in Benin's cotton sector focusing primarily on the transfer of SONAPRA's economic activities to firms in the private sector. In 1994, the CFA franc was devalued making cotton and other exports from countries in the UEMOA less expensive on the world market.

According to some observers, however, these progressive moves risk being undermined by the agricultural policies pursued in wealthy countries. Agricultural subsidies encourage production in the industrialized countries and this extra output is sold on world markets where it depresses the prices received by unsubsidized farmers in low-income countries. U.S. cotton subsidies reached $3 billion in 2001 and totaled more than $19 billion over the period 1995 to 2005 (Environmental Working Group). In 2002, Benin's gross domestic product (GDP) was $2.7 billion compared with $2.4 billion in U.S. cotton subsidies for that year. According to the Environmental Working Group (EWG), 85 percent of U.S. cotton subsidies are distributed among only 25,000 cotton farmers (see also Oxfam International, 2002). With annual U.S. subsidies averaging about $2.3 billion over the period 2000–4, this translates into an annual transfer on the order of $78,000 per cotton farmer. Compare this with per capita GDP in Benin of $400–$500 per year. According to a study by the IMF (2004), costs of producing cotton in Benin are lower than many other countries and only about half the cost of production in the United States. This suggests that without the subsidies, U.S. cotton exports would not be competitive with those of Benin and many other cotton producers.

In 2002, Brazil filed a dispute settlement case with the WTO, claiming that U.S. cotton subsidies violated U.S. commitments under the WTO Agreement on Agriculture. As noted earlier, Benin, Mali, Chad, and Burkina Faso successfully petitioned the WTO in 2003 for the creation of a cotton initiative with the goal of eliminating cotton subsidies in high-income countries. Several economic studies were done around this time in an effort to measure the precise impact of the subsidies being challenged by Brazil and the African countries. Sumner (2008a,b) estimated that world cotton prices over the period 1999–2002 would have been almost 13 percent higher if there had been no U.S. cotton subsidies.[7] He argued further that an increase in world prices of this magnitude would have a significant impact on poverty reduction and the economic well-being of cotton growers in low-income countries (see also Dugger, 2007). Several other studies came to similar conclusions (Gillson *et al.*, 2004; Baffes, 2005). On the other hand, Shepherd (2004) reports results of a statistical analysis that show limited effects of U.S. subsidies on world cotton prices. Another study found that the price increase following the elimination of U.S. subsidies would be substantially less than predicted by Sumner and the increase would be eroded fairly quickly as farmers expand production in response to the higher prices (Pan *et al.*, 2004).

Although there is disagreement about some of the details, most analysts appear to concur that cotton subsidies in the industrialized countries have depressed world prices at least to some extent. This is also the consensus of those publishing less formal analyses (Oxfam, 2002; FAO, 2004; de Rato, 2005). In addition, there is some evidence that lower world cotton prices have a negative impact on the economic well-being of rural people in low-income, cotton-exporting countries. Minot and Daniels (2002) use a farm-level survey to model the impact of a decline in cotton prices on rural poverty in Benin, finding that a 40 percent decline in cotton prices would lead to a fall in rural per capita income of 5–7 percent and a substantial increase in rural poverty.

---

[7]   Sumner conducted his analysis as background for Brazil's case before the WTO. One version of the analysis was submitted to the WTO dispute resolution panel for Brazil's cotton case as Annex I. Annex I and another unpublished version of the study are available at the internet addresses listed in the references.

Between 2000 and 2002, world cotton prices fell by more than 20 percent (IMF, 2008). The IMF (2004) study of Benin's cotton sector also concludes that elimination of cotton subsidies would make a significant contribution to poverty reduction and increased farm income. Boccanfuso and Savard (2007) found that the elimination of cotton subsidies would also reduce poverty significantly in Mali.

It is not just small African countries that may be harmed by agricultural subsidies. In the early 1990s, many countries in Latin America and Asia embraced globalization and free-market trade policies in the hope that these strategies would finally bring the economic prosperity that had so long eluded them. The newfound enthusiasm for trade and globalization in Latin America followed a long period during which Latin American countries had pioneered the kinds of socialist development strategies noted above, including protectionism, overvalued exchange rates, loose monetary policy, and government budget deficits. These policies combined with worldwide inflation, low interest rates, and other global developments in the 1970s and 1980s led to the severe Latin American debt crises of the 1980s. The international community agreed to reschedule or cancel much of that debt but demanded that extensive policy reform, referred to as structural adjustment programs (SAP), be undertaken to avoid a repeat of these problems. The SAP generally included currency devaluation, reductions in government spending, tight monetary policies, and trade liberalization. The rationale for these measures is often referred to as the "Washington consensus" because of the role in their implementation played by the World Bank and IMF, both located in Washington, DC. In the 1990s, Latin American governments began to take more active roles in carrying out the new policy orientation. Mexico joined the United States and Canada in the North American Free Trade Agreement (NAFTA) in 1994 and Argentina, Brazil, Paraguay, and Uruguay expanded their 1991 trade pact known as MERCOSUR (MERCOSUL in Brazil), the southern cone common market. Other Latin American countries entered into trade agreements and many of the former autocratic regimes were replaced with democratically elected governments.

Less than a decade later, the enthusiasm for globalization and free trade in Latin America evaporated as first Brazil and then Argentina began to experience financial strains and reduced standards of living (*The Economist*, May 20, 2006). Since 2000, several left-wing governments have taken power in Latin America and there appears to be widespread skepticism about the benefits of the Washington consensus, now frequently referred to as "neoliberalism," a term that is meant to be derogatory. Whether this skepticism is warranted or not will be hotly debated for many years to come. For many economists, the problems in Latin America and other developing countries do not stem from globalization as such but rather from poor policy decisions by governments in both the industrialized and developing countries as well as by the World Bank and the IMF. Joseph Stiglitz, one of the winners of the 2001 Nobel Prize in economics, has argued quite forcefully that unthinking application by the World Bank, IMF, and some Western governments of policies based on trade liberalization and fiscal and monetary austerity in countries that lack the legal institutions needed for markets to function effectively has caused untold damage to people in low-income countries (Stiglitz, 2003). The financial crisis in Argentina was exacerbated by decisions in the United States as well as some of the policies of the Argentine government itself. From this perspective, globalization is not the cause of economic stagnation in low-income countries and, in fact, can be a force for economic growth and development if managed appropriately. The problem is to discover how to avoid the policy mistakes that compromise the ability of all countries to take advantage of the beneficial aspects of globalization.

Agricultural subsidies in high-income countries are considered by many to be one of the worst of these policy errors reducing the benefits to low-income countries of actively participating in world trade. The editorial page of the *New York Times* has been quite outspoken on the immorality of farm subsidies in the United States, the European Union (EU), and other high-income countries.[8] Articles in the *Washington Post* have drawn attention to the cost of farm programs and a 2008 public television broadcast of Bill Moyers Journal focused on the impact of these programs on U.S. taxpayers and world hunger (Morgan, 1979; Bill Moyers Journal, 2008). The charitable development organization, Oxfam International, has also weighed in with extensive criticisms of U.S. and EU agricultural policies.[9] As noted in the Prologue to this volume, it was widely reported at the 2002 World Food Summit in Rome that the wealthy countries are spending a billion dollars a day to subsidize their farmers with disastrous effects on farmers in low-income countries.

These criticisms have not remained empty intellectual exercises. In September 2004, the WTO ruled in favor of Brazil's complaint about U.S. cotton subsidies. The United States modified some of the offending policies while it appealed the WTO decision. In June of 2008, the appeals process reached its conclusion with most of the original ruling upheld. This left the

---

[8]   See, for example, "The Hypocrisy of Farm Subsidies," December 1, 2002; "The Case Against King Cotton," December 7, 2003; "Those Illegal Farm Subsidies," April 28, 2004, or "Cow Politics," October 27, 2005; all from the editorial pages of the *New York Times*.

[9]   Among many others, see "The Great EU Sugar Scam," August 6, 2004; "Cultivating Poverty: The Impact of US Cotton Subsidies on Africa," September 25, 2002; "A Little Blue Lie: Harmful Subsidies Need to be Reduced not Redefined," July 21, 2005; all available at www.oxfam.org.

United States with a choice between modifying its cotton policies in a way that would satisfy Brazil or doing nothing which would mean that the WTO would give Brazil the green light to impose retaliatory trade barriers on U.S. products (WTO, 2008c). In August 2004, the WTO established a cotton sub-committee in response to the proposal by the four African countries, and the Doha Development Round of WTO trade negotiations that began in 2001 has included much discussion aimed at reducing agricultural subsidies and other barriers to trade in agricultural goods.

There has also been serious discussion in the high-income countries themselves about the desirability of costly subsidies that often seem to have more to do with pork-barrel politics than saving family farms. Some have suggested that the farm subsidies actually are of greater benefit to large agribusinesses than to U.S. or European farmers, although it is likely that some of these farmers would go out of business without the subsidies. In June 2007, the EWG published the names of all the recipients of U.S. government subsidy payments from 2003 to 2005 on its website. Many of the beneficiaries listed in the EWG database turned out to be wealthy individuals with fairly tenuous connections to farming (see Berga, 2007). The story about rich Americans who receive agricultural subsidies created something of a furor and was picked up by numerous media outlets across the country (EWG, 2007). The overall tone of this discussion was highly critical of U.S. farm programs.

Assessing the actual impact of agricultural subsidies in wealthy countries on the poor who live in low-income countries is not simple. As in the case of the impact of U.S. cotton subsidies on world cotton prices, analysts often come to different conclusions about the precise effect such subsidies have on world agricultural markets. In addition, even if one accepts that the additional output induced by the subsidies depresses world prices, such an outcome may not be detrimental to all people living in low-income countries. On average, Nigerians spend 75 percent of their income on food (ERS, 2008e). Low-income house-holds in Nigeria, a country that is a net importer of food, may actually benefit from the lower food prices caused by Western agricultural subsidies. Of course, one reason a country like Nigeria imports much of its food is that its govern-ment has traditionally pursued cheap food policies that result in low food prices. These low prices in turn discourage Nigerian farmers from adopting new technologies that would make the country's agricultural sector more productive and the country less dependent on imported food. Moreover, if the goal is to provide low-cost food to poor consumers in developing countries, direct cash transfers would be a more efficient way to achieve this result than to subsidize farmers in wealthy countries. Nevertheless, the fact that farm sub-sidies may give rise to positive effects that offset some of their negative consequences will need to be kept in mind in assessing these policies.

So far, I have not defined the subsidies that have been the object of so much criticism. As will become evident when we examine the OECD data on agricultural subsidies in greater detail in a later chapter, deciding just what constitutes a subsidy and what does not is not without controversy. A clear understanding of the nature and scope of these subsidies is needed, however, to assess their impact, in both low-income countries and in the wealthy countries themselves, and to investigate the reasons why governments have elected to establish costly agricultural policy mechanisms in the first place. For the time being, let us define an agricultural subsidy as any government intervention that causes agricultural prices, firm revenues, or farm household incomes to differ from what they would be in the absence of the intervention. Some subsidies involve direct government payments. In the United States, for example, the government has provided a supplement to the market price (known as a loan deficiency payment) so that farmers may receive a final price higher than the market price. The higher price encourages them to produce more, depressing the market price and widening the gap between that price and the price received by the farmer. In the absence of this program, there would be only one price which would fall between the depressed market price and the subsidized price received by farmers. The gap between the two prices is financed by the government using revenue from taxpayers to write the checks.

In other cases, the subsidy is financed by consumers rather than taxpayers. This is the case when trade barriers such as import tariffs or customs duties are applied to imported goods so that their price within the country is higher than the world price. U.S. trade barriers on imported sugar raise the U.S. price well above the world price, protecting U.S. sugar producers from foreign competition. In this book, farm subsidies are understood to include both those financed through the government budget and those that are supported by real or implicit taxes on traded goods. Not all subsidies are directed exclusively at producers, however. Low-income countries often use subsidies to lower food prices as does the United States with its food stamp program. It turns out that the suggestion that the wealthy countries are spending a billion dollars a day on agricultural subsidies is based on the inclusion of food stamps, publicly supported agricultural research, and other similar programs as well as trade barriers and programs aimed more directly at farmers. On the other hand, the subsidies reported by the Environmental Working Group, the $19 billion in cotton subsidies over the period 1995 to 2005 noted earlier, for example, include only government expenditures on producer subsidies, excluding subsidies created by trade barriers as well as such subsidies as food stamps and publicly funded research. The purpose of this book is to develop as clear a picture as possible of the nature and effects of the farm subsidies that have become such an important public policy issue, as well as to critically assess the justifications offered in support of these policies and the arguments against them.

Organization of the Book

Accomplishing these goals will require substantial background information as a basis for a more detailed examination of the problem. The next three chapters are designed to provide that information. Chapter 2 is a review of some basic economic arguments concerning government intervention in markets. Its main purpose is to introduce some technical concepts and terminology that will facilitate subsequent discussions. In general, economists believe that prices act as signals that influence individual decisions and that the best decisions are made if prices are not distorted by government policy interventions or by other types of market imperfections. A case can be made for government intervention if there is a market failure, that is, a situation which leads to prices that do not accurately reflect the underlying costs and benefits associated with a particular good or service. Economic reasoning provides a justification for government intervention only in these special circumstances and one of the objectives of Chapter 2 is to provide a foundation for studying the extent to which actual farm policies are consistent with such justifications.

Chapter 3 describes the structure of the world food system including the production, exchange, and consumption of food throughout the world. Over the past 200 years, Malthus's predictions that population growth would outstrip increases in food production have turned out to be completely wrong. Because of technological advances, there is more food available today, on average, for each person on earth than at any previous time in history. The stupendous increases in food production have occurred as world population has more than sextupled, increasing from around a billion at the time Malthus wrote his *Essay on the Principle of Population* in 1798, to more than 6.6 billion in 2007. Despite the fact that more than enough food is produced each year to feed everyone adequately, some 854 million people, about 13 percent of the world population, are undernourished (FAO, 2006). While food production has been increasing around the world, the ways in which agricultural products are processed, traded, and consumed have also evolved. Complex global interconnections call into question food and agricultural policies that have been driven primarily by domestic concerns and that were initiated in a substantially different economic setting. In Chapter 4, the implications of globalization for food and agriculture are examined with particular attention to the role of the WTO in dealing with broad international trade policies and disputes over national agricultural policies that have an impact on trade.

The next part of the book is devoted to a detailed examination of the agricultural subsidies described in the OECD database. Chapter 5 identifies broad subsidy categories and presents summary statistics on the amounts spent by OECD member states either through government transfers directly to producers and consumers or through import barriers that drive a wedge between domestic and world prices. The next three chapters discuss the agricultural policies of some of the central parties to this debate, the United States, the European Union, and the Pacific Rim countries of Japan, Korea, Australia, and New Zealand. Each chapter contains a brief history of agricultural policy in the country or region under review along with descriptions of the types of policy mechanisms chosen and special political and philosophical perspectives that condition the country's approach to food and agriculture. Agricultural policies in low-income countries are the subject of Chapter 9 in which a distinction is made between developing countries that are major exporters of food and agricultural products and those that are importers.

The final chapter summarizes what has been learned about this issue and draws out the implications of these results for public policy and the debate about farm subsidies. Although there is wide variation in the estimated impacts of eliminating farm subsidies, most analysts find that the net effect of such a change would be positive. The political impediments to agricultural policy reform are formidable, however, and it is not clear that politicians in wealthy countries will be able to muster the strength to overcome the opposition. The ethical dilemma, of course, is that wealthy countries with the means to find other ways to provide social insurance to their vulnerable farmers have chosen methods that shift the burden onto the shoulders of poor farmers in low-income countries. It is worth noting that the agricultural policy debate has changed substantially in the past 15 years. Previously, belief in the virtues of family farmers coupled with the sense that these hard-working individuals are generally less well-off than others have made farm policies a kind of, with apologies, sacred cow in many industrialized countries. As the industrialization of the farm sector becomes more evident in the high-income countries, it is more difficult to maintain the myth of poor, hard-working farmers deserving of special protection even if that protection comes at the expense of poor farmers in developing countries and consumers and taxpayers in the wealthy countries themselves. This book will provide a basis for evaluating arguments for and against farm subsidies highlighting the economic and political realities that are at the base of current agricultural policies.

2

The Economics of Government Intervention

Introduction

One of the great intellectual cleavages in human history has been between those who believe that individual liberty should take precedence over all other considerations and those who feel that individual freedoms ought to be subordinated to the collective needs of society as a whole. This division often arises in discussions of the appropriate roles for governments and markets in the organization of social interaction. For some, markets are benign institutions that allow people to freely realize their objectives while governments use their power of coercion to channel individual behavior in directions deemed to be of benefit to the wider society. From this perspective, individuals freely pursue their personal interests in markets and in so doing, are led by Adam Smith's famous invisible hand to act in ways that end up enhancing the well-being of society even though that was not their intention. In contrast, governments rely on their monopoly on the use of force to compel individuals to sacrifice some of their desires for the good of the whole. Thomas Paine wrote about society rather than the market but it may not be too great a stretch to suggest that he defended such a position at the beginning of *Common Sense*:

> Some writers have so confounded society with government, as to leave, little or no distinction between them; whereas they are not only different, but have different origins. Society is produced by our wants, and government by our wickedness; the former promotes our happiness *positively* by uniting our affections, the latter *negatively* by restraining our vices (Paine, 1997, pp. 2–3, italics in original).

An alternative perspective views markets as operating in a kind of anarchy in which the strong are able to exploit the weak while governments are seen as the preeminent means for insuring that everyone is treated fairly, softening the harsh blows of unfettered market capitalism. This view is central to socialist and Marxist ideas on social organization, although the ultimate Marxist hope was that the state would fade away as individuals came to understand the value of spontaneous cooperation. According to Roemer:

> Both neoclassical economics and Marxism view agents under capitalism as pursuing their material self-interest; but whereas neoclassical economics derives (under certain conditions) the unintended good consequences of such pursuits, Marxism characterizes the result as anarchical and inefficient. Capitalism is a system in which there is a vast misallocation of resources, the most obvious of which is unemployment ... (Roemer, 1988, p. 150).

Each of these perspectives has been elucidated in a wide range of forms, from moderate to extreme. An extreme form of the pro-market view can be found among market anarchists who believe that society would be freer and fairer if all the functions presently carried out by governments were left to the "voluntary, consensual forces of market society" (Molinari Institute, 2006). At the other end of the spectrum, socialists continue to call for the abolition of private property and replacement of market mechanisms by a central authority that would coordinate the democratic determination of resource allocation and distribution (World Socialist Party, 2006).

A more moderate position than either of these extremes would recognize the importance of individual liberty but would also note that such liberty is itself contingent on a well-defined legal system enforced by a state with a monopoly on the use of force. That is the perspective adopted in this book. Of course, even among moderates, the devil is always in the details and there is a great deal of room for disagreement over the relative importance of markets and governments in coordinating social interaction in particular cases. European social democracies, for example, assign a much larger role to the government in providing services such as health insurance, retirement pensions, and income support than is the case in the United States. Many of the conflicts between the European Union (EU) and the United States over policies affecting food and agriculture can be traced to differing perceptions of the virtues and vices of states and markets. National differences in the roles ascribed to markets and governments probably stem primarily from the particular histories of these regions and the prevailing values to which such experiences have given rise. This does not mean, however, that no general principles concerning the responsibilities of states and markets in coordinating social interaction can be formulated. It is the purpose of this chapter to do just that.[1] The account presented here will draw particularly on economics although it will become evident as the discussion progresses that any assessment of the appropriateness of government intervention must involve political, social, and ethical judgments as well as the use of economic principles.

In the next section, the theory of the invisible hand is described along with the special and necessary conditions alluded to by Roemer in the quotation above. Violations of these conditions, often referred to as market failures, are discussed in the third part of the chapter. Market failures lead to inefficiencies in the allocation of resources and the distribution of goods and services and many economists believe that the economic role of the government ought to be limited to interventions that remove these inefficiencies. A vexing question is whether the unequal distribution of income and wealth that so often arises under laissez-faire capitalism is caused by a form of market failure or whether it is simply a side-effect of economic activity best dealt with through political processes. It turns out that much government intervention works to redistribute wealth and income and even policies that clearly target economic efficiency generally have distributional consequences as well. The tension between economic efficiency and equity or distributive justice is at the heart of many of the topics to be addressed in later chapters.

The Invisible Hand

According to Roemer (1988), both neoclassical economics and Marxism are based on the assumption that individuals are motivated primarily by the pursuit of their own self-interest, a behavioral supposition that is often referred to as "economic rationality." Some have objected to the assumption of economic rationality on the grounds that it cannot account for the many cases when people do not seem to be pursuing their self-interest. One might think of this as the Mother Theresa problem: was Mother Theresa really just pursuing self-interest as she worked with destitute people in the slums of Calcutta? Some feel that she was indeed behaving rationally given her expectations of life after death or the pleasure she got from helping others. Others would surely

---

[1] Readers familiar with general equilibrium and welfare economics may wish to skip this chapter. Those with limited economic background may find some of the discussion somewhat confusing. Little will be lost by these readers in skipping the chapter although there will be some technical terminology in later chapters that may not make a lot of sense without the economic foundations developed in this section. Technical presentations of the theory can be found in any microeconomic textbook (Baumol and Blinder, 1991, is clear and accessible).

object to this contention on the grounds that it fails to recognize Mother Theresa's special virtue in sacrificing her personal safety and comfort to help people with few resources and little hope for better lives. No doubt a full understanding of human motivation and human behavior would recognize that we often behave in ways that cannot be entirely explained as the rational pursuit of self-interest. In addition, recent research by behavioral economists has shown that individuals frequently do not behave in the strictly rational manner assumed in many economic models (Thaler, 1994).

Admitting that the concept of economic rationality cannot explain the full diversity of human behavior, however, does not mean that it does not explain anything at all. Consider the response of U.S. citizens to increased gasoline prices in recent years. These price increases have been caused by an expansion of world demand for petroleum as China and India realize higher rates of economic growth and by supply disruptions due to natural disasters such as hurricanes Katrina and Rita and political strife in oil-producing countries. In response to the higher prices, some consumers have changed their behavior by driving less and shifting their automobile purchases from gas-guzzling behemoths to more fuel-efficient cars (Krauss, 2008; Vlasic, 2008). They did not do this because they wished to save the environment, although that may have been a factor in some of the decisions that were made. Nor did they do it because they altruistically wanted to share the more limited gasoline available with fellow citizens who might be in greater need. Rather, the main reason for these behavioral changes was that they were consistent with individual self-interest: the value of continuing to spend a lot of time driving large cars is less than the value of the things people would have to give up to be able to maintain their old driving habits, and so continuing to practice those habits would lower their well-being. In other words, the response to the higher prices was entirely consistent with the idea that people are strongly motivated by the rational pursuit of their own self-interest.

Of greater interest, perhaps, is the realization that the response of consumers to the higher prices was exactly what was needed to bring demand for gasoline back in line with the lowered supplies. There was no need for the government to ration gasoline or to place constraints on the amount of time individuals would be permitted to use their cars. Despite a lot of complaining about the prices, gasoline rationing and reduced driving were freely chosen by individual automobile owners themselves in response to the price signals being generated in the market. The result is that gasoline consumption has automatically adjusted to the available supplies without serious social or economic disruption and without the intervention of the government. In making rational choices, consumers ended up advancing not only their own interests, given the circumstances, but those of the broader society as well.

It seems counterintuitive to think that the selfish pursuit of one's personal interests along with similar pursuits by everyone else can give rise to beneficial consequences. In the sixteenth and seventeenth centuries, philosophers as diverse as Thomas Hobbes, Nicolò Machiavelli, and Baruch de Spinoza saw the pursuit of self-interest as a major characteristic of human beings, taking this behavioral assumption as a basis for their reflections on the state and political authority (Stewart, 2006). Hobbes suggested that the most likely result of the pursuit of self-interest would be social discord as individuals seeking to advance their interests through greater power and control over their circumstances would inevitably come into conflict with others pursuing similar goals. He argued that without a sovereign power to control these selfish individuals, there would be nothing but conflict ("... a warre, as is of every man against every man") and life would be "... solitary, poore, nasty, brutish, and short" (Hobbes, 1988, pp. 64–5). For many, the conclusion that individual pursuit of self-interest will inevitably lead to conflict and strife probably seems obvious. Hobbes's view of human behavior and the role of the sovereign was echoed about a century later, for example, in Thomas Paine's assertion that government is made necessary by our "wickedness."

Not everyone agreed with these rather grim visions of the human prospect, however. Albert Hirschman (1977) has argued that various seventeenth- and eighteenth-century thinkers developed the idea that social relations might be coordinated by letting certain human passions serve as countervailing forces to moderate the others. Thus, instead of relying on a central authority to restrain people's passions, a particular passion, selfishness or greed, might be called on to control the others. From the idea of a countervailing passion, it is but a short step to Adam Smith's famous statement in *The Wealth of Nations*:

> As every individual, therefore, endeavors as much as he can both to employ his capital in the support of domestic industry, and so to direct that industry that its produce may be of the greatest value; every individual necessarily labors to render the annual revenue of society as great as he can. He generally, indeed, neither intends to promote the public interest, nor knows how much he is promoting it. By preferring the support of domestic to that of foreign industry, he intends only his own security; and by directing that industry in such a manner as its produce may be of the greatest value, he intends only his own gain, and he is in this, as in many other cases, led by an invisible hand to promote an end that was no part of his intention. Nor is it always the worse for society that it was no part of it. By pursuing his own interest he frequently promotes that of society more effectually than when he really intends to promote it (Smith, 1976, pp. 477–8).

In this passage, Smith is following up on an earlier observation in his book to the effect that "[i]t is not from the benevolence of the butcher, the brewer, or the baker, that we expect our dinner, but from their regard to their own interest" (p. 18). For Smith, not only is it the case that the pursuit of self-interest does not automatically lead to conflict, but even more, it actually serves society well because people interacting in markets will find that it is in their interest to behave in ways that turn out to advance the general welfare. This is a remarkable result. If true, instead of Hobbes's sovereign with absolute authority over people's lives, we can simply leave everything up to individuals exercising their freedom to exchange goods and services in free markets. Unlike some of his interpreters, Smith clearly saw the need for a government to provide the institutional and legal context within which markets operate. But the invisible hand is a compelling metaphor for the market as a self-regulating system in which individual actions are coordinated with little or no external coercive force.[2]

While one can imagine situations in which the incentive structure is such that individuals have good reasons to behave in ways that generate benefits for others as well as for themselves, it is also possible to think of cases where the incentives are likely to lead to antisocial behavior. In the case of rising U.S. gasoline prices, for example, many people felt that the higher prices were the result of manipulation by the small number of gigantic companies that control petroleum refining and distribution. If the petroleum companies are able to manipulate gasoline prices to increase their profits, the rational pursuit of their self-interest would dictate that they do so. And if they do, the invisible hand of the market may leave consumers worse off. This would be the case if the total gains to the small number of companies were smaller than the total losses to millions of consumers. The obvious question is why the market seems to serve society well some of the time, while in other situations self-interested behavior leads to profiteering, exploitation, manipulation, or waste.

Economists have developed a complex theoretical apparatus to answer this question and in the process have worked out the specific conditions that are required for the pursuit of self-interest in the market to result in desirable social outcomes. A sketch of this theory is provided in Appendix 2.1 at the end of this chapter and more complete accounts can be found in many economic textbooks (see, for example, Baumol and Blinder, 1991). For present purposes, it will probably be sufficient to briefly summarize the broad conclusions of these theoretical considerations focusing on the special conditions that are required for markets to perform as indicated by the theory. A first

---

[2]   The invisible-hand metaphor has been used to describe a variety of self-regulating processes by the philosopher Robert Nozick who includes evolutionary theory, the ecological regulation of animal populations, and Thomas Schelling's account of how residential segregation arises, even though no one intends to create segregated neighborhoods, as further examples of invisible-hand explanations (Nozick, 1974, pp. 20–1).

point to make in this context is that the theory of the invisible hand identifies efficiency as the *summum bonum* of economic activity. In an efficient economy, productive resources are put to their best use and the result is the production of greater amounts of desirable goods than would be the case if there is rampant waste and inefficiency. The precise definitions of efficiency used by economists are discussed in Appendix 2.1.

The significant theoretical conclusion from this theory is that self-interested individuals behaving rationally in markets that are perfectly competitive will automatically act in ways that guarantee efficiency in production and distribution. Economists define perfect competition as a price system in which everyone faces the same prices and no individual through her behavior can influence these prices. Note that the variables that do all the work in this theory are prices. It is in rational responses to price signals that individuals advance both their own interests and those of the broader society. If prices are distorted in some way, inefficiencies will be introduced into the economy. As noted in the discussion of gasoline prices, some believe that the large petroleum companies are manipulating market prices to advance their economic or political interests. If they are right, petroleum markets would not be characterized by economists as perfectly competitive and there would be economic losses due to the inefficiencies brought about by these distortions.

But if markets are perfectly competitive, individuals will find that their self-interest is best served by economic behavior that also advances the common good. Perfect competition is one of the conditions referred to by Roemer in the quotation cited earlier but it is not the only one. Markets can fail in a variety of ways as shown in the next section of this chapter. Moreover, while rational individuals operating in a perfectly competitive economy will automatically realize economic efficiency, efficiency is not the only economic factor that is important. It turns out that it is theoretically possible to realize efficiency in the production and distribution of desirable goods and services but leave great inequalities in the amounts of goods available to different individuals. The invisible hand is powerless when faced with economic inequality even if all the conditions for efficiency are met.

Market Failures

The theoretical sketch presented in Appendix 2.1 is based on a highly simplified economic model. It turns out that the basic conclusions of that analysis hold for much more complex models as well. Using sophisticated mathematical methods, economists have proved that an economic system with perfectly competitive prices and rational consumers and producers will automatically reach an equilibrium that is efficient. Economic rationality and a perfectly competitive price system are necessary for the invisible hand to work its magic but they do not exhaust the requirements for economic efficiency. In real economies with many consumers and producers, it is not always the case that individual agents have full information about prices or other economic variables. They may not know that there is a potentially beneficial trade that could be made or they may be unable to predict the effects of a particular pattern of consumption. It is likely, for example, that many young smokers began smoking on the basis of inaccurate assessments of its long-term costs and benefits. An initial mistake about the value of smoking can have very serious consequences given the addictive nature of tobacco consumption.

Thus, in addition to perfect competition and economic rationality, information and foresight have to be sufficiently accurate to prevent serious errors in the rational pursuit of self-interest. The problem is that these basic conditions are violated with some frequency in most economic systems. Imperfect competition can give rise to distorted price signals, information asymmetries can derail mutually beneficial exchanges, and insurance markets may fail to cover all the risks and uncertainties about the future that people face. In addition, even if the basic conditions are fully met, there may still be cases when a market generates faulty price signals because of imperfections in the way markets work or because there is no market to generate any price signals at all. Beautiful sunsets and biodiversity both have value despite the fact that they are not traded in markets and, consequently, do not have prices. A final set of problems concerns the inability of markets to correct underlying inequalities in income or wealth as noted at the end of the preceding section. Let us examine these three sets of problems in greater detail.

Violations of the basic conditions: imperfect competition, information, and risk

The first problem for the invisible hand is that the basic conditions for the automatic realization of efficiency are often not met in the real world. In modern economies, imperfectly competitive markets are the norm rather than the exception. Imperfectly competitive firms may have enough market power to distort prices in their favor and this can lead to economic inefficiency. It turns out, however, that even powerful monopolies are constrained in their behavior by market forces. Consider the case of the Organization of Petroleum Exporting Countries (OPEC). OPEC is a cartel made up of oil-producing countries that use their control over large amounts of petroleum to manipulate market prices. But even this powerful cartel is unable to simply decree what the price of petroleum will be. In fact, when the OPEC oil ministers meet to discuss pricing strategies, they actually spend most of their time discussing production quotas, that is, limits to the amounts of petroleum each member can produce. If the OPEC cartel wishes to increase petroleum prices, its members have to agree to restrict their output.

Suppose that petroleum is priced at $100 a barrel and that, at that price, world consumption is 80 million barrels a day. If OPEC successfully raises petroleum prices to $110 per barrel, world consumption will not remain constant at 80 million barrels per day. No one from OPEC can hold a gun to the head of every consumer to force her to continue consuming petroleum products at the same rate despite the higher prices. We have already seen how rational consumers may lower their energy consumption when prices increase. Suppose that the level of world consumption that is consistent with a price of $110 per barrel is 76 million barrels a day. The only way OPEC can raise the price to $110 is by cutting its production by 4 million barrels a day so that the total available on the world market is reduced to 76 million barrels. This "shortage" will lead to OPEC's desired price increase through the normal operation of the market. Any monopoly that wishes to maximize its profits will find that it can only do so by lowering the amount of the good it places on the market relative to the amount that would be supplied by a set of perfectly competitive firms. In pursuing its self-interest, the monopolist is able to increase the market price so that it no longer reflects underlying economic values.

Monopolies are unstable unless the firm can prevent the entry of new competitors. A firm earning monopoly profits is an indicator to other firms that this particular market is ripe for further exploitation. OPEC was partially successful in acting as a monopoly in the 1970s restricting its output to raise prices quite substantially. But the higher petroleum prices encouraged exploration and new sources of petroleum were located in the North Sea, Alaska, and elsewhere. In 1970, OPEC accounted for about 51 percent of world petroleum production compared with around 42 percent in 2007 (Energy Information Administration, 2008). This change was not due to a fall in OPEC's output (OPEC production increased by almost 50 percent between 1970 and 2007) but rather to expanded production from countries such as Mexico, Norway, and the United Kingdom which are not members of the cartel. World petroleum production increased 69 percent between 1970 and 2007 with much of this increase coming from non-OPEC countries.

OPEC was unable to prevent petroleum discovered in the aftermath of its price increases from entering the market and this lessened its control over the world petroleum price. Moreover, the OPEC countries realized that it is not in their long-term interests to raise prices so high that it disrupts the economies of their clients. Note that if the world petroleum market were competitive, one would expect the price of petroleum to increase over time as this non-renewable resource becomes ever scarcer. By limiting its own output, OPEC has managed to advance the timetable for these inevitable price increases to its advantage and, no doubt, put off the day when petroleum will have become so scarce that its price becomes too high for it to be used at all. Sometimes, monopolistic firms are able to prevent the entry of competitors and maintain their monopoly control for longer periods of time. For example, if a firm possesses a specialized technology that is not generally available, other firms may be unable to enter the market. The same would be true if the firm has exclusive control of a resource that is essential for the manufacture of the product and can prevent other firms from obtaining this key input.

Sometimes, governments actually help firms to establish a temporary monopoly through the issuance of a patent. The rationale for granting patents, of course, is that the government wishes to encourage innovation by making it worthwhile for firms to conduct research and development. Most of the time, one would expect that the government would intervene in markets to promote competition. Patents are an interesting example of using one kind of market failure (a monopoly) to correct another. The particular market failure in this case is that innovations become generally available as soon as products are released. This feature is one of the characteristics of public goods which will be discussed in more detail later. The fact that a firm's competitors are likely to be able to take advantage of any innovations it generates through its own research and development activities acts as a disincentive for pursuing such activities in the first place. Without patent protection, there would be less innovation and lower standards of living. The price of these innovations, however, is the inefficiency generated by the legal monopoly granted to the patent-holder. An ideal patent system would result in the equation of the marginal cost of allowing a firm to exercise market power with the marginal benefit of the innovations generated by firms in response to potential patent protection.

Occasionally, the technical nature of an industry is such that there are natural barriers to entry and a natural tendency for the market to be monopolized. These natural monopolies arise when the costs of production decline as a firm expands the scale of its operations. If the costs of production continue to decline as the firm becomes ever larger, it will be able to sell its product at ever lower prices. This will benefit consumers but if the process continues long enough, the firm may eventually become so large that there is no room in the market for any other firms. Additional firms could not enter the market because they would have to start at a smaller size with production costs that would not be competitive with those of the large firm that is enjoying extensive economies of scale. Utilities such as telephones or electricity are examples of natural monopolies. In the United States, natural monopolies are often operated by private firms under government regulation. In other countries, nationalized telecommunications, electricity, and gas utilities are often run by the government. Left to their own devices, natural monopolies are likely to sell their products at prices that differ from those that would prevail in perfect competition so there may be a role for the government in preventing inefficiencies in such industries through regulation or public supply.

Monopolies are not the only example of imperfect competition. Market power can also be exercised by a single buyer, a situation referred to as a monopsony. In addition, markets in which there is a small number of producers (an oligopoly) or consumers (an oligopsony) may also be subject to price manipulation. In the United States, there are only a few firms that purchase fattened cattle for slaughter. Many cattle producers feel that these meat-packing firms can find ways to coordinate their price setting even though such collusion is supposed to be illegal. Some have suggested that the firms act as oligopsonies when purchasing cattle (paying low prices to producers) and oligopolies when selling meat (charging high prices to consumers). It turns out that many industries in highly industrialized countries are more properly characterized as some version of an oligopoly or oligopsony than as being perfectly competitive. To the extent that firms in such industries are able to manipulate the prices they pay or receive, the price signals that are supposed to be guiding the invisible hand will be distorted. These distortions will not be automatically eliminated by the market. It is not because of market pressures that Microsoft's operations in the EU have had to be modified but rather because of EU competition policy. In other words, governments can play a positive role in the economy by promoting competition and regulating imperfectly competitive industries.

Perfect competition is not the only basic condition required for the effective operation of markets that is often violated in real-world economies. Individuals may lack information about opportunities to advance their own interests and this in turn renders the invisible hand inoperative. A shortage of hay in a particular region, for example, will be indicated by high prices. In some other region, there may be an abundance of hay and, consequently, relatively low prices. If the transportation costs between these two regions are less than the difference in hay prices, an individual could benefit by buying hay in the region with low prices, transporting it to the high-priced region and selling it for a profit. As others see this opportunity more hay will flow from the region where it is in surplus to the region where it is in short supply. This process is known as arbitrage, and while some individuals may be able to realize economic gains from arbitraging the price difference, it is also true that their actions are of broad social benefit. Lowered milk production in one region due to lack of adequate hay while perfectly good hay is going to waste in another region is a paradigm of inefficiency. The problem, of course, is that if information about hay prices in various regions is unavailable, such inefficiencies may persist.

Clearly, information can be of great value and it is not uncommon for governments to assist private enterprises to make sure information is widely available to all. The value of information can be seen in the elaborate procedures followed by public agencies in announcing commodity forecasts and other economic predictions as well as in the laws against insider trading.[3] Other information problems have been highlighted by Joseph Stiglitz, Michael Spence and George Akerlof who together won the 2001 Nobel prize in economics for their work on information asymmetries. An information asymmetry arises when one party to a potential transaction has more information about the item being exchanged than the other. Akerlof's (1970) classic article about the market for used cars showed that beneficial trades could be blocked if the buyer and seller have different information about the quality of a used car. One way out of such a situation would be for an impartial judge to publicize accurate information backed up by some form of guarantee so that the parties to the transaction can reach a bargain with some confidence that they are not making a terrible mistake. One candidate for the role of impartial judge would be a public agency charged with regulating markets in which information asymmetries occur.

A final condition concerns decision making about future events. Clearly, the future cannot be known with certainty and the potential for making a wrong decision relative to unforeseen future events can significantly affect behavior in the present. One way to protect against the risks of an unknown future is to purchase insurance. If insurance markets are competitive and meet all the other requirements for the efficient operation of the invisible hand, individuals will be able to reduce their exposure to risk. Unfortunately, insurance markets are frequently not perfect leaving risk as a serious source of economic inefficiency. Consider, for example, insurance against the risk of hurricanes, earthquakes, and other natural disasters. The probability that a particular region will be devastated may be fairly low but if it is struck by a natural disaster, damage is likely to be widespread and severe. It has been estimated, for example, that Hurricane Katrina, which struck New Orleans

---

[3]   In the 1983 film *Trading Places*, the lead characters discover that two business tycoons who had played a trick on them are trying to make a killing on orange juice futures by intercepting a report on the orange harvest prior to its official release and using that information to buy or sell futures contracts according to the information in the report. The heroes arrange for a false report to be delivered to the tycoons who subsequently lose everything by taking the wrong position on the market.

and much of the U.S. Gulf Coast in 2005, cost insurers between $40 billion and $55 billion (Reuters, 2005). The total cost of the hurricanes that hit the Gulf Coast is even greater ($200 billion) because many things were not insured (Streitfeld, 2005).[4] Since such events are rare, it is difficult to establish a premium that would cover the costs when they do occur. Moreover, it is likely that any actuarially fair premium would be so high that few property owners would buy the insurance.

The potential difficulties of establishing efficient private markets for insurance are compounded by two kinds of market failure peculiar to insurance markets. The first, moral hazard, arises when the behavior of individuals who are insured changes because of the insurance protection. If an automobile is insured against theft, the owner may be less inclined to take precautions to prevent the car from being stolen. If all owners behave this way, more cars will be stolen than anticipated by the insurer who will have to raise the premiums to cover the costs. At the higher premium, many who might like to purchase insurance may be forced to do without it. The second problem with insurance markets is known as adverse selection. Suppose that a health insurer cannot distinguish smokers from nonsmokers. The fair rate for the group as a whole will be attractive to smokers, who face a higher probability of disease, but unattractive to nonsmokers. If the pool of insured begins to include more smokers and fewer nonsmokers, the premiums will have to rise and fewer nonsmokers will find the insurance attractive. If the health insurer could identify smokers and nonsmokers, it would be able to offer different actuarially fair rates to the two groups. Because the insurer cannot make this distinction, there is a market failure. Moral hazard and adverse selection inhibit the functioning of insurance markets leading to inefficiencies in the handling of risk.

It turns out that much economic intervention by the governments of high-income countries can be characterized as social insurance for such vicissitudes of life as unemployment, natural disasters, old age, disabilities, and so on. The economic justification for such programs is the problem of providing private insurance at actuarially fair rates as a result of moral hazard, adverse selection, and other market failures. It should be noted, however, that many of these programs actually result in a redistribution of income among different

---

[4] See also "A Policy of Deceit" by Jim Hood (Op-Ed page, *New York Times*, November 19, 2005). Hood, attorney general for the state of Mississippi, noted that insurance companies were trying to reduce their liabilities by claiming that much of the damage was due to flooding rather than the hurricane winds for which Gulf Coast residents had insurance coverage. Hood suggested that the insurance companies might save $2 billion to $4 billion if they could avoid paying for damage resulting from the storm surge caused by the hurricanes.

groups. Whether such redistribution is justified or not is independent of the market failures associated with risk. We will have more to say about redistribution later.

Public goods and externalities

Even if markets satisfy all the basic conditions described in the preceding sections, it is still possible for them to give rise to resource misallocations and other inefficiencies. These problems generally arise because of particular characteristics of goods or the ways in which legal ownership is defined. Public goods, mentioned briefly in the discussion of patents, are an important example of this problem. Public goods have two characteristics that make them very different from normal goods. The first, referred to as non-rivalry, is that consumption by one individual does not reduce the amount available for consumption by others. The second is that it is difficult to prevent individuals from consuming the good once it becomes available. It is this second characteristic that gives rise to the problem that patents are designed to alleviate. Once an innovation is introduced, competitors can often reverse engineer the product to figure out how it is made. In the absence of patent protection, competitors will have an economic advantage because they can begin producing and marketing the good without having had to invest in any of the research that led to its invention. This type of behavior is known as free-riding (see Appendix 2.2). Free-riding is economically rational but unless there is some way to prevent it, such behavior will reduce the potential benefits to the innovator and, therefore, lower the incentives to fund research and development.

Classic examples of public goods include national defense and a country's legal system, both of which were identified by Adam Smith as part of the responsibilities of governments. In both cases, the amounts of security or justice available is the same for everyone, one person's consumption of the goods does not diminish the amounts available for others, and it is difficult to prevent citizens of the country in question from enjoying the benefits of the goods. If the provision of national defense and a country's legal institutions were left to the market, as suggested by market anarchists, for example, the likely result would be less than optimal amounts of the two goods as a result of free-riding. Individuals would have an incentive to hide their true preferences for national defense and legal protection to avoid having to pay for them and, because they cannot be prevented from consuming the goods which become available to everyone as soon as they are produced, they could still expect to be able to enjoy the security and protection they provide. This type of market failure constitutes an important rationale for government intervention in the economy.

There are many other examples of economic goods that are non-rival and characterized by difficult exclusion. In the days before cable, television broadcasts were public goods because once broadcast, the programs became available to everyone with a television receiver. The problem for the networks was to find a way to force free-riding viewers to pay. In the United States, the solution was advertizing. In France, television broadcasting was for many years at least partly financed through the government which collects an annual tax on television sets. As shown by the case of television broadcasts, the term "public goods" is a bit infelicitous because such goods are sometimes supplied by private firms rather than the public. If a private cartel restricts output to raise prices, it provides a kind of public good (higher prices) to all of its members even if some choose to free-ride. Although the members of OPEC are national governments, its actions are generally similar to those of a private cartel. When OPEC began restricting its petroleum production to raise prices, the higher prices were available to all oil-producing entities whether they belonged to OPEC or not. Within OPEC, some of the members have chosen on occasion to cheat by exceeding their production quotas. Their expectation may have been that Saudi Arabia, the largest petroleum producer in the world, would offset their excesses by further reducing its output so they would not seriously undermine the cartel's efforts to raise prices. In fact, this uncooperative behavior along with the increased output from non-OPEC countries did undermine OPEC's ability to maintain high prices. Recent increases in petroleum prices may be due more to growing demand in Asia than to any price-enhancing efforts by OPEC (see Appendix 2.2).

Another type of market failure occurs when some of the costs or benefits of an economic activity are not taken into account by the decision makers directly involved in that activity. Because it is usually relatively inexpensive, farmers often apply nitrogen fertilizers to their fields at rates that exceed the amounts that will be taken up by their crops. While this may seem wasteful, the exact amount of fertilizer that will be absorbed by plants cannot be known in advance and erring on the side of over- application is a reasonable strategy to reduce risk. In the soil, nitrogen is converted to nitrates that can be absorbed by plants. Excess nitrates in the soil can leach into the groundwater contaminating water supplies and leading to health problems, particularly in infants who may suffer from methemoglobinemia, also known as "blue-baby syndrome," an impairment of the blood's ability to transport oxygen. From the perspective of the farmer, decisions on the amount of fertilizer to apply depend on the fertilizer cost, the application costs, the likely impact on crop yields, and output prices. The potential cost to others of nitrate contamination of the groundwater does not enter into the farmer's calculations. But the cost of nitrate contamination is a real cost that has to be borne by somebody. Moreover, it is part of the crop production costs. If this part of the costs of production is covered by someone else, the farmer is, in essence, receiving a subsidy that reduces the full cost of applying fertilizer.

In the simple economy described in Appendix 2.1, rational producers choose to purchase inputs up to the point where the value of the marginal product of the input is equal to its price. In the case of nitrogen fertilizer, the cost has been reduced because the farmer can ignore the costs of groundwater contamination. Consequently, the farmer uses more fertilizer and produces more output than would be socially optimal. This type of inefficiency is known as an externality. Nitrate contamination and other types of pollution are negative externalities which generally lead to greater output than is socially optimal. Positive externalities arise when an economic agent does not receive compensation for a beneficial contribution to some other economic activity. For example, there is a positive externality associated with education. The more educated an individual is, the greater will be his likely contribution to the economic, political, and social systems in which he lives. Obtaining a high level of education, however, requires substantial sacrifices of current income and consumption. The current sacrifices are compensated for in part by the expectation of a higher future salary. But there may be no compensation for the positive contribution to economic, political, and social life that the educated person is likely to make. In this case, there may be a tendency to under-invest in education because of the uncompensated externality.

Externalities arise when the social benefits or costs of some activity differ from the private benefits or costs. Because individual decisions are driven by private benefits and costs, this divergence means that the invisible hand of the market leads to incorrect economic decisions. Sometimes individuals can negotiate arrangements that internalize the externalities. For example, there are positive externalities associated with honey production. Bees need to collect nectar from flowers to produce honey. Flowering plants have evolved to provide nectar as a way to attract bees and other insects that inadvertently transport pollen thereby assisting in the plant's reproduction. Cheung (1973) found that where honey production is highly dependent on desirable blossoms in fruit orchards, bee keepers often pay the orchard owners to be able to place their hives in proximity to the orchard. In contrast, orchard owners who are particularly dependent on bees for pollination often pay the bee keepers to locate hives near their orchards. The positive externalities involving bees, pollination, and honey have been internalized by voluntary arrangements between private individuals with no government intervention. In fact, markets for pollination services and nectar have developed more or less spontaneously.

The theoretical basis for this result was derived by Ronald Coase in a famous article published in 1960. Coase showed that if the costs of bargaining are negligible and the ownership of the property involved is clearly defined, rational individuals will find ways to internalize externalities. Suppose that there are 100 coal-burning electricity plants in the U.S. Midwest that produce nitrous oxide and sulfur dioxide emissions in addition to the electricity sold to their customers. These substances combine with water vapor to fall as acid rain in New England. The acid rain damages crops, forests, and buildings. Suppose the annual cost of this damage is $100 million and that the acid rain can be eliminated through the installation of scrubbers on the smokestacks of the electricity plants at a total cost of $80 million. Society would clearly be better off with the scrubbers because their cost is less than the damage being incurred in New England. The question Coase examined concerned the way in which ownership is legally defined. If the owners of the electricity plants have implicit ownership of the air, there would be no law against using the air as a repository for their pollution. In this case, if there were no costs of making a deal, rational property owners in New England would find it in their interest to pay for the scrubbers themselves. They would incur a cost of $80 million but save themselves $100 million in damage. On the other hand, if the New England property owners have legal title to the air, they could demand compensation for the damage from the acid rain to be paid by the plant owners. Rather than paying $100 million in damages, the electricity plant owners would find it in their interests to install the scrubbers for $80 million, saving themselves $20 million.

Thus, either way, the outcome will be the same: scrubbers will be installed, the acid rain will be eliminated, and society as a whole will be better off by $20 million. The only difference is who will have to pay for the scrubbers and that depends on how property rights are assigned. This result would appear to be a further triumph of the invisible hand as markets arise spontaneously to eliminate the inefficiencies associated with externalities. But note that in addition to low bargaining costs, this result requires clearly defined property rights, something that is accomplished by the public good that is a nation's legal system. The link between externalities and property rights is one example of the need for legal institutions as a prerequisite for a market economy. In the absence of such institutions, it is impossible to know who owns what, contracts have little or no meaning, and business transactions will not be carried out. If there is no government to establish a legal system and back it up with force if necessary, these functions may be taken over by organized crime. In the immediate aftermath of the dissolution of the Soviet Union, economic transactions were frequently coordinated by criminal gangs because the governments of the former Soviet republics had not established mechanisms to make and enforce laws on contracts, exchange, property, and so on.

The link between legal institutions, property rights, and market failures can be further illustrated by a special kind of externality known as a common pool or common property resource. Such resources are owned collectively and often allow open access for all who share ownership. The problem is that individuals do not bear the full costs of their use of the resource because these costs are shared among all the owners. As a consequence, there is a tendency for common pool resources to be over-exploited. This problem was first analyzed by Garrett Hardin (1968) in a well-known article entitled "The Tragedy of the Commons." The commons was an area used by all members of the community who were allowed to graze their sheep on the land. Hardin explained the tendency for the commons to be overgrazed by noting that the marginal cost to an individual shepherd was lower than the marginal social cost for the group as a whole because the costs of grazing each animal were shared by all those using the commons. As a result, individuals had an incentive to put as many of their animals as they could on the common grazing land. Privately held grazing land would not suffer this problem because the marginal cost of adding an animal to the grazing flock is fully borne by the private owner (see Appendix 2.2).

The implication of Hardin's analysis was that defining property rights to common pool resources would eliminate the externality because the costs of using the resource would no longer be shared with others. It turns out that defining private property rights is not the only way common pool resources can be managed. Many societies have developed norms that allow regulation of individual access to collectively held resources. The Tsembaga, a group of hunter-gatherers in New Guinea, developed a complex system of stylized warfare, taboos, and religious ritual that regulated access to commonly held wildlife stocks so that these and other resources were not depleted through over-exploitation (Rappaport, 1979). At the same time, there are many examples of common pool resources that have been or are being destroyed because access cannot be controlled. Ocean fisheries, which have been dramatically overfished, are a primary example of this problem. Reducing the rate at which fish stocks are being depleted requires that all fishing operations reduce their catches. But unless an individual fishing captain can be sure that others will work to conserve the resource, she has no incentive to do so unilaterally. After all, if I limit my catch, my income will be lower and if others do not limit their catches as well, the fishery will be destroyed anyway. As shown in Appendix 2.2, this is an example of a situation where rational self-interest leads not to efficient outcomes but rather to the destruction of valuable resources.

A final case of market failure is the situation described earlier in which there is no market for something that, nevertheless, has economic value. Suppose, for example, that a firm has decided to build a multistory office complex to serve as its new headquarters. Such a decision would normally be based on expected building costs along with assessments of the economic benefits such an office complex would generate. But if the office complex interferes with the scenic view that was previously available to residents of a neighboring apartment building, there is a cost that is not being taken into account by the firm. The apartment residents may have had to pay higher prices for their dwellings because their view was more attractive than from lower-priced apartments in a less desirable location. In this case, the construction costs for the office complex are underestimated because the cost to the residents of losing their scenic view has not been taken into account. Other examples of valuable things for which there is no market and therefore no market price include human life, endangered species, historic and archaeological sites, and many more. Because there is no market price for these goods, the invisible hand of the market cannot provide incentives for individuals to make socially optimal decisions.

Income distribution, poverty, and inequality

Imperfect competition, information problems, risk and market failures such as public goods, externalities, common pool resources, and missing markets can all lead to situations where the invisible hand of the market does not lead to efficient outcomes. Often, it will turn out that government intervention can improve the operation of the economy when these defects in the market system are present. In fact, one particular public good, the legal institutions related to contracts, property, and criminal activity, is necessary for the market economy to function at all. For many economists, the economic role of the government should be limited to the elimination of inefficiencies arising from market failures. From this perspective the social goal of economic efficiency should not be confused with other social goals such as those related to distributive justice, for example. This view is common among libertarians who argue for a minimal government charged with addressing certain market failures but leaving problems of poverty and inequality to private charity.[5]

One difficulty with this view is that government policies designed to correct market failures usually have an impact on the distribution of income as well.

---

[5]   See Robert Nozick (1974) and James M. Buchanan (1975). Nozick and Buchanan use very different conceptual approaches to arrive at similar conclusions about the role of the state. Nozick argues that a minimal state would arise through a series of voluntary agreements in which no individual rights would be violated. He believes that income redistribution by the state would violate individual rights and suggests that as long as the final economic situation has been achieved through just acquisition and exchange, that situation is just even if there is extensive poverty. Buchanan, who won the Nobel prize in economics in 1986, argues for a protective state that would assign property rights and enforce contracts in order to escape from the prisoners' dilemma that plagues social interaction but would not redistribute income or wealth.

For example, the Coasian solution to the problem of acid rain showed that an efficient outcome would be reached if bargaining costs were negligible and property rights were clearly assigned. It turns out, however, that the way in which the property rights are assigned determines who would have to pay for the scrubbers. The U.S. Conservation Reserve Program (CRP) pays farmers to remove fragile land from cultivation as a way to reduce soil erosion and other types of environmental degradation. The CRP targets an environmental externality and can be thought of as a government program aimed at correcting a market failure and increasing economic efficiency. At the same time, however, the CRP operates through compensating farmers for economic losses incurred when they cease to despoil the environment. It would have been possible to achieve similar efficiency results by fining farmers for the harm they were doing to the environment rather than paying them to stop. The way the CRP is structured means that taxpayers, rather than farmers, are forced to pay for correcting the externality. The decision to set the program up this way was based more on political realities than on economic or ethical considerations.

As these examples show, it is often impossible to disentangle the effects of public policies on economic efficiency and the distribution of income or wealth. It might be argued that economic efficiency and distributive justice are determined simultaneously so that any public policy needs to be evaluated in terms of both efficiency and equity. Such a position is not popular with many economists who believe that economic analysis can address issues of efficiency but must remain silent on value judgments about the fair distribution of economic and social goods (Robbins, 1932; Brennan, 1996, p. 133). For others, however, injustices in the distribution of income are seen as an additional example of a market failure (Peterson, 2001). From this perspective, the fact that the invisible hand of the market does not automatically lead to a distribution of income and wealth that would be accepted by all as fair and equitable means that there may be a role for the government in using its powers of taxation and expenditure to advance the social goal of distributive justice. Regardless of the how one approaches the associated problems of efficiency and equity, it is undeniable that government policies almost always have consequences for both and that some government interventions have income redistribution as their primary purpose.

Conclusion

Markets are extraordinary institutions that can be relied upon to coordinate a wide range of economic activity in ways that ensure efficiency while allowing individual agents a great deal of freedom in the pursuit of their ends.

The economic framework developed in this chapter recognizes that there are market failures that may be corrected by government intervention but the implication of the analysis is that if there is no market failure, the government should allow the market to operate freely. At the same time, because government interventions are likely to have multiple impacts, the specific market failures or distributional issues that are identified and the way in which they are attacked cannot easily be separated from political, ethical, and broad social considerations. Government policies will never be entirely determined by the cool calculation of costs and benefits as will become evident in the closer examination of agricultural policies that follow. Still, as a general principle, the notion that government economic policies should be justifiable with reference to identifiable imperfections in the way markets work seems to be a sound starting point in any evaluation of such policies, including those related to food and agriculture.

Appendix 2.1: The Theory of the Invisible Hand

For economists, a well-functioning economy is one that is efficient. Efficiency means that the greatest amount of goods and services possible are produced given the quantities of productive resources (labor, capital, raw materials) that are available. Efficiency in this sense means that nothing is wasted and all resources are fully employed. In an efficient economy, there is no way to increase the output of one good, say, chocolate ice-cream, without reducing the output of some other good or goods. The reason for this is that increasing chocolate ice-cream output would require that more resources be allocated to its production. But if all resources are already being used to produce goods and services, allocating more resources to chocolate ice-cream production means withdrawing them from other productive activities and this in turn means reduced output of something. Output of all goods in this economy can be increased over time but only if the amount of resources available increases or if the existing resources become more productive as a result of technological innovation.

A well-functioning economy should not only produce goods and services efficiently but should also distribute them among consumers in an efficient manner. Economists refer to distributional efficiency as Pareto optimality,[6] defined as a situation in which no one can be made better off without making someone else worse off. This is clearly analogous to productive efficiency as

---

[6]   Pareto optimality is named for the Italian economist, Vilfredo Pareto (1848–1923), who first developed the concept.

defined above, but applies to the distribution of goods and services among consumers. Why is Pareto optimality desirable? Many economists are utilitarians who believe that the best society is one that maximizes social well-being, often referred to as "utility." Utility is thought to depend on the amounts of goods and services individuals are able to consume and the good society is one in which the maximum possible utility is attained. If a redistribution of utility-producing goods and services would increase one individual's utility without reducing the utility of anyone else, such a change would necessarily increase total utility. Once all such changes have been made, it will no longer be possible to redistribute goods and services so as to increase one person's utility without reducing the utility of someone else. In other words, Pareto optimality will have been attained. Note that once Pareto optimality has been achieved, the society is in a zero-sum game: if someone gains, someone else necessarily has to lose.

With these definitions in mind, the task is to show how rational individuals pursuing their self-interests and with no external coercive force will automatically generate an efficient and Pareto optimal economic equilibrium. Any economic system must solve three problems (see Baumol and Blinder, 1991, pp. 562–3):

1. How should the goods and services that are produced be distributed among consumers?
2. How much of each available input should be allocated to the production of a particular good or service?
3. How much of each good or service should be produced?

These problems are clearly quite complicated given the large number of goods, services, consumers, inputs, and firms that make up the building blocks for any economic system. Little is lost, however, by simplifying the analysis to assume that there are only two consumers and two firms, each using two inputs to produce one of two goods. Even in this simpler problem, there are substantial complexities because inputs can be used in many ways to produce large numbers of combinations of the two goods which can then be distributed between the two consumers in many different manners. Moreover, the question is not just how an economic system can solve the three problems but how it can do so in a way that results in allocative efficiency and Pareto optimality.

The theory of the invisible hand requires that all agents behave rationally. For an individual consumer, this is generally represented as the desire to maximize utility. The economic problem is that consumption is constrained by the size of the individual's budget. Suppose that the two goods in this example are wheat and rice. The budget constraint means that consumers cannot expand their rice and wheat consumption to a point at which they would be completely satiated. The normal consumer will have to make a choice in allocating her budgetary resources between the goods. The choices made will reflect tastes and preferences. If the consumer likes wheat more than rice, a greater share of her budget will be used to purchase wheat than would be the case if she had different preferences. To avoid additional layers of complexity, assume that there is no money so the price of wheat is the amount of rice that has to be sacrificed to obtain additional wheat. Under these circumstances, the rational consumer will increase wheat consumption until the last unit purchased brings an increase in utility that is just equal to the price of the wheat, that is, the loss of utility due to giving up a certain amount of rice.

To show why such a process leads to the greatest utility, imagine that the consumer is considering the purchase of an additional kilogram of wheat and that the price for this wheat is two kilograms of rice. If an additional kilogram of wheat will increase the consumer's utility more than the loss of utility caused by having to give up two kilograms of rice, then the rational consumer will make the purchase and realize an increase in total utility (the benefits of the additional wheat are greater than the costs in foregone rice). Most consumers would probably like to have some variety in the foods consumed so even though this individual may prefer wheat, it is unlikely that she will trade all of her rice for wheat. In fact, it is generally the case that the value of each successive unit of a good will decline as consumption increases. A second beer may bring a substantial increase in one's happiness. The third one may still bring an increase in utility but probably not as large an increase as did the second. If one continues to consume additional beers, the value of each successive beer is likely to decline until, perhaps, the prospect of another one begins to seem like a very bad idea.

This shows that while utility is positively related to consumption of a good, the rate at which utility increases as additional units of the good are consumed is not constant. This rate of change is known as marginal utility and the expectation is that it will decline as additional units are consumed. The optimum for the individual consumer is when the value (the increase in utility) of the last unit purchased is just equal to its price. At that point, an additional kilogram of wheat would not bring as much of an increase in utility as would be lost by giving up two kilograms of rice. An identical story can be told for firms deciding how much of an input to purchase. Suppose the rice farmer uses labor and fertilizer to produce his crop. There are many combinations of labor and fertilizer that will generate a unit of output. For example, using a small amount of fertilizer with a lot of labor may give the same output as would be obtained using a lot of fertilizer so that less labor would be needed to keep out the weeds that compete with the plants for soil nutrients. As in the case of the consumers, the addition to the rice output for each increment of one of the inputs declines. Economists refer to the effect of an input on total output as the marginal product and the expected decline in the marginal product is an example of the law of diminishing returns. For consumers, the optimum is attained when the marginal utility of wheat consumption is equal to its price defined as the amount of rice that is given up to purchase a unit of wheat. For the firms in this story, the optimum combination of inputs is achieved when the marginal product of the last unit of fertilizer purchased is equal to its price defined as the amount of labor that could be traded for a unit of fertilizer.

So far, we have considered the rational decision making of one of the consumers and one of the producers. It is time to bring in the other players. The second consumer is also assumed to be rational so like the first, the optimal allocation of his budget between rice and wheat will be at the point where the marginal utility of the last unit of wheat purchased is just equal to its price. Because both consumers are rational and they both face the same price, they will both choose the consumption combination that results in equating their marginal utilities to the price of wheat. At these consumption points, it will also be true that their marginal utilities will be equal to each other as well.[7] It turns out that consumption where marginal utilities are equal is a Pareto optimum. Suppose that for some reason the first consumer was consuming at a point where her marginal utility was three while the second was at a point where his marginal utility was one. In this situation, the first consumer would be willing to give up three units of rice to obtain an additional unit of wheat. The second consumer on the other hand values the wheat at one unit of rice and would be happy to trade some of his wheat at any price above one. For example, if the first consumer offered to pay two kilograms of rice in exchange for one kilogram of wheat, the second would find that an attractive offer because he is getting an amount of rice that has a greater value than the value of the wheat being given up. In other words, both would be better off as a result of the trade. In fact, they would have an incentive to continue trading

---

[7]   Let MU_1 stand for the marginal utility of the first consumer, MU_2 that of the second consumer, and P the price of wheat in terms of rice. The optimum for the first consumer is where MU_1 = P. The optimum for the second consumer is also where MU_2 = P. Since both marginal utilities are equal to P they are also equal to each other, $MU_1 = MU_2$. Note that equality of the marginal utilities does not mean that the two individuals are consuming identical amounts of the two goods. The value each consumer attaches to an additional unit of one of the goods depends on that individual's tastes and preferences and how much he or she is presently consuming. It could turn out that the marginal utilities would both be equal at a point where one consumer is consuming a lot of rice and only a little wheat while the other exhibits a very different pattern of consumption.

until their marginal utilities are equal, at which point they can no longer gain from trade because they both attach the same relative value to the two goods.

The only requirement for a Pareto optimum besides rational behavior and diminishing marginal utilities is that both consumers face the same price. This is a very important result. The market failures examined in the main text usually involve situations where prices have been distorted, are not the same for various groups of consumers or producers, or do not exist at all. The result is that the invisible hand cannot lead individuals to the point where their marginal utilities are equal, a point that is Pareto optimal. On the production side, the result is the same. If both firms face common input prices, they will choose to purchase inputs so as to equate the marginal product of one of the inputs to its price (defined as the cost in terms of the other input) and, therefore, end up in a situation where the marginal products of the two firms are equal. As in the case of the consumers, if the marginal products of the two firms were not equal to each other, the firms would value the inputs differently and they would be able to increase their outputs by exchanging resources. In other words, only when the inputs are allocated between the firms in a way that brings the marginal products into equality is the economy operating efficiently in the sense that there will be no way to reassign the two inputs that would increase the output of one firm without decreasing the output of the other.

An economic system in which all economic agents face a common set of prices is referred to as perfect competition. With perfect competition, consumers and producers are price takers in the sense that they cannot influence market prices through a change in behavior. Recall that some U.S. gasoline consumers suspect that the large petroleum companies are using their market power to raise prices. If these firms were perfectly competitive price takers, they would be unable to charge prices higher than the prevailing market price because there would be numerous alternatives for consumers who would simply take their business to competitors with lower prices. With perfect competition, market prices reflect the values consumers attach to various goods as well as the resource costs incurred by producers to bring the goods to market. Rational consumers and producers respond to these prices with the result that the distribution of the goods between the consumers is Pareto optimal and the inputs used to produce them are allocated efficiently. The first two problems listed above are, thus, resolved automatically in an economic system with perfectly competitive prices.

There is one final challenge for the invisible hand of the competitive market. This is the problem of determining how much of each of the outputs to produce. So far, we have focused on the relation of inputs to outputs in analyzing production decisions. But we could also think about the cost of producing more of one good in terms of the amount of the other good that would have to be given up to do so given that productive resources are not unlimited. Suppose that all labor and fertilizer were allocated to the production of wheat. A lot of wheat would be produced but there would be no rice production at all. If some labor and fertilizer were shifted from wheat production to rice production, the amount of wheat produced would fall. The cost of producing rice in this case is the amount of wheat given up. A related concept, opportunity cost, is defined as the value of the best alternative to a particular course of action. Choosing to employ resources in rice production means that they are unavailable for wheat production, the next best alternative in this simple economy. The opportunity cost of using scarce resources to produce rice is the value of the wheat that could have been produced had the resources been used for wheat production instead. Opportunity cost may not be constant. As resources are removed from wheat production, there may initially be a large increase in rice production because some of the resources previously allocated to wheat are better adapted to rice production. Once substantial amounts of resources have been removed from wheat production, additional resource shifts may not generate large increases in rice output. For this analysis, we assume non-constant (or nonlinear) opportunity costs.

The value to society of wheat and rice can be determined by considering either the marginal opportunity cost or the value to consumers of the two goods. In a competitive equilibrium, the marginal utility of wheat is the same for both consumers and this value can then be taken to represent the social marginal utility. Suppose the marginal utility of wheat is three units of rice while the marginal opportunity cost of additional wheat production is one, that is, an additional unit of wheat can be produced by giving up a unit of rice. This situation is not optimal because the value to consumers of additional wheat is greater than the cost of producing the additional wheat. Suppose the figures were reversed so that the marginal utility of wheat is one and the marginal cost is three. Now the value to consumers of wheat is less than its cost which implies in this particular case that the value of rice to consumers is greater than its cost in terms of the wheat that would have to be given up to produce the additional rice. Either way, society would be better off adjusting wheat and rice output until the marginal cost of each good is equal to the marginal utility of the two consumers.

There is one additional theoretical result needed to complete the analysis. The optimum combination of inputs for a firm that is maximizing its profits has been shown to depend on the prices of the inputs. The optimal total output for each of the two firms in this example depends on the output price. Profit-maximizing firms will produce where marginal cost is equal to the output price. Suppose that the cost of producing an additional unit of wheat is less than the price the producer will receive for the additional wheat. It would be in that producer's interest to produce more wheat and to continue expanding wheat production until the marginal cost is equal to the price. But this price is the same as the price paid by consumers. As long as prices are competitive, consumers and producers will face the same market price and rational pursuit of self-interest will lead them to equate marginal utility and marginal cost to this price. As before, if two things are both equal to the same amount, they have to be equal to each other. So at the competitive optimum, social marginal cost will be equal to social marginal utility and it will not be possible to find another combination of outputs that would make one consumer better off without reducing the well-being of the other. The invisible hand operating through competitive prices has given rise to an efficient resource allocation in production, a Pareto-optimal distribution of the goods between the consumers, and a Pareto-optimal combination of outputs.

Appendix 2.2: The Prisoners' Dilemma

The prisoners' dilemma can be used to show how individuals rationally pursuing their self-interest may end up reducing social welfare. In the classic story, two individuals have been arrested on suspicion of robbing a bank. The police can charge them with the crime of carrying a concealed weapon but are certain that these individuals committed the more serious crime of bank robbery. Unfortunately, there are no credible witnesses so the police need a confession from the two thieves if they are to get a conviction on the more serious charge. Having carefully read their economics textbooks, the police offer the prisoners the following deal shown in Figure 2.1:

Number of years in prison if:	Prisoner 1 Confesses	Prisoner 1 Stonewalls
Prisoner 2 Confesses	(6,6)	(12,0)
Prisoner 2 Stonewalls	(0,12)	(1,1)

Figure 2.1 Payoff matrix for the prisoners' dilemma

The figures in parentheses indicate the number of years the prisoners will be jailed if they confess or refuse to confess (stonewall) with the number of years for the first prisoner shown on the left of the parenthetical expression and that of the second on the right. If both confess, they will each receive a sentence of six years in prison. If they both stonewall, the police will only be able to get a conviction on the concealed weapons charge and they will each receive sentences of one year. If, on the other hand, one confesses while the other stonewalls, the one who confesses and testifies against the other will serve no jail time and the stonewalling prisoner will receive a particularly severe sentence of 12 years. For example, in the upper, right-hand cell of Figure 2.1, prisoner 1 receives a sentence of 12 years because he refused to confess while prisoner 2 is released because she cooperated with police and confessed to the bank robbery. The reverse would be the case if the first prisoner confessed while the second stonewalled.

The dominant strategy for both prisoners is to confess with the result that they will each be sentenced to six years in jail. To see why this is the case, imagine that you and a friend are the two prisoners and that, prior to appearing before a judge to enter your pleas, you both agree to stonewall. If this strategy can be carried out, you will each serve a year in jail which is clearly better than sentences of six or 12 years. The problem is you may not be able to trust your friend to stick to the agreed strategy. Suppose the judge asks you first how you wish to plead in the case. If you reply "not guilty, your honor," your disloyal friend has only to say "I confess" and he will go free while you are sent up the river for 12 years. Knowing this, unless there is absolute trust or some way of insuring that the agreement that was made will be enforced, the only rational thing for you to do is to confess. And once you have confessed, your friend would be crazy to stonewall because then he would get the long sentence while you go free. No matter how the other prisoner pleads, your best strategy is to confess. If he confesses, your best course of action is to confess and if he stonewalls, your best strategy is still to confess. This is true for both prisoners making confession the dominant strategy in this game.

So both prisoners confess and wind up with a total of 12 years of prison time. From the point of view of the prisoners, this is clearly inferior to the situation if both had stonewalled for a total of two years in jail although the police would no doubt see things differently. In the language of Appendix 2.1, the results in a prisoners' dilemma are not Pareto optimal. Rational individuals pursuing their self-interest end up in a situation in which both could be made better off, the opposite of what would occur if the invisible hand were at work. The prisoners' dilemma is particularly useful in explaining the tendency for individuals to free-ride in the provision of public goods and to over-exploit common pool resources. In these cases, social welfare would be enhanced by cooperative behavior but the individual incentives are to behave uncooperatively. The problem of overfishing described earlier is an example of such a situation. The fishing boat captains are caught in a prisoners' dilemma with the incentives all pointing in the direction of fishing as much as possible before the stocks are completely exhausted.

Experimental economists have discovered a number of ways to overcome defection in prisoners' dilemma games. For example, the dominant strategy if the game is repeated over an indefinite period with the final game left unidentified is known as "tit-for-tat." This strategy calls for the participants to respond on each successive game as the other player did on the previous game. Tit-for-tat strategies can give rise to stable equilibria in which the players both cooperate. If there is a pre-announced final game, however, the temptation to defect in the last game may be hard to resist. Another way to overcome defection in prisoners' dilemma games is through establishing enforceable contracts. If the prisoners in the original story were both members of an organized crime syndicate such as the Mafia, their verbal agreement might have been sufficient to prevent defection as they would know that cooperating with the police would almost certainly bring swift and deadly retribution. James M. Buchanan (1975) has argued that Hobbes's state of nature (the war of all against all) is a giant prisoners' dilemma which can be resolved by the creation of a state that is responsible for enforcing contracts so that people can do business. Buchanan's view is similar to our earlier conclusion that legal institutions created and enforced by the state are a necessary prerequisite for a market economy to function.

There are many examples of situations that can be characterized as prisoners' dilemmas. During the Cold War, the arms race between the Soviet Union and the United States was a prisoners' dilemma. While both countries would have been better off using scarce resources to produce goods of greater benefit than nuclear arms and missiles, the dominant strategy was to build more arms. As the leaders of the two countries continued negotiations on arms control, somewhat greater trust developed allowing them to accept some verification of compliance by the other country. This verification served as an enforcement mechanism for the agreements on arms control that were reached. Another example of a prisoners' dilemma is advertizing by Coca-Cola and Pepsi. Advertisements are costly and may actually have little effect on total sales. If one of the companies stopped advertising, however, it would probably see its share of the market erode as its competitor continued to advertize. To avoid this both continue to spend a lot of money on advertisements that do little to increase company profits. If the two companies could reach an agreement with some mechanism to ensure that the contract would be enforced, they could both save a great deal of money. Of course, any contractual arrangement on advertizing between Coca-Cola and Pepsi would probably appear to be collusion and, as such, run afoul of antitrust laws. As these and other examples suggest, there may be many situations that have the characteristics of a prisoners' dilemma. In these cases, the rational pursuit of self-interest will lead to free-riding, defection, and other forms of uncooperative behavior rather than the Pareto optimal outcomes associated with the invisible hand.

3

The Structure of the World Food System

Introduction

As noted in Chapter 1, Malthus's prediction that population growth would outpace food production and result in famine, war and death, has not been corroborated over the past two centuries. This is not to say that there have been no famines, wars, or other disasters causing loss of human life but only that population has not grown more rapidly than food production. In fact, there is more food available per person today than at any previous time in human history despite the fact that world population has increased by a factor of six since Malthus wrote his essay (Fogel, 2004). Although statistical data for the nineteenth century are scarce and unreliable, there is evidence that agricultural output has expanded over the past 200 years at a rate that has frequently been greater than the rate of increase of world population. Federico (2005) reports data showing that the amount of food available per person remained largely constant between 1800 and 1870 for the world as a whole and that this remained true for much of the world until 1938. Some countries in Europe and North and South America began to experience more rapid growth in per capita food availability after 1870 and per capita food output took off almost everywhere after the Second World War (Federico, 2005). Federico (2005) reports estimates that world agricultural output grew at an average annual rate of 2.3 percent between 1950 and 2000 compared with average annual world population growth of 1.7 percent during that period. Based on statistics from the FAO, average daily caloric intake per person increased 35 percent between 1961 and 2005 (FAOSTAT, http://faostat.fao.org/site).

The main reason that Malthus missed the mark in his original prediction is that he underestimated the potential for technological innovation to increase agricultural output. During the nineteenth century, much of the increase in food production was due to increases in the amount of land being cultivated.

Some of these increases in cultivated land stemmed from colonization and settlement in North and South America and Africa but, according to Federico (2005), even in densely populated Asian countries, the total amounts of land used for agriculture increased during this period. Cultivated land was not the only agricultural input that grew during the nineteenth century. Agricultural labor, capital inputs, and other resources used in agricultural production all expanded along with the growing acreage planted and these changes meant that world agricultural production increased. If food production increases are brought about exclusively by growth in the amount of inputs used, however, per capita food availability is likely to remain relatively constant. More people using more land and other inputs will end up producing more food in total but may not raise the amounts available per person. Data reported by Federico (2005) showing relatively constant levels of per capita food availability until the Second World War are consistent with this observation.

In the twentieth century, the amounts of many of the traditional agricultural inputs (land and labor) being used ceased growing and in some cases began to decline, yet total food production grew dramatically. This growth was due to technological innovation and increasing agricultural productivity. Technological change is indicated by changes in measures of total factor productivity (TFP) defined as the amount of output that can be obtained from a given set of inputs. Federico (2005) reports evidence showing that TFP in agriculture grew slowly even in the period leading up to the First World War. Following the Second World War, however, agricultural TFP began to grow at substantially higher rates in most parts of the world. Growth in agricultural productivity over the past 50 years has been fueled by the development of scientific research in both the industrialized and low-income countries. Much agricultural research has been supported by public expenditures although in recent years research and development by private firms has taken on increased importance in sustaining the rate of growth of agricultural productivity.

Of course, the fact that world food production has grown more rapidly than world population even during the population growth surge that took place following the Second World War, does not guarantee that these successes will continue indefinitely. Dramatic food price increases in 2008 gave rise to concerns that the long-term trend of declining food prices that had prevailed in the post-war period had come to an end. In addition, many analysts worry that the ability of plant and animal breeders and other scientists to continue making the dramatic scientific discoveries that have fueled productivity growth over the past century may be declining at a time when current agricultural practices have begun to put strains on the environment. A report issued by a group of scientists sponsored by the FAO and the Consultative Group on International Agricultural Research (CGIAR), an umbrella organization for the network of international agricultural research centers that have played important roles in increased agricultural productivity in developing countries, predicted that the world's water supplies could be exhausted within 50 years (CGIAR, 2006). The scientists suggested that water shortages may lead to conflict between countries, declining food supplies, and further environmental degradation. The sustainability of world economic activity, including food production, has been an important issue since the 1970s when the first United Nations conference on the environment was held in Stockholm, Sweden. The relationship between environmental degradation and economic growth and development was a major theme of the 1992 Earth Summit held in Rio de Janeiro as well as in the follow-up conference held in Johannesburg, South Africa in 2002 (Division for Sustainable Development, 2002).

Producing adequate amounts of food to feed growing populations without destroying the environment on which human life depends is not the only problem confronting the world food system. Current food production is sufficient to provide every human being with more than enough food to live a healthy and productive life but there are still more than 850 million people, about 13 percent of the world population, who are hungry and undernourished. The reason hunger is still prevalent is because of widespread poverty not insufficient food production. The poor lack the means to purchase adequate amounts of food. Runge *et al.* (2003) describe a poor family in Bangladesh with an annual income of about $400 for a household of six people. Income is earned through the father's work pulling a rickshaw and from other heavy labor done by family members. Some of the food needs are met from the family's agricultural production on land holdings totaling less than half an acre. The adults in the household consume a little more than half the recommended daily allowance of calories given the energy required for the work they perform and the children also suffer from severe under-nutrition. It is not because of insufficient food production in Bangladesh that the members of this family are so severely under-nourished but rather because of their extreme poverty.

If some individuals consume less than adequate amounts of food at the same time that sufficient food is produced to feed everyone well, it has to be the case that some people are consuming more food than is strictly necessary for survival and good health. The other side of under-nutrition among the poor is over-nutrition for much of the world's population. Obesity has been a health problem in the United States for decades and is becoming a more serious threat to health in Europe and even in some developing countries. The world food system that has achieved such stunning success in generating enough food to feed a rapidly expanding world population has been less successful in assuring sustainable food security and healthy diets for all. The purpose of this chapter is to describe the basic structure of this world food system. In the next section, the history and evolution of the ways in which food has been acquired, processed, and consumed are briefly summarized. This is followed by a profile of today's global food system.

Historical Perspectives

It is helpful to think of the network of organizations, institutions, and individual agents that produce, process, transport, and distribute food as a system. Systems transform sets of outside inputs into outputs. Within the system itself there may be complex connections and feedback mechanisms. An airplane, for example, is a system that uses inputs such as fuel and skilled labor to produce an output, transportation services. The airplane and its crew work together to generate the thrust that moves the plane through the air making adjustments in its operation in light of feedback obtained from monitoring its performance. Likewise, a food system uses various resources (labor, raw materials, land, and capital) to obtain raw food products and transform them into consumable food that contributes to health and well-being. The specific actions carried out to achieve these tasks are subject to long-term evolution and short-term adjustment in light of changing circumstances and feedback related to differences between the desired and actual performance of the system.

Any food system has to solve three sets of problems. First, edible raw food materials have to be obtained in some way. Second, these raw food products have to be transported, processed, stored, and distributed to potential consumers. Finally, finished food products are cooked and consumed. It turns out that each of these functions can be accomplished in a wide range of manners leading to great variation in the ways in which people around the world and through time have fed themselves. Food systems include subsystems for dealing with each of the three problem areas. The production subsystem uses such inputs as human and animal labor, fishing boats and equipment, farm machinery, energy, fertilizers, animal feeds, and pesticides to produce raw food products. It is important to note that the output of the production subsystem almost always needs a lot of further manipulation before it can be consumed. Ears of maize in a field in the U.S. Midwest are of little use to anyone until they have been collected, transported, and transformed into meat, high-fructose maize syrup, ethanol, breakfast cereals, or some other consumable good. The output from the production subsystem is one of the inputs used by the second component of the food system, the post-harvest subsystem. Other inputs for this system include labor, capital and other resources and the output is finished food products delivered to consumers. The post-harvest subsystem carries out such activities as transportation, processing, storage, and marketing. The output of the post-harvest subsystem is an input into the final component, the consumption subsystem. As for the other subsystems, various inputs are combined with the output of the post-harvest subsystem to generate an output, in this case, human well-being and nutritional health.

This vision of food systems provides a framework for describing the many different ways human populations have found to feed themselves. For most of human history, small groups of human beings satisfied their food needs by hunting wild animals and foraging for edible wild plants and insects. Hunting and gathering are still practiced in some parts of Africa, South America, and Asia but have been replaced with systems based on agricultural production in most of the world. Traditional hunting and gathering were very effective solutions to the food problems identified earlier requiring relatively little work and allowing a great deal of leisure time (Weisdorf, 2003). Food was generally eaten where it was found so there was little need for elaborate transportation, storage, or processing activities. If the diets of modern hunter-gatherers such as the Khoisan in Southern Africa are a reliable indication, our hunter-gatherer ancestors obtained most of their calories from animal products and fiber-rich nuts and tubers (Cordain *et al.*, 2000). Some analysts have argued that the shift from hunting and gathering to sedentary agriculture resulted in a less healthy diet as well as increased disease as a result of living in close proximity to domesticated animals (Diamond, 1999) or because of increased carbohydrate consumption from cereal grains and a less-active lifestyle (Larsen, 2003).

Given the advantages of hunting and gathering, many scholars have wondered why humans elected to develop sedentary agriculture some 10,000 years ago. Weisdorf (2003) suggests that many factors may have contributed to this change including climate modification, competition with other groups for resources, and declines in wild animal populations. It is important to recognize that, in the heyday of hunting and gathering, life expectancies were probably less than 30 years and population densities were low. Hunter-gatherer bands require large areas over which to forage so this kind of lifestyle would not be possible in a densely populated world. As population densities have increased, settled agriculturalists have encroached on land over which small bands of hunter-gatherers used to roam, often with devastating impacts on the hunter-gatherers. O'Keefe and Lavendar (1989) report that there has been a serious decline in the nutritional status of Khoisan hunter-gatherers in Namibia who have been forced to abandon their traditional lifestyle. On the other hand, the development of agriculture, sometimes referred to as the Neolithic Revolution, does seem to have set in motion a process that has led to increased life expectancies, larger populations, and, perhaps, much of modern civilization. Diamond (1999) notes that population densities began to rise with the creation of agriculture and suggests that the food surpluses that could be generated by sedentary farmers allowed for the development of stratified societies with differentiated roles for craftsmen, political and religious leaders, poets, scholars and scientists.

The Neolithic Revolution represented a major shift in the way in which human beings solved the problem of procuring edible raw food products. Both Diamond (1999) and Pringle (1998) argue that the initial domestication of plants and animals occurred gradually as hunter-gatherers began growing certain plants as supplements to their normal diets. Eventually, sedentary settlements were established and hunting and gathering began to decline as a food source while the cultivation of domesticated plants took on ever greater importance (Pringle, 1999). Sedentary agriculture appears to have developed independently in several places, most notably in the Fertile Crescent (Iraq), China, and Mesoamerica. In these three areas, cereal grains (wheat, barley, maize, rice, and millet) and pulses (lentils, peas, soybeans, and other beans) were the main crops (Diamond, 1999). Food surpluses from these agricultural production systems made the development of great civilizations possible although the majority of people continued to live in relatively small communities that practiced subsistence agriculture. Most of the food produced in these subsistence systems was processed, cooked, and consumed within households.

Purely subsistence agriculture is still found in some of the more remote areas of the world. As in the case of hunter-gatherer systems, subsistence agriculturalists have limited contact with markets and make use of few inputs from the outside world. Beckerman (1987) describes a typical subsistence food system as practiced by the Bari who live in the upper reaches of the Amazon river basin. The Bari employ slash-and-burn cultivation techniques similar to the maize production system in Benin described in the first chapter. In this case, however, the staple food is cassava which is produced on plots that are used for five to 10 years and then left fallow for 25 to 50 years. Bananas, plantains, and maize are also produced. A few steel tools such as machetes are purchased from the outside but everything else used for cultivation, the construction of shelter, cooking and other household activities is hand crafted within the village. The only fertilizer used is the ash that is left on the field after burning the vegetation, which was cut down when the field was first cleared for cultivation. Pigs and chickens are raised for food and diets are supplemented with foodstuffs obtained through hunting and gathering. The post-harvest and consumption subsystems are internal to the village with extended families working together to process, store, cook, and consume food produced through their own endeavors. Beckerman suggests that the Bari produce the equivalent of about 1.2 metric tons of grain per hectare, significantly less than average maize yields in the United States (9.5 metric tons per hectare in 2007). Some subsistence food systems can be quite productive, however.

Rappaport (1979) estimates that a group of subsistence agriculturalists in the highlands of New Guinea obtained food with an energy content of 17 calories for every calorie expended to produce the food compared with the U.S. Great Plains where each calorie used to produce wheat results in food with an energy content of only 11 calories.

Over the past several hundred years, most groups practicing a pure subsistence agriculture have gradually been transformed through contact with the wider society. In Africa, Asia and Latin America, large numbers of people continue to practice slash-and-burn agriculture and to obtain much of their food from household production. Kelley (1990) estimates that about 30 percent of arable land in developing countries is cultivated with slash-and-burn methods (see also Palm *et al.*, 2005 and Dixon *et al.*, 2001). This type of production subsystem is perfectly sustainable as long as population densities remain low. During the 1960s and 1970s, the World Health Organization (WHO) of the United Nations began widespread vaccinations against smallpox all over the world. In Benin, prior to the WHO vaccination campaign, smallpox resulted in the deaths of about half the children born before they reached the age of five. Vaccinations and other improvements in health care contribute to reduced mortality and high population growth rates.[1] Between 1961 and 2006, Benin's population grew from about 2.27 million to 8.76 million, an average annual population growth rate of 3.0 percent (FAOSTAT, http://faostat.fao.org/site). Rapid increases in population can lead to increased population densities and pressures to bring land back into cultivation before the full fallow period needed to rejuvenate the soils has elapsed. In addition, larger populations often cause deforestation as farmers in need of more land colonize new areas and put previously virgin forest into cultivation. Both these outcomes lead to environmental damage and reduce the sustainability of slash-and-burn production systems.[2]

[1]   In Benin, smallpox was such an important disease that a smallpox deity had become part of the traditional religion. Traditional religious beliefs in southern Benin were the basis for the development of Voodoo in Haiti. The word Voodoo comes from *vodun* in the Fon language of southern Benin, a word that signifies the pantheon of animistic spirits and gods that could be called upon by the living for help. Shrines where offerings are made to the smallpox spirit (referred to as a fetish by French-speaking Beninese) and others such as the god of war and metal (Ogun known in Haiti as Ogun-ferraille) or the sexually prolific Legba who speaks all the languages of the gods and men, are common in rural Benin. The WHO smallpox vaccination campaign successfully resulted in the eradication of this scourge in the 1970s. The last reported case was in Somalia in 1977 (http://www.bt.cdc.gov/agent/smallpox/overview/disease-facts.asp).

[2]   The impact of slash-and-burn agriculture, particularly in the Brazilian Amazon, is viewed as so negative by many that a consortium of non-governmental organizations (NGOs), universities, and others was formed in 1992 at the end of the Rio Earth Summit organized by the United Nations. The Alternatives to Slash-and-Burn (ASB) consortium works to reduce the practice of slash-and-burn agriculture that has caused extensive deforestation. See Palm *et al.* (2005).

These environmental problems create pressures to modify traditional agricultural systems. In addition, the availability of a much broader range of goods in the local markets means that farmers have an incentive to produce more than is strictly needed for household consumption. The need for a marketed surplus to serve as a source of income that can be used to purchase modern household goods and other consumer items adds to the pressure to modernize the traditional food system. As market connections become more prominent, activities previously carried out within the household may be outsourced to specialized entrepreneurs. In southern Benin, a network of roads connects periodic markets that are rotated in a four-day cycle among market towns in a particular region. Much of the local marketing is done by women who sell tomatoes and other fresh produce, maize, and a variety of other goods on market days in the town nearest to their villages. The markets are also attended by itinerant traders, mostly men from the Yoruba ethnic group who specialize in cooking utensils, thread, and other household goods. The range of goods available in a typical West African periodic market is extraordinary, including talismans and herbs used in traditional medicine, used and new clothing, bicycles, kerosene lamps, and much more.

The income generated from sales in these markets allows households to purchase tools and other goods as well as various services. For example, grain produced by a household has to be processed through removal of husks and, perhaps, grinding into flour or meal that can be used in cooking. In a purely subsistence food system, post-harvest activities such as grain milling are done within the household and this used to be the case in West Africa, where grain milling was traditionally done by women using a mortar and pestle. Today in countries like Benin, maize is frequently ground into meal by a diesel-powered mill owned and operated by someone in the village who charges a fee for this service. The evolution of food systems has largely been a process of increasing specialization as the role of markets in coordinating food production, processing, transportation, and consumption has expanded. In the United States, for example, farm households produce a narrow range of commodities using inputs that are purchased from specialized firms. The commodities are transferred to agribusiness firms that take care of all the post-harvest activities and then distribute the food to retailers and restaurants where consumers, including the farmers who produced the original commodities, select the food items to be consumed.

Dorel (1987) describes a modern food system in the Champagne region of France. Much of the land used in this system was reclaimed after the Second World War and planted initially to wheat. European Union (EU) policies have provided substantial support for grains, sugar beets, and various livestock enterprises. In the region described by Dorel, the incentive structure created by these policies worked to encourage the cultivation of sugar beets and alfalfa at the expense of wheat, although wheat remains the most widely cultivated crop. The region is characterized by relatively low rainfall with very large farms by French standards. According to Dorel, the average farm size was 60 hectares (about 150 acres) much larger than a typical French farm (25 hectares) but smaller than an average U.S. farm (about 180 hectares or 444 acres in 2005). The production subsystem in this region is based on the use of manufactured inputs including petroleum, fertilizer, pesticides, machinery, and equipment. Of special note is the significance of purchased seeds multiplied and distributed by specialized seed companies. In traditional agricultural systems, seeds are generally retained from last year's crop rather than purchased from seed companies. In addition, farms in the Champagne region rely on credit markets to finance their operations. Credit is needed because large expenditures for purchased inputs must be made well before any crops are harvested and sold.

Output from the production subsystem is sold to specialized agribusiness firms that store, process, and commercialize the food. Sugar beets, for example are sold to local mills that operate under rules and support systems established by the EU's Common Agricultural Policy (CAP). The CAP insures that sugar in the EU commands a price that is much higher than the world price and this price support translates into better prices for the beet producers as well. Virtually all of the functions carried out by the post-harvest subsystem are handled by agribusiness firms and cooperatives that are connected to the farmers by markets. The food products produced by this subsystem are passed to a modern wholesale and retail system that distributes food to consumers primarily through supermarket chains. About 23 percent of consumer expenditures for food in France are made for food away from home (Ministère de l'Agriculture et de la Peche, 2006). French farmers in the Champagne region may have a small vegetable garden for home consumption as do many French citizens working in non-agricultural occupations, but the farmers and other consumers purchase the vast majority of the food they consume from modern retail outlets where they find food products produced in France and imported from all over the world.

The World Food System

The most striking aspect of the evolution of food systems from hunting and gathering to complex modern systems is the increasing role played by firms, governments, agricultural researchers, traders, and many others in executing the activities related to the provision of food. Operations previously carried out within rural households are increasingly handled by specialized firms and organizations that operate through markets to obtain inputs and commercialize their outputs. In addition, the markets that have come to play such important roles in national food systems are becoming increasingly global. The world food system is made up of national food systems that are linked to each other through trade, investment, labor movements, and foreign aid. Although trade in food, agricultural commodities and agricultural inputs such as fertilizer has increased dramatically since the Second World War, most countries still rely on their domestic producers and post-harvest industries for much of their food supplies. Still, the influence of world market conditions on domestic prices and other national economic conditions has become highly significant. Global interdependencies were vividly illustrated in 2008 by worldwide increases in food prices that resulted from such diverse phenomena as income growth in China and India, biofuel policies in the EU and United States, drought in Australia, export restrictions in food exporting countries such as Argentina and Thailand, and rising prices for petroleum-based inputs.

Tables 3.1 to 3.6 have been designed to provide a statistical profile of the world food system. In some of the tables, China and India have been separated from the rest of the Asian region because of their size and importance. With populations of more than a billion in each of these countries, they account for some 38 percent of total world population. Over half the world's population is found in Asia, which has long been the most populous region on the planet. Of the five countries with the largest populations, three (China, India, and Indonesia) are in Asia. The other two countries in the top five are the United States (third on the list) and Brazil (fifth). If the EU is counted as a single entity rather than 27 separate countries, it would come in third on the list. About 84 percent of the world's population live in low- and middle-income developing countries. Because population growth rates tend to be higher in developing countries, the proportion of the world population living in these countries is likely to increase (UNDP, 2008). Population growth rates have begun to decline and it seems likely that world population will stabilize at about nine to 10 billion toward the middle of the twenty-first century. Several countries in Europe have begun to record negative population growth rates and the UNDP predicts that the countries comprising Eastern and Central Europe and the former Soviet Union will see declining populations over the period 2005–15.

Population growth is measured by the difference between annual births and deaths in a country with adjustments for net migration. For most countries, net migration (immigrants minus emigrants) is of limited significance and the main factors in population growth are the birth and death rates. Countries with high population growth rates (in excess of 2 percent per year) will end up with

Table 3.1 World population and land use (2006)

Region	Population, millions (2006)	Total land area (million hectares)	Total agricultural land (million hectares)	% agricultural land that is arable	% agricultural land in permanent crops	% agricultural land in permanent pasture	% arable land that is irrigated
Sub-Saharan Africa	750.5	2,334	947	17.0	2.2	80.8	3.5
China & India	2,480.3	1,289	736	41.2	2.9	55.9	36.4
Other Asia	1,503.6	1,433	635	24.8	6.5	68.7	39.8
Australia/N. Zealand	24.7	801	457	10.8	0.5	88.7	5.7
Europe*	588.1	590	267	60.4	5.6	34.0	7.7
Russia	143.2	1,710	216	56.7	0.8	42.5	3.8
Latin America/ Caribbean	565.0	2,055	726	19.7	2.7	77.6	13.0
Near East/N. Africa	408.8	1,268	458	19.1	2.5	78.4	33.6
North America	335.5	2,003	477	45.9	1.8	52.3	10.6
World	6,592.8	13,432	4,973	28.2	2.8	69.0	19.8

* Excluding the Russian Federation.

Source: FAOSTAT (http://faostat.fao.org/site/) and author's calculations. See Appendix 3.1 for country groupings.

young populations as the additions to the population through birth are much greater than the subtractions due to death. Between 1975 and 2005, the annual population growth rate in Sub-Saharan Africa averaged 2.8 percent and in 2005, 44 percent of the population were aged less than 15 years. In contrast, high-income countries registered average annual population growth of 0.6 percent over the same period and in 2005, only 18 percent of their populations were under 15 (UNDP, 2008). Conversely, countries with low or negative population growth rates will have more older people. The UNDP predicts that there will be no population growth in Japan between 2005 and 2015 and that 26 percent of Japan's population will be 65 or older in 2015. This can be compared to the situation in Ireland where the population growth rate for the period 2005–15 is expected to average 1.5 percent per year and only 12 percent of the population will be 65 or older in 2015 (UNDP, 2008). In some parts of Europe and in North America, immigration may partly offset the effects of low population growth rates on the age distribution of the population.

The amount of fertile land available is of critical importance for food production systems based on agriculture. As shown in Table 3.1, some regions are more favorably endowed with arable land than others. In Sub-Saharan Africa, for example, only 17 percent of agricultural land is arable with most of the rest in permanent pasture. Of course, much of the African continent is covered by deserts, notably the Sahara Desert, the largest on earth. In contrast, China, India, Europe, Russia, and North America have extensive land resources that can be used for agricultural production. Irrigation is more highly developed in Asia where rice is the staple food than in other regions where rain-fed cultivation is more widespread. Tropical soils are generally of lower quality than temperate zone soils which were deposited more recently as a result of volcanic activity and glaciation. Sometimes, relatively fertile soils may be left uncultivated because of particular environmental conditions. In Burkina Faso, the fertile valleys of the three rivers that come together in Ghana to form the Volta River were uninhabited for many years because of the presence of a fly that transmits the parasites that cause onchocerciasis (river blindness). A campaign to eradicate the fly led to the successful colonization of these river valleys (McMillan, 1995).

Cereal grains are the main staple food throughout the world although the type of grain cultivated and consumed varies from one region to another (see Tables 3.2 and 3.3). Wheat and barley which originated in the Fertile Crescent are still the main types of cereal grain in Europe, the Middle East, and Russia while rice is the most widely cultivated grain in Asia. Maize which is indigenous to the Americas is widely cultivated in temperate climatic zones along with wheat and barley but the United States is the dominant maize producer with about 41 percent of world production. Other important crops grown

Table 3.2 World production of major agricultural commodity groups and percentages of the total produced in various regions (2007)

Agricultural commodity group	World production (million metric tons)	% world production in Sub-Saharan Africa	% world production in China & India	% world production in other Asian countries	% world production in North Africa/ Near East	% world production in Europe	% world production in Latin America/ Caribbean	% world production in North America
Cereal grains	2,340.7	4.7	30.4	17.3	3.5	16.9	7.4	19.8
Oilseed crops	407.9	2.8	18.8	21.2	1.3	5.4	28.9	21.6
Pulses	61.3	17.1	33.8	11.4	5.2	11.1	11.1	10.3
Fiber crops	29.1	4.8	47.1	18.5	5.8	2.1	6.2	15.5
Starchy roots	742.1	27.7	28.1	12.8	2.3	17.5	7.9	3.2
Sugar beet/cane	1484.9	4.6	10.1	17.4	3.3	11.4	49.1	4.1
Coffee, tea, cacao	15.6	27.6	15.4	24.9	–	–	32.1	–
Fruit	498.2	9.7	28.9	14.2	7.4	14.1	20.6	5.1
Vegetables	890.6	2.9	58.2	11.3	8.0	10.6	4.5	4.5
Meat	283.8	3.0	32.5	12.4	3.1	18.5	14.2	16.3
Milk	635.3	2.7	16.4	15.9	6.0	33.6	10.9	14.5
Fish, seafood*	128.2	3.5	38.7	23.5	1.8	13.6	13.8	5.1
% world population in region**	100.0	11.4	37.6	22.8	6.2	11.1	8.6	5.1

* 2005.

** World population in 2006 was about 6.59 billion.

Source: FAOSTAT (http://faostat.fao.org/site/) and author's calculations. See Appendix 3.1 for country groupings.

Table 3.3 World consumption of major agricultural commodity groups and percentages of the total consumed in various regions (2003)

Agricultural commodity group	World consumption (million metric tons)	% world consumption in Sub-Saharan Africa	% world consumption in China & India	% world consumption in other Asian countries*	% world consumption in North Africa/ Near East	% world consumption in Europe	% world consumption in Latin America/ Caribbean	% world consumption in North America
Cereal grains	1,911.8	5.2	27.1	16.0	7.7	19.4	9.0	15.5
Oilseed crops	407.1	3.3	25.9	17.8	3.0	15.7	19.1	15.2
Pulses	57.0	15.3	34.8	11.3	7.6	14.4	12.4	4.1
Fiber crops	24.9	2.3	51.0	19.7	7.1	6.2	8.0	5.7
Starchy roots	703.46	24.4	32.1	9.4	2.6	20.0	7.6	3.9
Sugar, raw equivalent	172.2	4.5	21.7	17.2	7.1	20.3	15.7	13.5
Coffee, tea, cacao	14.7	7.1	9.2	15.5	6.1	31.3	15.4	15.4
Fruit	489.1	8.9	25.1	14.3	9.1	19.9	14.0	8.6
Vegetables	846.5	2.8	57.1	10.1	8.9	12.1	3.9	5.1
Meat	251.7	3.0	30.7	11.3	3.8	21.7	13.7	15.8
Milk	612.8	0.3	18.7	16.4	6.4	33.2	10.6	14.3
Fish, seafood	126.4	1.2	42.0	27.0	2.0	16.6	4.5	6.6
% world population in region**	100.0	11.4	37.6	22.8	6.2	11.1	8.6	5.1

* Includes Australia and New Zealand.
** 2006. World population in 2006 was 6.59 billion.
Source: FAOSTAT (http://faostat.fao.org/site/) and author's calculations. See Appendix 3.1 for country groupings.

around the world include oilseeds, starchy roots and tubers, pulses, fruits, vegetables, sugar crops, stimulants (coffee, tea, and cacao), and fiber crops (see Appendix 3.1 for definitions of these commodity groups). Oilseeds such as soybeans, rape seed, groundnuts, sunflower seed, and many others often serve two purposes as the residue after the oil has been extracted is generally rich in protein making it an excellent feed for livestock. In addition, much of world cereal grain production is used for livestock feeding rather than for human consumption. In 2007, 47 percent of U.S. maize production was consumed in the United States as livestock feed and much of the 19 percent of U.S. production that was exported was probably used to feed livestock as well (ERS, 2008d).

Domesticated animals are an important part of the world food system. For arid regions, land that has little value for crop production can often provide enough grass for cattle, camels, horses, sheep, and goats to graze, thereby making use of a resource that could not be directly consumed by humans. These animals provide milk, blood, wool, hides and skins as well as meat. In much of Africa, cattle, sheep, and goats are managed by nomadic herders who often take care of animals owned by sedentary farmers in return for payment in the form of blood, milk, or newborn animals. In contrast, in North America cattle are usually fed a mixture of grain and oilseed cake (meal) by specialized firms that purchase the young animals after a relatively short period spent grazing pasture land. The concentrated feed consumed by these animals leads to greater meat output than would be the case if the animals were raised entirely on grass and it also has an effect on the texture and flavor of the meat. Of course, cattle and other animals evolved to be able to consume and process grass so the maize and soybean cake concentrate they are fed is an unnatural diet. Some have criticized modern systems because rather than using livestock to extract valuable food from otherwise unusable land, modern practices use perfectly good food to feed animals for whom such substances may even be unhealthy (Pollan, 2006).

Not all domesticated animals are grass eaters. Pigs and poultry have long been raised for meat, although some societies have chosen to prohibit the consumption of pork. Harris (1974) explains the taboos on pork consumption among Jews and Moslems by noting that pigs are omnivores and consume the same kinds of food as humans. In arid areas such as the Middle East, instead of converting inedible grasses into meat, pigs would compete for the same foods as the human population. Because pork is tasty and highly desirable, Harris argues, it is necessary to convince people that the meat is somehow unclean so they will not be tempted to keep pigs, an animal that is simply too expensive for the Middle Eastern ecosystem. According to Harris, religious injunctions were added to make the prohibition even stronger. In contrast, forest peoples in New Guinea, for example, have put the raising of pigs at the center of their food systems. In the forests of New Guinea, pigs are able to find adequate food for themselves without competing with humans for the same plants and animals (Harris, 1974).

In Tables 3.2 and 3.3, the bottom row has been included to help interpret the percentages in the body of the tables. With 11.4 percent of world population, Sub-Saharan Africa accounts for only 4.7 percent of world cereal production but for 27.7 percent of world production of starchy roots. This suggests that roots and tubers such as yams, sweet potatoes, and cassava are more important in Africa than, for example, in Asia. In 2003, the average Sub-Saharan African consumer obtained almost 18 percent of her total daily caloric intake from roots and tubers compared with about 4 percent in Asia. Conversely, the average South Asian consumer got about 60 percent of his daily caloric intake from cereal grains compared with around 47 percent in Sub-Saharan Africa (FAOSTAT). Other figures that stand out are those for the production of coffee, tea, and cacao in Sub-Saharan Africa and the Latin America–Caribbean region, vegetables in China and India, and cereal grains and livestock products in Europe and North America. In all these cases, the region accounts for a larger share of world production than is reflected in its share of world population. In contrast, Europe, the Near East and North Africa, and North America produce no coffee, tea, or cacao—all of which are tropical products not adapted to the temperate climates in Europe and North America or the more arid regions in North Africa and the Near East.

Turning to Table 3.3, it appears that consumption is much more evenly distributed than production. At this writing, the FAO data used to construct the consumption table are only available through 2003. More recent data, however, would not significantly alter the consumption patterns shown in the table. Although Europe and North America produce no coffee, tea or cacao, these products are consumed much more extensively in these regions than in the regions where they are produced. Along with such tropical fruits as bananas and pineapples, these commodities are classic examples of the kinds of goods exchanged in the North–South trade that was established through colonialism. Colonial plantations were set up in Africa, Asia, and Latin America to take advantage of the favorable climate for the production of goods that were destined primarily for the European market. The amounts of the various commodities produced and consumed in the different regions can differ because of international trade. For example, North America accounts for 18.6 percent of world cereal grain production but only 15.5 percent of world cereal grain consumption suggesting that this region is a net exporter of cereal grains. Likewise, Sub-Saharan Africa accounts for 27.6 percent of world production of coffee, tea and cacao but only 7.1 percent of world consumption, again suggesting that this region is a net exporter of these commodities. North Africa and the Near East produce only 3.5 percent of the world's cereal grains but through imports are able to consume 7.7 percent of total world cereal consumption. Food production depends in part on climate and other conditions that may limit the type of plants and animals that can be exploited in a particular region. Through trade, these variations in production can be evened out so that consumers are not strictly bound by what can be produced in their part of the world.

World trade is described in Tables 3.4 to 3.6. Both goods and services are traded internationally. Trade in goods is often referred to as merchandise trade which includes agricultural commodities and processed foods as well as other goods. In Table 3.4, data on merchandise trade since 1948 are organized by region. The first seven rows show total world merchandise exports and the shares of this total accounted for by the various regions. The bottom rows of the table contain the same type of information for imports. The export and import values are in current dollars and much of the increase shown in the table is due to world inflation. Using estimates of long-term economic growth developed by Maddison (2001), the value of world merchandise exports corrected for inflation appears to have increased more than 19-fold since the end of the Second World War. In addition, Maddison reports estimates suggesting that the proportion of world output that is traded has increased from less than 5 percent in the late 1800s to 17 percent in 1998. According to the UNDP (2008), 26 percent of world GDP was traded in 2005.

Although trade in services (banking and financial services, education, technical consultation, health care, communications, and much more) has grown rapidly in recent years, it is still less important than merchandise trade. In 2007, the total value of merchandise trade was more than four times the value of trade in services (WTO, 2008). The shares of world merchandise exports from North America, Latin America and the Caribbean, and Africa have fallen since 1948 while the shares of Europe and Asia have grown substantially. Increases in the Asian share of world exports were driven initially by the powerful Japanese economy. More recently, China's economy has taken off and with its accession to the WTO in 2001, its exports have grown substantially. It is important to note that figures for Europe include trade among the members of the EU. Intra-EU trade has grown very rapidly with the elimination of trade barriers among the member states as called for in the treaties establishing the EU. If intra-EU trade is excluded, Europe's share of world exports in 2007 is about 12.5 percent rather than 42.4 percent as shown in Table 3.4.

In general, the variation in world merchandise import shares is somewhat less than that for the export shares, although there has been substantial growth in the share of world imports flowing to Asian countries. The decline in the share of world merchandise exports to Latin America may be due to the

Table 3.4   World merchandise trade (billions of current dollars) and regional shares (percentages), 1948–2007 (selected years)

	1948	1953	1963	1973	1983	1993	2003	2007
World exports*	58	84	157	579	1,838	3,670	7,342	13,619
North America (%)	28.3	24.9	19.9	17.3	16.8	18.0	15.8	13.6
South & Central America (%)	11.4	9.8	6.3	4.3	4.4	3.0	2.9	3.7
Europe** (%)	31.5	34.9	41.4	45.4	43.5	45.4	46.1	42.4
Africa (%)	7.3	6.5	5.7	4.8	4.5	2.5	2.4	3.1
Middle East (%)	2.0	2.7	3.2	4.1	6.8	3.4	4.1	5.6
CIS*** (%)	5.9	8.1	11.1	9.2	4.9	1.6	2.6	3.7
Asia (%)	13.6	13.1	12.4	14.9	19.1	26.1	26.1	27.9
World imports*	66	84	163	589	1,881	3,768	7,623	13,968
North America (%)	20.6	20.7	16.2	17.3	18.5	21.5	22.7	19.4
South & Central America (%)	9.8	8.3	6.0	4.4	3.8	3.3	2.5	3.3
Europe** (%)	40.4	39.4	45.4	47.4	44.2	44.8	45.4	43.4
Africa (%)	7.6	7.0	5.5	4.0	4.6	2.6	2.2	2.6
Middle East (%)	1.7	2.0	2.3	2.8	6.2	3.3	2.6	3.4
CIS*** (%)	5.9	7.5	10.4	9.0	4.2	1.2	1.6	2.7
Asia (%)	14.2	15.1	14.2	15.1	18.5	23.3	23.0	25.3

* Billions of current dollars.
** Includes trade among the members of the EU. In 2007, exports from EU countries to countries outside the EU were $1,695 billion (12.5 percent of world exports) and imports were $1,949 billion (14.0 percent of world imports) compared with U.S. exports of $1,163 billion (8.6 percent of world exports) and imports of $2,017 billion (14.5 percent of world imports).
*** Commonwealth of Independent States
Source: WTO, 2008.

impact of protectionist trade policies common in Latin America until the 1990s. While it is always possible for the value of total imports to differ from the value of total exports in a country or a region, total world exports should equal total world imports. In Table 3.4, world exports are not equal to world imports and this is something of a puzzle. The main reason for this discrepancy is that there may be goods that are in transit or in storage as the date changes from one year to the next. Other factors that may contribute to the difference include smuggling and errors made in recording exports and imports. In any case, the difference between world exports and imports in any year is usually relatively small.

The majority of the merchandise that is traded is made up of manufactured goods (Table 3.5). Agricultural products and the output of mining industries (including petroleum) account for a little more than a quarter of world exports and imports. Within the various regions, however, the importance of manufactured, agricultural, and mining products trade varies significantly. For Latin America and the Caribbean, the Commonwealth of Independent States (CIS), Africa and the Middle East, agriculture and mining account for 66 to 78 percent of total exports compared with 28 percent for the world as a whole. In fact, fuel and mining exports account for about two-thirds of the value of total exports in the CIS and Africa and almost three-quarters in the Middle East mainly because of the importance of petroleum in these regions. Agriculture generally accounts for less than 10 percent of merchandise exports although the proportion is somewhat higher in Latin America. Manufactured goods make up the largest share of imports in all the regions, accounting for between 64 and 77 percent of total imports.

Table 3.6 contains data on agricultural exports and imports for the world and by region in 2005, the most recent year for which aggregate commodity data are available from the FAO. Fruits and vegetables account for about one-sixth of agricultural trade while meat and meat preparations and cereals and cereal products each represent between 10 and 13 percent of the total. Historically, the main agricultural goods traded were bulk commodities such as unprocessed grain and oilseeds which are storable and easy to handle. Over the past 25 years, trade in processed and higher value food products has expanded dramatically while trade in bulk commodities has remained relatively constant. According to data reported by Gelhar and Coyle (2001), bulk agricultural commodities accounted for more than 40 percent of world food and agricultural trade in 1980 but less than 30 percent by the end of the last century. In the United States, bulk commodities accounted for 70 percent of total agricultural exports in 1976 compared to only 37 percent in 2005 (ERS/FATUS, www.ers.usda.gov/Data/FATUS/index.htm#summary). High-value agricultural products include processed foods, alcoholic beverages, fresh fruits and vegetables, meat, and dairy products. Many of these products are perishable and it has only been through improved and lower cost transportation that it has become possible to exchange such goods over long distances. An interesting example of trade in perishable products is the export of fresh fruit from Chile to the United States. Chile's summer coincides with winter in the United States and this means that fresh produce can be grown in Chile and sold in the United States at a time when many fresh fruits and vegetables are unavailable. In a similar manner, Kenya and other African countries in the southern hemisphere as well as Australia and New Zealand export fresh fruits, vegetables, and flowers to Europe during the European winter.

Table 3.5 Structure of world trade (2007)†

	World	North America	South/Central America	Europe**	CIS***	Africa	Middle East	Asia
Merchandise exports*	13,619	1,854	499	5,772	510	424	760	3,800
Agricultural share (%)	8.3	9.6	25.1	9.0	7.6	8.1	2.5	5.6
Fuels & mining share (%)	19.5	13.9	41.2	10.5	65.5	69.7	74.4	10.4
Manufacturing share (%)	69.8	72.2	30.9	78.6	20.1	18.8	21.0	81.6
Merchandise imports*	13,968	2,710	461	6,062	370	363	475	3,527
Agricultural share (%)	8.3	6.0	8.7	9.2	10.9	14.0	10.2	7.4
Fuels & mining share (%)	19.5	19.0	19.2	16.9	11.1	15.4	11.1	26.6
Manufacturing share (%)	69.8	72.8	69.1	72.1	76.7	68.0	75.7	63.7
Service exports*	3,292	536	92	1,703	66	78	77	740
Service imports*	3,086	440	99	1,461	91	102	133	760

† Shares are the percentage of a region's exports or imports accounted for by each of the three main categories of merchandise trade (agriculture, fuels and mining products, and manufactured goods). The three shares may not sum to 100 percent because of other exports or imports not included in these categories.

* Billions of current dollars.

** Includes trade among the members of the EU.

*** Commonwealth of Independent States (former USSR).

Source: WTO, 2008.

Table 3.6 Value of agricultural exports and imports by region, 2005 (billions of current dollars)

	World exports	Sub-Saharan Africa exports	China & India exports	Other Asian countries* exports	North Africa/ Near East exports	Europe exports**	Latin America/ Caribbean exports	North America exports
All agricultural goods	654.4	17.7	29.5	91.2	20.5	322.9	85.5	87.1
Cereals & preparations	77.6	0.7	3.7	11.2	2.0	36.0	5.3	18.7
Oilseeds	23.2	0.6	1.0	0.6	0.3	3.1	8.8	8.8
Fruits & vegetables	112.5	3.0	9.2	9.7	8.2	51.8	16.5	14.1
Sugar & honey	24.6	1.3	0.7	3.2	1.0	10.3	6.7	1.4
Feeding stuffs	27.9	0.2	1.7	1.7	0.1	11.8	7.6	4.8
Coffee, tea, cacao, spice	44.2	6.0	2.1	5.7	0.9	19.0	8.1	2.4
Meat & meat preparations	73.3	0.2	2.6	10.0	0.3	37.4	12.0	10.8
Dairy products & eggs	42.8	0.1	1.4	6.3	0.9	32.1	1.5	1.5

	World imports	Sub-Saharan Africa imports	China & India imports	Other Asian countries* imports	North Africa/ Near East imports	Europe imports**	Latin America/ Caribbean imports	North America imports
All agricultural goods	672.1	17.9	38.9	113.0	46.4	340.9	37.4	77.6
Cereals & preparations	82.9	6.5	3.0	17.9	12.6	28.1	9.1	5.7
Oilseeds	26.3	0.1	8.7	4.9	1.7	8.1	2.1	0.7
Fruits & vegetables	118.7	1.2	3.6	13.5	4.6	72.8	3.8	19.2
Sugar & honey	25.9	1.5	0.9	4.4	3.0	11.8	1.1	3.2
Feeding stuffs	30.5	0.3	0.6	6.7	1.8	17.1	2.5	1.5
Coffee, tea, cacao, spice	44.2	0.4	0.6	5.8	2.6	25.6	1.2	8.0
Meat & meat preparations	70.7	1.1	1.1	14.8	3.0	39.6	4.0	7.1
Dairy products & eggs	41.8	1.2	0.7	5.6	3.9	26.1	2.5	1.8

* Includes Australia and New Zealand.

** Includes the former USSR and trade among the member countries of the EU.

Source: FAOSTAT (http://faostat.fao.org/site/) and author's calculations. See Appendix 3.1 for country groupings.

Agribusiness, Government, and Science

The world food system includes both traditional production, post-harvest, and consumption systems as well as modern, industrialized versions of these three food-system components. Both within countries with such industrialized food systems and on international markets, large multinational agribusiness firms have become dominant forces in the provision of inputs and the processing and commercialization of agricultural commodities and high-value food products. It is not uncommon for particular markets to be controlled by a relatively small number of these large firms, which often conduct a wide range of activities that may affect several economic sectors. Archer Daniels Midland Company (ADM), for example, processes maize, soybeans, wheat, and cocoa to produce goods as diverse as ethanol, chocolate, livestock feed, vegetable oils, flour, and many more, producing and selling these products in countries around the world. The company also carries out a wide range of other activities such as grain trading, for example, in support of its processing and manufacturing enterprises (ADM, www.admworld.com).

Some large agribusiness firms are vertically integrated in the sense that everything from the supply of inputs to the commercialization of final products is carried out within a single firm. For example, Tyson Foods handles everything in the production and commercialization of poultry products through its own offices except for the actual growing of the chickens and turkeys which is done by poultry farmers under contract with Tyson. The farmers receive baby chicks, feed, veterinary supplies, operating instructions, and everything else needed to raise the chickens from Tyson. When the chickens reach the appropriate size, Tyson buys them from the growers at a pre-set price, slaughters them, and processes the birds for domestic and international sales (Tyson Foods). In this vertically integrated industry, transactions that were previously handled by markets have become internal to the firm. Thus, the food manufacturers who in the past would have used a market to locate the dressed chickens they needed to produce frozen TV dinners have been absorbed into the vertically integrated firm. The market that used to bring poultry suppliers and food manufacturers together no longer exists. Note that Tyson is not a monopoly as there are other vertically integrated poultry firms operating in the United States and in other countries. In some cases, however, Tyson may be the only poultry firm in a particular region and this may allow it to act as a local monopolist. In addition, it is frequently the case that poultry farmers in a particular area have no alternative but to contract with Tyson Foods and this may allow the firm to act as a monopsonist, lowering the prices it pays its growers.

The fact that many agricultural markets are dominated by a small number of large multinational firms has given rise to occasional concerns about abuses of their market power. Although there are many firms that engage in international grain trading, this market has long been dominated by a small number of multinational corporations. In 1982 the General Accounting Office (GAO, now the Government Accountability Office) conducted several studies of the export market for U.S. grain. At the time of the GAO studies, five multinational firms (Cargill, Continental Grain, Bunge, Louis Dreyfus, and Cook Industries) were responsible for about half the grain and soybeans exported from the United States. A popular book (Morgan, 1979) had made the case that these five secretive companies were able to manipulate prices to enhance their profits at the expense of farmers and consumers. The GAO (1982) concluded that world grain markets were competitive despite the apparent oligopoly. This issue came up again in 1998 when Cargill and Continental Grain decided to merge. The U.S. Department of Justice filed a complaint on the grounds that the merger of these two large firms would reduce competition in grain export markets. The negotiated settlement allowing the merger to go forward required that Cargill and Continental divest themselves of several of their facilities to maintain overall competition at the level that prevailed prior to the merger (Hayenga and Wisner, 2000).

International grain markets are further complicated by the presence of government actors and government policies. Canada's grain exports are managed by the Canadian Wheat Board, a government agency that purchases and commercializes Canadian wheat and barley. Prior to the dissolution of the Soviet Union, Soviet grain imports were handled by a state trading agency and many other countries had state-owned enterprises that handled some or all of the trade in grains and oilseeds. In addition, even when no state trading agencies are involved, many governments have established policies that affect grain prices and the quantities that enter international markets. For example, in the 1980s, the United States initiated export subsidies for agricultural goods under the Export Enhancement Program (EEP) with the intent of countering EU export subsidies. Export subsidies implemented by countries that control a large share of world trade in a particular commodity, such as the United States, EU or Canada, have the effect of raising internal prices and depressing world prices. When the United States and Canada formed a free trade agreement, trade barriers between the two countries were lowered or eliminated. In the early 1990s, there was a dramatic increase in Canadian wheat exports to the United States and some argued that the increase was the result of using the EEP to subsidize U.S. wheat exports. According to this argument, Canada shipped wheat to the United States under the terms of the free trade agreement to take advantage of higher U.S. prices resulting from the EEP subsidies rather than selling wheat on the world market at the depressed world price (see Mohanty, 1995).

The preceding example illustrates an important principle related to globalization. As markets in different countries become increasingly interdependent, governments lose some flexibility in establishing and carrying out many public policies. If a country does not participate in international food and agricultural trade, its government is free to set up whatever type of public policy it deems appropriate. As soon as a country's leaders elect to take advantage of the gains that can be had through international trade, however, any domestic policy that has the effect of differentiating internal market conditions (prices, product characteristics, and so on) from the corresponding world market conditions will be undermined unless some sort of trade barrier is put in place. Thus, for example, if a government decides to ban the use of hormones in livestock production on the grounds that there may be some risk to human health, it will have to set up barriers to prevent imports from countries in which hormones are used or try to convince the governments of those countries to join in the ban. Likewise, differences of opinion about the safety of genetically modified food are of no great significance as long as the countries with different views on this question do not trade with each other. If they do trade with each other, something has to be done to reconcile or accommodate the differences. We will return to this theme in the next chapter.

Genetically modified crops are created through the application of modern scientific methods. Such methods have become an increasingly significant part of the modern world food system over the past 50 years. Since the first domestication of plants and animals, human beings have selected seeds from the best plants for future propagation and bred the strongest animals in hopes of producing the best offspring. In *The Origin of Species* (1859/2003), Darwin pointed to agricultural selection as a model for the natural selection that formed the basis of his explanation of evolution. Plant and animal breeding took on new force in the twentieth century with greater understanding of genetics and, more recently, the ability to manipulate genetic material in new ways. Historically, plant and livestock breeders could only work through crossing organisms from a single species. With the discovery of methods to identify and separate particular genes and to transfer this genetic material to a different organism, scientists were able to create varieties with characteristics taken from a completely different species. Thus, insect-resistant varieties of cotton have been created by introducing into the cotton genome genetic material from an unrelated species, the bacterium *Bacillus thurengensis* (Bt), which produces insect toxins. The application of advances in scientific understanding to agricultural production, processing, and consumption is the main reason the world food system has been able to forestall Malthus's prediction that food production would never be able to keep up with population growth.

Conclusion

The world food system is highly complex and diverse. It includes subsistence farmers relying on slash-and-burn agricultural methods, farmers using global positioning technology to cultivate enormous expanses in the Great Plains of the United States, highly trained geneticists and other scientists, multinational corporations, and government bureaucrats. Underlying physical and technical realities serve as constraints on individual and collective decisions, government policies, and corporate and organizational strategies. This complicated system is able to produce and distribute enormous amounts of food and other useful products but is in need of continual change and adjustment to improve its performance on such problems as hunger, malnutrition, food safety, and environmental sustainability. In an ideal world, the food and agricultural policies implemented by national governments would correct market failures and provide the incentives needed to promote behavior that would lead to the solution of these problems. Ours is not an ideal world, however, and many government policies end up serving narrow interests rather than broad social goals related to food and agriculture. On the other hand, non-government organizations operating both domestically and internationally along with international organizations such as the WTO and various United Nations agencies can help to channel national policies in constructive directions. In the next chapter, the role of the WTO in establishing rules for international trade, including international agricultural trade, is described as a prelude to the closer examination of farm subsidies and agricultural policies in later chapters.

Appendix 3.1: Country and Commodity Classifications used in Statistical Tables

Country groups:

- Sub-Saharan Africa: All countries on the African Continent except Morocco, Algeria, Tunisia, Libya, Sudan, and Egypt as well as the islands of Madagascar, Cape Verde, Comoros, Mauritius, Reunion, Sao Tome and Principe, and the Seychelles.
- Other Asian countries: All countries in South and Southeast Asia except China and India as well as Pacific Islands and Australia and New Zealand unless otherwise indicated.
- Europe: All countries in Eastern and Western Europe, Scandinavia and the Russian Federation unless otherwise indicated.

- Near East and North Africa: Afghanistan, Bahrain, Cyprus, Palestinian Authority, Iran, Iraq, Israel, Jordan, Kuwait, Lebanon, Qatar, Saudi Arabia, Syria, Oman, Turkey, United Arab Emirates, Yemen, Sudan, Morocco, Algeria, Tunisia, Libya, and Egypt.
- Latin America and Caribbean: Countries in South and Central America (including Mexico) and Caribbean islands (including Martinique and Guadeloupe).
- North America: Canada, Greenland, Bermuda, and the United States.

Commodity groups:

- Cereal grains: Cereals including wheat, rice, barley, maize, popcorn, rye, oats, millet, sorghum, buckwheat, quinoa, fonio, triticale, canary seed and mixed grain and products (flour, etc.) from these commodities.
- Oilseed crops: Soybeans, groundnuts, coconuts, palm and palm kernel, olives, shea nuts, castor beans, sunflower seed, rapeseed (canola), tung nuts, safflower seed, sesame seed, mustard seed, poppy seed, melon seed, tallow tree seed, kapok fruit, seed cotton, linseed, and hemp seed.
- Pulses: Dry beans, dry broad beans, dry peas, chick-peas, dry cow peas, lentils, pigeon peas, bambara beans, vetches, and lupins.
- Fiber crops: Cotton lint, jute, sisal, hemp, flax.
- Starchy roots: Potatoes, sweet potatoes, cassava, cocoyam, taro, and yams.
- Sugar (raw equivalent): Semi-refined sugar from sugar beets and sugar cane.
- Fruits: Bananas, plantains, oranges, tangerines, mandarins, clementines, satsumas, lemons, limes, grapefruit, pomelo, apples, pears, quinces, apricots, sour cherries, cherries, peaches, nectarines, plums, strawberries, raspberries, gooseberries, currants, blueberries, cranberries, grapes, figs, persimmon, kiwi, mangoes, avocados, pineapples, dates, cashew apple, and papaya.
- Vegetables: Cabbages, artichokes, asparagus, lettuce, spinach, cassava leaves, fresh tomatoes, cauliflower, pumpkins, cucumbers and gherkins, eggplants, chilies and peppers, green onions, dry onions, garlic, leeks, green beans, green peas, green broad beans, string beans, carrots, okra, green corn, mushrooms, watermelons, cantaloupes, and melons.
- Meat: Beef and veal, mutton and lamb, goat meat, pig meat, buffalo meat, poultry, horsemeat, camel meat, ass meat, mule meat, rabbit meat, and game meat.
- Milk: Milk from buffalos, cows, camels, sheep and goats.
- Fish and seafood: Freshwater and ocean fish, shellfish, and other seafood.

4

Global Institutions and the World Trade Organization

Introduction

As noted in the last chapter, national governments face few constraints in setting up whatever institutions and policies they may deem appropriate for their
country's food system as long as that country is not involved in international
trade. The government of a non-trading country might decide, for example, to
ban the sale of certain types of strawberry jam judged to be unhealthy because
they contain more sugar than fruit. Some citizens of the country who like
sugary jams might object and work to get the decision overturned through
whatever courses of action are available within the country but there would be
no reason for other countries to be upset because the country was not trading
strawberry jam to begin with. If the country is engaged in international trade,
however, there would be international repercussions that would have to be
taken into account. If the government really believes that strawberry jam containing more sugar than fruit represents a health threat, it will want to prevent
not only the sale of such jams by domestic firms but also their importation as
well and that means some kind of trade barrier.[1] Because virtually all countries do allow international trade, the implementation of special food and agricultural policies designed to achieve national goals may well lead to conflicts
with trading partners.

[1] Within the EU, national differences in the ways in which processed food products are made
led to efforts by some countries to block imports from other EU members of products such as
jams, beer, alcoholic beverages, sausages, and so on. Restrictions on the free flow of these
goods within the EU violate the basic principle of an economic union. To avoid this problem,
EU bureaucrats first tried to harmonize food standards by specifying precisely the ingredients
and their proportions that would be permitted in a particular food product. The hope was that
if the composition of strawberry jam, for example, could be agreed upon by all members, all
strawberry jam produced in the union would have the same composition so there would be no

In 1985, the EU adopted a directive banning the use of various hormonal substances in livestock production following earlier experiences with carcinogenic hormonal agents that had been found in baby food. The directive was extended to traded livestock products in 1988 and resulted in the elimination of U.S. meat exports (mostly edible offal[2]) to the EU worth about $100 million at that time much to the consternation of U.S. meat producers (Peterson, 2001). Natural and artificial hormones were then and continue today to be used by beef cattle producers in the United States and other countries to improve the conversion of feed into meat and to speed up growth rates. Hormone use dramatically increases returns at a relatively small cost and these substances are widely employed outside the EU. Even within the EU, some producers have continued clandestinely to employ the illegal hormones, or synthetic substitutes that are also illegal there, because the positive economic effects of these practices are so great.

There is no clear scientific evidence that the proper use of hormones in livestock production is harmful to human health and U.S. beef producers argue that the EU ban is really a trade barrier designed to reduce foreign competition for EU beef producers. Policy makers in the EU counter that the hormone ban was put into place to protect consumers from potentially unsafe products, invoking the "precautionary principle" in justifying their policy decision. The precautionary principle states that it may make sense to prevent or regulate a particular course of action even if scientific evidence of risk is not yet available because that course of action might turn out one day to be harmful. The problem with this principle, of course, is that it seems to require proof of a negative, that is, proof that something is not harmful and such proofs are

---

justification for trade barriers. Reaching agreement on these specifications was not simple, however. Vogel (1995) points out that European authorities spent 14 years negotiating a regulation on the composition of jams and jellies. Eventually, the EU concluded that the only way to handle these differences was to abandon the effort to standardize product characteristics and to require that EU members allow products from other countries to enter their markets even if they differed from traditional domestic products in some way as long as they posed no health hazard.

[2] Edible offal, sometimes referred to as variety meats, includes kidneys, tongue, tripe, sweetbreads, liver, and other organ meat. In the United States, such products are often used in pet food or to make processed meat products but are less common as main courses at U.S. dinner tables. In Europe and many other countries, however, these goods are often treated as delicacies figuring prominently on the menus of some of the finest restaurants: the three-star Parisian restaurant "L'Arpège" was offering grilled calf sweetbreads à la carte for 90 euro—$115.00—in November 2006. The ability to sell edible offal to Europeans willing to pay relatively high prices was a great advantage for U.S. packing plants that would otherwise have had to sell these products for much less to pet food manufacturers.

notoriously difficult to pull off. In any case, many European consumers have come to believe that meat from hormone-treated animals is either unsafe or of poor quality. These consumers support the EU policy even though it has the effect of raising the prices they pay for livestock products.

The conflict between the EU and the United States over hormones is just one part of a broader disagreement over policies affecting food and agriculture that has been going on since the 1970s. In the aftermath of the Second World War, much of Europe's agriculture was in ruins making countries in Western Europe dependent on imported food. As their economies began to recover after the war, Europe became a major market for food exports from North America and other parts of the world less affected by the war. In 1958, France, Germany, Italy, and the Benelux countries established the European Economic Community (EEC) which eventually evolved into the EU after a series of name changes and expansion in the number of participating countries. The accession of Romania and Bulgaria in January 2007 brought EU membership to 27 and there are many other countries that hope to be admitted to the club. By the mid-1960s, the EEC had created the Common Agricultural Policy (CAP) which afforded very generous support to European farmers. The response to these farm subsidies was a rapid increase in output and a reduction in the need for imports. By the 1970s, the EU (known at that time as the European Communities, EC) had made the transition from being a major net importer of food to being a major net exporter, competing on world markets with the United States and other food exporting countries (see Chapter 7).

The CAP used a combination of internal price supports and trade barriers to insulate EU agricultural markets from foreign competition. From the point of view of the United States, the loss of an important export market was bad enough but what made matters even worse was the fact that the EU began to chip away at U.S. domination of world markets for temperate-zone agricultural products. As noted earlier, the United States implemented an export subsidy program (the EEP) in the 1980s aimed at countering EU subsidies that were making EU agricultural products more competitive on world markets. It was in the context of this subsidy war that the conflict over hormones in livestock production arose. In 1986, 103 countries that were signatories to the General Agreement on Tariffs and Trade (GATT) undertook multilateral trade negotiations that led in 1995 to the creation of the WTO, the Uruguay Round Agreement on Agriculture (AA), the Sanitary and Phytosanitary Agreement (SPS), and new regulations affecting numerous other areas. Drawing on the provisions in the new SPS, the United States and Canada filed a complaint over the EU's hormone ban. A WTO dispute resolution panel ruled in favor of the U.S. and Canadian petition but the EU has refused to modify its policies so a low-level trade war has been underway ever since.

Beyond the hormone and subsidy conflicts, the EU and the United States also disagree about genetically modified (GM) foods which are viewed very negatively by many European consumers but are found in almost all the processed foods consumed in the United States. According to a report published in *Eurobarometer* (2006), an EU survey and polling organization, a majority of Europeans feel that GM foods are morally problematic and pose a potential health risk. The different attitudes toward genetic manipulation on the two sides of the Atlantic raise the potential for further conflicts over traded food items. Of course, trade disputes are not limited to conflicts between the United States and the EU as we saw earlier in the cotton case brought before the WTO by Brazil. Because the potential for trade disputes over food and agricultural goods, as well as over most other goods and services that are traded, is so great, some mechanism for adjudicating these conflicts is critical if the world is to avoid descending into an all-out trade war as happened during the 1930s. The primary mechanism for coordinating international trade policies, the WTO, is described in the next section of this chapter.

The World Trade Organization

In 1930, the U.S. Congress adopted the Smoot–Hawley tariff which raised average industrial tariffs in the United States from 38 percent to 52 percent (Hoekman and Kostecki, 1995). This legislation was adopted in a climate of economic crisis following the 1929 stock market crash. In retaliation, other countries raised their tariff rates and world trade contracted severely. While the Smoot–Hawley tariff did not cause the Great Depression, it contributed to the length and severity of the economic crisis which rapidly spread to other countries. In addition to the contraction of international trade, the 1930s were marked by financial crises that resulted in the general abandonment of the gold standard for coordinating international financial transactions (Samuelson, 2006). The economic stimulus provided by the Second World War brought the Great Depression to an end in the United States but the international economic crisis of the 1930s showed that the pre-existing world economic order was no longer viable. Even before the war had ended, the need to construct new international institutions that would be less subject to the social and economic instability that had characterized the inter-war years had become apparent to leaders in Europe and North America. Beginning in 1944, European and American diplomats undertook discussions that resulted in the construction of such international organizations as the United Nations, the International Monetary Fund (IMF), the World Bank, and the GATT. The economic and financial organizations created at the end of the war supplied the framework for regulating international economic interaction for the next 25 years.

Within countries, legal institutions are available to resolve commercial conflicts, regulate financial and monetary instruments, promote peace and security, and generally establish the rules and regulations that allow people to live and do business together. As noted in Chapter 2, legal institutions have the characteristics of public goods and this means that they are unlikely to arise spontaneously through the voluntary efforts of private citizens. The problem of free-riding in the provision of public goods is overcome within countries by governments that are empowered to make and enforce laws. At the international level, there is no central government that could play a similar role. This is a problem because such legal institutions are needed to coordinate international relations for the same reasons they are needed in domestic settings. The solution to the problem of these international public goods is to negotiate international agreements that create legal institutions and the organizations needed to administer them. Because international organizations have no way to enforce the laws that are agreed upon, the treaties and agreements through which such organizations are established usually include a requirement that the governments of the participating countries incorporate the provisions of the agreement into their national legal systems. In other words, enforcement of international rules and laws is the responsibility of the governments of the countries that have signed on to the agreement.

In 1944, delegates meeting in Bretton Woods, New Hampshire under the leadership of the well-known British economist John Maynard Keynes and the U.S. Secretary of the Treasury Harry Dexler White established the IMF and the World Bank (World Bank, 2004). The international monetary system created at Bretton Woods was based on adjustable exchange rates pegged to the U.S. dollar which was backed up by U.S. gold reserves. In principle, the United States stood ready to redeem dollars with gold at a fixed rate of $35 to an ounce of gold. Countries were required to peg their currencies to the U.S. dollar but were allowed to adjust these rates if warranted by economic conditions. The Bretton Woods monetary system ended in 1971 when President Nixon suspended the convertibility of dollars into gold during an international financial crisis after which the world gradually moved to a system in which the exchange rates of major currencies are determined by market forces. Today, the IMF assists countries with balance of payments problems and manages other international financial issues. The World Bank's official name is the International Bank for Reconstruction and Development (IBRD) and its original purpose was to assist in post-war reconstruction. In the years since its creation, it has evolved into a group of agencies focusing on economic development in low-income countries. Both the IMF and World Bank are affiliated with the United Nations (UN) which was established in October 1945 with an initial membership of 51 countries. Today, there are 192 UN members and most of these countries also participate in the IMF and World Bank as well as numerous other UN agencies.

The delegates to the Bretton Woods conference had also planned to establish an International Trade Organization (ITO) with the same status as the IMF and World Bank but were unable to reach agreement because of opposition from the United States (Braithwaite and Drahos, 2000). In 1947, the GATT was created to serve as a stopgap arrangement until a true international trade organization could be created. Such an organization was approved at a conference in Havana, Cuba in 1948 but the U.S. Congress refused to ratify the agreement (Hoekman and Kostecki, 1995). As a result, the GATT served as the mechanism for coordinating international trade until 1995 when it was incorporated into the newly created WTO. The GATT and its successor have both carried out two primary types of operations. The first is the periodic organization of trade negotiations referred to as "rounds." Eight rounds of multilateral trade negotiations (MTN) have been completed and the ninth, known as the Doha Round, was launched in 2001. During these negotiations, national representatives attempt to reach agreement on rules to reduce trade barriers and establish principles to govern other areas of conflict in international trade. The second function of the GATT/WTO is to maintain a permanent secretariat which, among other things, is charged with convening panels of experts to hear arguments and render judgments in disputes between countries on the meaning and import of the rules to which they have agreed during the MTN. These are the panels that have rendered decisions on U.S. cotton subsidies and the EU hormone ban.

From an economic standpoint, the common language of WTO trade negotiations is somewhat peculiar. The discussions are usually organized around "concessions" that are offered by the member states. These concessions generally take the form of a reduction in some barrier to trade. The early rounds of GATT trade negotiations, when only 23 to 33 countries were parties to the agreement, resulted in substantial reductions of industrial tariffs, for example. Reducing barriers to trade can lead to losses for certain industries or economic sectors but the gains from increased trade are always greater than these losses so the country ends up better off than it would be if it did not reduce the trade barrier.[3] This suggests that offers to reduce trade barriers are advantageous to

---

[3] The advantages and disadvantages of free international trade have been debated for many centuries. A prominent argument in Adam Smith's great work on the wealth of nations is that the trade barriers known as the Corn Laws reduced national wealth by enriching land owners at the expense of workers and capitalists who were the driving forces in the new industrial

the country itself and should not be seen as concessions, that is, something desirable a country offers to give up in exchange for similar offerings from other countries. A possible reason for this kind of language is that governments may find it politically useful to argue that the harm the policy change may occasion is offset by harms (concessions) inflicted upon other countries rather than by the general benefits to consumers or other groups in the country itself. In any case, exchanging concessions is the bread and butter of WTO trade negotiations.

An important principle undergirding the GATT and WTO is the principle of "normal trade relations" previously known as "most favored nation status." This principle requires that tariff reductions or other concessions offered to another WTO member be extended to all other members. It is this principle of non-discrimination that makes the rules and regulations adopted by the 152 member countries truly multilateral. The principle has been undermined somewhat by numerous exceptions. To begin with, the WTO permits countries to set up regional trade agreements such as the EU or the North American Free Trade Agreement (NAFTA). The fundamental characteristic of such arrangements is that the members treat the other members differently from non-members. In other words, the EU, NAFTA, and other regional trade agreements are based on discrimination, thus violating the principle of normal trade relations. In addition, the WTO specifically stipulates that "special and differential treatment" should be granted to low-income countries. These countries are often allowed to reduce their trade barriers more slowly or less severely than other countries and they fall under the special provisions of the Generalized System of Preferences (GSP), an arrangement that gives developing countries greater access to markets in high-income countries.

Agriculture in the WTO

Despite these exceptions, there has been extensive trade liberalization under the GATT and the WTO and the general reduction in trade barriers is an

---

economy. For the purposes of this book, trade liberalization, the process of reducing trade barriers and moving world markets closer to free trade, is taken to generate social benefits that are greater than social costs. This position can be justified through logical argument and empirical evidence but to do so would require an entire book in itself and so the case for trade liberalization will be only partly elucidated in this and subsequent chapters. Irwin (1996) provides a good summary of the arguments for and against free trade and more technical treatments of this question can be found in any textbook on international trade.

important reason why international trade has grown so rapidly since the end of the Second World War. For most of the last 50 years, however, agriculture was left out of the process of trade liberalization. During the early rounds of GATT negotiations, the U.S. government was operating highly interventionist agricultural programs and resisted any trade agreements that might undermine these policies. As a result, agriculture was not subject to the GATT provisions for other goods and such barriers to trade as quantitative restrictions and export subsidies that had been eliminated for industrial goods continued to be applied to agricultural trade (Hoekman and Kostecki, 1995). As the EU and Japan developed their own interventionist agricultural policies, there was little interest from the countries with the largest economies in liberalizing agricultural trade. This began to change in the 1980s, however, when the United States pressed for inclusion of agriculture in the Uruguay Round of trade negotiations launched in 1986. As it turned out, the agricultural negotiations were so contentious that they almost caused the entire Uruguay Round to collapse.

The agricultural policies that were in place in the United States, the EU, and Japan when the Uruguay Round began included a variety of domestic subsidies coupled with non-tariff barriers that insulated agricultural markets from the effects of world market variations. Tariffs are taxes on imported goods that have the effect of raising their prices to levels at or above the prices of similar goods produced in the country applying the tax. Non-tariff barriers (NTB) to trade afford protection similar to that of the tariff but operate in different ways. An import quota, for example, is an NTB that sets a limit to the quantity of imports of a particular good that will be allowed in the country. This limitation means that the amount of the good placed on the market is less than it was before the imposition of the quota and this artificial shortage will result in a higher price through the normal operation of supply and demand. In other words, tariffs raise the price of imports, reducing the quantity imported, while quotas limit the quantity imported to raise the price.[4] The problem with both

---

[4] While a tariff and an equivalent quota have the same effects on prices and quantities, their dynamic effects are quite different. Suppose that there is seasonal variation in the world price for some commodity. With a tariff in place, that seasonal variation will be reflected in the internal market of the importing country. For example, if the world price is 100 euro and a 10 percent tariff is being levied, the domestic price will be raised to 110 euro. If the world price falls to 94 euro, the internal market price will fall to 103.40 (= 94 × 1.10) euro. At this lower price, the country is likely to import more than it did when the price was 110 euro. In contrast, if a quota is being used to raise the price to 110 euro, the amount imported can never change regardless of what happens to the world price. The only effect of world price variation in this case is to increase or decrease the quota rents. Since the quantity placed on the market has not changed, there is no reason for the domestic price to fall. The most likely reason for the fall in the world price is that a greater amount of the commodity is available. With either free trade or a world in which only tariffs are practiced, changing supply or demand conditions

tariffs and quotas is that other countries often retaliate by introducing trade barriers of their own as happened in the aftermath of the Smoot–Hawley tariff, for example. The ensuing trade war may have serious economic consequences.

One way to mitigate this problem is to use another type of NTB known as a voluntary export restraint (VER). A VER is a quota on exports levied by the exporting country. To understand why a country would agree to limit its exports voluntarily, it is first necessary to understand what these trade barriers do. Suppose that Beninese rice producers are selling rice to consumers in Niger at a price of 200 CFA francs per kilogram. If rice producers in Niger need to sell their rice for 220 CFA francs to cover their costs of production, the government of Niger could levy a 10 percent tariff raising the price of rice from Benin to 220 CFA francs and preventing the Beninese rice from undercutting the price of Nigerien rice. Assuming the price of rice in Benin does not change and that Niger continues to import some rice from Benin, the government will collect the tax of 20 CFA francs per kilogram imported.[5] If Niger elected to restrict imports with an import quota rather than a tariff, the price in Niger would still increase. Suppose the import quota is set to limit the quantity imported to a level that raises the Nigerien price by the same amount as the tariff and that the government of Niger sets up a state agency to handle imports. The agency would be able to purchase rice up to the amount determined by the quota in Benin at 200 CFA francs per kilogram and then sell it in Niger for 220 CFA francs. For every kilogram that is imported under the quota, the agency collects the difference between the Nigerien and Beninese

---

that cause changes in the world price triggers responses that tend to stabilize the world market. In the case described above, the world price decline may be limited as countries respond to the lower prices by purchasing more. With quotas or VERs, however, there is no change in domestic consumption because the quantities imported are frozen by the quota. Thus, quotas and other forms of NTB such as the EU's variable levy (see Chapter 7) tend to increase instability relative to the situation that would exist if an equivalent tariff were employed. It is this difference that has led the international community to work to replace quantitative restrictions with equivalent tariffs.

[5]   In many cases, a tariff can actually affect prices in both countries. When a very large country such as the United States restricts imports of sugar in an effort to protect its sugar growers, for example, it may reduce world demand so much that world prices are depressed. This is precisely the problem with farm subsidies in wealthy countries that lead to excess production dumped on world markets increasing the supply and depressing prices. World prices may be altered by either a change in demand or a change in supply. They will be depressed if demand is reduced or supply increased and raised if supply is decreased or demand increases. In the case of Benin and Niger, I assume that these countries are too small to have an impact on the world price so Niger's decision to restrict imports does not change the price in Benin. See Krugman and Obstfeld (2000) or any textbook on international trade for a full explanation of the effects of different barriers to trade.

prices. This revenue is referred to as a quota rent. A VER has the same impact as an import quota except that, because it is administered by the exporting country, the quota rent is captured by the exporter rather than by individuals or a government agency in the importing country.

From 1981 to 1985, the United States negotiated a VER on automobile exports from Japan. The Japanese government agreed to limit the number of automobiles sold to the United States first to 1.68 million cars and later to 1.85 million (Krugman and Obstfeld, 2000). Japan was willing to do this in part because the quota rent from the VER was retained in Japan as partial compensation for the reduced exports. If the alternative to a VER is a tariff or import quota, the exporting country would prefer the VER because of the quota rent it would be able to retain. According to Krugman and Obstfeld (2000), the VER on Japanese automobiles cost the United States more than $3 billion in 1984 and most of this was captured by Japan as quota rent. During the 1980s, the VER became a preferred method for protecting U.S. agricultural markets and was applied to beef, sugar, and dairy imports. In the EU, a variable import tariff that had effects similar to those of an import quota was in force and Japan and Korea blocked all imports of rice to protect their domestic producers. In addition to the NTBs used to protect domestic markets from imports, the EU and the United States were using export subsidies to increase the competitiveness of their agricultural exports. These policies left world agricultural markets in disarray and one of the goals of the Uruguay Round of trade negotiations was to establish rules that would bring some order to these markets.

At the beginning of the Uruguay Round trade negotiations, the United States and the EU staked out very different negotiating positions. The U.S. agricultural proposal called for the elimination of all trade barriers and all subsidies affecting international trade. Domestic policies with no impact on trade would have been permitted. Such policies are often referred to as "decoupled" support because they are presumed to have no influence on producer decisions about how much to produce and, therefore, how much will be sold on international markets. The EU wanted reductions in the level of intervention in certain markets along with broader trade liberalization based on reducing the overall level of support. Under the EU proposal, countries would have been able to retain particular policy instruments and levels of protection as long as they introduced sufficient reductions in other areas to result in the required lowering of overall agricultural support (Anania, Carter and McCalla, 1994).

The only other countries that actively participated in the early negotiations were some smaller agricultural exporters known as the Cairns Group which includes Australia, Canada, New Zealand, Thailand, Brazil, Argentina, and others. The Cairns Group tabled an initial proposal on price supports but eventually joined the United States in a proposal calling for the elimination of export subsidies, the conversion of NTB into tariffs (a process referred to as "tariffication") followed by reductions of the resulting tariffs, and the elimination of trade-distorting domestic policies. South Korea and Japan sided with the EU, forming a more protectionist block to face off against the U.S.–Cairns Group alliance. Most developing countries did not enter actively into the Uruguay Round negotiations on agriculture.

By 1990, the two negotiating groups had tabled what they considered to be final proposals that actually differed only a little from their initial positions. It appeared unlikely that a reasonable compromise could be found despite four years of negotiation. In 1991, the Director-General of the GATT, Arthur Dunkel, drafted a proposal for an overall negotiating framework that began to relieve the deadlock and eventually became the basis for the AA. Earlier efforts to find a compromise position had led to the division of the talks into three areas: market access (that is, reduction of import barriers); export subsidies; and trade-distorting domestic policies (Tangermann, 1994). The Dunkel proposal retained this structure and added some more specific detail. First, to increase market access, delegates would agree to tariffication of all NTB followed by gradual reduction of the level of these tariffs. Second, expenditures on export subsidies as well as the volume of subsidized exports were to be reduced. Finally, reduction of trade-distorting domestic policies was to be made on the basis of a measure of the general level of protection and known as the aggregate measure of support (AMS) but calculated for specific commodities (Anania, Carter and McCalla, 1994). In 1992, a breakthrough was made during a meeting at the Blair House in Washington, D.C. The meeting had originally been organized to work on resolving a long-standing U.S.–EU trade dispute over oilseeds. In addition to solving the oilseed problems the EU and U.S. representatives were able to reach agreement on a compromise text that would subsequently become the AA (Anania, Carter and McCalla, 1994).

In the final agreement, market access was to be increased by tariffication[6] of NTB and other import barriers and reduction of the resulting tariffs by 36

[6]   The actual process of tariffication involved the use of "tariff-rate quotas" (TRQ). A TRQ establishes a quota for a good that is less than historic levels of importation. Goods are imported with no tariff or with a reduced tariff as long as the quota has not been exceeded. Once the quota level has been reached any further imports are subject to much higher tariffs. Overall, it is expected that in the first year after implementing this policy change, the quantities imported will be about the same as during the period prior to the policy change. In other words, the low-duty or duty-free quota will be set low enough that additional imports are likely and these imports will be taxed at the higher tariff rate. Liberalization of these systems requires the gradual reduction of the tariff and, usually, the gradual increase in the low-duty or duty-free quota.

percent over six years for industrialized countries and by 24 percent over 10 years for developing countries (WTO, 2008a). Very poor countries were not required to comply with the market access provisions which also included minimum access levels and safeguards in case of an import surge. The AA stipulates that the value of expenditures on export subsidies is to be reduced by 36 percent and the volume of subsidized exports by 21 percent both over a period of six years. Food aid (that is, subsidized food exports directed at low-income countries for humanitarian and emergency purposes) was largely exempted from the export subsidy requirements (WTO, 2008a). For domestic subsidies, the AA created three categories referred to as "boxes." Trade-distorting policies[7] are placed in the "amber box" and governments are required to reduce these subsidies by 20 percent over six years relative to an AMS that reflects general agricultural support rather than being based on commodity-specific support levels. Domestic policies such as government-funded research, direct payments for conservation programs, and others thought to have very limited impact on trade are placed in the "green box" and are not subject to any requirements for reduction. The EU and the United States agreed to allow certain agricultural subsidies to be placed in a "blue box" with no requirements for reduction. Blue-box policies included subsidies that are tied to limitations on production and other direct payments to farmers not thought to have significant effects on trade (WTO, 2008a).

---

[7] Agricultural policies include interventions that operate through trade barriers (import restrictions and export subsidies) as well as those considered to be only indirectly related to trade. An example of the latter is the U.S. program for peanuts (groundnuts) that was in effect until 2002. The peanut program supported prices through a system of marketing quotas. Producers who did not own a peanut quota could only sell peanuts for oil on the world market. Those with a peanut quota could sell peanuts in the United States at prices significantly higher than the world price. Because of the difference between the U.S. and world price, the domestic peanut program had to be complemented with a trade barrier. The trade barrier itself was trade distorting but the requirement that non-quota peanuts be sold on the world market added to the distortions caused by this program. An example of a domestic program not considered to be trade distorting is the U.S. Conservation Reserve Program (CRP) which provides monetary compensation to farmers who agree to remove land that is particularly subject to erosion or environmentally fragile in some other way from production putting it into approved conservation uses. The goal of the CRP is to reduce environmental damage within the United States, a goal that appears to be unrelated to international trade. The problem with this interpretation is that removing this land from production could have an impact on total output and such changes could, in turn, affect trade in the commodities that previously were produced on the land put into the reserve. It is significant that when world grain prices began to rise in 2007 and 2008, U.S. farmers who were eligible to do so, began taking land out of the CRP to increase their cultivated areas. The distinction between domestic agricultural policies that are trade distorting and those that are not is considerably less clear than it might seem when reading WTO documents.

The Uruguay Round of trade negotiations addressed a wide range of issues in addition to agriculture including textiles and clothing, technical barriers to trade, trade-related investment measures (TRIMs), trade-related intellectual property (TRIP), and dispute settlement procedures. Of particular interest for food and agriculture is the Uruguay Round's Sanitary and Phytosanitary Agreement. The SPS stipulates that countries can establish standards for food safety and quality but if such standards are more restrictive than existing international standards, such as those contained in the Codex Alimentarius maintained by the FAO, they must be based on scientific evidence. The SPS also calls for non-discrimination and the use of the least restrictive measures consistent with protecting human, animal, or plant life (WTO, 2008h). Prior to the adoption of the SPS, U.S. efforts to obtain a favorable resolution to the dispute over hormones had been stymied by GATT rules that focused on final products and ruled out consideration of disputes over production methods. For example, the GATT could have considered a dispute over beef from countries in which foot and mouth disease had not been eradicated because the final product in this case (meat and meat products) is a threat to animal health. But the GATT rules did not cover products that differed only in the way they were produced which meant that the U.S.–EU dispute over hormones was simply not considered to be part of the GATT mandate.

With adoption of the SPS, however, the newly formed WTO did have jurisdiction over this case and a dispute resolution panel was duly convened. The panel ruled against the EU on the grounds that the hormone ban was more restrictive than existing standards and that the greater restrictiveness could not be justified on the basis of scientific evidence. When a country loses a dispute resolution case at the WTO, there are several options available. First, of course, the losing country can simply eliminate the contested policy so that it is in compliance with the rules. In most cases, however, the country undertakes negotiations with the countries that filed the complaint in an effort to work out an accommodation that is acceptable to both sides. Sometimes agreement can be reached ending the trade dispute. Such was the case with a trade dispute between Mexico and the United States over tuna and dolphins. In 1972, the United States adopted the Marine Mammal Protection Act (MMPA) in an effort to protect dolphins, whales, seals, and other marine mammals. In parts of the Pacific Ocean, dolphins tend to swim near the surface above schools of tuna and dolphin sightings were often used by tuna fishers to place their nets. As the nets were drawn in, many dolphins were drowned. U.S. tuna vessels were subject to the MMPA and forced to alter their methods to reduce dolphin mortality (Vogel, 1995).

The MMPA is a U.S. not an international law and so it did not apply to Mexico or other countries less concerned about dolphin welfare. Some

Mexican tuna boats continued to use the practices that were resulting in collateral damage among dolphins. In addition, some U.S. tuna boats re-registered in Mexico to avoid the MMPA. In response, the U.S. government banned tuna imports from Mexico and other countries in 1990. The countries subject to the ban subsequently filed a complaint with the GATT. A dispute resolution panel was formed and in 1991 it ruled against the United States pointing out that the unilateral application of U.S. laws in international situations was inconsistent with GATT rules. The GATT ruling was followed by consultations between the United States, Mexico, and other countries with tuna fleets that led not only to the lifting of the U.S. tuna import ban but also to international agreements on fishing methods that would protect dolphins. Today, dolphin mortality related to tuna fishing has been significantly reduced and countries with fleets fishing in the Pacific have mechanisms for discussing a full range of issues related to marine mammal protection (Vogel, 1995).

In this case, the application of a trade barrier was not the best approach to solving the problem (dolphin killings) and the GATT intervention allowed the various parties to find ways not only to resolve the immediate conflict but also to address underlying issues. In the case of the hormone ban, however, results were less satisfactory. The conflict was not resolved by consultations between the EU and the United States and Canada. The EU refused to eliminate its ban on imported meat from animals treated with hormones and the United States and Canada refused to drop their case. If after consultations, the losing country still refuses to change its policy, the WTO grants the countries that filed the complaint the right to retaliate by imposing equivalent trade barriers on imports from the losing country. The WTO Dispute Settlement Body (DSB) determined that the value of lost U.S. exports as a result of the hormone ban was US$116.8 million while Canada suffered a loss of CDN$11.3 million (WTO, 2008d). The two countries were allowed to levy trade barriers of an equivalent value on goods exported by the EU. In the language of the WTO, the United States and Canada have been allowed to "suspend their obligations" to observe the rules of the WTO in dealing with the EU. The United States has placed import duties on such products as prosciutto ham, white wine, and other European food products. These trade barriers are not considered violations of normal trade relations or other actionable provisions of WTO agreements so the EU cannot file a complaint about these barriers against the two countries.

In 2004, the EU did file a complaint, however, on the grounds that a new EU directive had been adopted that put the EU in compliance with the decision of the dispute resolution panel. One of the arguments in the original decision was that the EU had failed to do a risk assessment study to support its contention that the use of hormones posed a substantial health risk. In 2003, the EU did conduct a risk assessment as background for a new directive outlawing the use of certain hormones and the importation of meat produced with these hormones, claiming that the fact that a risk assessment was conducted put them in compliance with WTO requirements (WTO, 2008d). Not surprisingly, the EU's risk assessment identified enough uncertainty to invoke the precautionary principle as justification for maintaining its ban. The United States and Canada rejected this argument (see USTR, 2006; WTO, 2008j).

Recall that this conflict began in 1988 and it was not until 1999 that the case was more or less resolved[8] with the initiation of retaliatory tariffs by the United States and Canada after the EU had failed to comply with the decision of the dispute resolution panel. But that resolution was short-lived as shown by the renewed discussions over whether or not the EU has complied with the requirements of the 1999 decision. In January 2007, the chair of the panel hearing this new case indicated that although the panel had hoped to finish its work in 2006, "… due to the complexity of the scientific issues involved and due to the difficulties in scheduling the second open hearing of the Panel with the parties and experts consulted by the Panel, it was not possible to meet that time line" (WTO, 2008j). The panel delivered a report in March 2008 ruling on certain issues but final resolution of the issue had not been achieved as of mid-2008.

Given the amount of time and energy spent on this still-unresolved trade dispute, some might question the WTO's effectiveness. Prior to the creation of the WTO, a common joke was to refer to the GATT as the General Agreement to Talk and Talk. But this cynicism may not be entirely warranted. Many disputes have been settled and it may be that the best one can hope for in the complex world of global trade is a way for countries to discuss their differences with the hope that some agreement can be reached. In the absence of the WTO, there is every reason to expect that countries would immediately start a trade war when confronted with a conflict rather than falling back on that response as a last resort. Still, the hormone dispute illustrates the range of difficulties that can arise when addressing economic relations among sovereign states. Moreover, the problem of finding common ground in multilateral trade negotiations has always been more acute for agriculture than for other economic sectors. Not only was agriculture specifically excluded from the original GATT talks but efforts during subsequent rounds to bring agriculture under GATT disciplines were unsuccessful until the Uruguay Round which almost failed because of differences between the EU and the United States

---

[8]   Note that the "resolution" in this case is to punish the EU by taxing Americans and Canadians. This is a peculiar result. Because the EU has a policy the U.S. and Canadian governments dislike, Americans and Canadians are forced to pay more for European food items they may wish to buy.

over agriculture. The reasons agriculture has always been such a problem for international trade negotiations will be explored in later chapters as we examine the origin and nature of national farm policies.

The AA that was hammered out with such difficulty was actually quite modest. Most analysts would probably agree that the major accomplishment of the negotiations leading to the AA was the simple act of bringing agriculture into the WTO and making it subject for the first time to a uniform set of rules governing international trade (See OECD, 2001b; Ingco and Croome; 2004; Diakosavvas, 2003). Because many of the barriers were high to begin with, their tariffication and reduction by 36 percent still left many high tariffs in place. Not all trade-distorting domestic policies were actually subject to amber-box reductions and those that were had to be reduced by fairly modest amounts. On the other hand, the AA rules on export subsidies did have some effect particularly in the EU and the United States. In addition, Article 20 of the AA stipulated that further discussions of market access, export subsidies, and trade-distorting domestic policies be undertaken in 2000 once the main provisions of the AA had been implemented. It was originally thought that these agricultural negotiations would be part of a new round of trade talks to be launched at a 1999 WTO Ministerial meeting in Seattle. That Ministerial was marked by street protests by groups opposing globalization and international trade and the delegates adjourned the meeting without reaching agreement on the terms of a new round (Olson, 1999). Thus, the agricultural negotiations called for in Article 20 and launched in 2000 were not initially part of broader trade talks.

In 2001, delegates to the WTO Ministerial in Doha, Qatar, succeeded in agreeing on terms for multilateral trade negotiations and the ongoing agricultural talks were incorporated into this new round. The Ministerial Declaration for these talks emphasized the importance of helping developing countries to fully benefit from world trade and the new round is referred to as the Doha Development Round. In contrast to the Uruguay Round during which the AA was crafted almost exclusively by the United States and the EU, developing countries adopted a much more active negotiating stance on agriculture as these talks were initiated. Individual developing countries as well as coalitions of low-income countries tabled a wide range of proposals for agricultural policy reform. Many of these proposals targeted the farm subsidies of the high-income countries on the grounds that these subsidies depressed world prices for the agricultural goods widely exported by developing countries. Because of their impressive economic growth in the years leading up to the Doha Round, China and India were able to play much more influential roles in the negotiations and their desire to protect domestic agricultural producers from competition would eventually contribute to the collapse of the talks in 2008.

In September 2003, a Ministerial Conference was held in Cancun, Mexico to take stock of the progress made in the negotiations. This meeting ended in disagreement over agriculture and several issues of particular interest to developing countries. The cotton initiative proposed by Benin, Mali, Burkina Faso, and Chad in April 2003 was introduced at the Cancun Ministerial and has been a separate negotiating item ever since. In 2004, agreement was reached in Geneva on a set of negotiating frameworks that offered some promise that the Doha Round might actually be brought to a successful conclusion. In December 2005, delegates to another Ministerial Conference held in Hong Kong agreed to a timetable for completion by the end of 2006. Unfortunately, the WTO Director-General concluded in July 2006 that so little progress was being made that the negotiations were temporarily suspended.

Not surprisingly, agriculture was one of the main reasons for this development. In earlier discussions, it had been agreed that the agricultural negotiations would aim to make further progress on the three central problem areas of the AA: market access; export subsidies; and trade-distorting domestic policies. Once the general orientation of the negotiations has been established, the next step is to define numerical targets for achieving the goals of improved market access, reductions or elimination of export subsidies, and reductions in trade-distorting domestic policies. These targets are referred to as "modalities" and their establishment is probably the most critical part of trade negotiations. In July 2006, the WTO Director-General concluded that there was insufficient time for the delegates to reach consensus on the agricultural modalities before the deadline for completion of the talks in December 2006. The suspension of the negotiations was supposed to allow time for reflection and the expectation was that the talks would be resumed fairly quickly. Delays of this nature have happened in previous trade negotiations. For example, the Uruguay Round was originally supposed to be completed by the end of 1990 but actually lasted until 1994.

For the Doha Round, however, the suspension of the negotiations represented a real risk because of some special circumstances in the United States. The U.S. constitution gives the legislative branch authority over international agreements. Because it would be unwieldy for the Senate and House of Representatives to participate directly in WTO trade talks, it has been the custom for these bodies to grant negotiating authority to the executive branch. This authority was referred to as "fast track authority" until 2000 when it was re-christened "trade promotion authority" (TPA). In granting negotiation authority to the executive branch, the U.S. Congress and Senate agree to consider any negotiated trade agreements in a simple vote for or against ratification, giving up their right to make amendments. TPA is granted for a specific period during which the U.S. Trade Representative is empowered to participate in multilateral negotiations as well as any bilateral or regional trade negotiations that may be on the table. The problem for the Doha Round is that the TPA under which the United States was participating in the negotiations expired at the end of June 2007. Without TPA, it is not clear how the U.S. Congress would deal with a new multilateral trade agreement.

That question became somewhat less pressing at the end of July 2008 when the Doha Round negotiations collapsed because of differences related to agriculture. The WTO Director-General indicated that he expected the talks to resume eventually and emphasized the importance of the progress that had been made in the talks prior to the breakdown (Lamy, 2008). According to *The Economist* (August 2, 2008), the WTO delegates had reached agreement on 18 of 20 outstanding issues after nine days of grueling negotiations but deadlocked on the nineteenth (safeguards against import surges) and did not address the twentieth (cotton). The issue that ended the talks concerned rules to allow countries to raise import tariffs if they experience a sudden surge of agricultural imports. India wanted to be able to implement safeguards after relatively low import increases while the United States wanted the threshold for invoking the safeguards set much higher. China backed India on this issue and the United States was unwilling to compromise given its sense that it had already made substantial concessions in the agricultural negotiations (*The Economist*, August 2, 2008). While these events do not mean that the Doha Round is terminated, it is not clear how much longer it will take for serious negotiations to resume given U.S. presidential elections in late 2008, the lack of TPA in the United States, and elections in India and other countries in 2008 and 2009.

Trade and Development

It might be argued that the WTO has taken on too broad a mandate and that it would be better to focus on traditional industrial trade barriers rather than on trying to find common ground on such divisive topics as agriculture, intellectual property rights (the globalization of patent laws), environmental regulations, and so on. It has also been suggested that multilateral negotiations in which decisions can only be made by consensus are simply too complicated to pull off and greater benefits would be realized if countries devoted their efforts to working out regional and bilateral agreements instead (Burfisher and Jones, 1998). The international institutional landscape already includes many bilateral and regional trade agreements. In addition to membership in NAFTA, the United States has an agreement with the Central American Free Trade Agreement-Dominican Republic (CAFTA-DR) and is participating in discussions related to several other regional agreements (the Free Trade Area of the Americas, Asia-Pacific Economic Cooperation, and others). Since 2000, the United States has entered into bilateral trade agreements with Australia, Chile, Singapore, Morocco, Oman, Peru, Bahrain, and the Southern Africa Customs Union. Three more agreements (Colombia, Panama, and Korea) are awaiting ratification and negotiations are under way with Malaysia, Thailand, and other countries (USTR, 2008). Other countries have also been busy negotiating regional and bilateral deals. As of July 2007, 205 regional trade agreements were in force and as many as 400 plus were either being planned or negotiated (WTO, 2008g). The 2008 collapse of the Doha multilateral trade negotiations is likely to give added impetus to these trends.

The proliferation of regional and bilateral agreements raises an important question about the best way to liberalize international trade. For some, regional and bilateral agreements are easier to negotiate and can serve as stepping stones to broader agreements that lower the general level of protection. The essence of any trade agreement is to lower tariffs and other barriers to trade and it would seem that partial liberalization in various regions would be better than no liberalization at all. As noted earlier, however, regional and bilateral trade agreements are based on discrimination and some have argued that giving up on efforts to realize multilateral trade agreements through the WTO could actually slow the movement toward a more liberal world trade regime (Gilpin, 2000). The worry is that regional blocks within which free trade is practiced could end up in significant and destructive trade wars with other regional trade groups. At the very least, large numbers of overlapping trade blocks based on discrimination against countries not party to one of the agreements seems likely to make the international trade regime less transparent and more confusing.

Another potential problem with regional free trade agreements concerns their effects on national welfare. Free trade agreements (FTA) and customs unions are the two main types of regional trade agreement and both involve reduction or elimination of trade barriers among the countries that are parties to the agreement. Customs unions differ from FTAs because in addition to lowering barriers to trade within the union, the countries also agree to harmonize their trade policies so that they apply the same types and levels of trade barriers to non-members. Both FTAs and customs unions can have the perverse effect of making countries worse off economically if the reduction in trade barriers causes a country to discontinue trade with a country outside the union that can produce goods at lower cost and to begin trading with a higher cost country that is a member of the FTA or customs union. This effect is known as trade diversion. Trade creation occurs when regional integration gives rise to expanded trade with low-cost producers that are included in the

FTA or customs union. If trade diversion is greater than trade creation, it is possible that national welfare will be lowered by the regional agreement.[9]

It is likely that the formation of the EEC and the implementation of the CAP led to substantial trade diversion in Western Europe as agricultural imports from North America, Australia, and New Zealand were replaced with similar goods produced within the EEC. Economic welfare in Italy or Belgium may have fallen as their imports of wheat from Canada, a low-cost wheat producer not in the EEC, were replaced with imports from France, a relatively high-cost wheat producer belonging to the EEC. Of course, it is also quite likely that the formation of the EEC and the subsequent further integration of European economies led to a great deal of trade creation in non-agricultural sectors making the overall effect of this regional integration positive. Krugman and Obstfeld (2000) discuss a World Bank study that found evidence of extensive trade diversion following the creation of MERCOSUR (MERCOSUL). A major source of these efficiency losses was that the higher-cost Brazilian automobile industry was able to displace Argentine imports from lower cost producers in Asia.

For the time being, it is likely that countries will continue to pursue regional and bilateral trade deals at the same time that they work on multilateral talks through the WTO. All types of trade negotiations are politically controversial. While those who favor trade liberalization are often impressed with the ineffectiveness of the WTO in reducing trade barriers and resolving trade disputes, trade opponents sometimes attribute a great deal more influence to trade agreements than would seem to be merited by the underlying facts. 1992 presidential candidate Ross Perot predicted that passage of NAFTA would create a "giant sucking sound" as U.S. jobs were lost to Mexico. Choate (1993) argued that almost half of all U.S. manufacturing jobs were likely to disappear as a result of NAFTA. These predictions have proved to be wrong although many continue to claim that NAFTA has cost the United States thousands of jobs. Based on statistics from the *U.S. Statistical Abstract*, the bare facts of the matter are that the U.S. unemployment rate was 6.9 percent in 1993 just prior to NAFTA's entry into force and that it declined in every subsequent year until the recession of 2001. In 2000, the unemployment rate was 4.0 percent and it did not reach the pre-NAFTA level even during the 2001–2 recession. From the middle of 1992 until the end of 2000, there was a net job gain (number of new jobs created minus jobs lost) of about 21.7 million and the total number of jobs gained through 2006 was about 24 million despite net losses of 3.7

---

[9] Technically, the theory of customs unions is an example of the theory of the second best. A full explanation of these theoretical considerations can be found in most textbooks on international trade. See Krugman and Obstfeld (2000) for example.

million during the recession (U.S. Bureau of the Census, 2008). These positive developments cannot be attributed to NAFTA as they probably would have occurred even if the NAFTA agreement had been defeated. But they do show that the predictions of economic disaster following the adoption of NAFTA were hyperbolic. Most economists would probably agree that NAFTA has had almost no effect on the number of jobs in the United States.

The main effect of trade liberalization is to increase the flows of traded goods and services as countries shift resources to their more competitive sectors. The economic concept of comparative advantage, described in more detail in Appendix 4.1, is central to discussions of the benefits and costs of trade liberalization. In a world of free trade and perfect competition, countries with different internal economic conditions would specialize in the production of goods for which they have a comparative advantage turning to world markets for at least some of the other goods they need. As Paul Krugman, winner of the 2008 Nobel Prize in economics, has shown, countries may benefit from international trade even when world markets are not perfectly competitive and there are few if any economic differences between them. While comparative advantage does not account for trade under the circumstances described by Krugman, it is still a driving force in some industries, agriculture in particular, and provides an important rationale for trade liberalization. The specialization that results under free trade means that production is carried out where the opportunity cost of these productive activities is lowest and this means that there will be greater total output for a given amount of world resources. How the increased amounts of goods made possible by specialization will be distributed depends not only on the economic circumstances of economic agents around the world but on the institutional framework as well. Most empirical analyses show that the benefits of trade liberalization are greater than any costs occasioned by such changes.

It is true, however, that trade agreements and trade policy reforms can have both positive and negative effects on jobs and economic returns in particular industries, on the environment and on development. Protectionism is always popular among those who may see their jobs displaced or their wages lowered as a result of competition from foreign firms even though such harms are generally not as extensive as many may think. Those who stand to gain from trade include consumers who face lower prices and workers who benefit from the jobs created as a result of trade liberalization. While the gains from international trade are greater than the losses, they are spread more thinly over larger numbers of people. Those who see lower wages or fewer jobs for which they are qualified in the aftermath of a trade agreement constitute a smaller number of people but their individual traumas may be severe. Trade policies are often more strongly influenced by the small number who fear great loss than by the much larger number of beneficiaries who stand to realize gains that may be quite modest. It is interesting to note that more jobs are created and destroyed by technological change than by trade. Few wish to forego the benefits of technological advancement in order to preserve jobs that are becoming obsolete but many seem more than willing to give up the gains from international trade to protect industries that have lost their competitiveness.

Given that the gains from trade are unevenly distributed, an appropriate policy would be to dip into these broad gains to compensate those who have been harmed by trade liberalization. Even with compensation, the net gains from trade will be positive. The U.S. Trade Adjustment Assistance Act is designed to do just that, providing training, health insurance, and tax credits to workers who can show they have lost their jobs as a result of a trade agreement (Department of Labor, 2006). Another approach that has gained some attention is to introduce side constraints into international trade agreements that make access to domestic markets contingent on some internationally agreed labor standards or minimum wages. The idea is to require all countries benefitting from WTO normal trade relations to establish some minimum level of worker protection that would "level the playing field." Of course, many developing countries lack the means to match labor conditions in the wealthy countries and are unlikely to agree to any international labor standards that would have the effect of eliminating wage differentials between countries. As shown in Appendix 4.1, allowing countries to exploit their comparative advantages levels the playing field (trade evens out the uneven distribution of the world's resources) although not in the way those favoring protectionism would like to see that leveling accomplished. In any case, a labor side agreement is part of NAFTA and labor standards have become another area of discussion at the WTO.

In a similar manner, many environmentalists favor side agreements or some other mechanism that would ensure environmental protection in the globalizing world economy. Their concern is that removal of trade barriers will allow firms in the industrialized countries to relocate their operations in developing countries to avoid the more rigorous environmental standards in the wealthy countries. Some environmentalists may also favor using trade barriers to discourage economic activity in other countries that might harm the environment. The tuna–dolphin trade dispute described earlier is an example of an attempt to use trade barriers to influence behavior in other countries. As a general rule, such efforts have been ineffective (Vogel, 1995). In addition to the labor side agreement, however, NAFTA also includes an environmental side agreement and the relationship between trade and the environment is another important subject of discussion at the WTO (WTO, 2008i). In 2007, Democratic Congressional leaders in the United States reached an understanding with the

President to include labor and environmental side agreements in current and future trade talks (Weisman, 2007).

Organized labor and environmental activists have been prominent in the periodic anti-globalization demonstrations that often take place in conjunction with international economic conferences. A third group participating in the anti-globalization movement is made up of people who see trade as a way for multinational corporations and rich people in high-income countries to exploit the poor in the developing countries. The foundation for this type of argument goes back to Karl Marx and the explanation of imperialism advanced by Rosa Luxembourg, Lenin, and others at the beginning of the twentieth century. For Marx, capitalists could be expected to employ various strategies to slow the arrival of capitalism's inevitable demise as a result of its internal contradictions. Among these strategies, Marx pointed to the need to spread growing amounts of capital over larger numbers of workers to increase the amount of exploitation that was the basis for maintaining capitalist profits (Blaug, 1979). Lenin internationalized this argument, contending that imperialist exploitation of workers in developing countries was the inevitable and final stage of capitalist development (Lenin, 1996/1916). For these thinkers, trade was just one element in a system of exploitation of low-income people in the periphery by wealthy capitalists in the center (Griffin and Gurley, 1985).

In the 1960s and 1970s, some of these ideas were adopted by economists at the UN Economic Commission for Latin America (ECLA) and the UN Commission on Trade and Development (UNCTAD) and combined with a theory of economic development known as dependency theory (Dos Santos, 1970). Two leading figures in this understanding of development were Raul Prebisch and Hans Singer who argued that the prices received by developing countries for their agricultural exports grew more slowly than the prices they paid for their industrial imports. This terms-of-trade effect was seen as disadvantageous and led to the policy recommendation that developing countries use high trade barriers to promote the industrialization of their economies (Lynn, 2003). Details of the neo-Marxist and dependency theories of development are beyond the scope of this book but it can be noted that these intellectual positions were the basis for many of the Latin American policies described in the first chapter. Because economic relations with wealthy countries were seen as exploitative and of benefit only to rich capitalists in the North, policies that prevented economic incursions by the industrialized countries were favored. These policies included trade barriers and nationalization of foreign-owned firms as well as loose monetary policies and undervalued exchange rates. As noted in Chapter 1, such policies were unsustainable making macroeconomic policy reforms inevitable.

The notion that economic relations between rich and poor countries are exploitative is still widespread as shown by the enthusiastic participation in anti-globalization demonstrations of many advocates for the poor. On the other side, most economists tend to believe that international trade is not a zero sum gain in which gains for one party necessarily mean losses for the other. These analysts point out that if the gains from international trade flowed to only one of the parties to the transaction, the other party would have no incentive to make a deal. Low-income countries generally lack the heavy industries that produce capital and intermediate goods used in the production of final consumer goods and must, therefore, rely on importation to establish industries producing consumer goods. Likewise, exports of goods that can be produced at low cost in a developing country can be a source of income that can be invested to increase productivity and output or used to finance consumption of food and other basic needs. There is some empirical evidence that countries that are open to trade fare better than those that attempt to follow the Prebisch–Singer thesis that industrialization and economic growth are best promoted behind extensive barriers to trade. The Asian Tigers (Taiwan, South Korea, Singapore, and Hong Kong) are often cited as countries with open economies that have experienced rapid growth and development through the promotion of exports.

Of course, even if active participation in international trade contributes to increased economic growth, it may still be the case that the benefits of this growth are not widely shared. Figini and Santarelli (2006) do find evidence that open trade policies contribute to reductions in poverty but others find great variation in the effects of trade liberalization on poverty in developing countries. Winters, McCulloch and McKay (2004) point out that trade liberalization will lead to adjustment as firms that were previously protected by trade barriers are faced with greater foreign competition while those that are internationally competitive see new opportunities to expand their operations. These adjustments may or may not be of benefit to the poor in a developing country. In their survey of the evidence, Winters, McCulloch and McKay (2004) find that the particular circumstances of developing countries are so varied that it is possible to find examples of countries that have benefitted from trade liberalization as well as other countries that have not. The Nobel Laureate in economics Joseph Stiglitz has made similar points noting that institutions in many developing countries may be so weak that the gains from trade are inevitably captured by foreigners or domestic business and political elites (Stiglitz, 2003).

The implication of these analyses, however, is not that protectionism is a better policy than trade liberalization but rather that complementary policies may be required to assure that the benefits of international trade are widely shared and the adjustment costs incurred by particular individuals or industries are mitigated. Some of the needed policies are the responsibility of the governments of developing countries themselves but others involve the international institutions described in this chapter. Although many still see trade as exploitation, there appears to be a growing consensus that with appropriate institutional changes, trade can be an important element in the fight against poverty (Sachs, 2005). Even some charitable organizations that might at one time have been skeptical about the benefits of trade liberalization have begun to recognize the potential for trade to play a positive role in development. Oxfam, for example, calls for increased international trade under a system of fair rules and regulations (Oxfam, 2008). As noted earlier, Oxfam is particularly concerned by the double standards of wealthy countries that insist on opening markets in developing countries while continuing to protect their agricultural producers with trade barriers and subsidies. Likewise the charitable organization founded by the rock singer Bono (Debt, AIDS, Trade, Africa) sees trade as a central element for development and poverty reduction as long as the wealthy countries open their markets to goods produced in low-income countries (DATA, 2007). The trade barriers and subsidies that are central to agricultural policies in high-income countries and that are thought by many to reduce the benefits of globalization for low-income countries are described in the following chapters.

Appendix 4.1: Comparative Advantage

The concept of comparative advantage is one of the most important discoveries in the history of economics. According to Jones and Neary (1984), Paul Samuelson pointed to comparative advantage in response to a challenge to name a social science principle that is "both true and non-trivial." To support his contention, Samuelson (1954) noted that the principle is obviously true (given the assumptions that underlie it) and as evidence that it is non-trivial he pointed to "... the thousands of important and intelligent men (sic) who have never been able to grasp the doctrine for themselves or to believe it after it was explained to them." For comparative advantage to arise, the economy must be perfectly competitive and countries must be sufficiently different in some way to give rise to different sets of relative prices when they are not trading (that is, when they are in a state of autarky). Under those conditions, countries will generally find that there is a trading partner from whom they can obtain certain goods at lower cost than they can obtain them from their own domestic industry.

Suppose there are two countries (Benin and Niger) producing and consuming two goods (food and clothing). Let P_{BF} and P_{BC} be the prices of food and clothing, respectively, in Benin, while P_{NF} and P_{NC} are food and clothing prices in Niger. Comparative advantage is determined by examining the relative prices for food and clothing when the two countries are in autarky. Benin has a comparative advantage in the production and trade of food if, in autarky, $P_{BF}/P_{BC} < P_{NF}/P_{NC}$. In other words, Benin has a comparative advantage in the good with a lower relative price as compared to Niger which has a comparative advantage in the other good, clothing. Note that comparative advantage has to do with relative prices, or, what amounts to the same thing in a world of perfect competition, relative costs. It is helpful to think of this in terms of opportunity costs, that is, what has to be given up to pursue an alternative activity (see Appendix 2.1). For Benin, producing an extra unit of food requires giving up less clothing than is the case in Niger where food is relatively more expensive in terms of the amount of clothing that has to be given up to obtain it. Because comparative advantage is based on a comparison of the relative internal opportunity costs, it is possible for a country to have an absolute advantage in both goods but a comparative advantage in only one. For example the absolute costs of production could be lower for both goods in Benin but Niger would still have a comparative advantage in one of them.

A classic story about comparative advantage may be helpful. A doctor and a nurse can both give shots and treat pneumonia. The doctor may be a better shot-giver and a better pneumonia-treater than the nurse, having an absolute advantage in both. But the doctor is probably much better at treating pneumonia than the nurse while, perhaps, being only slightly better at giving shots. If the doctor has to spend time giving shots, she will have less time for treating pneumonia—the opportunity cost of giving shots for the doctor is high. If the nurse specializes in shot-giving, the doctor will be free to spend more time on treating pneumonia, the activity in which she has a comparative advantage. Although the nurse has an absolute disadvantage at shot-giving (the doctor is better at both functions), he has a comparative advantage in giving shots. Their patients will be better off if the nurse and doctor each specialize in the activity in which she or he has a comparative advantage.

To see why specialization according to comparative advantage is economically beneficial, suppose that labor is the only input (and therefore the only "cost") and that Benin and Niger, in autarky, produce food and clothing according to the following:

Units of food/clothing that can be produced with 1 unit of labor:

In:	Food	Clothing
Benin	9	5
Niger	5	4

Note that Benin has an absolute advantage in both goods: a unit of labor produces more food and more clothing in Benin than a unit of labor in Niger. Suppose that each country has 100 units of labor and in autarky, they allocate 60 units to food production and 40 units to clothing production. Then Benin produces (and consumes) 540 (9 × 60) units of food and 200 (5 × 40) units of clothing while Niger produces/consumes 300 (5 × 60) units of food and 160 (4 × 40) units of clothing. Total production is, thus, 840 units of food and 360 units of clothing.

Now consider the autarky opportunity cost ratios. Shifting a unit of labor from food to cloth production in Benin means giving up 9 units of food in return for 5 units of cloth. In other words, 9 units of food are "worth" 5 units of cloth in Benin. This means that 1 unit of food in Benin is worth 5/9 (0.5556) unit of clothing (9 food = 5 clothing; divide both sides by 9 to get 9/9 = 1 = 5/9). The same procedure in Niger yields a value of food in terms of cloth equal to 4/5 (0.8000). The opportunity cost of producing food in Benin is lower than it is in Niger (5/9 < 4/5) so Benin has a comparative advantage in food production and Niger has a comparative advantage in clothing. With trade, each country specializes according to comparative advantage allocating all of its labor to one or the other of the goods. The result is that Benin produces 900 units of food while Niger produces 400 units of clothing. In total, there are 60 more units of food and 40 more units of clothing than there were in autarky. There have clearly been gains from specialization as there is more of both goods available in the world than there was in autarky.

It would take some more work to show that this result applies for all possible initial resource allocations and to extend the analysis to more realistic situations in which the opportunity costs are not constant. In addition, without further information, it is not possible to determine where the world price would settle although it would have to be between the autarky relative prices (5/9 and 4/5). The reader is referred to any international trade textbook for further details on these aspects of comparative advantage. There is one other question related to comparative advantage that is worth pursuing here, however, and that is the question of why autarky relative opportunity costs might differ in the first place. The conventional explanations are that countries have different technologies, different consumer tastes and preferences, different resource endowments, or some combination of these differences. All of these differences can give rise to different relative autarky prices but the last explanation is the one that has received the most attention in the literature. If one assumes that both countries have the same tastes and technologies, comparative advantage is explained by differences in the amounts of labor, capital, and other resources found in the various countries.

This explanation was developed by two Swedish economists, Eli Heckscher and Bertil Ohlin. Heckscher and Ohlin suggested that the technologies available for producing different goods might be characterized as intensive in a particular resource. Suppose, for example, that there are two productive resources, capital and labor, and that textile production is a labor-intensive industry while computer production is capital-intensive. If China is well endowed with labor but does not have a lot of capital, labor will be relatively cheap and capital expensive. In autarky, China would be forced to produce both textiles and computers. If the Chinese market is opened to trade, it will have a comparative advantage in textile production which requires a lot of China's relatively inexpensive labor. If Japan has relatively more capital and less labor than China, it will have a comparative advantage in computers which require more of Japan's relatively inexpensive capital. So, with free trade, China specializes in textiles and Japan in computers and the two countries trade with each other to satisfy final consumer demand.

One implication of this model is that trade actually represents the exchange of resources that are embodied in the goods that are traded. In other words, the uneven distribution of resources around the world is smoothed out by trade. Areas with little capital will still be able to consume capital-intensive goods through trade using their abundant resources to produce goods that have a lower internal opportunity cost than the capital-intensive goods that are now imported. It follows from this that free trade can affect returns to different resources. The United States has abundant land and capital but relatively scarce labor. In autarky, U.S. wages will be high. With free trade, U.S. wages fall as the relative labor scarcity is offset by the importation of labor-intensive goods. This, of course, is why U.S. labor unions always oppose trade liberalization. The Heckscher–Ohlin model explains only part of international trade but may be particularly relevant for agriculture. Agriculture is a land-intensive industry so countries that have relatively abundant land, such as the United States, Canada, Australia, New Zealand, Brazil, and Argentina, are likely to have a comparative advantage in agriculture. Countries with relatively limited amounts of agricultural land as a result, for example, of extensive mountainous terrain, deserts or high population densities, will not have a comparative advantage in agricultural activities that require abundant land resources.

5

The Nature and Scope of Agricultural Subsidies in High-Income Countries

Introduction

The term "agricultural subsidies" is applied to a wide range of mechanisms employed by governments to manage and support the food and agricultural sectors of their economies. In general, food and agricultural policies can be designed to correct market failures as described in Chapter 2 or to promote the interests of particular industries, farmers, or consumers. In wealthy countries, agricultural policies have generally been oriented toward increasing the well-being of farmers although policies to advance the general welfare by correcting the inefficiencies associated with market failures as well as policies benefitting consumers are not uncommon. Subsidies can be thought of as being the opposite of taxes and as such constitute policy instruments that encourage particular patterns of behavior or support certain activities. We might think of these subsidies, then, as any government intervention that causes food or agricultural prices, firm profits, or household incomes to be more favorable for the economic agents concerned than they would be in the absence of the government action. Examples include interventions that increase the prices farmers receive for their output or that lower the prices they pay for farm inputs, direct monetary transfers that raise farm household incomes, monetary compensation for losses due to natural or manmade disasters, and actions that lower food prices for low-income consumers.

In 1993, the Environmental Working Group (EWG) began requesting detailed information on farm subsidies from the U.S. Department of Agriculture (USDA) under the Freedom of Information Act. This act requires federal agencies to comply with information requests unless there is good reason to keep the information confidential. EWG has been able to obtain detailed data on U.S. government payments to farmers from 1995 to the present. According to statistics published on the group's website, U.S. farm subsidies in 2006 totaled \$13.4 billion, down from \$21.1 billion in 2005, with \$11.2 billion allocated to farm income support, \$2.0 billion to conservation programs and \$0.2 billion to disaster payments (EWG, www.ewg.org/farm/index.php). Historical statistical tables included with the 2009 U.S. Federal Budget indicate that the government spent \$21.4 billion on farm income support in 2006 and an additional \$4.6 billion on research and other services to agriculture for a total of \$26.0 billion (Government Printing Office, 2008).

The differences in these two expenditure estimates may be due to the use of different systems of classification and terminology. For example, the figures for farm income support in the Federal Budget no doubt include all three of the categories that make up the subsidy total reported by EWG. The way in which spending on government policies is reported will be influenced by the objectives of the group or organization doing the reporting. EWG is particularly interested in environmental questions and may want to highlight the contrast between the amount spent on conservation compared with the amount spent to support farm incomes. From another perspective, however, the conservation programs generate payments to farmers and could properly be seen as part of the broad income support afforded to farm households. While our objective in this and subsequent chapters is to examine the farm subsidies that have an impact on world markets and low-income countries, it is useful to adopt a broad classification at the outset to better understand the full range of policy interventions that may affect prices and world food markets. The broadest set of agricultural policy data available is published by the Organization for Economic Cooperation and Development (OECD, 2008c).[1]

The OECD database is updated annually in its publication *Producer and Consumer Support Estimates* which includes data not only on direct government spending but also on the contributions of consumers who pay prices that differ from world prices as a result of trade barriers (OECD, 2008c). In addition, the OECD reports the amounts spent for services such as agricultural research or marketing and promotion programs. In the next section, the objectives of agricultural policy are examined along with descriptions of the nature and scope of various types of agricultural policy tools. This overview is followed by a detailed description of the OECD data on agricultural subsidies

---

[1] The OECD includes 30 high-income countries in North America, Europe, and the Pacific rim: Canada, the United States, Mexico, Japan, South Korea, Australia, New Zealand, certain countries in the EU (Netherlands, Belgium, Luxembourg, France, Germany, Italy, United Kingdom, Ireland, Denmark, Greece, Spain, Portugal, Finland, Austria, Sweden, Hungary, Poland, Czech Republic and Slovak Republic), Norway, Iceland, Turkey, and Switzerland. Its headquarters are in Paris (www.oecd.org).

and a statistical profile of producer and consumer support in OECD countries. In the final section of the chapter, some of the evidence concerning the effects of agricultural subsidies in OECD countries is reviewed.

Agricultural Policy Objectives and Tools

According to the National Priorities Project (NPP, 2008), the United States had spent more than $540 billion on the war in Iraq as of mid-2008. In 2005, world military spending reached $1.12 trillion (almost half of which was spent by the United States), about three times the $376 billion spent on agricultural support in that year (NPP, 2008a; OECD, 2008c). The 2006 budget of the United States was some $2.4 trillion while U.S. GDP was $13.2 trillion and the total GDP of all countries in the world was roughly $48.2 trillion (World Bank, 2008b). Compared to these numbers, 2007 agricultural support spending by the OECD countries of $365 billion may not appear to be too far out of proportion. On the other hand, the value of total world agricultural trade in 2006 was just $945 billion (WTO, 2007). Moreover, World Bank (2008b) data show that total GDP for all the countries in Sub-Saharan Africa was only $710 billion in 2006. Finally, the OECD data show that support to agricultural producers in OECD countries has often represented about a third of total farm income (see Table 5.1). These figures suggest that while agricultural subsidies are small relative to the size of the world economy, they are really quite substantial when compared to world agricultural trade, farm income in the OECD, and the size of the economies of low-income countries.

Why do the wealthy countries choose to implement these policies? The rationale for government economic intervention described in Chapter 2 points to market failures as the primary justification for public policies related to the economy. Because agriculture depends critically on such capricious phenomena as the weather, it is likely to be characterized by a great deal of instability. If the weather is particularly clement, harvests may be abundant causing market prices to fall. These low prices can cause hardship for producers some of whom may be forced out of business. Subsequently, a spell of bad weather may lead to much lower production and rising prices that adversely affect consumers. The risk of adverse price movements as a result of highly variable weather could be managed if appropriate insurance instruments were available. But markets for crop insurance can suffer the kinds of failures (adverse selection and moral hazard) described in Chapter 2 and such insurance may therefore be extremely expensive or difficult to find. Government provision of subsidized crop insurance may correct this market failure and lead to greater efficiency.

Table 5.1 Total OECD producer and consumer support estimates, selected years (billions of current dollars)

	1986	1995	2000	2005	2007
Value of production (farm gate)	**538.7**	**775.1**	**660.9**	**834.7**	**1,002.8**
Producer support estimate (PSE)	**230.2**	**267.5**	**243.7**	**272.1**	**258.2**
*PSE/farm income (%)**	*39*	*31*	*32*	*28*	*23*
Market price support	176.4	183.5	150.6	146.8	127.0
Payments based on output	12.6	7.7	18.1	16.4	5.0
Payments based on input use	18.4	23.2	20.9	27.6	32.5
Payments based on current prod.	19.2	44.6	38.1	38.1	27.7
Payments—historic production**	0.9	0.5	0.1	0.1	1.5
Payments—historic production**	2.2	3.0	14.6	38.8	60.6
Payments—non-commodity	0.3	3.5	2.9	4.0	3.7
Miscellaneous payments	0.3	1.5	−0.8	−0.4	0.1
General services support estimate (GSSE)	**38.8**	**70.5**	**56.2**	**74.0**	**77.6**
Research and development	3.2	5.7	5.1	6.7	7.8
Agricultural schools	0.8	1.5	1.4	2.1	2.2
Inspection services	1.0	1.4	1.8	3.2	3.4
Infrastructure	13.4	29.9	19.8	22.2	22.2
Marketing and promotion	12.7	28.1	23.6	35.6	37.8
Public stockholding	6.3	1.8	1.8	1.8	1.5
Miscellaneous	1.5	2.2	2.7	2.5	2.6
Consumer support estimate (CSE)	**−150.8**	**−191.6**	**−144.4**	**−135.7**	**−115.9**
Consumer transfers to producers	−162.9	−182.5	−148.3	−145.8	−125.3
Other transfers from consumers	−19.5	−38.4	−20.2	−21.4	−22.2
Taxpayer transfers to consumers	18.2	24.9	22.2	29.5	29.2
Excess feed cost	13.3	4.4	1.9	2.0	2.3
Total support estimate (TSE)	**287.3**	**362.9**	**322.2**	**375.6**	**365.1**
Transfers from consumers	182.4	222.8	168.5	167.3	147.4
Transfers from taxpayers	124.4	180.4	173.8	229.7	239.8
Budget revenues	−19.5	−38.4	−20.2	−21.4	−22.2

* Farm income is equal to the value of production at the farm gate plus direct payments from national budgets.
** The first set of payments based on historic output requires production, the second does not.
Source: OECD, 2008c.

It was noted in Chapter 2 that governments also intervene frequently to redistribute income. In some cases, the motivation is to promote distributive justice by providing financial assistance to individuals who may be unable to provide adequately for themselves. Part of the original justification for farm policies in many of the OECD countries was that farm households had lower incomes on average than other households. Because these low incomes were perceived to be the result of forces outside the control of the farm household, they were seen as unfair and the government felt political pressure to correct the disparity. It is also the case, however, that politicians may choose to distort taxation and spending policies in favor of individuals and groups that are willing and able to make large campaign contributions. Much of the criticism of agricultural policy both from within the high-income countries themselves and from advocates for the poor in low-income countries is based on the perception that farm subsidies represent political responses to a favored special-interest group rather than policies aimed at correcting market failures or distributive inequities.

The specific goals of national agricultural policies vary from country to country and depend on a variety of special national circumstances that will be described in later chapters. As noted earlier, however, for the countries belonging to the OECD, the broad objective of agricultural policy has generally been to increase the well-being of farmers. Other goals have been important, of course. After the Second World War, for example, European governments were particularly interested in rebuilding their rural economies to insure that there would be adequate food available for urban consumers. Likewise in the United States, public policies related to the dairy industry were originally designed to insure that there would be adequate fluid milk supplies across the entire country and throughout the year. Nevertheless, farm income has always been an important objective of agricultural policy in the OECD countries and in recent decades would seem to have become the overriding concern (see Anderson, Martin and van der Mensbrugghe, 2006a). Increasing farm household income can be accomplished by raising the prices farmers receive for their output, lowering the prices they pay for inputs, providing direct income supplements or providing support services at government expense.

As detailed in Chapter 3, trade has become an important part of virtually all countries' food systems. In the absence of government intervention, prices for agricultural inputs and farm products will be equal to the world price adjusted for transportation costs between a local market and a port of origin. If these prices are too low to insure that a country's farm income objectives are met, they can be raised through the imposition of trade barriers. Importing countries can raise internal prices by levying tariffs on imported goods. The tariff raises the price of the cheaper imports to a level equal to the more expensive domestic product. For countries that export a particular good, prices can be increased by implementing an export subsidy. Export subsidies work by allowing an exporting firm to purchase goods at a high internal price and to sell them at the lower world price with the government making up the difference. Note that tariffs raise revenue for the national treasury while export subsidies require budgetary expenditures. Both tariffs and export subsidies raise the prices producers receive and they also increase the prices consumers have to pay. Thus, some or all of the cost of these subsidies is borne by consumers in the form of higher prices.

Some have argued that price modifications brought about by trade barriers should not be counted as agricultural subsidies on the grounds that only interventions that require budgetary expenditures are properly identified as subsidies (Wise, 2004). In fact, the EWG and Federal Budget figures on farm subsidies cited earlier include only payments made through the budget. Many policy analysts make a distinction between agricultural subsidies financed through government budgets and agricultural trade barriers that alter world and domestic prices treating each type of intervention as a separate form of farm support (FAPRI, 2002; Anderson *et al.*, 2006a; Schmitz *et al.*, 2006). The OECD defines agricultural support to include both trade barriers and domestic farm programs. This definition is actually an appropriate indicator of the effect of agricultural policies on world markets because trade barriers frequently have a more significant impact on world prices than programs that provide income supplements or farm services. The most important farm policy in Japan is a trade barrier applied to rice imports that has on occasion raised internal rice prices to more than seven times the level of the world price (OECD, 2008c). This policy is financed by consumers and does not show up anywhere in Japan's government budget. Transfers from consumers through trade barriers accounted for 72 percent of Japan's total agricultural support in 2007 (OECD, 2008c). It would be highly inaccurate to ignore these important subsidies just because they are financed by consumers rather than through the government budget. Some conceptual problems in deriving appropriate estimates of the magnitude of these trade-related subsidies are discussed in the next section.

Another way to raise farm incomes is to provide income supplements. In contrast to the price increases brought about through trade barriers, income supplements are financed entirely from government budgets. An important distinction concerns whether these subsidies are tied to farm production or not. Many of the direct income payments that are made to farmers are based on the amount of particular goods produced. In the United States, for example, farmers can sell their crops at prices that are lower than a guaranteed floor price and the government will, in essence, make up the difference.[2] The

---

[2]   The program being described here is the loan deficiency payment. The precise way in which this program works is extremely complicated. In later chapters, additional details on how loan deficiency payments and other types of income supplements will be provided as necessary for the discussion. At this stage, the important point is that payments tied to output are likely to influence producer decisions and lead to increased output while those that are not tied to output (the so-called decoupled payments) are not thought to have this effect.

payments provided by the government are calculated by multiplying the payment rate (expressed as a price, that is, monetary units per bushel, pound, ton or some other quantitative measure of a specific commodity such as maize or wheat) multiplied by the quantity marketed by the producer. This means that the more of the particular commodity a farmer produces, the greater will be the total payment received (of course, so too will be the costs of production). Payments of this nature are sometimes referred to as "coupled" payments in contrast to "decoupled" payments that are not tied to production (see Chapter 4).

In 2003, the EU initiated reforms of the CAP aimed at decoupling farm subsidies from production (European Commission, 2008b). The main element of this new approach is known as the "single farm payment" which stipulates that farmers receive direct payments with no requirements that they produce particular crops. The hope is that producers will respond to market signals in their decisions on the types and amounts of agricultural commodities to produce rather than being influenced by subsidies that are tied to cereal grains, oilseeds, or other specific goods.[3] The distinction between coupled and decoupled payments is important for compliance with the provisions of the WTO Agreement on Agriculture. Decoupled payments are not considered to be trade distorting and so are not subject to requirements that they be reduced as is the case for the coupled or trade-distorting domestic policies.

In addition to price supports and income supplements, governments also provide farmers with services at taxpayer expense. In the United States, for example, the government subsidizes housing costs of rural farm labor and finances the promotion of U.S. farm products overseas. In some cases, government-provided agricultural services are of benefit to both producers and consumers. Publicly funded agricultural research, for example, leads to technological innovations that lower the costs of agricultural production. Because farming is a competitive industry unable to exercise market power (as would be the case for a monopoly), these cost reductions are eventually passed along to consumers in the form of lower prices.[4] Research generally has at least one

---

[3] As noted in an OECD report, "... all payments that are contingent upon being a farmer will have some impact on output" (OECD, 2003). Even if payments are not tied to the production of specific commodities, by supporting farmers in their continued production activities, agricultural output will be greater than it would have been had these individuals not received payments and elected to move into some other line of work. Still, such programs have less impact on production and are less trade distorting than those that create incentives to expand production of specific crops to which payments may be tied. See also OECD, 2006b.

[4] Publicly funded agricultural research in the United States has contributed to a highly productive U.S. agricultural sector that produces immense quantities of low-cost food. Because food is relatively cheap and Americans are quite wealthy, the proportion, on average, of an individual's income that has to be spent on food is extremely low. According to the Economic

of the characteristics of a public good in that once a research result has been realized it rapidly becomes available to everyone making it difficult to prevent those who did not contribute to the research from benefitting from it. Because of this characteristic, less than socially optimal amounts of certain kinds of research would be conducted in the absence of government funding.[5] Most estimates of the economic returns to public expenditures on agricultural research range from about 25 percent to more than 100 percent, suggesting that there is a very high payoff to this type of economic intervention (Fuglie *et al.*, 1996). As noted in Chapter 2, governments also encourage research through issuing patents on technical innovations in order to overcome the free-rider problem and encourage privately funded research. Until the late 1970s, public and private agricultural research expenditures in the United States were about equal but since then private spending on research and development has surpassed that of the public sector (Fuglie *et al.*, 1996).

Agricultural Subsidies in OECD Countries

Table 5.1 contains statistics on producer and consumer support in the 30 OECD countries for selected years. The total support estimate (TSE) includes income supplements, food subsidies, and farm services paid for through government budgets as well as transfers from consumers resulting from trade barriers. This support is divided into three parts: the producer support estimate (PSE); the general services support estimate (GSSE); and the consumer support estimate (CSE). Since 1986, the TSE has surpassed $365 billion (that is, a billion dollars a day) on three occasions (2004, 2005, and 2007) and surpassed $350 billion an additional eight times (1991, 1992, 1993, 1994, 1995, 1999, 2003, and 2006). The TSE for the OECD countries has declined from 2.76 percent of their aggregate GDP in 1986 to 0.89 percent in 2007. Producer support is by far the most important element in the TSE accounting for 71 percent of the total in 2007. Note that the CSE is negative because the transfers

---

Research Service (USDA), U.S. consumers devote less than 10 percent of their total consumer expenditures to food compared with 13 percent in Germany, 15 percent in France and Japan, 16 percent in Norway and the UK, 27 percent in Mexico, 34 percent in Russia, 51 percent in Indonesia, and 73 percent in Nigeria. See ERS (2008e).

[5] Basic research usually does not lead directly to the creation of a new product that can be patented. This type of research concerns the discovery of new knowledge that may form the basis for research that does lead to patentable products or may simply add to the stock of human knowledge with little or no effect on practical innovations. It is basic research that is likely to be under-supplied by the private sector because it does not lead directly to new products from which economic returns can be captured by private enterprises.

from consumers to producers as a result of trade barriers are greater than the transfers from taxpayers to consumers through such programs as the U.S. food stamp program.

Table 5.1 is derived from the TSE statistics on the OECD internet site (OECD, 2008c). These statistics are computed from a series of national tables that in turn are derived from data on production, prices, and various types of support for particular commodities in the 30 OECD countries. The method employed to develop the estimates is described in detail in a manual available online (OECD, 2008b; see also Legg, 2003). Some observations about the entries in the table may help to understand how the data are structured. To begin with, note that the values for "Market price support" under PSE are very close to the values entered for "Consumer transfers to producers" under CSE, albeit with opposite signs. In fact, these values should be about equal in absolute value because they refer to the same thing, that is, the subsidy financed by consumers who pay higher prices for traded goods as a result of tariffs and export subsidies. For consumers this value is a tax and is therefore entered with a negative sign. For producers, it is a subsidy so it is entered in the table with a positive sign.

Market price support (or consumer transfers to producers) is based on the difference between internal domestic prices and world prices for the main commodities traded by a country. For the OECD as a whole, the commodities used to compute market price support make up about 67 percent of total agricultural production. The value of market price support for these commodities is then increased by about 49 percent (one divided by 0.67 minus one) to obtain an estimate for all agricultural support. The implicit assumption, thus, is that the amount of support afforded commodities not used to calculate the initial estimate is in the same proportion as for the main commodities. Such an assumption may lead to overestimates of the value of market price support if, in fact, the commodities that are not included in the basic estimate receive less protection than those for which data are collected.

Market price support is generated by both tariffs on imported goods and subsidies on exports. In the case of imports, the tariff raises the domestic price above the world price. Consumers pay this higher price for both domestically produced products and imports of the same goods. Producers receive the difference between the domestic and the world price multiplied by the amount they market in the country and this subsidy is paid for by consumers. Consumers also pay the higher price on imported goods sold in the country and the revenue from this tariff is transferred to the government. In other words, the tariff on imported goods generates a cost to consumers that is divided between the producer subsidy and the tariff revenue collected by the government. In Table 5.1, the tariff revenue is shown as "Other transfers from

Table 5.2 Market price support for rice in Japan

	Units	1990	2000	2007
a. Domestic production	1,000 metric tons	10,499.0	9,490.0	8,714.0
b. Producer price (farm gate)	yen/kg	275.0	225.5	205.29
c. Value of production (a × b)	billion yen	2,887.23	2,140.0	1,788.86
d. Domestic consumption	1,000 metric tons	10,484.0	9,790.0	9,091.10
e. Consumption price (farm)	yen/kg	275.0	225.5	205.29
f. Value of consumption (d × e)	billion yen	2,883.10	2,207.65	1,866.27
g. Reference price (farm gate)	yen/kg	62.09	30.90	60.10
– World price	US$/ton	284	–	–
– Transportation cost	US$/ton	28.4	–	–
– Exchange rate (yen/US$)	yen/US$	144.80	–	–
– Conversion milled to husked	rate	0.91	0.91	0.91
– Quality adjustment	rate	0.66	0.66	0.66
h. Market price differential	yen/kg	212.91	194.60	145.19
i. Market transfers	billion yen	2,232.11	1,905.13	1,319.90
– from consumers to producers	billion yen	2,232.11	1,846.75	1,265.15
– other transfers from consumers	billion yen	0	58.38	54.75
j. Budgetary transfers	billion yen	24.99	1.90	0.10
– from taxpayers to producers	billion yen	3.19	0	0
– from taxpayers to consumers	billion yen	21.80	1.90	0.10
k. Market price support	billion yen	2,235.30	1,846.75	1,265.15

Source: Japanese tables and explanatory notes at OECD, 2008c.

consumers" and entered at the bottom of the table as "Budget revenues." Export subsidies also generate two kinds of transfers. First, the higher domestic price that results from the export subsidy means that consumers transfer to producers an amount equal to the difference between the internal price and the lower world price multiplied by the domestic output sold within the country. This consumer cost is included in the measure of market price support. For the portion of domestic production that is exported, there is a transfer from taxpayers equal to the difference between the internal and world prices multiplied by the amount that is exported. This subsidy is also included in the market price support measure even though it is financed by taxpayers through the government budget rather than by consumers.

Table 5.2 is based on the OECD table used to determine the price support from consumers and taxpayers for rice in Japan and can be used to illustrate the calculation of price support levels. Until 1995, the reference price used was the FOB[6] Thai price for milled rice expressed in U.S. dollars per metric ton and converted to Japanese yen per kilogram using the exchange rate and conversion factors to take account of quality variations and differences in the processing stage. Since 1996, the reference price is the average import price expressed in yen per kilogram. In 2007, the reference price was 60.10 yen per kilogram. Subtracting this price from the farm-gate price of 205.29 yen per kg gives a market price differential of 145.19 yen per kg. This differential is paid for by consumers and the total value of the subsidy, 1,319.9 billion yen, is obtained by multiplying the price differential by domestic consumption. Of this, 54.75 billion yen represent consumer transfers to the government budget. These other transfers are subtracted from the total to obtain market price support for rice of $1,265.15 billion yen.

Support for rice is only part of the story, of course, as other commodities also receive protection. In 2007, market price support for other commodities amounted to 1,060.95 billion yen so the total was 2,326.10 billion yen. This figure, however, is for only the commodities that the OECD tracks for Japan and these commodities in 2007 represented just 65.8 percent of all agricultural commodities receiving price support. To estimate the total value of market price support, therefore, the total for the selected commodities is divided by 0.658. The result is about 3,535 billion yen. The rest of the value of the PSE is made up of various direct payments from the government. Some 85 percent of the Japanese PSE in 2007 (4,149 billion yen) came from consumer transfers with only 15 percent being channeled through the government budget.

Japanese rice policies are somewhat unusual in that they have effectively prevented rice imports from entering the country. As a result, market price support is made up almost entirely of the transfer from consumers to producers. In other countries where trade barriers are used to raise the price, part of the consumer transfer represents revenue for the government budget, classified as other consumer transfers in the OECD tables as noted earlier. For Japanese rice this element is either missing entirely or relatively small. Prior to the Uruguay Round, Japan banned rice imports altogether. The AA required minimal market access for rice so Japan has imported small amounts since its implementation. If a tariff is set to prevent imports altogether, no tariff revenue will be raised. Because Japan does not export a great deal of agricultural

---

[6]   FOB stands for "free on board." The FOB price is the price at the farm gate plus transportation and all other transactions costs incurred in moving the commodity from the farm to a port, including any costs associated with clearing customs. An alternative measure of the world price is the CIF (cartage, insurance, freight) price which is the price at the port of destination prior to the levying of any customs duties. The CIF price differs from the FOB price by international maritime costs including shipping, insurance, and any other legal or transactions costs associated with the international movement of goods.

goods, there are no export subsidies and no taxpayer transfers to producers from this type of policy tool.

There is a conceptual issue related to the calculation of market price support that was alluded to earlier. In calculating the value of this subsidy, it is necessary to use a reference price against which the internal price can be compared. As shown in the example of Japanese rice, OECD analysts have developed methods to take account of the fact that price observations may relate to commodities at different stages of processing or of varying quality. As a result it is possible to express all prices used in the computation of market price support as farm-gate prices for equivalent goods. The problem is that the world prices used as references in these calculations have been distorted by the very policies that are being measured. In the United States, for example, a tariff-rate quota (TRQ) is used to maintain the U.S. price for raw sugar at about $0.21 per pound. Measuring U.S. market price support for sugar is based on comparing the domestic price to a world price that has varied between $0.06 and $0.16 per pound over the past 20 years (OECD, 2008c). In 2007, the world reference price was $0.12 (after having averaged $0.10 per pound for the period 2000 to 2006) so the price difference was about $0.09 per pound. Based on this price differential, the value of the consumer transfer to producers was $806 million dollars while the value of the other consumer transfers (that is, the amount collected by the government in tariff revenue and included in the budget revenue category at the bottom of Table 5.1) was $818 million (OECD, 2008c). Because the United States is a very large market, however, its policies have an impact on the world prices that are actually observed. This is, of course, part of the argument against farm subsidies which are alleged to have the effect of lowering world prices to the detriment of low-income agricultural exporters.

Some have argued that it is inappropriate to use observed world prices because if the policies were eliminated these prices would be higher so basing the calculations on actual depressed world prices exaggerates the value of the subsidy (see Tangermann, 2005). The suggested alternative is to use estimates of what the world price would be in the absence of all the price-distorting policies. Such estimates could be derived from one or more of the statistical models used to analyze the impact of policy changes (see Hertel, 1999; Hertel and Ivanic, 2006; Anderson *et al.*, 2006b). The problems with such an alternative are both practical and conceptual. On the practical side, statistical models are generally sensitive to the assumptions made in building and running them with the result that a wide variety of quite different price estimates could be generated with little hope of reaching consensus on which of the various hypothetical prices is most appropriate. In addition, whether it is preferable to use actual or hypothetical prices depends on the purpose of the analysis being conducted. For the OECD, actual expenditure on agricultural subsidies is more appropriate than the theoretical value of such subsidies if the policies that gave rise to them were eliminated. The advantage of the OECD approach is that it is based on actual price observations and, as Tangermann argues, it accurately reflects the "... intensity of effort needed to keep domestic prices at given levels...." (2005, p. 4).

The other elements included in the PSE are various kinds of direct payments to producers from government budgets. For the OECD as a whole, these direct payments constituted about 51 percent of total producer support in 2007. This level of direct support marks a substantial increase in the use of such policies, however, compared to 1986 when only 23 percent of the OECD PSE was accounted for by budget transfers. This change is due primarily to policy reform in the EU where the use of trade barriers has been reduced because of the entry of new members and the requirements of the AA. The OECD estimates divide the payments to producers according to the ways in which they are calculated. For example, the U.S. loan deficiency payment program is classed as a payment based on output of specific commodities. The 2008 U.S. Farm Bill established a price floor (loan rate) for wheat of $2.75 per bushel. If the average market price for wheat settles at $2.50 per bushel, wheat producers would be eligible for a payment of $0.25 per bushel on part of their wheat output.

The TSE is not the simple sum of the PSE, CSE and GSSE, because of the way in which consumer transfers are treated. To obtain the TSE, the PSE, including the transfer from consumers, is added to the GSSE and the part of the CSE that is positive (taxpayer transfers to consumers). The reason that the negative elements in the CSE are not subtracted from the other measures to determine the TSE is that these consumer transfers are counted as subsidies elsewhere in the table where they are entered with positive signs. Thus, the OECD TSE for 2007 ($365 billion) is equal to the PSE ($258 billion, including $127 billion in consumer transfers) plus the GSSE ($78 billion) plus the transfers to consumers from taxpayers ($29 billion). In essence, the TSE is made up of consumer transfers to producers, government transfers to producers, general services to agriculture provided by the government, and government transfers to consumers.

This last element merits further reflection. In most of the debates about agricultural subsidies, the focus is on support for farmers and agribusinesses. Taxpayer contributions to consumers are made through food subsidies such as food stamps and other types of food assistance usually for the benefit of low-income consumers. Such consumer subsidies may actually be of some benefit to producers as well because they increase demand and lead to somewhat higher domestic prices. The dual impact of the U.S. food stamp program is explicitly recognized in the OECD producer and consumer support data. One of the services included in the GSSE is "marketing and promotion," government intervention aimed at increasing demand for domestic agricultural products. Sixty-four percent of the costs of the food stamp program are included under marketing and promotion while the other 36 percent are counted as part of the transfer to consumers from taxpayers (OECD, 2008c).[7] In the United States, the food stamp, child nutrition, and school lunch programs are part of the farm policy legislation that is revised every five years or so. Since 1972, such programs have been administered by the U.S. Department of Agriculture (USDA) along with the programs that support farm incomes and this is no accident. More people in the United States live in urban and suburban areas than in rural areas and this distribution is reflected in the membership of the House of Representatives. Urban representatives have little interest in farm incomes but may be persuaded to support general farm legislation by the inclusion in that legislation of consumer food subsidies which are of interest to them.

The United States accounts for about 90 percent of the OECD taxpayer transfers to consumers (see Table 5.3). For the OECD as a whole, the taxes on consumers far outweigh consumer subsidies so the overall CSE is a large negative number. This would not be the case for all countries. In fact, as we will see in Chapter 9, many developing countries have historically taxed their agricultural sectors and subsidized their urban food consumers, an approach to food policy that is the opposite of the one commonly found in the high-income countries (see also Bilal, 2000). The OECD has collected data on Chinese agricultural policies and arranged them in the same format as for the producer and consumer support estimates for OECD countries (OECD, 2008c). In several years, the Chinese CSE is positive and in 1993 the PSE was negative. The reason for this state of affairs is that Chinese food policies occasionally result in domestic farm prices that are lower than the world price and this represents a consumer subsidy.

The data in Table 5.3 show that the United States, the EU, and Japan provide the largest amount of support, accounting for about 81 percent of the OECD TSE.[8] The way in which this support is distributed, however, differs

---

[7] The following statement can be found in an explanatory note for the U.S. producer and consumer support tables (OECD, 2008c): "USDA budget expenditure on administrative expenses on domestic food assistance programs (Food Program Administration), and the 'delivery cost' of the Food Stamp Program, calculated as 64 percent of the total budgetary expenditure." It is not clear what the basis is for using 64 percent of total expenditures as the "delivery cost" of the program.

[8] Of course the United States, the EU, and Japan also account for most of the population of the OECD as well as most of total economic and agricultural output. Based on OECD data, these countries have about 75 percent of the OECD population, account for 86 percent of the aggregate GDP for the 30 countries belonging to the OECD, and generate 78 percent of the total value of OECD agricultural output.

Table 5.3   Agricultural support in 2007 (billions of current dollars and percentages)

	OECD	United States	EU	Japan	Other OECD
Total support[a]	365.1	100.8	153.4	45.3	69.7
% OECD total[b]	100.0	27.6	42.0	12.4	18.8
Producer support	258.2	32.7	134.3	35.2	59.8
% country total[c]	70.7	32.4	87.5	77.7	85.8
General support	77.6	41.9	16.2	10.1	10.0
% country total[c]	21.3	41.6	10.6	22.3	14.2
Consumer support	29.2	26.2	2.9	0.0	0.1
% country total[c]	8.0	26.0	1.9	–	0.2
% TSE from taxpayers	61.9	87.1	68.6	28.0	–
% TSE from consumers	38.1	12.9	31.4	72.0	–
Number of farms, 2005[d]	–	2.1 million	10.0 million	2.6 million	–
Producer support per farm, 2005[e]	–	$20,333	$13,386	$18,231	–

[a] Total support estimate (TSE) made up of producer support, general services, and consumer support.
[b] Percent of TSE for all OECD countries accounted for by given country.
[c] Percent of a given country's TSE accounted for by producer, general service, or consumer support.
[d] EU Commission, http://ec.europa.eu/agriculture/agrista/2006/table_en/index.htm.
[e] Producer support estimate (PSE) divided by the number of farms.
Source: OECD, 2008c.

quite substantially among the three. Japan registered almost no taxpayer transfers to consumers in 2007 while such transfers represented 26 percent of the U.S. TSE. The U.S. PSE also accounts for a smaller proportion (about 32 percent) of total support than in the EU and Japan where the PSE amounts to 88 and 77 percent of the total, respectively. In addition, the two bottom rows of Table 5.3 show significant differences in the way in which total support is financed.[9] In the United States, most support is channeled through the

[9]   To compute the proportions of the TSE accounted for by taxpayers and consumers, it is necessary to deal with the problem of the negative budget revenues shown in the bottom row of Table 5.1. These revenues reflect transfers from consumers to the government budget as a result of trade barriers that raise the prices paid for imports. They do not benefit producers but they are a real cost to consumers. It turns out that part of this cost is borne by foreign producers who experience lower prices as a result of the trade barrier. But in the OECD method, a cost to domestic consumers is estimated and included as part of the consumer contribution to TSE. In Table 5.3, consumer and taxpayer transfers are added and the proportions in each category computed on the basis of this total. Thus, for the OECD as a whole, consumer trans-

government budget with less than 13 percent of the TSE paid for by consumers as a result of trade barriers. In contrast, 72 percent of Japan's TSE comes from consumer pocketbooks. It is also interesting to compare the proportion of PSE that comes from trade barriers. For 2007, 49 percent of the OECD PSE came in the form of market price support (trade barriers) with the rest being provided through direct payments. The corresponding figures for the United States, the EU, and Japan were 37 percent, 36 percent, and 85 percent, respectively. In later chapters, the particular agricultural policies that are found in the United States, the EU, Japan, and other countries will be described in greater detail with attention to the historical evolution of government intervention over time. It will turn out that quite significant changes have been made in EU agricultural policy. In 1986, only about 23 percent of total EU support came from the EU budget, the rest being financed by consumer transfers, while in 2007, 69 percent of total support was charged to taxpayers.

Another way to think about farm support in the United States, the EU, and Japan is to consider the average producer support per farm. There are considerably more farms in the EU than in either the United States or Japan so the per-farm average is likely to be lower in the EU than in the two countries with fewer farms. This comparison is made difficult by incompatible definitions of farms used by national statistical offices in different countries. In the United States, for example, anything with sales of agricultural goods worth more than $1,000 is counted as a farm while in Japan the minimum sales needed to be considered a farm is 500,000 yen (about $4,200). The European Commission reports that the number of farms in the 25 members of the EU was just under 10 million in 2005 compared with 2.6 million in Japan and 2.1 million in the United States in the same year (European Commission, 2006a). The figures for the United States and Japan are consistent with numbers reported by the Japanese Ministry of Agriculture, Forestry and Fisheries (www.maff.go.jp/toukei/abstract/index.htm) and the Economic Research Service of USDA (Hoppe and Banker, 2006). Dividing these figures into the values for producer support in 2005 gives estimates of the average producer support per farm in the EU, the United States, and Japan of $13,386, $20,333, and $18,231, respectively. From this perspective, the United States has the most generous farm programs of the three.

fers in 2007 were US$147.4 billion while taxpayer transfers were US$239.8 billion. Adding these two numbers gives US$387.2 billion rather than the TSE of US$365.1 billion reported in the table. Dividing consumer and taxpayer contributions by US$387.2 billion gives percentages that sum to 100 (38.1 percent for consumers and 61.9 percent for taxpayers). If this adjustment were not made, the figures for the OECD would be 65.7 percent for taxpayers, 40.4 percent for consumers, and -6.1 percent in budget revenues.

Of course, it is likely that the distribution of producer support is not evenly spread across all farm operations. The EWG reports, for example, that the top 10 percent of farm payment recipients in the United States (about 144,628 of the recipients included in the EWG database) received 62 percent of the USDA payments in 2006 suggesting a per-farm average for this group of $57,665. The EWG data do not include estimates of market price support due to trade barriers. Using the EWG number of recipients and the OECD figure for U.S. producer support in 2006, the average per-recipient support for these large farmers is $132,293. Note that the top 10 percent of farms account for the bulk of U.S. agricultural production as well, about 75 percent of total farm output in 2004 (Hoppe *et al.*, 2007a). In any case, if there are significant differences between the concentration of farm subsidies in the EU, the United States, and Japan, the average per-farm support might not accurately reflect the true generosity of the three programs. Suppose, for example, that all U.S. payments are distributed to half the farms (the other half receiving nothing) while Japanese support is fairly evenly distributed over 75 percent of the country's farms. Such a situation would suggest that actual per-farm support for the farms receiving support in Japan in 2005 averaged $24,308 compared with $40,667 in the United States rather than $18,231 and $20,333 respectively as reported above.

It is also instructive to consider producer support relative to the value of farm income from agricultural activities in the different OECD countries. In 2007, producer support for the OECD as a whole was equal to 23 percent of farm income defined as the value of agricultural production at the farm gate plus all of the direct payments made through the government budgets. Comparing the three countries in Table 5.3, the United States had the lowest percentage (10 percent) while Japan registered the highest at 45 percent and the EU occupied an intermediate position with about 26 percent of the value of farm income coming from the various subsidies included in the PSE. The countries with the lowest support relative to income were Australia and New Zealand at 6 percent and 1 percent, respectively. The level of support in Mexico was also relatively low at about 14 percent while the figure for Canada was 18 percent. At the other extreme, producer support in Korea, Iceland, Norway, and Switzerland in 2007 was equal to 50 percent or more of the value of farm income.

So far, discussion of the general support services has been limited to the comments on research and the inclusion of the U.S. food stamp program in the GSSE marketing and promotion category. It turns out that the United States accounted for about 85 percent of the total 2007 OECD expenditures for marketing and promotion and most of that was due to the food stamp program. Another U.S. program included in the marketing and promotion category is the Food for Peace program (Public Law 480 or P.L. 480). This program provides food assistance to low-income countries in support of development and for emergencies when there is a threat of famine. In 2007, about $2.6 billion was spent by the United States on food aid according to OECD figures. The reason this program is counted as a subsidy under the GSSE is that it requires that the food distributed be purchased in the United States and that it be shipped on U.S. vessels and therefore acts as a subsidy for both the agricultural and maritime transportation industries. In 2007, the Bush Administration proposed using some of the P.L. 480 funds to make cash transfers, thereby allowing food to be purchased locally or in neighboring countries (Lak, 2007). Local purchases would reduce the amount of time it takes to deliver emergency food relief and eliminate most of the high transportation costs that absorb a large portion of the funds allocated to this program. This proposal was rejected by the U.S. Congress for political reasons.

P.L. 480 is not the only U.S. international food assistance program and other high-income countries also provide food aid. Lak (2007) reports that about 59 percent of total food aid is contributed by the United States, 25 percent by the EU, and smaller shares by Japan, Canada, and Australia. Food aid has long been controversial because of the perception that it is mainly a surplus disposal program for the high-income countries and that it contributes to lower prices in recipient countries to the detriment of local farmers (Oxfam, 2005). In emergency situations, surplus food from high-income countries is donated to relief organizations working in conjunction with the United Nations World Food Program. Other food assistance is usually donated to the governments of developing countries which sell the food at low prices to raise funds for general development programs. In either case, farmers in recipient countries often find the prices they receive for their products depressed by this subsidized food. Because food aid has effects similar to those of an export subsidy, a policy tool that was specifically targeted in the WTO Agreement on Agriculture, a decision had to be made about whether food aid should be reduced in line with the reductions required for other types of export subsidies or not. The decision was that food aid would not be counted as part of a country's export subsidies so no restrictions on this policy have been established.

OECD governments provide a wide variety of services to agriculture in addition to the marketing and promotion programs and agricultural research noted earlier. Infrastructure services include rural electricity subsidies, rural housing programs, roads, irrigation facilities, and many more. Support for agricultural schools and inspection services are also included in the GSSE. In the United States, some general service support is provided by state governments. Similarly in the EU, national governments fund certain general services while others are supported through the guidance component of the CAP.

Individual states in the United States and EU member countries also contribute to producer and consumer support. The data in Table 5.3 show that general services support accounts for a larger share of the U.S. TSE than is the case in other OECD countries although the Japanese government does spend substantial amounts on infrastructure.

Effects of OECD Agricultural Subsidies

The policy interventions included in the OECD database as described in the preceding section take many forms and are likely to have diverse and, occasionally, conflicting effects on food and agricultural markets. Agricultural research, for example, can be expected to lead to long-run declines in food prices while market price support leads to domestic food price increases. Some of the items shown in Table 5.1 can be justified on the grounds that they represent efforts to correct market failures and, thus, lead to efficiency gains of general social benefit. As noted earlier, publicly funded agricultural research serves to correct the market failure associated with the public-good characteristics of such research and empirical estimates indicate that it generates high rates of economic return for society as a whole. Other types of producer and consumer support discussed above serve primarily to redistribute income, often as part of a country's social safety net. The U.S. food stamp program, for example, is a publicly funded social insurance program that targets low-income consumers. The public provision of insurance against some of life's vicissitudes can often be justified on grounds of market failures in private-sector insurance markets. In addition, one could argue that redistribution aimed at reducing income and wealth disparities and poverty is an essential part of governments' responsibilities whether there are clear-cut market failures involved or not.

Of course, not all agricultural subsidies can be rationalized with reference to market failures or economic justice. Most of the subsidies included in the PSE have little to do with either of these justifications. One of the arguments for the establishment of agricultural policies in the United States in the 1930s was that farmers were poorer than the rest of society. Today, however, the median income of U.S. farm operator households is higher than the median income for all U.S. households (Hoppe and Banker, 2006). As a result, the contention that poor, hard-working farmers deserve income supplements and protection from foreign competition in the name of economic justice may have lost much of its force. The data reported by the EWG show that many recipients of farm subsidies are far from being poor and that much of the producer support distributed in the United States goes to very large farms and agribusinesses (EWG, 2007). Such subsidies are difficult to justify on the basis of the economic criteria described in Chapter 2. Many see farm subsidies simply as a political response to a powerful special interest group.

There is a counter-argument, based on the concept of multifunctionality, that is often invoked in Europe and Japan. According to this argument, farmers carry out multiple functions contributing to a well-ordered countryside and rural amenities of one sort or another in addition to producing food. They are paid, however, only for the food they produce and are therefore short-changed in terms of their other positive contributions. It has been suggested, for example, that farmers in the Mediterranean regions of Southern France provide a useful public service in controlling summer brush fires because they clear some of the excess vegetation and provide early warnings when fires first appear. In Austria, high dairy price supports are sometimes justified, at least in part, by the scenic value of cows with interesting cow-bells grazing on the slopes of Alpine valleys. In economic terms, these arguments are pointing to positive externalities that accompany agricultural production and for which farmers are not remunerated. From this perspective, farm subsidies are justified because they compensate farmers for externalities that benefit the wider society. One problem with this argument is that there may be negative externalities associated with farming as well (e.g., pesticide and fertilizer runoff that contaminates rivers and lakes) that are not being taken into consideration. Valuing both the positive and negative externalities could very well lead to a net social cost rather than a net social benefit. In any case, it would clearly cost consumers and taxpayers less to simply pay the dairy farmers in the Alps a salary in return for their contribution to the Austrian tourist industry rather than using trade barriers and income supplements that support not only the Alpine farmers but also those in flatter regions where more efficient and lower cost production is possible.

As exhaustive as the OECD database is, some types of agricultural support are left out. A recent EWG report points to water subsidies in the Central Valley Project (CVP) in California that are funded by the U.S. Bureau of Reclamation in the Department of the Interior (EWG, 2007). The CVP manages dams that generate hydroelectric power and distributes large volumes of irrigation water using electricity generated by the dams to power the pumps. Farmers are charged only a fraction of the true costs of the power used to move the irrigation water (EWG, 2007). According to EWG, the value of this subsidy in 2002–3 was over $100 million. There are many other subsidies associated with publicly financed irrigation schemes in the Western United States (see Reisner, 2001) as well as with the use of public lands for grazing and a variety of other public policies. For example, U.S. ethanol blenders receive subsidies that reduce the price of ethyl alcohol made from maize, making it profitable to include this fuel in gasoline blends. The ethanol subsidies have increased demand for maize in the United States and contributed to higher producer prices. These subsidies have not been included in the OECD measures of producer support although the 2008 version of the database includes rows in the U.S. spreadsheet for various biofuel subsidies suggesting that these subsidies will be included in the future.

There will be more to say about these issues in later chapters on national farm policies. Because the focus of this book is on the impact of OECD agricultural subsidies on low-income countries, it may make sense to concentrate mainly on the subsidies that affect world prices and consequently the economic well-being of producers and consumers in developing countries. For example, it could be argued that government support for agricultural research and agricultural schools and the government subsidies to low-income consumers (transfers to consumers from taxpayers) may not have significant effects on world agricultural markets. If these three items are left out of the total support estimate for 2007, for example, the result would be a subsidy estimate of US$325 billion, some US$39 billion less than the full TSE but still representing a pretty hefty amount.[10] In fact, for most analyses of farm subsidies in OECD countries, the PSE is considered to be an adequate measure of the extent of government intervention. It turns out that it corresponds well to the three pillars of the WTO Agreement on Agriculture: market access; export subsidies; and trade-distorting domestic farm policies. The PSE includes market price support which is derived from import barriers (market access) and export subsidies along with various government payments to producers (domestic farm policies).

---

[10] Readers who share the author's enthusiasm for tables full of numbers will have noticed that there is an item in Table 5.1 that remains unexplained. "Excess feed cost" is entered as a subsidy to consumers. It is computed by adding up commodity-specific values for differences between world prices and the prices of domestically produced grains and oilseeds that are used for feed. These values are recorded in the tables used to calculate market price support (MPS). From the explanatory notes (OECD, 2008b), MPS is net of "... the market price support on domestically produced coarse grains and oilseeds used as animal feed (d. Excess feed cost)." In fact, it appears that measures of excess feed cost based on amounts recorded in the tables for various livestock commodities (in which the monetary value of the feed is not included in the total value of the livestock subsidy) are subtracted from consumer transfers to crop producers. The data are then collected and entered as positive excess feed costs under the CSE and explained as "... the producer contribution (as consumers of domestically produced crops) to the market price support on crops used in animal feed" (OECD, 2008b). The idea is that producers are effecting transfers to themselves through the higher costs of feed that result from market price support and this offsets some of the consumer transfers that serve the same purpose.

Agricultural economists have produced a very large number of studies of the impact of particular agricultural policies on domestic and world markets. Over the past two or three decades, the methods used for these studies have become increasingly sophisticated. For studies of the impact of agricultural subsidies on world markets, a common procedure is to build a large multi-equation model to simulate the operation of world and national agricultural economies.[11] Such models can be used to perform experiments in which economic variables of interest are projected some years into the future according to alternative scenarios. Initial simulations are done to establish a baseline which represents the likely evolution of prices and other economic variables assuming that there are no significant policy changes. The baseline projections can then be compared to the model predictions when adjustments are made to reflect particular policy changes. For example, such models can be used to predict what would happen if all agricultural subsidies were eliminated or if only some (e.g., agricultural trade barriers) were eliminated. Generally, the models include representations of important countries or regional groupings so that it is possible to examine the likely effects if there is trade liberalization only in selected areas. The results of these policy analyses show the degree to which world prices would increase if various markets were liberalized. To get a sense of how much prices are being depressed by current policies, it suffices to simply reverse the signs on the predicted changes.

Among many others, there are three groups in particular that have been actively analyzing the effects of agricultural policies on world markets. A representative sample of their results is presented in Table 5.4. The OECD (2007b) study compares a baseline projection over the period 2004 to 2013 to a series of scenarios reflecting various degrees of policy reform. The results reported in Table 5.4 are for scenarios in which there is first a 50 percent reduction in producer support in the OECD countries and then a 50 percent reduction in producer support coupled with a 50 percent reduction of trade barriers in non-agricultural sectors. Anderson, Martin, van der Mensbrugghe and others at the World Bank have published numerous studies of agricultural policy reform. The one included in Table 5.4 is an analysis of the impact of removing all trade barriers and all agricultural subsidies over the period 2001 to 2015. As noted by the authors, such a scenario is somewhat unrealistic as it

---

[11] Many of these models are computable general equilibrium (CGE) models (see Hertel, 1999, for example). Such models are similar to the climate models used to analyze global warming. Climate models aim to predict global climate conditions under alternative scenarios reflecting different behavior patterns relative to energy use and the generation of greenhouse gases. Likewise, CGE models are designed to predict the likely economic conditions that would prevail if particular economic policies are modified.

Table 5.4   Percentage increases for world prices of selected commodities compared to baseline projections in three representative studies of agricultural policy reform (various years)

Commodity	OECD[a]	World Bank[b]	FAPRI[c]
Wheat	−0.014 to −0.27	5.0	4.77 to 7.60
Rice	1.61 to 1.92	4.2	10.32 to 10.65
Other grains	1.73 to 1.83	7.0	5.67 to 6.23
Oilseeds	−0.14 to −0.25	15.1	2.83 to 3.14
Oilseed meals	−2.49 to −2.70	–	3.83 to 4.16
Vegetable oils	2.64 to 2.78	1.9	6.17 to 6.98
Cotton	–	20.8	2.93 to 11.44
Sugar	–	2.5	–
Beef	0.86 to 2.86	–	3.28 to 3.77
Pork	0.72 to 1.26	–	10.30 to 10.92
Dairy	4.87 to 13.55	11.9	22.34 to 39.56

[a] OECD (2007b). The range reported is for scenarios based on a 50 percent reduction in all agricultural support and a 50 percent reduction in all agricultural support plus a 50 percent reduction in manufacturing protection.

[b] Anderson, Martin and van der Mensbrugghe (2006). Full liberalization of all merchandise trade (agricultural and non-agricultural trade). Livestock and processed meat prices are predicted to be 2.5 and 4.3 percent higher, respectively.

[c] FAPRI (2002). The ranges reported are for two scenarios, one of which simulates the elimination of both trade barriers and domestic farm programs and the other reflecting only the elimination of trade barriers. The FAPRI report breaks oilseeds, oilseed meals, and vegetable oils into soy, rape, sunflower, peanut, and palm. The figures reported in the table are for soybeans, soy meal, and soy oil. The results for dairy products are reported for butter, cheese, skim milk powder, and whole milk powder. The figures in the table are the largest and smallest increases across all of these types of dairy products.

is unlikely that governments will agree to eliminate all of these interventions any time soon. Nevertheless, such an analysis can be useful as a guide to the full effects of these policies. Finally, researchers at the Food and Agricultural Policy Research Institute (FAPRI) at Iowa State University have also conducted a number of studies of these issues. The one reported in Table 5.4 is an analysis of the impact of reducing agricultural trade barriers and domestic farm programs in the OECD countries over the period 2002 to 2011.

All of these studies report predictions of production, consumption, and trade as well as the price changes shown in Table 5.4. I have chosen to record only the predicted world price changes in the interest of space and because these prices are the clearest indicator of the overall impact of agricultural subsidies. All of the studies use their models to predict prices over some time horizon. The figures in Table 5.4 are the averages of the predicted values. The first thing that stands out is the modesty of the price increases for many of the commodities. All three groups predict substantial increases in dairy prices and the studies that included cotton indicate that prices for that commodity would be likely to increase fairly significantly if those markets were liberalized. Recall that Sumner (2008) predicted that cotton prices would have been 13 percent higher over the period 1999 to 2002 if U.S. cotton programs had been eliminated (see Chapter 1). The World Bank prediction of the effect of liberalization on sugar prices is lower than other estimates. World sugar markets are severely distorted by U.S. and EU policies. Elobeid and Beghin (2006) find that removal of these distortions would lead to world price increases of 27 to 48 percent depending on the particular assumptions made while van der Mensbrugghe *et al.* (2003) predict a 21 percent increase in the world price as a result of sugar policy reforms. For grains, oilseeds, and non-dairy livestock products, however, the predicted world price increases are far less dramatic. It is worth noting that cotton and sugar are particularly important export crops in many developing countries while grains and oilseeds are often significant for both producers and consumers in these countries.

The World Bank estimates are supposed to reflect more complete trade liberalization than is the case for the other analyses but for most commodities their results are not very different from those of the FAPRI group which analyzed agricultural liberalization alone. The OECD results seem significantly lower than the others and for some commodities they show that policy reform would lead to a fall in world prices. All three groups find that import barriers and export subsidies have greater impacts on world prices than do domestic farm programs although the OECD study shows that liberalizing only the market access and export subsidy pillars can lead to less desirable changes than if all three pillars are addressed simultaneously. In a related study, van der Mensbrugghe and Beghin (2004) find that full liberalization of all merchandise trade (including food and agriculture) would generate $385 billion in income gains for the world as a whole with about $196 billion going to developing countries. Most of these income gains, about $265 billion, stem from the liberalization of agricultural markets because non-agricultural merchandise trade is already fairly free. Martin and Anderson (2006) also find that agricultural policy reform is likely to have a greater impact than further trade liberalization of non-agricultural markets, estimating that 63 percent of total gains of about $287 billion from full trade liberalization would stem from food and agricultural trade reform.

An important result in these analyses concerns the impact of policy reform in developing countries. According to van der Mensbrugghe and Beghin (2004), global income gains are reduced to $102 billion if only the high-income countries reform their agricultural policies. For developing countries, the benefits of agricultural policy reform are about $129 billion if both they and the high-income countries reform their policies but only $10 billion if agricultural policy reform occurs only in the high-income countries. Martin and Anderson (2006) find that the benefits to developing countries resulting from both agricultural and non-agricultural trade reform in high-income countries are about equal to the benefits generated by trade reforms in the developing countries themselves. These results are consistent with an analysis by Hertel and Ivanic (2006) which shows that cutting tariffs in the developing countries themselves would have a greater impact on poverty than if agricultural trade policies are reformed only in the wealthy countries. A corollary of these results is that the main beneficiaries of agricultural and merchandise trade policy reform by the high-income countries are the high-income countries themselves.

Conclusion

Although the results of these analyses are broadly similar, there is often fairly wide divergence with respect to some of the details. Predicting the effects of agricultural policy reform is not an exact science. Nevertheless, much can be learned from these studies. For example, much of the public debate about agricultural subsidies concerns the impacts of the subsidies provided by governments in wealthy countries on farmers in poor countries. Discussions of this issue often ignore the idea that there might be some benefit to low-income countries from changes in their own agricultural policies. In fact, a key concept that underlies WTO trade negotiations, and upon which the governments of many developing countries insist with particular vehemence, is the idea that low-income countries should receive "special and differential treatment." This generally amounts to exemptions from trade policy reforms adopted by the other WTO parties or the right to implement milder changes over a longer period of time (WTO, 2008k). The empirical studies reviewed above would suggest that this principle may be misguided. In addition, the benefits of farm subsidies in the OECD countries that lower prices for low-income food consumers in developing countries are frequently overlooked. These issues need to be kept in mind as we examine the origin, history, and current state of agricultural policies in the main parties to this debate in the following chapters.

6

U.S. Agricultural Policy:
How Not to Save the Family Farm

Introduction

Agricultural policy is developed in particular contexts that serve to color and constrain the options most likely to be pursued. While the particular context that has given rise to the farm policies found today in the United States includes the complex interaction of many political, economic, social, and physical phenomena, there is one element that has obviously been of great importance in the evolution of U.S. agriculture and agricultural policy: the abundance of arable land and the relative scarcity of labor to work it. When European colonists first began settling in North America, the continent was fairly sparsely populated. Great controversy surrounds the question of how many Native Americans were living in North America in the seventeenth century but most estimates appear to place the number between 2 million and 18 million (MSN Encarta; see also Dobyns, 1983; Trabich, 1997). Even the larger of these estimates is quite small relative to the number of people, thought to be about 100 million, inhabiting Europe west of the Ural Mountains in the middle of the seventeenth century (Lucas, 2003). Much of the early history of the United States concerned the acquisition of more land through purchase, conquest, ethnic cleansing (the "Indian Wars") or some combination of these methods and the subsequent distribution of this land to European settlers through sales, land grants, and homesteading.

Despite the influx of European settlers during the seventeenth and eighteenth centuries, farm labor remained relatively scarce. Cochrane (1979) argues that New England farmers responded to the need for more workers by having large families while Southern plantation owners became ever more reliant on imported African slaves. According to data published by the U.S. Census Bureau (1975), individuals of African origin made up 1.3 percent of the total U.S. population in 1630, 11.1 percent in 1700, 20.2 percent in 1750, and 20.7

percent in 1780. In the nineteenth century the proportion of the total U.S. population made up of African Americans began to decline falling to 15.7 percent in 1850 and 12.1 percent in 1900. The proportion in 2006 was 12.8 percent having changed little since 1900. The shift in proportions in the nineteenth century came about as the slave trade was eliminated and large numbers of European immigrants arrived in the United States. During the period of high immigration between 1850 and 1920, U.S. population grew from 23.2 million to 106.0 million, a net addition of 82.8 million people. Over this same period, some 27.9 million immigrants entered the United States, representing about a third of the net addition to the total population, not counting their children. Of these immigrants, 84 percent (23.3 million) were from Europe (author's calculations based on data from the U.S. Census Bureau, 1975).

During the seventeenth, eighteenth, and nineteenth centuries, most Americans lived in rural areas and made their living from farming or activities related to farming (Table 6.1). From 1850 to 1935, the number of farms continued to increase as newly acquired land was settled and homesteaded although the rapid growth of the urban population meant that the proportion of the total population working as farmers began to decline. The number of farms in the United States reached a peak of 6.8 million in 1935 when about 44 percent of the U.S. population lived in rural areas and 24.4 percent of the U.S. labor force was employed in agriculture.[1] Since then the number of farms, the farm population, and the amount of land in farms have all declined although the amount of land used for agriculture has fallen less steeply than the number of farms and the farm population. The result has been an increase in the average farm size from 62.8 hectares (155 acres) in 1935 to 179.8 hectares (444 acres) in 2005 (U.S. Census Bureau, 1975; Hoppe *et al.*, 2007b). Over this same period, agricultural productivity in the United States began to grow at much higher rates. It was noted in Chapter 3 that growth in agricultural total factor productivity (TFP) took off in most parts of the world after the Second World War. Gardner (2002) summarizes productivity estimates for U.S. agriculture showing that productivity grew at an annual rate of only about 0.2 percent between 1910 and 1939 compared with estimates ranging from 1.3 to 2.0 percent per year after 1940.

The technological innovations that have driven agricultural productivity increases in the United States have generally been labor saving (Gardner,

---

[1]   Dimitri, Effland, and Conklin (2005) estimate the proportion of the US workforce employed in agriculture to be 21.5 percent in 1930 and 16 percent in 1945. The figure of 24.4 percent for 1935 was obtained using data from the U.S. Census Bureau (1975). Based on the Census data, the percentage of the labor force working in agriculture was 25.8 percent and 18.6 percent for 1930 and 1945, respectively.

Table 6.1 Rural population and farm structure, United States, 1790–2005

Year	Rural population as % of total population	Farm population as % of total population	Number of farms (1,000)	Land in farms (million hectares)	Average farm size (hectares)
1790	94.9	NA	NA	NA	NA
1800	93.9	71.8*	NA	NA	NA
1850	84.6	45.2	1,449	118.9	82.2
1900	60.4	21.1	5,740	340.5	59.3
1950	36.0	7.6	5,338	470.2	88.0
2000	21.0	2.2	2,158	381.8	176.9
2005	19.2	1.9	2,101	377.9	179.8

*1820.
Sources: Column 1 from U.S. Census data summary at www.census.gov/population/census-data/table-4.pdf and FAO population data at www.faostat.fao.org/site/348/default.aspx. Column 2 from U.S. Census Bureau, *Historical Statistics of the United States*, Millennial Edition Online and FAO population data. Columns 3–5, *Historical Statistics of the United States*, Millennial Edition Online and Hoppe *et al.*, 2007b.

1992). This is consistent with the observation that labor in the United States is relatively scarce. One explanation of technological change in agriculture, the theory of induced innovation, is based on the idea that the development of new technologies is driven by the desire to make greater use of resources that are abundant and, therefore, relatively less expensive while conserving scarce resources that are likely to be more costly (see Hayami and Ruttan, 1985). The induced innovation explanation of technological change would suggest that technological innovations will tend to substitute abundant land and capital resources for labor if labor is scarce. While this is consistent with the early development of U.S. agriculture, the circumstances appear to have changed in the twentieth century. After the Second World War, the number of farms declined and many farm workers began to leave the agricultural sector, which has often been characterized by low wages and income. Low wages and income and the continuing rural exodus would suggest that there has been too much labor employed in agriculture over the past 70 years (see Boulding, 1968).

It appears that once the frontier had been settled and technological progress began to accelerate, the original labor scarcities in agriculture were offset by labor-saving technological changes that led to food surpluses and low commodity prices even as the farm population declined. Gardner (2002) offers an alternative explanation based on the observation that rapid growth in manufacturing wages attracted agricultural workers so that rural labor scarcities persisted and induced labor-saving technological change. Either way, the persistence of surplus agricultural output and low farm prices has been a major factor in the evolution of U.S. farm policy in the twentieth century. In fact, the first formal government programs designed to address the problem of low prices and incomes in the farm sector were implemented in 1933 at the beginning of both the acceleration of agricultural productivity growth and the decline in the farm population. The purpose of this chapter is to describe and explain the evolution of U.S. agricultural policy. In the next section, an historical overview of U.S. farm policy is presented along with a more detailed description of current policies. The third part of the chapter explores the general effects of these policies both within the United States and on world markets and the domestic markets of other countries, particularly those in low-income developing countries. The final part of the chapter draws on analytical work done by agricultural economists to explain why the U.S. government provides such generous support to an economic sector that is relatively small and of modest strategic importance.

Historical Overview of U.S. Farm Policy[2]

Governments establish the legal and institutional framework needed for market economies to function. This framework includes laws on property, contracts, competition, interregional commerce, and much more. In addition, governments have traditionally played a role in creating and regulating a country's currency including policies for both exchange rates and interest rates and they have used taxation and government spending to provide public goods (e.g., national defense) and to redistribute income. From its inception, the U.S. government has carried out a wide range of economic policies that have had an impact on the agricultural sector although in many cases the policies have targeted the general economy rather than any specific sector. In the

---

[2] There are numerous accounts of the history and evolution of agricultural policy in the United States. In 1984, Bowers, Rasmussen and Baker published a detailed history of modern agricultural policy between 1933 and 1984 for the Economic Research Service (ERS), USDA. ERS also regularly publishes historical accounts of farm policy as background for the Farm Bills that are adopted every five years or so. Brandow (1977), Cochrane (1979, 2003), Gardner (1985, 1992, 2002), Hallberg (1992), Pasour and Rucker (2005), and many others provide detailed histories of the nature and effects of farm programs, primarily during the twentieth century. The description presented in this chapter is necessarily far less detailed than the accounts in these publications. It is designed to highlight the aspects of U.S. agricultural policy that are particularly relevant to themes being addressed in this book.

twentieth century, government interventions focusing specifically on agricultural prices and farm incomes expanded significantly, culminating in a complex system of price supports, trade barriers, production controls, and a host of other provisions some of which are directed at related policy issues such as nutrition, environmental protection, or poverty.

Of course, government intervention in agricultural markets runs counter to the dominant economic philosophy in the United States which has generally favored reliance on the private sector and a limited role for the government in economic activity. Historically, the tension between free-market economics and interventionist farm policies has been resolved by pointing to the "farm problem." This problem arises because farm incomes are thought to be lower and less stable than incomes in other sectors of the economy as a result of weather variability, slow growth in demand, and productivity increases that cause supply to expand and agricultural prices to decline (Gardner 1992). The slow increase in demand can be explained by Engel's law which suggests that as incomes grow, the proportion of the average consumer budget allocated to food declines. The result is that growth in food consumption is slower than growth in income. Productivity increases should lower the costs of production so falling output prices only represent a problem for farm households if the output and input prices are declining at different rates or if the lower costs occur later in time than the falling prices. In any case, the idea that farmers are honest, hard-working individuals who are nevertheless less well-off than their urban counterparts as a result of falling farm prices has long provided a rationale for active government intervention in agricultural markets.

The types of policy interventions formalized in the 1930s did not grow out of a vacuum. Effland (2000) argues that there have been four overlapping periods in U.S. agricultural policy beginning with the period 1785 to 1890, the date conventionally thought to signal the closing of the frontier, during which land distribution policies were the primary form of government intervention affecting agriculture. An important land distribution policy during this period was the 1862 Homestead Act that allowed individuals and families to take possession of unowned public land provided they agreed to live and work on it (Cochrane, 1979). According to Effland (2000), policies during this period grew out of a debate between those who saw the vast amounts of land acquired by the federal government as a source of government revenue and those who believed the land should be used to create a class of property-owning small farmers. The former favored selling land at high prices to raise government revenue while the latter favored the wide distribution of land to small, independent family farmers.

Those who argued for low selling prices and wide distribution of land ownership represented an important tradition in U.S. agriculture that has often been traced back to Thomas Jefferson. Jefferson believed that U.S. democracy would be more secure if based on a large, land-owning class of independent farmers (Thompson, 1988). Variations on this agrarian theme have been present in agricultural policy debates ever since (see Comstock, 1987) and have played an important role in creating and maintaining legislative support for agriculture. The idea that there is something particularly virtuous about farming coupled with the perception that family farmers are unfairly disadvantaged relative to the rest of U.S. society have made agriculture much less vulnerable to criticism for its reliance on government subsidies.

The second agricultural policy era identified by Effland (2000) was a period of public investment in agricultural research and education running from 1830 to 1914. Effland argues that the settling of the frontier and the establishment of large numbers of family farms in the new territories increased the level of competition faced by established farmers in the eastern United States. These farmers believed that scientific research and broad education in agricultural methods would lead to increased agricultural productivity, allowing them to remain competitive in the face of the increased agricultural output from the newly settled lands. One of the most significant government interventions of this period was the Morrill Land-Grant Act of 1862 which created universities to promote "... the liberal and practical education of the industrial classes in the several pursuits and professions in life" (U.S. Congress, 1862).[3] This act transferred land owned by the federal government to the states which were expected to use the proceeds from the sale of the land to establish universities focusing on practical education. Most of the "pursuits and professions in life" at that time were related to agriculture with a third of the population in 1860 identified as farmers and 80 percent of the total population living in rural areas (U.S. Census Bureau, 1975). This meant that education in agricultural practices was an important, although not the only, focus of the new educational institutions.

In 1887, the U.S. Congress passed the Hatch Act which established agricultural research stations connected to the Land-Grant University in each of the states. In 1914, the Smith–Lever Cooperative Extension Act entered into force, adding adult education in agriculture to the research and teaching activities put in place by the Morrill and Hatch Acts (Cochrane, 1979). This three-part

---

[3] Passed in the midst of the Civil War, the Morrill Land Grant Act had a distinctly populist flavor. Justin Morrill was arguing for higher education for the children of working-class families in contrast to the education being provided to the children of the business and political elite by Harvard, Princeton, Yale, and other selective universities. According to Parker (1924, p. 263) the objective of the Act was to educate "... farmers and mechanics and all those who must win their bread by labor...."

land-grant system has been highly effective at developing productivity-enhancing technologies that are transferred to farmers through the educational and extension activities of the Land-Grant University in each state. In addition to the state agricultural research stations, the U.S. Department of Agriculture has supported national agricultural research activities under the Agricultural Research Service (ARS). Fuglie and Heisey (2007) report estimates of the returns to publicly funded agricultural research that are much higher than the returns generally observed for other types of investment although public research has not escaped criticism. Several authors in a book edited by Thu and Durrenberger (1998), for example, blame the Land-Grant Universities for the development of confinement hog production which they see as damaging to the environment and rural communities and Hightower (1978) severely criticized the land-grant system for conducting research that benefits large agribusiness firms while destroying rural communities and lowering the quality of the food consumed in the United States.

The third policy period (1870–1933) discussed by Effland (2000) was characterized by increasing concern for the economic disparities between the agricultural sector and other industries. Toward the end of the nineteenth century, farm output increased rapidly and prices and farm household income declined. At the same time, there was a wave of mergers and consolidations in a wide range of industries that resulted in the monopolization of numerous economic activities. In response to public complaints about monopolistic price fixing, the U.S. Congress passed the Sherman Anti-Trust Act in 1890 (Hartman, 2007). This law and later amendments aim to promote competition by making it illegal for firms and individuals to collude on price setting, enter into contractual arrangements between buyers and sellers that bypass the market, and merge with other firms in ways that reduce the level of competition in a particular industry (Hartman, 2007). The conceptual basis for these policies is the standard economic notion discussed in Chapter 2 that competitive markets insure low consumer prices and the efficient allocation of resources while monopolization has the opposite effects.

In the early twentieth century, agricultural producers began calling for the creation of marketing cooperatives that would allow them to counter the market power held by processing firms that, despite antitrust legislation, were often able to manipulate the prices they paid because of the perishability of agricultural products and the inability of producers to withhold their output as they bargained over prices (Gardner, 2002). The problem was that allowing farmers to collude through their cooperatives in the sale of agricultural products violated the new antitrust laws. The Capper–Volstead Marketing Act of 1922 exempted agricultural cooperatives from the provisions of the developing antitrust legislation, allowing rapid growth in farmer-owned cooperatives

(Gardner, 2002). The number of marketing and purchasing cooperatives increased by almost 47 percent from 7,374 in 1921 to 10,803 in 1926 (U.S. Census Bureau, 1975).

Effland's final policy era began in 1924 and is still continuing today. This period is characterized by government policies designed to increase farm household income through market interventions aimed at raising prices. From 1910 to 1920, agricultural prices had been highly favorable spurred in part by increased demand during the First World War. Once the war had ended, commodity prices fell causing great hardship for many farmers and leading to calls for market regulations that would protect them from the effects of low prices (Gardner, 2002). In 1924, legislation to directly influence market prices was introduced by Senator Charles McNary and Representative Gilbert Haugen. The McNary–Haugen farm legislation called for insulating U.S. farm prices from falling world prices through the use of tariffs and export subsidies and for fair prices within the United States through the regulation of supplies to the domestic market. The goal was to raise U.S. prices to levels that would re-establish the "parity" with industrial prices that had existed prior to the First World War (Cochrane, 1979). The McNary–Haugen legislation was introduced several times but did not win Congressional approval until 1927 when it was vetoed by President Coolidge and again in 1928. Elements of the McNary–Haugen farm bills were included in the 1933 Agricultural Adjustment Act (AAA) which was signed into law as part of Franklin Roosevelt's New Deal legislation (Cochrane, 1979).

The concept of parity has been highly significant in the history of U.S. farm policy. Boulding (1968) argues that farmers believe the prices they receive are unfair, contending that a fair price would maintain the purchasing power of the farmer's output over time. If a bushel of wheat in the past could be sold for a price equal to that of a pound of nails, the fair price for wheat in later time periods would also be equal to the price of a pound of nails at the later time. Formally, parity is measured by computing an index of the prices farmers receive for their output and an index of the prices paid for inputs and other expenses. The parity index in agriculture is the ratio of the index of prices received to the index of prices paid.[4] Both indexes are set up with the same

---

[4]   The original parity index took the period 1909–14 as the base years. This was later changed to 1910–14 after 1948 (Bowers *et al.*, 1984). The base period for the calculation of the indexes has been changed many times although USDA has continued to report price indexes based on the 1910–14 base period. For 2006, the parity ratio based on the 1910–14 base period was 0.37 suggesting that, on average, agricultural prices received would need to be 2.7 times higher (one divided by 0.37) to maintain the 1910–14 purchasing power of agricultural commodities. Parity prices can be calculated for individual crops. The data in the 2006 summary report on agricultural prices (NASS, 2007) suggest that parity corn and cotton prices would

base period so if the parity ratio falls below one, as in fact it has, it is an indication that prices received are not increasing as rapidly as prices paid. The declining parity index was thought to provide strong evidence that falling commodity prices following the First World War were unfair because farm households could no longer exchange their products for the same amount of goods as they had been able to purchase in the past.

Boulding (1968) points out that the parity argument is an assertion about the terms of trade between agriculture and the rest of the economy. As noted in Chapter 4, Raul Prebisch and Hans Singer based their advice on development strategies for low-income countries on the claim that the terms of trade between developing and industrialized countries were deteriorating and that this harmed developing countries. The terms of trade studied by Prebisch and Singer were measured by the ratio of an index of prices received by primary commodity producers in low-income countries to an index of prices paid for imported manufactured goods. Prebisch and Singer believed they had evidence that this ratio was declining making it difficult for low-income countries to obtain the imports they needed with the revenues obtained from the sale of their export commodities. The terms-of-trade argument of Prebisch and Singer is clearly identical to the agricultural parity argument made by U.S. farm organizations.

Both arguments, however, are flawed. Empirically, the international terms of trade between primary commodities and manufactures did decline until the 1970s when petroleum price increases set off by the actions of OPEC along with more general commodity price increases reversed the earlier trends. Parity and the terms-of-trade ratios are highly sensitive to the items included in the index and the base year chosen. A decision to exclude petroleum prices from the terms-of-trade indexes, for example, would strengthen the evidence for their decline. The parity ratio was based on agricultural prices in 1909–14 while Prebisch and Singer took the period of the Korean War as the base for computing the international commodity terms of trade. Both base periods were characterized by unusually high commodity prices making it inevitable that the two ratios would decline in later years. In both cases, this decline was used to support calls for policies to raise the prices received. Choosing different base years and different sets of goods for inclusion in the indexes, however, would change the story dramatically.

be about five times the actual prices received for these commodities. In 2006, corn prices averaged $3.20 per bushel and cotton prices were $0.47 per pound. The corresponding parity prices (1910–14 base) would be $16.00 per bushel for corn and $2.35 per pound for cotton. Using 1990–2 as the base period, the parity ratio in 2006 is 0.78 suggesting that prices received for all farm products have not risen as rapidly as the prices paid by producers over the period 1990–2 to 2006.

The parity and terms-of-trade arguments are also defective because they are inconsistent with the expected functioning of markets. Adopting policies that would maintain parity or the terms of trade that prevailed in some base period has the effect of freezing relative prices. In dynamic market economies, however, relative prices shift constantly as technological innovation and increases in productivity, the evolution of consumer tastes and preferences, and other economic developments alter the basic supply and demand conditions. The primary virtue of a market economy is that flexible prices act as signals of changes in underlying market circumstances and provide incentives for consumers and producers to adjust their behavior to the altered situation. Imagine a policy to maintain the parity prices for oats and other crops used to feed horses and mules as the first automobiles and tractors began to come onto the market. In 1910, 27 percent of harvested acres in the United States were used to feed these animals. By 1960, this figure had fallen to 5 percent as resources were transferred out of the industries associated with the use of animal power which were declining as a result of technological innovations in transportation (U.S. Census Bureau, 1975). This resource reallocation came about naturally through individual responses to incentives created by changing relative prices. By freezing relative prices, parity prices would have prevented these incentives from developing thereby slowing the resource reallocation that was made necessary by the introduction of internal-combustion engines.

Of course, such arguments would probably have been unpersuasive to many of the early advocates of parity farm prices and those who argued for reversing the declining international terms of trade as both of these groups were likely to have been skeptical about the value of capitalism and free markets in the first place. In any case, the idea of parity for agricultural prices was enshrined in the Agricultural Adjustment Act (AAA) of 1933 and remained a prominent part of farm policy discussions until the 1970s (Bowers *et al.*, 1984). The economic crisis of the 1930s gave new life to the quest for parity prices that was at the heart of the McNary–Haugen policy initiatives. The 1929 stock market crash and the Great Depression that followed it led to reduced demand for agricultural goods and falling agricultural prices. Total net farm income from farming activities fell from $6.2 billion in 1929 to an average of $2.7 billion per year for the period 1931 to 1934 (author's calculations based on data from U.S. Census Bureau, 1975). The economic conditions of the agricultural sector were worsened further by the environmental disaster known as the Dust Bowl, a severe drought coupled with wind erosion in the Great Plains that lasted most of the decade of the 1930s. John Steinbeck's Pulitzer and Nobel prize-winning novel, *The Grapes of Wrath*, is a searing account of the trials faced by many families forced to leave their farms during these years.

The AAA was designed to increase prices by reducing output through limitations on planted acreage. Gardner (2002) reports that an average of about 30 million acres (12 million hectares) were left idle each year between 1934 and 1938, almost 10 percent of the total harvested acreage for those years. Coupled with the effects of the Dust Bowl which also reduced output, crop production fell substantially after 1933. Harvested maize acreage fell from an annual average of 106 million acres (43 million hectares) from 1930 to 1933 to about 93 million acres (38 million hectares) for the period 1934 to 1939 while annual maize production fell about 12 percent over the same periods (U.S. Census Bureau, 1975). Cochrane (1979) argues that the supply management programs of the AAA were relatively ineffective and suggests that reductions in agricultural output were due primarily to the drought.

An important policy tool introduced in the original AAA was the nonrecourse loan. This program establishes a price floor by offering farmers loans at harvest when prices generally fall. The amount of the loan is determined by the loan rate established by the government and the historical output of an individual farmer. Until the 1970s, loan rates for particular commodities were set in relation to the parity price for that commodity. The expectation was that farmers would pay off the loan later in the marketing year when prices had recovered from their post-harvest slump. If market prices remained low, farmers could default on their loans with no penalty to their credit ratings because of the nonrecourse feature. In such cases, the government takes possession of the crop which is held as collateral. As an example, the 1985 Food Security Act established a loan rate for wheat in 1986 of $3.00 per bushel (Glaser, 1986). Wheat growers were eligible for loans equal to the amount they produced historically multiplied by this loan rate. Farmers would have an interest in taking out a loan if market prices were at or below $3.00. Later in the year, if market prices rose above $3.00, the farmer would pay off the loan and sell the crop on the market for the higher price. If prices remained depressed, the farmer could simply keep the loan and the government would take possession of the crop. In this way, the loan rate becomes a minimum price for eligible commodities.

One of the main features of the AAA was the voluntary reduction of planted acreage or animal numbers for a set of basic commodities including food and feed grains, cotton, and certain livestock products. Note that the effort to raise prices by reducing output is what a private-sector monopolist might attempt to do. For agricultural producers, such a strategy cannot be implemented without government intervention because individual incentives favor free-riding, which undermines the ability of producers to control supplies on their own (see Appendix 2.2). The AAA supply management efforts were to be financed by a tax on agricultural processors (Bowers *et al.*, 1984). In 1936, the U.S.

Supreme Court ruled the processor tax unconstitutional, forcing Congress to develop new legislation for supply management. The approach that was eventually put in place involved using government payments to encourage farmers to shift crop land out of grains and other row crops and into legumes and cover crops that would help to conserve the soil (Gardner, 2002). The idea of encouraging farmers to limit output by putting some of their land into soil conservation programs is still a part of U.S. farm policy today. The basic commodity policies developed during the 1930s, including production controls and price supports through the loan program, remained in force throughout the following two decades although there were some modifications during the Second World War and the Korean War when commodity prices were higher and the government instead of trying to restrict output wished to encourage production in response to increased wartime demand.

These policies targeted the supply side of agricultural markets by attempting to restrict production and, if output could not be sufficiently limited, to correct the low prices that resulted with direct payments and price supports. In 1954, a new program designed to raise farm prices by increasing demand, the Agricultural Trade Development and Assistance Act, commonly known as Public Law 480 (P.L. 480), was added to this mix. P.L. 480 is the U.S. food aid program that uses surplus agricultural goods (often accumulated through the loan program when market prices are low) to provide emergency food relief during famine situations and subsidized food for development programs in low-income countries. P.L. 480 and another program designed to enhance demand, the Food Stamp Program, were both discussed briefly in Chapter 5 in the sections describing the general services support and consumer support estimates. An early food stamp program, lasting from 1939 to 1943, provided some 20 million low-income people with stamps that could be used to purchase surplus food. This program was terminated when food surpluses were exhausted and the Depression-era levels of unemployment had been reduced by the needs of the wartime economy. In 1961, a pilot food stamp program was initiated and it was made permanent in 1964 (FNS, 2007).

By the 1960s, an important principle in U.S. agricultural policy had been established. This was that farmers were required to restrict their production by reducing the acreage they planted to be eligible for government price and income support (Gardner, 2002). Farmers could choose not to participate in the government programs if they did not wish to take any of their land out of production. The attempt to use acreage controls to limit production and raise farm prices was often ineffective because, in complying with the acreage reduction requirement, farmers would idle their lowest quality land and farm their remaining land more intensively. Thus a requirement that 10 percent of farmland be idled would often lead to only a 2- or 3-percent reduction in output. In addition, export markets had begun to take on greater importance as a way to dispose of agricultural commodities produced in excess of domestic needs at the prevailing prices. Maintaining exports meant that support prices could not continue to be set in relation to parity because such price levels were well above world market prices. While the loan program was still useful in managing seasonal price variation, it was not very effective at enhancing farm household income.

In 1973, a new policy tool, the deficiency payment, was introduced to tackle the problem of farm incomes (Bowers *et al.*, 1984). Loan rates were lowered so that the U.S. price floor did not interfere with agricultural exports. A target price high enough to cover costs of production was set by the government and deficiency payment rates were determined as the difference between the target price and an estimate of average market prices.[5] The amount of land that had been planted to particular crops in recent years and the corresponding yields obtained were used to determine individual farm acreage bases and program yields. The actual payment was equal to the product of these three amounts (deficiency payment rate, base acreage, and program yield) or some proportion of that product. Farmers received the market price (or the loan rate if market prices were lower) plus the deficiency payment. The objective of this program was to insure farm income while allowing markets to clear at much lower prices. To the extent that farmers adjust their output in response to high target prices, the amount produced is greater than it would have been in the absence of this program. In such cases, the effect is to lower market prices making deficiency payments a subsidy to both producers and consumers (domestic and foreign) financed by taxpayers.

---

[5] Calculation of the actual amounts that farmers would receive in direct deficiency payments was extremely complicated. For most of the life of the original deficiency payment program, payments were computed as the product of a farmer's base acreage for a given crop, the farmer's program yield, and a deficiency payment rate based on an estimate of the average market price. For example, the target price for wheat in 1986 as set by the 1985 Farm Bill was $4.38 per bushel. The difference between this price and a national weighted average price was the deficiency payment rate. The weighted average wheat price for 1985/6 was $3.08 (wheat yearbook data at: http://www.ers.gov/Data/Wheat/Yearbook/WheatYearbookTable01-Full. htm) so the deficiency payment rate was about $1.30 per bushel. Farm base acreage for wheat was calculated as the average number of acres planted to wheat over the preceding five years. Program yield was equal to the average of yields obtained over the previous five years with the highest and lowest yields excluded (Glaser, 1986). To be eligible for these payments, farmers had to comply with requirements for reducing their wheat acreage if applicable. Over time, the formulae used to compute these payments were modified and in the 1990s, the payment rate was often set as some percentage of the average market price multiplied by the acreage base multiplied by the program yield. Note that the target price was set initially in relation to costs of production rather than parity as had been the case in previous legislation.

The loan program, deficiency payments, acreage controls, and demand-enhancing policies all remained in effect until 1996 although there were numerous variations including efforts to control costs by making direct payments on only a portion of a producer's harvest and setting loan rates well below market prices. It is important to note that these policies applied only to a set of program crops that included grains, oilseeds, and cotton. Although government expenditure for these commodity programs accounted for the bulk of the commodity support, there were many other provisions in this legislation. New farm bills are adopted every five years or so and have included as many as 18 different chapters known as "titles." The 2008 Farm Bill has 14 titles: commodity programs, conservation, trade (including P.L. 480), nutrition programs (including food stamps), credit programs, rural development, research, forestry, energy, horticulture and organic agriculture, livestock, crop insurance, commodity futures, and miscellaneous (U.S. Congress, 2008). The first two titles are the ones that most directly affect agricultural producers although as recognized in the OECD support estimates, nutritional programs such as food stamps, research, and many of the other programs can be seen as contributing to general agricultural support. Other commodities that have received support include dairy and other livestock products, peanuts, wool and mohair, honey, lentils, chickpeas, dry peas, sugar, and tobacco. Some of these commodities have been supported by protective trade barriers while others have received direct price supports through government purchases.

In the 1990s, concerns that agricultural policies were seriously distorting farmers' decisions gave rise to efforts to make them more market oriented. The 1996 Farm Bill eliminated production controls and deficiency payments replacing them with decoupled direct payments that were supposed to be phased out over time. The loan program, food stamps, and most other programs were retained. The 1996 legislation was passed at a time when farm prices were quite high and the favorable economic conditions made it easier to make fairly dramatic changes in agricultural policy. Of course, farmers responded to the favorable prices as they always do by expanding output so that by the time the 1996 act was set to expire, prices had fallen substantially and there was intense pressure to introduce new provisions that would provide additional support to farm incomes. In the 2002 Farm Bill, the direct payments that were supposed to be phased out were made permanent and counter-cyclical payments and marketing loans that allowed farmers to pay off loans at market prices lower than the loan rate and keep the difference were added. The marketing loan program also allowed for direct payments known as loan deficiency payments set equal to the difference between the loan rate and average market prices. Direct payments were made available to producers who entered into annual agreements with USDA but there was no requirement that producers reduce their planted acreage. Counter-cyclical payments are similar to the deficiency payment program in operation prior to 1996 (for full descriptions of these programs see ERS, 2008a).

To get a sense of how this program might work, consider the provisions for upland cotton, the most common type of cotton grown in the United States. The loan rate for 2004–7 was set at $0.52 per pound. Suppose a producer sells his 2004 crop at the average market price for that year which was $0.46 per pound (NASS, 2005). This would make him potentially eligible for a loan deficiency payment of $0.06 per pound. Counter-cyclical payments were available if the effective price, defined as the higher of the market price or the loan rate plus the direct payment, was lower than the target price. For upland cotton, the direct payment rate was $0.0667 per pound and the target price used in calculating the counter-cyclical payment was $0.724. Based on these figures, the effective price was $0.5867 per pound so the counter-cyclical payment was $0.1373 per pound. The producer would sell the cotton for $0.46 per pound and receive a loan deficiency payment (or its equivalent) of $0.06 per pound, direct payments of $0.0667 per pound and counter-cyclical payments of $0.1373 per pound. In the end, the producer receives $0.724 per pound for the portion of the crop covered by the program, a price that is 57 percent higher than the market price. These programs, along with subsidies to domestic cotton users and export credit guarantees, were found to violate U.S. commitments under the AA in the decision on Brazil's complaint about U.S. cotton policies (WTO, 2008c; see Chapter 1).

Provisions for other program crops were somewhat less generous than those for cotton but the movement away from the market orientation of the 1996 Bill and the generally lavish support for a fairly narrow range of commodities produced primarily by large farmers and agribusiness firms provoked widespread criticism. Some advocates for family farms argued that this legislation benefitted only the larger farms making it difficult for smaller family farms to survive (Christison, 2002; Mittal, 2002). Others noted that it would lead to excess production that would depress prices and harm farmers in low-income countries (Orden, 2003) and that the focus on commodity programs neglected the needs for broader rural development and conservation programs (Babcock and Hart, 2005). Babcock and Hart point out that the 2002 act included substantial increases in subsidies for U.S. producers at the same time that other countries were beginning to turn toward more market-oriented approaches to agricultural policy.

Tables 6.2 and 6.3 describe U.S. farm support from 1986 to 2007 using the OECD policy classification defined in Chapter 5. Recall that the OECD data include estimates of the economic costs of trade barriers (market price support) as well as of other government programs that actually entail budgetary

Table 6.2   U.S. agricultural support estimates, 1986–2007 (billions of current dollars)*

	TSE	PSE	PSE (MPS)	PSE (budget)	GSSE	CSE	MPS/PSE (%)
1986	66.4	38.4	12.4	26.0	18.3	−4.6	32.3
1990	65.7	31.9	14.5	17.4	21.2	−1.7	45.5
1995	67.9	20.8	9.3	11.5	29.8	6.8	44.7
2000	96.0	52.8	17.4	35.4	25.3	−1.1	33.0
2001	98.4	51.5	18.2	33.3	28.4	−1.7	35.3
2002	91.3	40.7	15.1	25.6	30.3	3.1	37.1
2003	91.8	36.0	10.3	25.7	34.1	9.4	28.6
2004	103.2	43.0	12.3	30.7	36.9	9.1	28.6
2005	105.5	41.0	8.4	32.6	39.7	14.7	20.5
2006	99.4	30.9	6.2	24.7	42.5	19.1	20.1
2007	100.8	32.7	11.8	20.9	41.9	13.0	36.1

* TSE (total support estimate), PSE (producer support estimate), GSSE (general services support estimate), CSE (consumer support estimate). PSE is divided into market price support (MPS) which comes from consumers through higher prices resulting from trade barriers and commodity programs financed through the government budget (see Chapter 5). The last column shows the share of producer support resulting from trade barriers (MPS/PSE). *Source*: OECD, 2008c.

expenditure. Although general service and consumer support do have an impact on farm prices and income, the most commonly used measure of farm subsidies is the producer support estimate (PSE). The last column of Table 6.2 shows the percentage of the total PSE that arises from trade barriers. Since 1986, this percentage has ranged from a low of 20.1 percent in 2006 to a high of 45.5 percent in 1990. As noted in Chapter 5, most of the Japanese producer support comes from trade barriers, about 85 percent in 2007, while the corresponding figure for the EU has declined from a high of 88 percent in 1986 to a level about equal to that of the United States (36 percent) in 2007.

Between 1986 and 2007, the U.S. PSE represented on average about 18 percent of the value of total farm income ranging from a low of 10 percent in 1995 and 2007 to a high of 26 percent in 1999. The proportion of farm income represented by these subsidies varies with economic conditions in the agricultural sector. High commodity prices and low or negative real interest rates caused by worldwide inflation in the 1970s led to high land values and increased farm operator debt. Falling real farm prices and interest rate increases in the 1980s triggered a crisis that resulted in the liquidation of a large number of farms (Gardner, 2002). During the farm crisis of the 1980s, government support for agriculture increased. As the farm economy recovered in the

Table 6.3 U.S. agricultural support estimates, selected years (billions of current dollars)

	1986	1995	2000	2005	2007
Value of production (farm gate)	**132.6**	**191.1**	**189.3**	**234.7**	**310.6**
Producer support estimate (PSE)	**38.4**	**20.8**	**52.8**	**41.0**	**32.7**
PSE/farm income* (%)	*24.0*	*10.0*	*24.0*	*15.0*	*10.0*
Market price support	12.4	9.3	17.4	8.4	11.8
Payments based on output	4.8	0.1	10.3	6.1	0.5
Payments based on input use	7.0	6.6	7.7	9.4	9.3
Payments based on current production	13.5	3.0	5.2	3.9	1.8
Payments—historic production	0	0	10.5	10.9	7.1
Payments—non-commodity	0	1.8	1.7	2.3	2.2
General services support estimate (GSSE)	**18.3**	**29.8**	**25.3**	**39.7**	**41.9**
Research and development	1.1	1.5	1.7	1.7	2.3
Agricultural schools	0.0	0.0	0.0	0.0	0.0
Inspection services	0.4	0.6	0.7	0.9	0.9
Infrastructure	5.3	3.2	3.1	5.5	4.4
Marketing and promotion	10.5	23.1	17.6	29.4	32.1
Public stockholding	0	0	0	0.1	0.1
Miscellaneous	1.1	1.4	2.1	2.2	2.2
Consumer support estimate (CSE)	**−4.6**	**6.9**	**−1.1**	**14.7**	**13.0**
Consumer transfers to producers	−13.0	−9.4	−17.4	−8.4	−11.8
Other transfers from consumers	−1.6	−1.1	−1.5	−1.6	−1.4
Taxpayer transfers to consumers	9.7	17.3	17.8	24.7	26.2
Excess feed cost	0.4	0.0	0.0	0.0	0.0
Total support estimate (TSE)	**66.4**	**67.9**	**96.0**	**105.5**	**100.8**
Transfers from consumers	14.7	10.5	18.9	10.0	13.2
Transfers from taxpayers	53.4	58.6	78.5	97.0	88.9
Budget revenues	−1.6	−1.1	−1.5	−1.5	−1.4

* Farm income is defined as the value of farm production at the farm gate plus all direct payments.
Source: OECD, 2008c.

1990s, farm subsidies began to represent a smaller proportion of farm income. By the end of the decade of the 1990s, prices were again falling and government support increased relative to income from agricultural activities. In recent years, prices have again risen dramatically and the importance of government intervention has diminished. The 2007 PSE represented only 10 percent of farm income and the exceptionally high commodity prices in 2008 mean that this trend will continue.

In 2007, the U.S. Congress began debating legislation to replace the 2002 Farm Bill. The administration proposed relatively minor modifications to the existing commodity programs with greater emphasis on environmental conservation and biofuel research (USDA, 2007). One issue addressed by the administration proposal that family farm advocates and other critics of current policies have taken up is the establishment of payment limitations. Consider a cotton farmer eligible for the subsidies described above with a market price of $0.46 per pound. The loan deficiency payment applies to the entire crop while the direct and counter-cyclical payments apply to 85 percent of the farmer's output as established by her program yield and base acreage. Suppose this producer has a program yield of 900 pounds per acre and base acreage of 5,000 acres. She would then be eligible for total government payments of $1,050,300. According to the EWG farm subsidy database, the Balmorel Farming Partnership received almost $3 million in government payments in 2005 while the average payment for the top 20 farming enterprises was a little more than $1.5 million each in that year (www.ewg.org/farm/index.php).

Granting such extravagant benefits to large firms that appear to be quite profitable even without the subsidies has given impetus to calls for limits on the size of the payments. The problem with payment limitations is that they create incentives for very large farms to divide their operations into several independent farms run by various members of the family with each one eligible for whatever is set as the maximum payment allowed. This largely defeats the purpose of the payment limitations. The administration proposal for the 2007 Farm Bill included calls to eliminate some of the loopholes in the payment limitations established in the 2002 Farm Bill (USDA). The final legislation reconciling the House and Senate versions of the Farm Bill, including some minor modifications in the application of payment limitations, was not completed until May 2008. That legislation was vetoed by the President in part because he felt the eligibility criteria and maximum amounts for government payments were too generous but the veto was overridden by a substantial margin.

The new Farm Bill generally maintains most of the provisions of the 2002 Farm Bill with a few modest changes (CRS, 2007). The marketing loan program, direct payments, and counter-cyclical payments are all continued with minor modifications. In addition, farmers will have the option of choosing between the current counter-cyclical program and a new program based on farm income rather than prices. Payments under this program will be made if the average farm revenue in a state is below historic state averages and an individual farmer's income from agriculture falls below recent averages for the farm (U.S. Congress, 2008). The new bill also includes a horticultural title that will, for the first time ever, extend government support to this sector mainly through programs to improve marketing channels, and a livestock title that includes mandatory country-of-origin labeling and improved monitoring of producer contracts in vertically integrated livestock industries.

The new legislation also maintains direct payments that are made even when prices are above the levels that would trigger loan-deficiency or counter-cyclical payments. In the 1990s, high farm prices made it easier to initiate significant reforms in the 1996 Farm Bill. In 2008, with prices that are even higher than was the case in the 1990s, Congress was unable to introduce any substantive policy reforms perhaps because 2008 was a presidential election year. In some cases, the new bill seems to be a step backward. Among the programs that were found to be in violation of U.S. commitments in the WTO cotton dispute brought by Brazil was a subsidy paid to cotton users and exporters in the United States to compensate for the difference between U.S. and world prices. Known as the Step 2 program, this subsidy was eliminated by the U.S. government in August 2006 in an apparent effort to comply with the WTO ruling (Abdelnour and Peterson, 2007). Section 1208 of the new farm bill, however, appears to reinstate this subsidy under a new name (U.S. Congress, 2008). Shortly after the new farm bill was adopted, the U.S. appeal of the cotton decision was rejected but the language in the new farm bill suggests that the United States has no intention of actually altering its cotton policies in line with the WTO ruling. According to Etter and Hitt (2008), national elections in 2008 coupled with fierce determination on the part of the farm lobby doomed the efforts that had been mounted to change the direction of agricultural policy.

The public debate on the 2008 Farm Bill has involved a diverse set of groups arguing for payment limitations and other reforms that they think would strengthen family farms, increase resources for food stamps and other nutrition programs, enhance rural development programs and the replacement of traditional commodity programs that depress prices received by farmers in developing countries with a system of revenue insurance (see Pollan, 2007; Bread for the World, 2008; Pearson, 2007; Center for Rural Affairs, 2007, among many others). According to World Public Opinion (2007), most U.S. citizens in both farm and nonfarm states favor subsidies to small farms when these farms encounter financial problems. Most do not support subsidies for large farms and oppose the provision of subsidies to all farms on a regular basis (as in the current system of entitlements) without consideration of financial need. The World Public Opinion survey also found that most Americans underestimate the degree to which farm subsidies are captured by large farms believing on average that 42 percent of the subsidies go to small farms when, in fact, 83 percent of program payments went to the top 20 percent of farms according to the EWG farm subsidy database. Although the new farm bill retains most of the features of the 2002 legislation, the case for a radical change in U.S. farm policy is being made with increasing passion by a wide range of interests.

The Impacts of U.S. Farm Subsidies

The results reported in Chapter 5 show the impact on world prices of agricultural subsidies practiced by all members of the OECD. It would be possible to estimate the impact of U.S. subsidies alone using the various models to predict prices if the United States eliminated its subsidies while all other countries maintained theirs. In general, economic analysts have not investigated this scenario. On the other hand, there have been studies of the impact of U.S. programs on world markets for specific commodities. The effects of eliminating U.S. cotton programs were described in Chapter 1. In a study of U.S. sugar policies, Beghin (2003) suggests that world sugar prices would be about 13 percent higher if the U.S. policies were eliminated.

For other commodities, it can be difficult to identify the effects of particular national policies because of special market circumstances. In the case of maize, for example, the United States accounts for more than 60 percent of world exports and effectively sets the world price. To the extent that the U.S. maize program encourages greater production than would be forthcoming in its absence, its effect is to lower the world price. This effect would be difficult to measure, however, as the observed U.S. and world prices will be the same. Still, many critics of the North American Free Trade Agreement (NAFTA) have asserted that subsidized U.S. maize has flooded the Mexican countryside lowering prices and forcing peasant farmers to abandon their farms (Oxfam, 2003; Aziz, 2007). Of course, when rising demand for maize in 2007 and 2008 triggered significant maize price increases in the United States, these events were blamed for rising tortilla prices that were thought to be harmful to Mexican consumers.[6] Interestingly, the higher Mexican maize prices were generally not seen as beneficial to the Mexican maize producers who had allegedly been harmed in the past by cheap surplus maize from the United States.

---

[6] Mexican tortillas are made from white corn while most U.S. corn exported to Mexico is yellow and used for livestock feed. Mesbah, Foster and Tyner (2008) argue that the markets for yellow and white corn are sufficiently distinct to prevent the conditions in one of the markets from significantly affecting prices in the other. De Janvry and Sadoulet (1995) have also shown that most Mexican peasant farmers are net purchasers of maize so that if U.S. maize exports do lead to lower prices, they may actually be of benefit to Mexican peasants.

The commodity programs involving market price support and direct payments are not the only subsidies that might have an impact on world agricultural markets. Food aid, agricultural research, domestic nutrition programs, and many other programs could influence supply and demand on both world and U.S. markets. Although these types of government intervention are not usually included in studies of the overall effects of agricultural policies, there have been many analyses of specific programs. Food aid, in particular, has been extensively studied to determine whether it contributes to or detracts from development in low-income countries (see for example Barrett and Maxwell, 2005). The problem with making a global assessment of all policies related to food and agriculture is the complexity of the many programs that are in place and the potential for contradictory effects. If food stamps lead to increased demand on U.S. markets, for example, they will raise prices offsetting to some extent the price-depressing effects of other farm subsidies.

Overall, U.S. agricultural policies have probably contributed to lower world prices in the cotton and sugar markets and may also have helped to depress prices for grains, oilseeds, dairy products, and other subsidized commodities. At the same time, studies of broad agricultural reform usually find that such reforms would have more appreciable effects in Japan and Europe than in countries such as the United States, Australia, Canada, or New Zealand suggesting that the Japanese and EU policies have the greatest impact on world prices (see Beghin and Roland-Horst, 2002). Japan, Korea, and some European countries rely more heavily on market price supports (trade barriers) in their agricultural policies than does the United States and several studies have found that this type of subsidy causes greater trade distortion than the direct payments that make up the most common form of U.S. commodity support (Anderson, Martin and Valenzuela, 2006). It seems likely that the impact of U.S. policies is somewhat less severe overall than that of EU and Japanese policies although in particular markets such as those for cotton and sugar, U.S. interventions probably have substantial impacts on world prices.

Of course the target of U.S. farm subsidies has been its domestic food and agricultural sectors and the international repercussions of these interventions are less an intended result than collateral damage. As noted earlier, the original farm policies were put in place to deal with the farm problem, that is, the fact that farm incomes were lower and less stable than incomes in other economic sectors. The desire to do something about this problem has been bolstered by the general perception that farming is a virtuous way of life and that a strong rural economy based on family farms is necessary for a thriving democratic society. Gardner (1992, 2002) has shown that on average farms were truly disadvantaged economically when the first farm programs were established in the 1930s. Since then, however, the median income of farm households has surpassed the median for all U.S. households. This result obscures the great variation among farm households in the United States but that diversity does not invalidate Gardner's conclusion that the farm problem that gave rise to government intervention in the first place has largely disappeared.

The Economic Research Service (ERS) of USDA has developed a farm typology for the United States (see Appendix 6.1).[7] Any entity that has agricultural sales of $1,000 or more is considered to be a farm and according to ERS data, there are about two million of these entities in the United States. Some of the characteristics of these farms are displayed in Table 6.4. The ERS farm typology classifies all but 2.2 percent of the two million farms as family farms and divides these into large and small family farms on the basis of gross sales. Large family farms and nonfamily farms accounted for 75.4 percent of U.S. agricultural output in 2004 although they represented less than 10 percent of the total number of farms. Most household income for the small family farms comes from off-farm work and even the large family farms obtain a substantial portion of total household income from non-agricultural activities. For all farms on average, only 17.5 percent of household income comes from farming (Hoppe *et al.*, 2007b).

The median annual income for all U.S. households in 2004 was $44,400 which was less than the median household income in that year for all family farms except the limited resource farms and those with sales less than $100,000 per year (Hoppe *et al.*, 2007b). Put differently, about 72 percent of all farm households had median incomes above the median for all U.S. households and most of their income did not come from farming. Finally, well over half of total government payments went to large family farms and nonfamily farms even though these enterprises made up only 9.7 percent of the total number of farms. If farms with medium sales are included with the large farms and the nonfamily farms, these enterprises, which make up 16 percent of all farms, collected about 73 percent of government payments. Hoppe *et al.* (2007b) divide government payments into commodity and conservation programs and their results show that about 80 percent of conservation program payments were received by small family farms while 62.5 percent of the commodity program payments went to large family farms and nonfamily farms. Retirement and residential/lifestyle farms have been more likely than others to enroll in the Conservation Reserve Program (CRP) which allows farmers to enter into contracts requiring land conservation in return for direct payments. It should

---

[7]   Briggeman *et al.* (2007) propose an alternative farm typology more closely tied to economic theories of household behavior. The categories they identify are quite different from the ERS classification but their analysis does not seriously alter the overall image of farm diversity and payment concentration shown in Table 6.4.

Table 6.4   Characteristics of U.S. farms in 2004

	% of total number of farms	*% of total value of production*	*Median household income ($)*	*% of income from farming*	*% of income from off-farm*	*% of farm payments received*
Small family farms	**90.3**	**24.6**	–	–	–	**44.6**
Limited resource	9.4	1.0	10,000	–76.8	176.8	2.1
Retirement	16.1	2.0	46,000	6.6	93.4	5.2
Residential/ lifestyle	39.7	5.3	69,000	–0.4	100.4	9.7
Farming occupation	*25.1*	*16.3*	–	–	–	27.6
Low sales	18.8	5.5	39,000	7.8	92.2	10.2
Medium sales	6.3	10.8	61,000	48.8	51.2	17.4
Large-scale family farms	**7.5**	**60.2**	–	–	–	**52.2**
Large family farms	4.1	14.8	99,000	64.1	35.9	21.4
Very large family farms	3.4	45.4	155,000	82.6	17.4	30.8
Nonfamily farms	**2.2**	**15.2**	**54,000**	–	–	**3.2**

Source: Hoppe *et al.*, 2007b.

be noted that commodity programs, the ones that are under attack at the WTO and by U.S. critics such as the EWG, accounted for 83 percent of total government payments in 2004 (Hoppe *et al.*, 2007b).

The current state of U.S. agriculture is vastly different from its condition when the first price and income support policies were established. It is likely that the farm policies of the past 80 years have contributed to these changes but it is important to recognize that many other factors, technological innovation, for example, have also played a role. Key and Roberts (2007) used data from recent censuses of agriculture to investigate the effect of commodity programs on farm structure, finding evidence that these programs have contributed to increases in average farm size. Because program payments have generally been tied to specific crops, farmers have little incentive to experiment with alternative crops. U.S. agriculture has always been characterized by concentration on a fairly narrow range of commodities with corn, wheat, other grains, soybeans, and cotton accounting for 70 percent of the harvested acreage in 1910 and 75 percent in 2007. Still, the fact that government support is provided for only some of the potential crops producers might grow has probably limited their desire to develop other agricultural markets.

In reviewing studies of the effects of government programs on farm incomes, Gardner (2002) finds contradictory results with some analyses showing that the programs have raised incomes while others find the opposite effect. From a broader perspective, Pasour and Rucker (2005) argue that the programs have important consequences for particular groups. Because some programs (e.g., deficiency payments for grains and oilseeds) lower food prices while others (e.g., the sugar and dairy programs) raise them, the overall effect on consumer prices is ambiguous. For taxpayers, agricultural policy is an important cost although the budgetary outlays are small relative to the overall budget. The $24 billion spent on direct commodity program payments in 2006 represent less than 1 percent of total federal expenditures of $2.66 trillion in that year.

Among agricultural producers themselves, however, Pasour and Rucker (2005) note important differences in benefits depending on the ownership of land and other assets. The prices of land and other specialized resources are determined by the returns they generate and these returns will be higher if prices are increased by government programs. The consequence is that farm subsidies are incorporated into land prices, for example, which are higher than they would be in the absence of the government programs. This benefits those who own land or other specialized assets but increases the costs of production for renters. Thus, while some producers do benefit from the government programs, others may not. Pasour and Rucker (2005) also point to inefficiencies brought about by programs that distort producer and consumer prices. Such inefficiencies represent a cost to society and these costs along with the direct budgetary costs, the costs to those who do not own land and other specialized resources, and the distortions stemming from trade barriers are likely to be much greater than any potential benefits.

Another way to evaluate farm subsidies is to assume that societal preferences include the desire that certain amounts be transferred to farmers and then to seek the least-cost system for accomplishing that transfer. The Government Accountability Office (GAO) analyzed the effects of U.S. sugar policies on producers and consumers estimating producer gains of $1.05 billion in 1998 compared with consumer costs of $1.94 billion in the same year. In this case, if the social preference is to support sugar growers with a transfer of $1.05 billion, consumers would save $890 million by replacing the current sugar policy with a direct payment to producers.[8] Babcock and Hart (2005) estimate target transfers for the main program crops based on the loan, counter-cyclical, and direct payment programs and compare these estimates with the actual amounts transferred through all government programs. They find many cases of overcompensation and recommend replacing the various programs with a single program designed to provide revenue insurance to producers. Their proposed revenue insurance program would achieve the same support target for farmers but at lower total cost. As noted earlier, the 2008 Farm Bill introduces a new support program based on farm revenue as an optional alternative to income supports based on prices (the counter-cyclical payments).

The Politics of U.S. Agricultural Policies

U.S. agricultural subsidies contribute to distortions of world markets that may be detrimental to the well-being of agricultural producers in low-income countries but their effects within the United States may be even greater. Most farm subsidies are distributed to large farms and contribute to the tendency for these enterprises to become larger, more concentrated, and less like the traditional image of a family farm. The subsidies represent a significant budgetary expenditure and, in some cases, raise consumer prices. The market distortions within the United States are as important as the international distortions and lead to inefficiencies in resource allocation that are costly to the general economy. Between 1999 and 2005, for example, $1.1 billion in farm subsidies were paid to farmers who had died, not all of them in the year the payment was received (Cohen, 2007). The original justification for these policies has disappeared as farm incomes have generally caught up with and in many cases surpassed the income of nonfarm households. And finally, if for some reason the U.S. citizenry wishes to continue providing subsidies to farmers, there are cheaper ways to accomplish the desired level of transfer than through the current programs.

---

[8]   Since the mid-1990s, the sugar program has relied on a tariff that actually generates revenue for the government. Earlier programs used import quotas known as voluntary export restraints (VERs) to increase domestic prices. With VERs, the revenue generated by the trade barrier is captured by the exporters. Either way, the savings from eliminating the sugar program include the foregone benefits of the tariff or VER revenue as well as a terms-of-trade effect (world sugar prices would increase). These elements mean that the actual savings are less than the $890 million difference between consumer costs and producer benefits. Nevertheless, the total benefits of the sugar program are less than the total costs because there will always be costs associated with the economic inefficiencies the program generates.

The widespread criticism of U.S. agricultural policies, the disappearance of the justification for these programs, and their unnecessary costliness beg the question of why they have become so entrenched. As noted in earlier chapters, a common economic justification for government intervention is the correction of market failures. Publicly funded agricultural research, for example, can be justified on the grounds that there is a market failure that would result in suboptimal amounts of research if these activities were left exclusively to the private sector. Many agricultural subsidies, however, do not correct market failures. In fact, commodity policies undermine the efficiency of agricultural markets by distorting prices and generating inaccurate signals to guide producer and consumer behavior. The other rationale for government intervention that is often invoked is the redistribution of income. Redistribution is usually justified by arguing that the beneficiaries deserve support because they are poor, elderly, disabled, or have some other special condition that warrants extra consideration. Arguments of this nature, of course, constituted much of the original justification for farm subsidies but it is not clear that such justifications make sense today.

For Pasour and Rucker (2005), current U.S. agricultural policies are the result of an inherent bias in the political system that favors continuing and expanding programs to benefit producers and agribusiness firms at the expense of the rest of the nation and have little to do with correcting market failures or justifiable redistribution. In the Senate, states have equal representation which increases the political clout of the many states with small populations but large agricultural sectors. The U.S. Department of Agriculture seems to have been captured by farm and agribusiness interests so that it contributes to the perpetuation of programs that benefit these groups. As the farm sector has declined in size, it has gained in its ability to organize itself as a special interest group. Olson (1971) demonstrated that relatively small groups with intense interests are better able to overcome the free-rider problem inherent in group efforts to obtain public goods for their members. From this perspective, well-organized farm groups and agribusiness firms that are able to influence their representatives in Congress have successfully fought for greater subsidies that are nothing more than political pork. On the other side, consumer and taxpayer groups are very large and not very well organized. In addition, the costs of the farm programs are spread over such a large number of people that each individual bears only a tiny fraction of the total and, thus, has little incentive to take the time to do battle with the farm lobby (see also de Gorter and Swinnen, 2002).

The political explanation of farm policies points to the self-interest of the farm lobby and the impotence of consumers and taxpayers in resisting its influence. This is fine as far as it goes but does not account for the fact that the farm lobby generally resists changes that would cost society less while leaving farmers and agribusiness firms no worse off than they are now. Stiglitz (1998) offers some insights on this question. As chair of the Council of Economic Advisers (CEA) in the 1990s, Stiglitz and the CEA argued for replacing the U.S. dairy program, which is based on restricting the amounts placed on the market in order to keep prices high, with a system of direct payments that would be equal in value to the extra revenue earned through the higher prices but would allow market prices to fall to the benefit of milk consumers. The direct payments would cost less than the price support policies but could be structured in a way that would leave dairy producers no worse off. This proposal was rejected by the dairy industry because direct payments are more visible and the milk producers were not convinced that the government would be able to defend these policies as well as it could the existing program. As a result, a program that would have lowered the cost of milk to low-income consumers while leaving dairy producers no worse off turned out to be politically unacceptable to the dairy lobby.

In 1994, Grossman and Helpman published an article in which they developed a theoretical model to explain why politicians often favor trade barriers that benefit a small number of constituents at the expense of the general public. Their model was based on the assumption that politicians are mainly concerned with pursuing their own self interest, including the interest of being re-elected. Grossman and Helpman modeled this political market as one in which politicians are influenced by contributions from lobbyists and by the welfare of voters. The lobbyists hope to use their campaign contributions to maximize the protection from foreign competition that they receive. The Grossman and Helpman model has been tested in several empirical applications and has generally provided interesting results. For example, Goldberg and Maggi (1999) used the model to analyze the structure of U.S. tariffs in 1983 and found that the empirical data were well described by the model. The most interesting result of their analysis was that the members of Congress appeared to attach much greater weight to the broad public interest than they did to campaign contributions.

Two relatively recent studies have used the Grossman and Helpman model to analyze the influence of campaign contributions on agricultural subsidies. Unlike the study by Goldberg and Maggi (1999), both Lopez (2001) and Gawande and Hoekman (2006) find that campaign contributions from agricultural interests have greater influence on politicians than concern for the general welfare. Lopez shows that the elimination of agricultural campaign contributions would substantially lower farm subsidies with a net benefit to society of $5.5 billion. He finds that each dollar invested by farm groups in lobbying for agricultural subsidies brings a return of $2,000 in government transfers. If the payoff is really this high, it is not surprising that farm organizations devote a lot of time and energy to their lobbying activities. Gawande and Hoekman also conclude that "… interest group money bends agricultural policy in the United States" (2006, p. 556). In addition, their results show that there is a great deal of inertia in the evolution of agricultural policy because governments are reluctant to change existing policies, perhaps for reasons similar to those enumerated by Stiglitz. Gawande and Hoekman note that this inertia makes it extremely difficult to reach an international consensus on agricultural policy reform and will complicate the realization of an agricultural agreement at the Doha Round of trade negotiations.

These results suggest that U.S. consumers and taxpayers are paying a fairly heavy price to provide subsidies to farmers and agribusiness firms that generally do not need them. Persuasive arguments can be made that the citizens of wealthy countries such as the United States ought to share their wealth with those who are less fortunate. If there are farmers among these less fortunate people, they would deserve the same consideration as any other low-income individuals not because they are farmers but because they are poor. The extent of the obligations to assist the poor may be the subject of intense debate as will be any decisions about what requirements should be met to be included among those deserving such assistance. The provision of government subsidies whether through trade barriers, direct government payments, or some other means, to individuals who are not poor or disadvantaged in some way, however, would seem to be outside the bounds of most reasonable assessments of our social obligations. Given the description of farm structure in Hoppe *et al.* (2007b), it is not even clear that the traditional family farm that has been so widely admired throughout U.S. history even exists today or that, to the extent that it does, farm policies have played any role in its preservation. Some would even argue that these policies have contributed to the demise of the family farm. The implication of these observations is that it would be in the national interest to eliminate farm subsidies that do not meet the tests of correcting market failures (e.g., agricultural research) or of income redistribution to support the needs of the poor or to save the family farm. Any further beneficial effects of such changes for the citizens of developing countries would be frosting on the cake.

Appendix 6.1: ERS Farm Typology

(The following descriptions are from "America's Diverse Family Farms," *Economic Information Bulletin*, Number 26, June 2007, ERS/USDA.)

The farm classification developed by ERS focuses on the "family farm," or any farm organized as a sole proprietorship, partnership, or family corporation. Family farms exclude farms organized as nonfamily corporations or cooperatives and farms with hired managers.

Small family farms (sales less than $250,000)

- *Limited resource*—Farms with gross sales less than $100,000 in 2003 and less than $105,000 in 2004. Operators of limited-resource farms must also receive low household income in both 2003 and 2004. Household income is considered low in a given year if it is less than the poverty level for a family of four, or it is less than half the county median household income. Operators may report any major occupation except hired manager.
- *Retirement*—Small farms whose operators report they are retired (excludes limited-resource farms operated by retired farmers).
- *Residential/lifestyle*—Small farms whose operators report a major occupation other than farming (excludes limited-resource farms with operators who report nonfarm work as their major occupation).
- *Farming-occupation*—Farms whose operators report farming as their major occupation (excludes limited-resource farms whose operators report farming as their major occupation).
  - *Low-sales*—Gross sales of less than $100,000.
  - *Medium-sales*—Gross sales between $100,000 and $249,999.

Large-scale family farms (sales of $250,000 or more)

- Large family farms—Farms with sales between $250,000 and $499,999.
- Very large family farms—Farms with sales of $500,000 or more.

Nonfamily farms

- Nonfamily farms—Farms organized as nonfamily corporations and cooperatives, as well as farms operated by hired managers. Also includes farms held in estates or trusts.

7

Agricultural Policy in the European Union: Europe's Sacred Cows

Introduction

It is commonly thought that there are about 2.7 billion people in the world who live on less than $2.00 a day, with more than a billion of these people living on less than $1.00 a day (World Bank, 2008c). Many have pointed out that cows in the European Union (EU) receive subsidies of $2.00 a day or more suggesting that it may be better to be a cow in Europe than a human being in many low-income countries (New York Times, 2003; Bleitrach, 2008; Hassett and Shapiro, 2003). Using data from the OECD statistical database on agricultural support (OECD, 2008c), the actual daily subsidies in the EU ranged from $1.41 per cow in 2006 to $2.92 per cow in 2004 and averaged $2.08 per cow for the period 2003 to 2006. In 2006, EU countries provided about $70 billion in total official development assistance (ODA)[1] compared with almost twice as much ($138 billion) in producer support for EU farmers (OECD, 2008a, 2008c). The countries belonging to the EU actually evince much greater generosity toward developing countries than does the United States, for example. EU ODA represented about 0.44 percent of their collective gross national income (GNI) in 2006 compared with U.S. ODA corresponding to only 0.18 percent of U.S. GNI (OECD, 2008a). Still, the EU's generosity toward its own farmers is impressive given that the producer support was distributed among less than 10 million people ($14,375 per person in the active farm population or $21,101 per farm, see Table 7.1) while the ODA

---

[1] ODA is made up of transfers from governments of wealthy countries (primarily those belonging to the OECD Development Aid Committee) to governments of low-income countries on terms (interest rates, repayment schedules, etc.) that are more favorable than can be obtained from private-sector lenders. It is what is normally thought of as foreign aid.

was spread over 5.5 billion people in low- and middle-income countries (a little less than $13.00 per person).

I concluded in the last chapter that the net benefits to the United States of eliminating U.S. farm subsidies would be greater than the net benefits to developing countries of such policy reforms. Given the high cost of farm supports for both consumers and taxpayers in the EU, it would seem likely that similar results will hold for the 27 countries that make up the EU today. There has been pressure on EU policy makers to undertake significant agricultural policy reforms for some time. Agricultural policy is one of the few policies coordinated and financed at the union level. Because many other public policies (e.g., national defense) are still financed by national governments, the CAP has ended up absorbing as much as two-thirds of the relatively small EU budget (European Commission, 2004). Expenditures on agriculture rose as farmers responded to generous price supports with increased output giving rise to costly surpluses. The high cost of the CAP has resulted in policy reforms designed to reduce its budgetary impact but agricultural spending in 2008 still amounted to about 43 percent of the EU budget, 55 billion euro out of a total of 129 billion euro (European Commission, 2008a). Note that the estimated national budgets for 2007 for the 27 countries in the EU totaled about $7.4 trillion (CIA, 2008), about 57 times the 2008 EU budget.

In addition to budget pressures, two other factors have played significant roles in encouraging CAP reform. The first is the successive enlargements which have increased the number of member states from six in the original European Economic Community (EEC) to 27 today (see Table 7.1). In particular, many analysts worried that the most recent enlargements, which added several Central and Eastern European countries with large rural sectors, would overwhelm the EU budget unless there were substantial changes in the CAP (Greer, 2005). New members of the EU become eligible for all the benefits provided by the CAP, although usually only after a transition period, and the potential budgetary impact of each of the six enlargements has been substantial. The other long-standing source of pressure on the CAP is the agricultural trade negotiations conducted by the GATT and WTO. The AA placed important limits on export subsidies, a mechanism frequently employed by the EU to get rid of its butter mountains, wine lakes, and other agricultural surpluses (Akrill, 2000). In response to these pressures, EU policy makers have made serious modifications to the CAP as originally set up, culminating in a set of reforms in 2003 that envision substantial decoupling of agricultural support (European Commission, 2008b).

In recent years, there has been additional pressure for reform from environmentalists and consumers worried about the sustainability of agricultural production and the safety of the food supply. These other voices increasingly

Table 7.1 Agricultural structure and external trade of the EEC, EC, and EU

	Number of farms (millions)[a]	Average farm size (hectares)[a]	Active farm population (millions)[b]	% of agricultural exports to exterior[c]	% of agricultural imports from exterior[d]
EEC (1958–72): France, Germany, Italy, Belgium, Netherlands, Luxembourg	5.30	12.06	10.74	36.82	71.95
EC9 (1973–80): EEC plus Ireland, Denmark, United Kingdom	5.17	16.91	8.31	34.57	48.02
EC10 (1981–5): EC9 plus Greece	5.11	16.65	8.10	36.98	40.45
EC12 (1986–94): EC10 plus Spain and Portugal	6.88	16.90	8.66	30.64	32.79
EU15 (1995–2003): EC12 plus Austria, Sweden, and Finland	6.84	18.68	6.98	29.97	31.44
EU25 (2003–6): EU15 plus 10 Eastern European countries[e]	6.54	24.7	9.60	19.55	21.92

[a] Data on the number of farms and average farm size are incomplete. The figures in columns 1 and 2 are simple averages of the available statistics: 1967 and 1970 for the EEC; 1973–5, 1977, and 1980 for the EC9; 1984 and 1985 for the EC10; 1987, 1989, and 1993 for the EC12; 1995, 1997, 2000, and 2003 for the EU15; and 2005 for the EU25.

[b] Data on the active farm population are also incomplete. Figures reported are simple averages for available years: EEC (1960, 1967–70, and 1972); EC9 (1973 and 1976–80); EC10 (1982–4); EC12 (1986, 1987–92, and 1994); EU15 (1995–6 and 1999–2003); EU25 (2004–5).

[c] Percentage of total agricultural exports from the EEC/EC/EU that were destined for third countries (extra-EU trade). Computed as the average percentage for all time periods except for that of the EEC which is based on data for 1968–72.

[d] Percentage of total agricultural imports into the EEC/EC/EU from third countries (extra-EU trade). Computed as the average percentage for all time periods except that of the EEC which is based on data for 1968–72.

[e] Estonia, Latvia, Lithuania, Poland, Hungary, Czech Republic, Slovak Republic, Slovenia, Malta, and Cyprus. Romania and Bulgaria entered the EU on January 1, 2007. Data for the EU27 are not yet available.

Sources: The Agricultural Situation in the Community, annual issues from 1972 to 1993; *The Agricultural Situation in the European Union*, annual issues from 1994 to 2000; and *Agriculture in the European Union—Statistical and Economic Information*, annual issues from 2001 to 2006, published by the European Commission, Brussels, Belgium. After 2000, the data were obtained online at http://ec.europa.eu/agriculture/agrista/index_en.htm.

set the tone of debates on policy reform in Europe (European Commission, 2004). At the same time, it is important to recognize that European consumers and taxpayers have considerable sympathy for farmers and, drawing on this public support, agricultural interests continue to successfully lobby for generous producer subsidies. Many Europeans feel that the amount spent on agriculture by the EU is about right and agree that supporting farm incomes is as important an objective of agricultural policy as a safe food supply and fair consumer prices (Eurobarometer, 2007). Tracy (1989) argues that European agriculture has been relatively uncompetitive since the end of the nineteenth century when cheap exports from the Americas, Australia, and New Zealand entered world markets and this fact has given rise to a long history of highly protectionist agricultural policies in the EU. In the absence of such policies, EU agricultural production would fall precipitously as cheaper imports flow into Europe. When the CAP was first established, about 72 percent of the total amount of food that was imported by the members of the EU came from countries that were not members, primarily Canada, the United States, Australia, and New Zealand (see Table 7.1). By 2006, this proportion had fallen to 18.2 percent as a result, primarily, of the CAP.

Further evidence of the effect of the CAP on international trade is shown in Table 7.2 which includes estimates of the net trade (exports minus imports) of particular agricultural commodities for the 15 countries making up the EU prior to the 2003 enlargement. Grains, oilseeds, sugar, and livestock products are the main temperate-zone products produced and traded by the EU, the United States, Canada, Australia, New Zealand and such developing countries as Brazil, Argentina, and South Africa. In the early 1960s, the 15 countries of the EU15 (nine of which were not yet members) imported more of all of the commodities shown in Table 7.2 than they exported. By the 1980s, the EU15 had become a net exporter of all of these commodities except oilseeds. Soybeans represent about three-quarters of the international trade in oilseeds and the United States and Brazil account for almost 80 percent of total soybean exports (FAOSTAT, http://faostat.fao.org/site/). The main reason the soybean market has not followed the same pattern as the other commodities is that EEC negotiators agreed to allow oilseeds to enter the community duty-free during the Dillon Round of GATT trade negotiations in 1960–1 (Akrill, 2000). The commitment not to place trade barriers on imported oilseeds remained in force through subsequent enlargements and trade negotiations and the net imports of these commodities have continued to grow. All the other commodities shown in Table 7.2 have received border protection and subsidies that have stimulated EU production and, eventually, dramatically increased exports.

The purpose of this chapter is to review the historical development of the EU and its agricultural policies and to assess the impact of these policies on

Table 7.2 Annual net trade of selected commodities (five-year averages), EU15* (1,000 metric tons)

	Coarse grains	Wheat	Oilseeds	Sugar	Bovine meat	Butter
1961–5	–17,880	–7,336	–6,188	–2,537	–671	–259
1966–70	–18,776	–4,058	–8,351	–2,782	–712	–174
1971–5	–19,722	–2,072	–11,490	–2,090	–551	–2
1976–80	–22,683	2,560	–16,050	798	–229	227
1981–5	–9,912	11,927	–16,082	2,958	286	343
1986–90	4,469	16,571	–14,726	2,990	577	420
1991–5	6,596	19,484	–16,449	3,813	766	193
1996–2000	6,617	12,378	–17,965	3,962	423	43
2001–4	5,209	5,229	–20,589	2,618	7	54

Note: The archival FAO data series on agricultural trade runs from 1961 to 2004. In 2006, the FAO statistical division inaugurated a new system that currently does not include variables for the EU15 as a distinct group. The new series are difficult to reconcile with the archival data so only the older data set is used. The archival data appear to have been adjusted to include the 15 countries that made up the EU in the 1990s rather than the smaller membership sets in earlier years. Thus, some of the data for the earlier periods include data for countries that were not yet members of the EU. The net trade estimates are derived from export and import data that include intra-EU trade (e.g., exports from France to Germany). The net trade figures, however, are actually fairly reliable estimates of the position of the EU vis-à-vis the rest of the world. Total EU15 exports are equal to intra-exports (trade within the EU15) plus extra-exports. Likewise, total imports are the sum of intra- and extra-imports. Let IX, XX, IM, and XM represent respectively intra-exports (France's exports to Germany), extra-exports (France's exports to Canada), intra-imports (Germany's imports from France), and extra-imports (Germany's imports from New Zealand). Net trade is defined as exports (X) minus imports (M), X – M. But total X and M are made up of intra and extra trade so X = (IX + XX) and M = (IM + XM). Then net trade is (IX + XX) – (IM + XM) = IX + XX – IM – XM. But IX and IM have to be equal (France's exports to Germany equal Germany's imports from France so that amount appears in both IX and IM) so those terms cancel. As a result, X – M will be approximately equal to XX – XM. Negative signs indicate that imports are greater than exports.

Source: Agricultural Statistical Databases (Archives) at www.faostat.fao.org/site/412/ DesktopDefault.aspx?PageID=412. Coarse grains include maize, barley, sorghum, and minor grains; wheat includes both wheat and wheat flour; sugar is all sugar measured in raw sugar equivalents; oilseeds include soybeans, sunflower seed, rape seed (canola), and others; bovine meat is beef and veal, fresh, frozen, and preserved in other ways; and butter is cow milk butter.

developing countries and on the EU itself. The next section includes a review of European agriculture and agricultural policy prior to the establishment of the EEC, description of the development of the CAP, and an assessment of the current state of EU agricultural policy using the OECD database. This section is followed by an evaluation of the effects of the CAP and discussion of the political, economic, and cultural forces that have shaped the evolution of agricultural policy in the EU.

Agricultural Policy in the European Union[2]

Evidence was presented in Chapter 3 that Malthus's predictions about population growth and food availability were incorrect. Growth in food production has been more rapid than population growth for the past 200 years. Malthus could not have known of the technological innovations that would arise in the centuries after he wrote his essay and he based his predictions on the history of Europe as he understood it in 1798. As it turns out, his understanding was perfectly sensible at that time. Europe appeared to have been caught in a Malthusian trap for centuries. From this perspective, any increase in living standards could only be temporary because population growth would be accelerated by the more opulent conditions, rapidly reaching rates that would surpass the potential for increased agricultural output. The consequence would be famine, war, pestilence, and vice (e.g., prostitution, infanticide) that would bring population and food availability back into balance at the standard of living that had prevailed before the increase. Abel (1980) notes that combining the Malthusian population model with some of the insights of another great nineteenth-century economist, David Ricardo, gave rise to an image of economic change that was largely accurate until the middle of that century. Ricardo developed the idea of diminishing returns pointing out that as more labor is applied to a constant amount of land, the increases in output associated with each successive labor increment will be smaller than the previous ones. This insight coupled with Malthus's population model suggested that land rents and food prices would increase more rapidly than the prices of

---

[2] As in the case of U.S. farm policy, there is an extensive literature describing agricultural policy in the EU and evaluating its effects. The account provided here draws on material originally developed for my previous book on agricultural policy (Peterson, 2001) and is necessarily somewhat abbreviated. More detailed descriptions of the origin and evolution of EU agricultural policy can be found in Fennell (1979, 1997), Harris *et al.* (1983), Tracy (1989), Kay (1998), Akrill (2000), Greer (2005), and many documents published online by the EU Commission (http://ec.europa.eu/agriculture/index_en.htm) as well as by USDA's Economic Research Service (http://www.ers.usda.gov/Briefing/EuropeanUnion).

industrial goods and wages and this was the case well into the nineteenth century (Abel, 1980).

There is much evidence, however, that the grim analyses of Malthus and Ricardo may have underestimated the potential for improvements in human living conditions.[3] There were important technological changes that occurred in agriculture and food production prior to the Industrial Revolution and standards of living probably trended upward during these periods albeit with periodic economic crises and widespread poverty. White (1962) traces the impact in Northern Europe of several agricultural innovations in the early Middle Ages (from about the sixth to the tenth centuries), including the development of the moldboard plow, the use of horse power to cultivate fields, and the three-field rotation system. He argues that these innovations raised the standard of living of peasant farmers giving them the means to purchase manufactured goods turned out by early industries and laying the foundation for the modern world characterized by increased urbanization and division of labor. According to the Malthusian population model, the gains in rural standards of living should have been eroded fairly rapidly by the increased population growth they were expected to induce. As White notes, however, the income gains were generated by increased food production and more nutritional diets which raised the ceiling on the Malthusian constraint allowing the persistence of larger populations with higher incomes.

Of course, Medieval and early modern Europe was full of wars and pestilence that acted to limit population growth. It is generally thought that the epidemics of bubonic plague in the sixth and fourteenth centuries caused declines in Europe's population of some 40 percent (Razi, 1986). Voigtländer and Voth (2007) show that the dramatic fall in population associated with the Black Death gave rise to wage increases that allowed higher living standards

---

[3]   Albert Hirschman (1991) has pointed to Malthus's essay as an example of a rhetorical device he labels the "perversity thesis" which holds that the effort being made to improve humankind's situation will not only fail to achieve its goals but will give rise to precisely the opposite effect. Malthus argued strongly against the poor laws, an early form of welfare for people living in poverty, on the grounds that raising the incomes of the poor would only lead to population growth that in the end would actually make the poor worse off than they had been before they received assistance. Hirschman's essay explores the types of rhetoric often employed by conservatives and reactionaries to oppose progressive changes. The other rhetorical approaches he identifies are futility (the poor are always with us so there is no point in trying to alleviate poverty) and jeopardy (progressive efforts will actually put other things that are of great value—democracy, for example—in jeopardy). Heilbroner (1953) contrasts "the gloomy world of Parson Malthus and David Ricardo" with the "wonderful world of Adam Smith" in his classic book on the history of economic thought.

that were not immediately eroded by population growth. They point out that higher urban wages attracted workers from the countryside to urban centers where disease was more prevalent and this fact coupled with the frequency of wars meant that population pressures were held in check despite the increases in income. Several authors have provided detailed accounts of the history of changes in agricultural production, incomes, and population prior to the Industrial Revolution that add important nuances to these accounts. Clark (2007) examined data on farm wages and income in England from 1209 to 1869 and found that although there was little technological change before 1600, agricultural productivity was already relatively high. After 1600, technological innovation in English agriculture picked up allowing both incomes and population to increase (Clark, 2007).

Duplessis (1997) documents substantial technological changes in European agriculture between 1650 and 1800. He suggests that part of the impetus for technical innovation was the need peasant farmers confronted to sell goods on the market to obtain cash income to pay rents and taxes. The most rapid growth in agricultural output occurred in England and the Netherlands where markets were more competitive and there were fewer communal institutions. In these areas, the technical progress in agriculture released large numbers of workers who moved into the developing industrial sector (Duplessis, 1997). Hopcroft (1999) also finds that agricultural systems organized on a more communal basis were less likely to experience early agricultural growth. She describes variations in the degree of community control of field rotations, grazing and other agricultural practices and argues that there was greater agricultural progress in areas where individuals with secure property rights, access to markets, and limited intrusion from feudal overlords were able to decide for themselves how to manage their farms rather than having such decisions made by the community.

Regional differences in technological innovation resulted in a European food system that was highly varied at the beginning of the twentieth century. In some areas farms were small and fragmented while in others the patchwork of small strips of land had been consolidated into larger, more productive farms. In 1901, about 40 percent of the working populations in France and Germany were in agricultural occupations compared with less than 10 percent in England (Tracy, 1989). In 1892, only 29 percent of French farms owned more than five hectares of land and 39 percent had less than one hectare (Cleary, 1989). In England, in 1870, almost half the farms (46 percent) held more than eight hectares of land with only 26 percent controlling less than two hectares (Tracy, 1989). As noted earlier, competition from producers in the Americas, Australia, and New Zealand put great pressure on European agriculture toward the end of the nineteenth century. Tracy argues that the appropriate response to this competition would have been to shift resources toward more labor-intensive production of dairy and livestock products, fruits and vegetables leaving the land-intensive commodities such as cereal grains to producers in the new world. Resource reallocation of this nature did take place to some extent in England, Denmark and the Netherlands, perhaps because the less communal agricultural systems in these countries were better able to adjust to changing circumstances. Elsewhere in Europe, the response was extensive protectionism and this tendency to erect trade barriers to shelter European farmers from foreign competition became more widespread and more entrenched with the economic crisis of the 1930s and in the aftermath of the Second World War (Tracy, 1989).

As European leaders set about the monumental task of rebuilding their countries after the ravishes of the Second World War, the need to rapidly increase agricultural production in the face of food shortages and a ruined countryside gave rise to extensive government intervention in agricultural markets. Because agricultural output was below pre-war levels, prices rose and scarce foreign exchange had to be used to pay for imported food (Tracy, 1989). Tracy shows that European agricultural output was re-established fairly rapidly through external assistance (Marshall Plan) and policies designed to encourage farm modernization, guarantee farm incomes and, as food shortages began to disappear, support falling farm prices. At this stage, of course, each government operated its own independent farm policy. There was great variation in the structure and level of productivity of the agricultural sectors of the countries that would eventually form the EEC stemming from both historical circumstances and the differential impact of the war. Despite these differences, however, most of continental Europe favored policies that protected domestic producers from foreign competition and provided price and income supports (Tracy, 1989).

In 1957, the governments of France, Germany, Italy, Belgium, the Netherlands, and Luxembourg signed the Treaty of Rome establishing the European Economic Community (EEC). Previous regional agreements among the countries of Western Europe had been organized around relatively narrow concerns, as in the case of the European Coal and Steel Community (ECSC) established in 1951. In contrast, the EEC treaty was a comprehensive agreement to remove trade barriers between the members of the community and to coordinate external trade policy. As noted above, agriculture in the six original members of the EEC was characterized by great diversity. Producers in France and the Netherlands were relatively productive, and exports were an important component of their agricultural economies. In contrast, producers in Germany, Italy, Belgium, and Luxembourg had small holdings and were less productive than their counterparts in France and the Netherlands. For French agricultural interests, the advantages of economic union consisted of access to German agricultural markets. The Germans expected to benefit from increased industrial sales in France (Akrill, 2000).

The diversity of the six national food systems complicated the establishment of common policies for agriculture. Fennell (1979) estimated that 30,000 different regulations had to be dealt with in setting up a common agricultural policy. Why was a common policy for agriculture needed? In establishing the EEC, a customs union (see Chapter 4), the member governments agreed to eliminate trade barriers among themselves and to adopt common external tariffs. Because the member states had pursued different policies, all of them protectionist to some extent, prior to the formation of the customs union, agricultural prices varied considerably from country to country. Such price differences cannot be sustained unless a tariff or some other measure is used to adjust the border prices of traded goods. Without trade barriers, it would be possible to purchase agricultural commodities in countries with low prices for sale in countries where policies to maintain high prices were in place. The resultant flow of goods would undermine the high-price policies. The elimination of internal barriers to trade, therefore, made it impossible for the member states to maintain different farm prices. The main economic advantage of a customs union, of course, is that production of particular goods is shifted from regions where it is costly to produce them to areas where production costs are lower. The formation of the EEC meant that agricultural policies had to be harmonized and this change was expected to generate widespread benefits in the form of lower prices due to more efficient production.

The CAP is based on several principles. The first, the principle of common prices, is unavoidable because of the creation of the customs union. A second principle is common financing. Each member of the EU contributes a portion of its tax revenues to the EU budget, which includes a central fund, known as the European Agricultural Guidance and Guarantee Fund (EAGGF), from which the CAP is financed. This fund replaces the financing of agricultural policy by the individual member states. Revenues from tariffs and levies applied to agricultural goods imported from countries outside the EU are also held in the central fund rather than by the treasuries of the countries that collected them. A final principle is the principle of community preference which means that no agricultural goods imported from countries outside the union can be sold at prices lower than the prices in countries belonging to the EU (Akrill, 2000).

Memories of difficult times during and after the Second World War also influenced the structure of the CAP. Price stability is seen as a major policy objective and the CAP is designed to isolate EU food markets from world market fluctuations. Fear of food shortages has led to a desire to increase the degree of food self-sufficiency, although that is not explicitly listed in the objectives of the CAP. Price stability and food security can be attained in many different ways. The particular approach to these issues followed by the EU has involved extensive government intervention, reflecting historical patterns of distrust for free markets in Europe. Agricultural policy has also been influenced by prevailing beliefs that rural life and family farms have special value and that it is important to maintain a relatively large rural population (Eurobarometer, 2007). These beliefs make it easier for EU consumers to accept the high food prices that have been induced by the CAP. In the United States, food absorbs less than 10 percent of consumer budgets compared with between 13 and 17 percent for such EU countries as France, Germany, Sweden, the United Kingdom, and the Netherlands (ERS, 2008c).

The CAP has two sets of programs corresponding to the two parts of the EAGGF: guidance and guarantee. Structural programs fall under the smaller guidance fund, while conventional price and income support programs are covered by the guarantee fund. As shown in Table 7.2, the EU was a net importer of many temperate-zone agricultural commodities when the CAP was being set up. The level of the common prices agreed upon by community policy makers was determined through a compromise that prevented individual members from experiencing price declines as the CAP was put in place. As a result, internal prices were set above world prices, making some form of external trade barrier essential. As in the United States, the policy makers who established the CAP were driven in part by the perception that farm incomes were lower than incomes in other sectors of the economy (Harris *et al.*, 1983). The original CAP included a wide range of market regulations aimed at maintaining high agricultural prices and preventing imported commodities from interfering with internal markets.

The programs for cereal grains can serve as an example of the types of market interventions initially practiced in the EU. Until the recent reforms, these programs were based on a politically determined target price representing the desired level of wholesale prices for a given commodity. The target price was used to calculate an internal support price, known as the intervention price, and a minimum import price, known as the threshold price. The intervention price was supported by government agencies that were required to purchase whatever producers wished to sell at that price which, thus, served as a floor for market prices. Unlike the early farm programs in the United States, producers were not initially required to reduce production to receive the benefits of market support. The threshold price, which was higher than the intervention price, was enforced through the application of a trade barrier known as the variable levy. The variable levy was set as the difference between the world price and the threshold price. Because the world price changes from day to day, the variable levy also varied on a daily basis to insure that imports would never enter the EU at prices lower than the threshold price.[4]

Initially, the EU was a net importer so internal prices tended to rise to the level of the threshold price and no grain was sold into intervention at the lower intervention price. As farmers began to respond to the high market prices, however, production expanded, imports fell, and surplus grain began to pile up in the intervention agencies. This led to the introduction of a new mechanism, the export restitution or export refund. Export restitutions were variable export subsidies calculated as the difference between the world price and the higher market prices in the EU. The increased production in the EU meant that market prices fell below the level of the threshold price, reaching the level of the intervention price as surplus stocks began to accumulate. The export restitution was designed as a mechanism for diverting the surplus production from the internal market to the world market. The combination of variable levies and export restitutions provided almost perfect insulation from world market variations for the EU's internal agricultural markets.

Not surprisingly, these agricultural policies generated a great deal of conflict with other exporting nations. For agricultural exporters, increased production in the EU meant the loss of an important foreign market and the rise of a major competitor on the world market. For the EU, the CAP led to price stability and increased self-sufficiency but at a high cost. Recall that the early CAP provided unrestricted support for whatever quantities were produced. By the 1970s, this open-ended support had become extremely costly so various mechanisms were introduced to force producers to help in the financing of the CAP and to limit the amounts that qualified for support (Akrill, 2000). These mechanisms included producer taxes (co-responsibility levies), production controls (dairy quotas and obligatory reductions in planted acreage), and guarantee thresholds that set maximum quantities eligible for support. The system of target, threshold and intervention prices, variable levies, and export restitutions remained intact, although there was an effort to restrain increases in price supports.

These reforms did not solve the problem of surplus agricultural production and the attendant budgetary costs. In 1992, more substantial policy reforms, often referred to as the MacSharry reforms for the EU agricultural commissioner at that time, were introduced (Kay, 1998). The MacSharry reforms represented a significant departure from earlier practices, instituting policies that were almost the same as those found in the United States at that time. Support prices for many commodities were lowered, with the loss in producer income

---

[4] The variable levy had a similar effect to that of an import quota because it does not allow imports to vary with changes in world prices (see footnote 4 in Chapter 4).

made up by direct payments similar to deficiency (counter-cyclical) payments in the United States. Production controls were expanded, eliminating entirely the open-ended support of agricultural production that had characterized the CAP in the past. This shift in policy took place in anticipation of potential international requirements that were being negotiated at the Uruguay Round (1986–94) trade talks. As noted earlier, the WTO Agreement on Agriculture did require significant changes in the CAP including replacement of the variable levy with tariffs and reductions in the use of export subsidies. The tariff levels negotiated by the EU were still quite high (155 percent of the intervention price for grains, for example) leaving considerable protection in place (ERS, 2008c).

In 1999, the EU adopted a set of policy reforms referred to as Agenda 2000. A principal objective of this new policy was to ease existing budget costs as well as those anticipated to arise with the entry of the Eastern European countries by freezing the CAP budget at the 1999 level. In addition, support prices for grains were reduced and other policy changes were made in an effort to comply with the Uruguay Round requirements and in light of expected further liberalization of the agricultural trade regime. A few years later in 2003, a new set of reforms was adopted with the intention of fundamentally changing the nature of the CAP. As noted in Chapter 4, the AA as well as the current Doha negotiations place great emphasis on shifting domestic support from policies that distort trade to decoupled payments that have little or no influence on producer decisions. The 2003 reforms envision a future in which virtually all producer subsidies will be decoupled (European Commission, 2008b). The vehicle for implementing this decision is known as the single farm payment (SFP) which has replaced the direct payments of the MacSharry reforms and is tied to a farm's historic compensation (ERS, 2008b). The SFP requires "cross-compliance," that is, respect for EU policies on the environment, food safety, and animal welfare as well as other provisions such as the requirement that farm land be maintained in good condition (European Commission, 2008b; Brasher, 2007).

Tables 7.3 and 7.4 show the OECD agricultural support estimates for selected years. Recall that these tables include measures of the support provided by consumers who pay higher prices for goods produced behind the protection of trade barriers. The figures in Table 7.3 show that the amounts transferred from consumers (market price support) have declined over time even though the number of member states has increased. As these are nominal figures, they underestimate the magnitude of the real decline. Note that the GSSE is quite modest relative to the PSE and that the CSE is negative because there are no EU-wide programs similar to the U.S. food stamp program that offset the consumer costs of the trade barriers. The last column of Table 7.4

Table 7.3 EU agricultural support estimates, selected years (billions of current euro)

	1986	1995	2000	2005	2007
Value of production (farm gate)	**212.8**	**232.2**	**242.5**	**271.4**	**318.8**
Producer support estimate (PSE)	**95.0**	**96.9**	**94.0**	**105.3**	**98.1**
PSE/farm income (%)	*42.0*	*36.0*	*34.0*	*32.0*	*26.0*
Market price support	83.5	56.6	52.7	48.8	35.4
Payments based on output	4.4	3.4	4.7	5.1	0.1
Payments based on input use	4.1	5.2	6.8	10.4	12.3
Payments based on current production	2.7	29.5	32.0	24.0	16.3
Payments—historic production**	0.0	0.0	0.0	16.1	32.5
Payments—non-commodity	0.3	1.3	1.2	1.3	1.1
Miscellaneous payments	0.1	0.9	−1.1	−0.4	0.0
General services support estimate (GSSE)	**9.0**	**5.8**	**8.1**	**12.2**	**11.9**
Research and development	1.0	1.5	1.7	1.9	2.0
Agricultural schools	0.2	0.5	0.8	1.2	1.1
Inspection services	0.2	0.2	0.3	0.8	0.7
Infrastructure	0.9	1.5	2.7	4.9	4.8
Marketing and promotion	1.6	1.8	1.5	2.7	3.1
Public stockholding	5.2	0.2	0.9	0.7	0.1
Miscellaneous	0.0	0.1	0.2	0.1	0.0
Consumer support estimate (CSE)	**−72.8**	**−50.5**	**−45.3**	**−43.4**	**−33.5**
Consumer transfers to producers	−83.6	−56.3	−49.9	−47.1	−35.3
Other transfers from consumers	−2.2	−1.6	−0.3	−0.8	−1.8
Taxpayer transfers to consumers	4.1	4.1	3.7	3.6	2.0
Excess feed cost	8.9	3.2	1.2	0.9	1.5
Total support estimate (TSE)	**108.1**	**106.8**	**108.2**	**121.1**	**112.0**
Transfers from consumers	85.8	57.8	50.2	47.9	37.0
Transfers from taxpayers	24.5	50.6	58.2	74.0	76.7
Budget revenues	−2.2	−1.6	−0.3	−0.8	−1.8

* Farm income is defined as the value of production at the farm gate plus direct budgetary payments.
** Decoupled single farm payments introduced in the 2003 reforms.
Source: OECD, 2008c.

Table 7.4   EU agricultural support estimates, 1986–2007 (billions of current euro)*

	TSE	PSE	PSE (MPS)	PSE (budget)	GSSE	CSE	MPS/ PSE (%)
1986	108.1	95.0	83.5	11.5	9.0	−72.8	87.9
1990	96.0	80.1	60.5	19.5	11.5	−52.8	75.5
1995	106.8	96.9	56.6	40.3	5.8	−50.5	58.4
2000	108.2	96.4	52.7	43.7	8.1	−45.3	54.7
2001	107.2	94.0	46.5	47.5	9.5	−40.8	49.5
2002	119.0	105.5	57.6	47.9	9.9	−53.3	54.6
2003	119.8	106.4	57.7	48.7	9.6	−51.8	54.2
2004	130.6	114.9	59.8	55.1	11.7	−52.9	52.0
2005	121.1	105.2	48.8	56.5	12.2	−43.4	46.3
2006	119.3	104.1	41.8	62.3	12.8	−39.6	40.2
2007	112.0	98.1	35.4	62.7	11.9	−33.5	36.1

* TSE (total support estimate), PSE (producer support estimate), GSSE (general services support estimate), CSE (consumer support estimate). PSE is divided into market price support (MPS) which comes from consumers through higher prices resulting from trade barriers and commodity programs financed through the government budget (see Chapter 5). The last column shows the share of producer support resulting from trade barriers (MPS/PSE).
Source: OECD, 2008c.

displays the proportion of total producer support made up of consumer transfers. This proportion has clearly fallen a great deal and was equal to that of the United States in 2007. The new policy direction can be seen in Table 7.3 for 2005 and 2007 where the payments based on historic production represent the decoupled single farm payments. These payments of 32.5 billion euro in 2007 mean that decoupled payments amounted to about half the total direct payments but only about a third of total producer support. Note that producer support in 2007 represents about 26 percent of farm income from agriculture, somewhat lower than in the previous years shown in Table 7.3. By comparison, U.S. producer support was about 10 percent of farm income in 2007.

The data in Tables 7.3 and 7.4 include both guarantee expenditures and the more limited spending on structural programs (guidance). In 1968, Sicco Mansholt, who was then serving as Commissioner of Agriculture, published a report calling for profound changes in the structure of European agriculture (Cahill and Hill, 2006). Mansholt and other analysts had already seen that there could be problems with growing expenditures on price and income supports for an agricultural sector that included many small farms of questionable economic viability. The Mansholt Plan called for a reduction in the number of farms and of the amount of land in farms and the establishment of larger farms that would be competitive at the much lower world prices (Akrill, 2000). Some elements of the Mansholt proposal were adopted but guidance expenditures have generally remained less than 10 percent of the amounts spent through the guarantee fund (Cahill and Hill, 2006). Cahill and Hill point out that guidance expenditures do not exhaust the amounts devoted to structural programs in the EU because there are national rural development programs as well as spending from the EU regional budget that are linked to agricultural structure. Nevertheless, structural and rural development programs have not yet had the effects envisioned by Mansholt who saw such initiatives as a way to rein in spending on farm subsidies.

The 2003 policy reforms have also exacerbated a tendency toward the renationalization of agricultural policy that first began to appear in the late 1960s. Agricultural policy prices are set by the agricultural commission in Brussels. Prior to the establishment of the European Monetary Union and the introduction of the euro, these prices were set in various accounting units such as the European Currency Unit (ECU) and then translated into national currencies by applying market exchange rates. This system is described in more detail in Appendix 7.1. Problems arose when countries began to adjust their exchange rates because the adjustments meant that agricultural support prices in the member states would also change. A solution of sorts was developed by allowing countries to use the old exchange rates (which came to be known as green rates) for agriculture. The result was two sets of exchange rates, one for agriculture and the other for everything else.

The dual exchange rate system meant that there were common prices in terms of the green rates but not in terms of the official market rates. As shown in Appendix 7.1, such a system cannot be sustained without border taxes and subsidies. In reality, what had happened was that the principle of common prices had fallen by the wayside. Farm prices differed between the member states and these price differentials were maintained by border taxes and subsidies known as monetary compensatory amounts (MCA). Although the governments did not have full control of farm prices, they were able to influence price levels through monetary and exchange rate policies. Thus, the agrimonetary system that was in place from 1969 until 1999 when the euro was introduced meant that agricultural support was no longer uniform across the member states.

The adoption of the euro eliminated the problem of exchange rate variation but other policy developments have meant that some control of agricultural policy has been returned to national governments. Rough calculations based on the OECD database for the EU suggest that national expenditures on agriculture increased from about 5 percent of the value of the PSE in 1986 to almost 18 percent in 2007. It should be pointed out that if one views the EU as a single entity, national expenditures would be equivalent to state and local expenditures in the United States. The U.S. data appear to incorporate some state and local spending to support agriculture but it is not clear that all non-federal spending is included, making the comparison between U.S. and EU support levels less clear. If one subtracts the national expenditures from the EU PSE in 2007, it would total about 80.8 billion euro (about $111 billion) instead of 98.1 billion euro ($134 billion) as reported in Table 7.3. Recall that the 2007 U.S. PSE was about $33 billion (24 billion euro).

The increase in significance of national agricultural spending in the EU is only one indication of the re-nationalization of agricultural policy. The 2003 reforms allowed substantial latitude to the member states in implementing the SFP. Governments were able to make the transition to the SFP at any time between 2005 and 2007 and could choose among alternative payment methods. There are provisions to strengthen rural development programs by shifting funds from conventional farm support to programs aimed at the structure of rural economies (ERS, 2008b). Greer (2005) has argued that the CAP has become less a common policy than one driven by disparate national interests and that it is a policy that has less to do with agriculture than it did in the past. In addition to the provisions on cross-compliance, many of the structural programs target environmental issues, regional development and socioeconomic concerns, and questions of food safety and food quality have begun to play important roles in policy discussions (see, for example, Brouwer and Lowe (2000) and Redclift *et al.*, 1999).

One factor that may have contributed to these trends is a shift in the rationale for agricultural policy. Low farm incomes and food security were the main justifications for extensive market interventions in the early CAP. While these concerns are still present, policy makers in the EU increasingly invoke the multifunctionality of agriculture as justification for agricultural policy interventions. Multifunctionality, which was briefly discussed in Chapter 5, draws attention to the multiple functions of agriculture including food production, of course, but also environmental protection and the stewardship of rural areas (Greer, 2005). It has become a subject for debate at the WTO where some countries argue that agricultural subsidies including subsidies that distort trade should be allowed as compensation for the many positive externalities created by agricultural producers (WTO, 2008f). EU policy makers favor subsidies that are carefully targeted at particular externalities (e.g., environmental protection) and that cause as little trade distortion as possible. Other countries such as Japan or Korea feel that subsidies tied to production should be permitted to assure the survival of uncompetitive agricultural industries that are needed for reasons of food security or to serve some other purpose. Many developing countries object to these arguments because they would allow wealthy countries to continue to subsidize their agricultural sectors even as they lower tariffs and export subsidies (WTO, 2008f).

In any case, the recent emphasis on multifunctionality in EU agriculture shifts attention to particular conditions in various parts of Europe and may lead to an expansion of the role of national governments in the design and implementation of agricultural policies. In fact, the intellectual basis for creating the EU is called into question by this new emphasis on local concerns. As noted earlier, the motivation for creating a customs union is to allow markets to direct the reorganization of economic activities so that industries that are inefficient or unproductive would decline while those that are more productive would expand. This reorganization would usually be expected to have implications for the spatial and regional distribution of economic activity. If the governments of areas in which farming is a high-cost activity claim that there are special benefits from having farms in that region anyway, they will want to prevent the reorganization that would be driven by markets in a normal customs union or free trade area.

Concerns for local circumstances may also be related to broader developments in the EU. The three main agencies that administer the EU are the European Commission, the Council of the EU and the European Parliament (Europa, 2008a). The Commission is a permanent bureaucracy based in Brussels that proposes statutes and laws and oversees their execution. The Council is made up of representatives of the governments of the member states and serves as the primary decision-making body for the EU. Elected representatives in the Parliament share some decision-making authority with the Council. For some time, there has been concern in the EU that the administrative agencies are disconnected from the lives and interests of ordinary citizens in the member states, a disconnection sometimes referred to as a "democratic deficit" (Europa, 2008b). The Parliament is the only body that is elected although voters do have some influence over the composition of the Council as its members are ministers representing democratically elected national governments.

In 1992, the Treaty of Rome was replaced by a new agreement known as the Treaty on European Union that included provisions reflecting worries about the democratic deficit. In particular, the new treaty established the principle of subsidiarity to regulate the division of administrative responsibility between local, national, and union officials (Brault *et al.*, 2005). This principle stipulates that the actions of the EU should be limited to matters relating clearly to union-wide issues leaving more local and national questions to authorities at those levels. If the emphasis of agricultural policy in the EU shifts from its current focus on broad price and income supports to rural development and other local concerns, the principle of subsidiarity would suggest an evolution toward greater policy responsibility at lower levels in the administrative hierarchy.

The Impact of the Common Agricultural Policy

Since 1992, there have been numerous attempts to sort out some of the contradictions in the governance of a union that includes 27 countries at widely different levels of development. Efforts to devise a constitution have so far been unsuccessful and the governing bodies and procedures of the EU continue to be set by treaties, the most recent of which is the Treaty of Lisbon signed in December 2007. This treaty, which would enter into force if ratified by all of the member states, addresses the democratic deficit by expanding the role of the European Parliament and clarifying the respective responsibilities of local, national, and union authorities. It also includes measures to streamline the voting mechanisms, introduces a charter on human rights, and strengthens the EU's ability to conduct relations with the exterior (Europa, 2008a). The first national referendum on the Lisbon Treaty was conducted in Ireland in June 2008. Irish voters rejected the proposed treaty leaving the future of EU governance up in the air.

Given the complexity of the EU, one might expect little more than bureaucratic red tape and organizational gridlock. In fact, the EU has been an extraordinary success. For one thing, European nations that had spent the better part of the twentieth century locked in vicious and brutal wars have been at peace for the past 60 years and the idea that they might one day again precipitate another world war has come to appear completely absurd. Countries such as Spain and Ireland that had languished economically and politically for generations have realized amazing levels of prosperity, the euro is well established as an important international currency and the EU is playing a greater role in international security efforts having taken over the peacekeeping operations in Bosnia. When Portugal joined the EU in 1986, its per capita GNP was lower than that of Algeria. In 2006, per capita income in Portugal was almost six times Algeria's and the level of per capita income in Ireland, historically one of Europe's poorest countries, was the ninth highest in the world and just ahead of that of the United States in 2006 (World Bank, 1990, 2008b).

The economic theory of customs unions and the concepts of trade creation and trade diversion were explained in Chapter 4. I suggested in that chapter that the CAP probably led to substantial trade diversion but noted also that the negative effects of these changes in Europe have almost certainly been more than offset by trade creation in other sectors along with the positive dynamic effects of regional economic integration. Tables 7.1 and 7.2 include evidence that supports the notion that the CAP led to considerable trade diversion in agriculture and this phenomenon is surely one of the more significant effects of the EU's agricultural policy. Trade diversion can lower welfare both for countries forming the customs union and for those outside it that see their exports fall. In the case of the EU, the external losses were incurred primarily by wealthy countries such as the United States, Canada, New Zealand, or Australia as these were the main export suppliers to Western Europe. Some developing countries may also have experienced agricultural export declines as the internal EU market became more fully unified. On the other hand, there are several ways in which at least some developing countries may have bene-fitted from European integration.

Eric Hobsbawm (1989) characterized the period from 1875 to 1914 as "The Age of Empire" and argued that "[i]n the course of the nineteenth century a few countries—mostly those bordering on the northern Atlantic—conquered the rest of the non-European globe with ridiculous ease" (Hobsbawm, 1994, pp. 199–200). Germany lost its colonies following the First World War but the United Kingdom, France, Belgium, Spain, Portugal, and the Netherlands all maintained colonial empires until well into the twen-tieth century. After the Second World War, these empires began to be disman-tled although independence did not generally mean a complete rupture between the former colonies and the European countries that had controlled them. In addition to relatively generous foreign aid programs directed at all developing countries, the members of the EU have instituted various finan-cial, commercial, military, and political agreements that benefit their former colonies in particular.

The Treaty of Rome that established the EEC recognized that some of the member states had special relations with former colonies and that these relationships needed to be respected by the new economic community (European Commission, 2008c). An example of one such relationship was the support that the French Treasury provided for the West African Monetary Union (Chapter 1) but broader economic and commercial links between the former colonial powers and the newly independent states were common. Some ties were formalized by the Yaoundé (Cameroon) Conventions of the 1960s in which the members of the EEC granted preferential access to the European market for France's former colonies in Africa. In 1975, a new preferential trade agreement was signed in Lomé, Togo, the first of four Lomé Conventions involving the growing EU and a set of former colonies in Africa, the Caribbean, and the Pacific (ACP). The Yaoundé and Lomé Conventions gave the ACP countries greater access to EU markets by implementing less restrictive trade barriers than those in effect for non-ACP countries. Currently, economic relations between the ACP countries and the EU are regulated by the Cotonou (Benin) Agreement which was signed in 2000. The Cotonou Agreement is much broader than the earlier pacts, including provisions related to governance, poverty eradication and financial cooperation as well as preferential trade arrangements (European Commission, 2008c).

It is important to emphasize that these agreements are discriminatory favoring only those developing countries that have had special historic ties to the members of the EU. Brenton and Ikezuki (2005) find that, in general, preferential trade arrangements have very limited impacts on income in developing countries although the provisions of the Cotonou Agreement, particularly those related to sugar, may have brought significant benefits to a limited number of countries (see also Lal and Rashmi, 2005). EU sugar policy reforms in 2006 lowered internal prices reducing the economic benefits that developing countries with preferential access to the EU market had realized prior to the policy changes (Elbehri *et al.*, 2008). Other developing countries may have somewhat greater access to the EU market through the WTO generalized system of preferences but they still generally face higher trade barriers than the ACP countries.

This disparity led to a curious trade dispute over bananas between the EU and several Latin American countries backed by the United States. In 1993, the EU replaced individual national policies on banana imports with new union-wide arrangements that granted preferential market access to the ACP countries along with such overseas territories as Martinique and Guadalupe which are part of metropolitan France (CNN, 2001). Latin American countries have long dominated the world banana market and some of them filed a complaint against the new EU policy with the WTO because of its impact on their exports. They were joined by the United States which is home to some of the multinational firms that handle fruit exports from Latin America. The WTO dispute resolution panel agreed with the Latin American and U.S. arguments and ruled in 1999 that these countries could apply retaliatory tariffs against EU exports because the EU had not complied with the ruling (CNN, 2001). This conflict came up again in 2007 when Ecuador challenged the EU claim that a new tariff regime was in compliance with previous WTO banana rulings (*International Herald Tribune*, 2007).

In addition to the special treatment afforded the ACP countries, some developing countries may have benefitted indirectly from EU agricultural policy. Recall that the CAP has maintained internal prices for cereal grains such as maize, wheat, and barley at levels that are much higher than world prices. These cereal grains, maize in particular, are used for livestock feed as well as for human consumption. Livestock feed rations are commonly composed of grain, which provides carbohydrates for energy, and high-protein meals (cake) that are byproducts of processing soybeans and other oilseeds for vegetable oils. Earlier, I noted that the EU had agreed not to levy tariffs on imported oilseeds or oilseed products (oils and meal) in 1961. Duty-free entry into the

EU was also granted to such products as maize gluten (a relatively high-protein byproduct of the maize wet milling process that produces the starch used for ethanol and high-fructose maize syrup), other agricultural byproducts that can be fed to livestock, and cassava (manioc, tapioca) flour which is almost pure starch. Because maize gluten and cassava flour were not taxed upon entry into the EU, it was less costly to make a kind of reconstituted maize from the cheap maize gluten and cassava starch than it was to use the high-priced maize produced or imported by the EU. The cassava–maize gluten mixture was combined with cheap imported soybean meal to make low-cost livestock rations that contained only limited amounts of feed ingredients produced in the EU. EU support prices for feed grains have been lowered over the past 10 to 15 years and imports of these cereal substitutes have declined (FAOSTAT, http://faostat.fao.org/site/).

For developing countries such as Indonesia and Thailand, the increased EU demand for cassava pellets in the 1970s and 1980s represented an important market for one of their relatively low-value products. This example and the banana case discussed above illustrate the complexity of the highly integrated global food system. They also show how trade barriers can have unintended consequences in the countries applying them. For many years, EU policy makers sought to undo their earlier agreement not to erect trade barriers on soybeans and cereal substitutes, arguing that these low-cost products were undermining EU grain markets, which, of course, they were. A similar situation exists in the United States where the application of trade barriers on sugar imports has resulted in high prices that make it economically advantageous to replace sugar in manufactured food products and soft drinks with high-fructose maize syrup, the production of which contributes to the supply of maize gluten that can be sold to European feed compounders to be mixed with Asian cassava and Brazilian soybean meal and fed to EU chickens and hogs.

If the CAP were eliminated, the market for Indonesian and Thai cassava pellets would decline further and that could affect farm incomes in those countries. Of course, the high price supports for grain were intended to increase farm incomes in the EU not to generate an economic windfall for cassava producers and processors in Asia. Elimination of the CAP would also mean that the preferential arrangements in the Cotonou Agreement related to agriculture would disappear. The effect of this preference erosion would probably be small, however, as most analysts find that trade preferences have limited impacts on incomes and poverty in developing countries. The broadest effect of the CAP is to lower world food prices which may be of benefit to consumers in low-income countries, many of which rely on imports to achieve food security. As noted previously, however, it would be much more efficient to transfer financial resources directly to developing countries to protect against food shortfalls than to implement policies that raise producer prices in the EU to induce European farmers to produce surpluses that can be dumped on the world market to lower world food prices.

In addition to studies cited in previous chapters, several analysts have tried to identify the particular effects of the CAP on world agricultural markets. Winters (2005) analyzes the implications of complete elimination of the CAP while all agricultural policies in countries outside the EU are left in place. The results suggest relatively modest increases in world prices for most food and agricultural products as compared to a baseline representing the situation in 2005 with no policy changes beyond those specified in the AA. The largest predicted price increase is for oilseeds at 4.3 percent above the baseline. The impact of EU agricultural policy reform on broader economic indicators in developing countries is also predicted to be small. The results show that while some developing countries would experience reduced poverty as a result of the elimination of the CAP, others would suffer increases in poverty because of the higher food prices (Winters, 2005). Other analysts also predict only minor changes in such variables as global GDP, trade and world prices as a result of agricultural policy reform in the EU (Fabiosa *et al.*, 2005; Bascou *et al.*, 2006; Oxford Economic Forecasting, 2006).

Within the EU itself, the effects of the CAP have been much more substantial. It has been estimated that EU consumers face food prices that are 23 percent higher than world prices as a result of the EU policies (Oxford Economic Forecasting, 2006). Studies of the impact of particular policy reforms often find only modest effects within the EU but this may be due in part to the fact that incremental changes are being compared to a status quo that includes a great many existing market distortions. For example, Bascou *et al.* (2006) analyze the impact of the 2003 policy reforms by predicting the evolution of agricultural prices, incomes, production, and trade with the reforms in place as compared to predictions based on the pre-existing Agenda 2000 policies. Analysis of policy changes of this nature may not reveal sizeable impacts on European agriculture. Even in studies that test the effects of complete elimination of the CAP, the effects are less severe within the EU than one might expect. Winters (2005) points out that agriculture represents only about 3 percent of the EU economy so even complete elimination of the CAP has only a small impact on poverty and income in the EU.

On the other hand, the effect of policy reform on EU agricultural producers would be substantially more dramatic. Anderson *et al.* (2006a) predict that agricultural output in the EU would decline by 12.3 percent relative to baseline projections by 2015 if all countries in the world including the EU reformed their trade policies to eliminate all trade distortions in markets for manufactured and agricultural goods. They also predict that farm employment and land prices in the EU would fall. Beghin and Aksoy (2003) find that broad agricultural trade liberalization would adversely affect EU producers of cotton, dairy products, and sugar while benefitting EU consumers of sugar and dairy products. The effects of policy reforms on cereal grains, oilseeds, and beef are more modest but also exhibit economic losses for producers and gains for consumers. Such results are consistent with Tracy's (1989) observation that much of European agriculture has not been internationally competitive since the end of the nineteenth century. The trade barriers and domestic subsidies that have protected EU agricultural sectors from foreign competition have resulted in a costly system that rewards producers at the expense of consumers and taxpayers. As in the United States, the EU subsidies flow disproportionately to large farms and agribusinesses as well as to some rather more unexpected individuals such as Queen Elizabeth II (Spiegel Online, 2006). Although the elimination of agricultural subsidies would cause serious disruption of the EU food system, most analyses show that the gains by consumers and taxpayers would be greater than the losses to producers.

As in the case of the United States, EU farm subsidies persist despite their obvious social costs in part because of the ability of farm organizations to form effective political groups to lobby for favorable treatment. The analysis of these activities is more complicated in the EU than in the United States, however, because political influence has to be exercised at both the national and union levels. There have been numerous analyses in which the authors characterize decision making on EU agricultural policy as a two-level strategic game in which politicians, bureaucrats, and voters first reach a national consensus and then conduct negotiations at the union level on the basis of these national positions to reach the final policy decision (Mahé and Roe, 1996; Olper, 1998; Pokrivcak and Swinnen, 2003). This complicated bargaining process appears to give rise to an inherent bias in favor of increasing the level of producer support, a bias that may stem from the same forces that led to the initially high support prices when the CAP was originally established. The bargain that was struck then set support prices high enough to prevent farm incomes from falling in any of the member countries even those with unproductive agricultural sectors. Likewise, the subsequent policy compromises have tended to result in higher prices that please farm interests in all member states rather than lower support levels that would be opposed by at least some of the countries.

There is some evidence that agricultural protection is greater in countries that have less competitive agricultural sectors internationally and this may be true for the EU as well. Olper (1998) shows that agricultural protectionism is higher in EU countries with uncompetitive agricultural sectors and that support prices rise when world market conditions are unfavorable for particular agricultural industries. Other analysts note the structure of EU institutions as a source of bias in agricultural support. Henning (2004) suggests that the Council of Agricultural Ministers, the body that makes decisions on agricultural policy, will always adopt higher levels of protection because of the requirement that decisions be unanimous. This voting rule means that the member state with the least competitive agricultural sector can veto any decision that does not support prices at levels that are satisfactory to its farmers. The other countries are likely to go along with these support levels because they generate windfall gains for farmers in their countries and this result generally leads to greater political support from the minister's agricultural constituents.

Of course, the willingness of politicians to promote policies that favor the economic interests of farmers is as puzzling in the EU as it is in the United States given that in both regions farmers make up only a small part of the population. As noted earlier, the general public in Europe seems highly supportive of agriculture. Part of this support stems from the close connections that still exist between urban residents and their rural ancestors. In addition, Europeans seem to have a very different attitude toward food than is found in the United States. It was Europeans after all who initiated the international slow-food movement in an effort to counteract that American icon of globalization, the fast-food restaurant (Slow Food, 2008). The conflict between the EU and the United States over genetically modified organisms (GMO) and the use of hormones in livestock production was described in Chapter 4. While most Americans appear to be indifferent to the inclusion of GMO in their food, the majority of Europeans see such products as morally problematic and risky (Eurobarometer, 2006). These attitudes make it politically acceptable to most Europeans to support more traditional agricultural systems even if such support leads to higher food prices. Many Europeans worry that the industrialization of agriculture as seen in the United States would eventually lead to poor quality food that may even be a danger to human health. From this perspective, the CAP helps to protect a desirable food system rather than the narrow economic interests of farm and agribusinesses lobbyists.

As noted previously, however, European interests in farming and food systems have widened to include such issues as food safety and environmental sustainability (see Ansell and Vogel, 2006). Ironically, there appear to have been more food safety problems in the EU than in the United States, the country with the most industrialized food system in the world. The most dramatic incident was the outbreak of bovine spongiform encephalopathy (BSE or mad-cow disease). BSE is a disease that is clearly the product of a highly industrialized food system that uses all parts of slaughtered animals in one way or another. Compared to the 185,000 cases of BSE that had been confirmed in the United Kingdom by the end of 2007, the three cases detected in U.S. cattle seem pretty insignificant (CDC, 2008). In any case, European consumers and environmentalists clearly have a growing influence on the direction of agricultural policy in the EU and the 2003 CAP reform appears to mark a much more substantial revision of traditional farm policies than has ever been achieved in the United States. The CAP is far from being a fully decoupled food safety and sustainability policy but movements in that direction appear to be gaining strength.

As with U.S. agricultural policy, the internal impacts of the CAP are probably greater than its effects on other countries. For the most part, external effects have fallen most heavily on high-income countries with the impact on developing countries being mixed. The special arrangements between the EU and the ACP countries and the lowered food prices faced by low-income food importers have probably been of some benefit to particular developing countries. At the same time, these benefits are at least partly offset by the damage the CAP has done to agricultural exporters in low-income countries that are not party to the Cotonou Agreement. Some ACP countries may also have been harmed by EU policies on such commodities as cotton, for example. Elimination of the CAP would no doubt have mixed impacts on developing countries but as Winters (2005) and others have concluded, such a change would generally be of great benefit to the EU itself and to the world as a whole. In the next chapter, we will examine the experience of two countries (Australia and New Zealand) that have eliminated their agricultural policies in contrast to two others (Japan and Korea) that most definitely have not.

Appendix 7.1: Green Currencies and the Re-Nationalization of the CAP

Recall that the CAP was supposed to replace the national agricultural policies that had resulted in different agricultural prices in the member states with a set of common policies that would lead to uniform prices. The mechanism put in place to accomplish this objective was the set of policy prices described earlier, most importantly, the politically determined target price from which the other policy prices were derived. Of course prices are expressed in terms of some currency and prior to 1999 when the euro was adopted as a common currency in 13 of the EU member states, most of the countries had different national currencies (Belgium and Luxembourg used the same currency). It would have been possible for policy makers to set the target price in German marks, for example, and then use prevailing exchange rates to translate that price into the various national currencies. That, however, was not the procedure adopted in the early years of the CAP. Instead, a basket of the member-state currencies was used to determine an accounting unit, policy prices were set in terms of this accounting unit and exchange rates between the accounting unit and national currencies were used to express the support prices in the various national currencies (see Harris *et al.*, 1983).

The accounting unit eventually became known as the European Currency Unit (ECU) and as with other currency baskets such as the special drawing rights (SDR) of the IMF was listed in exchange rate tables on financial pages even though these currencies are not normally used in standard market transactions. Suppose that the target price for wheat has been set at 100 ECU per metric ton. If the exchange rate between the French franc and the ECU is 0.20 (1 French franc equals 0.20 ECU or 1 ECU equals 5 French francs), the target price in France would be 500 francs per metric ton. Similar calculations would be done in the other countries to express the target price in national currencies. Such a system works fine as long as the exchange rates between the national currencies do not change. Suppose that the exchange rate between the German mark and the ECU is 4 marks equal to 1 ECU (1 mark equals 0.25 ECU). This implies that the exchange rate between the mark and the franc is 1 mark equals 1.25 francs. In Germany, the target price is 400 marks which is the same as the French price at the market exchange rate (if 1 mark equals 1.25 francs, then 400 marks equal 500 francs).

In the 1960s, the Bretton-Woods monetary system of exchange rates pegged to the U.S. dollar with the dollar backed by a fixed amount of gold (1/35th of an ounce) was still in effect. Under this system, exchange rates were fixed but could be adjusted in light of economic conditions. In 1968, France devalued the French franc against all other currencies including the mark and the accounting unit which we will refer to as the ECU, although that currency unit was actually created somewhat later. Suppose that the devaluation lowered the value of the franc to 0.1818 ECU (1 ECU equal to 5.5 francs). The devaluation would mean that the target price for wheat in France would automatically increase to 550 francs per metric ton. Because the devaluation was triggered by higher inflation in France than in its trading partners, the last thing the government wanted was an automatic increase in food prices. As a consequence, France was allowed to continue using the old exchange rate for agricultural policy prices. Subsequently, Germany elected to revalue the mark which would lead to an automatic lowering of the agricultural prices in Germany. Suppose that the mark was revalued to be equal to 0.2667 ECU (1 ECU equals 3.75 marks). That would mean the target price of 100 ECU per metric ton would become 375 marks instead of the original 400. As in France, this was seen as undesirable so Germany continued to use the old exchange rate for its agricultural prices as well.

These events mark the origin of what became known as "green" exchange rates.[5] As the parities between the various national currencies adjusted, the EU

---

[5]   Harris *et al.* (1983) and Akrill (2000) provide useful accounts of the origin and history of green currencies.

ended up with two exchange rate systems, one for agriculture and the other for everything else. The problem with this system is that there are common prices in terms of the green rates but not in terms of the market exchange rate. The market exchange rate between francs and marks given the assumptions in the preceding paragraph is 1 mark equals 1.4667 francs (1 franc equals 0.6818 mark). If the prices for wheat in France and Germany are equal to the target price computed at the green exchange rates (1 ECU equals 4 marks and 5 francs), they will be 500 francs and 400 marks, respectively. Under these conditions it would be possible to buy a ton of wheat in France for 500 francs, ship it to Germany where it would be sold for 400 marks. The 400 marks could then be taken to a bank and exchanged at the official rate for 586.68 francs (1.4667 multiplied by 400) for a profit of 86.68 francs. As more traders recognized the opportunity to arbitrage this price anomaly, more and more wheat would flow into the intervention agencies in Germany.

To prevent this outcome, a system of border taxes and subsidies known as monetary compensatory amounts (MCA) was adopted. The MCA had the effect of adjusting agricultural prices at the border so that they would be equal in the two countries in terms of the official exchange rate. Thus, in the preceding example, a tax of 86.68 francs would be applied to wheat being transferred from France to Germany to equalize the French and German wheat prices at the official exchange rate. German wheat exported to France would receive a subsidy to offset the price differential at the official exchange rates. This system solves the problems set in motion by the original exchange rate adjustments but completely violates the principles of a customs union. The MCAs are trade barriers that allow countries to differentiate their internal agricultural prices. In effect, Germany was able to maintain higher wheat prices than France through its exchange rate policies.

Of course, allowing prices to vary from one country to another also prevents the expected resource reallocation that was one of the reasons for establishing a customs union in the first place. The system of green currencies and MCAs made the CAP less common and more national. In 1999, however, the introduction of the euro rendered this agri-monetary system obsolete at least in the 15 countries that use the euro as their national currency (Bernstein, 1999). Vestiges of the old system still exist because the United Kingdom, Sweden, and Denmark have not joined the monetary union and still employ their national currencies. Aside from Slovenia, Malta, and Cyprus, the newer members of the EU are not members of the monetary union either but it does not appear that there has been any need to establish green currencies for these countries.

8

Agricultural Policy on the Pacific Rim: Non-Trade Concerns versus Comparative Advantage

Introduction

The evidence presented in the two previous chapters supports the conclusion that eliminating U.S. and EU agricultural subsidies would be broadly beneficial for the world as a whole although the main benefits of agricultural policy reform in these countries would flow to their own citizens. The political realities in the United States and the EU suggest, however, that such reforms will not be easy to accomplish. In both the Uruguay and Doha Rounds of trade talks at the WTO, agriculture has been the most difficult dossier to negotiate and the collapse of the Doha negotiations in July, 2008 was caused by differences over agricultural subsidies between some developing countries and the United States and the EU. There is little evidence of substantial efforts on the part of policy makers in the OECD countries to dismantle government farm programs despite the fact that farm prices in 2008 reached record levels. U.S. farm legislation adopted in 2008 maintains virtually all of the programs that were included in the 2002 Farm Bill and extends support to producers of horticultural crops who have not received subsidies in the past. Charter predicted that EU agriculture ministers would be unable to agree on significant CAP reforms in 2008 noting that representatives from France and Germany were arguing for continued farm subsidies to insure that farms would remain profitable at a time when food shortages and high food prices showed that the world needed all the farmers it could get. While there will be some reduction in the amount of subsidies received by U.S. and EU farmers as long as farm prices remain high, taxpayers and consumers in those countries seem likely to continue facing significant costs for agricultural support.

One explanation for the difficulty of reforming agricultural policies is that countries with internationally uncompetitive agricultural industries may be reluctant to undertake agricultural policy reforms that would lead to significant

Table 8.1   Percentage PSE* for OECD members, selected years

Country or region	1986	1990	1995	2000	2005	2007
Australia	11	10	6	4	4	6
Canada	38	33	19	19	22	18
EU	42	32	36	34	32	26
Iceland	75	76	62	63	70	61
Japan	65	52	62	59	51	45
Korea	65	74	72	66	62	60
Mexico	3	16	−5	23	13	14
New Zealand	20	2	2	0	1	1
Norway	71	71	65	66	67	53
Switzerland	77	73	65	69	68	50
Turkey	15	21	13	20	25	21
United States	24	17	10	24	15	10
OECD	39	32	31	32	28	23

* The percentage PSE is calculated as the monetary value of a country's PSE divided by the value of farm production at the farm gate plus total budgetary payments. Budgetary payments are the part of the PSE that is not accounted for by market price support.
Source: OECD, 2008c.

and politically unpopular economic adjustment of their farm sectors (see Olper, 1998). Table 8.1 contains indicators of the level of support for agriculture in all of the OECD countries. This measure is calculated as the producer support estimate (PSE) divided by farm income from agriculture defined as the value of agricultural production at the farm gate plus direct payments to farmers from the government budget. The most striking revelation in this table is the extremely low levels of producer support in Australia and New Zealand. In contrast, producer support in Iceland, Switzerland, Norway, and Korea accounts for more than half of farm income. The United States, Canada, the EU, Mexico, and Turkey seem to occupy intermediate positions. It is worth noting that the effects of rising world food prices are apparent in the lower percentage PSE values in 2007. For the OECD as a whole, producer support generally accounted for about 30 percent of farm income prior to 2005. The proportion recorded for 2007 (23 percent) is the lowest recorded between 1986 and 2007. In 2005, the percentage PSE for Brazil, China, Russia, South Africa, and Ukraine, computed in more or less the same manner as for the OECD countries, ranged from 6 percent to 15 percent placing these countries at the lower end of the support spectrum (OECD, 2008c).

Australia, New Zealand, Canada, Brazil, and South Africa are members of the Cairns Group, a 19-nation coalition of agricultural exporters (The Cairns

Group, 2008). In the language of economics, these countries have comparative advantages in such widely traded agricultural commodities as cereal grains, oilseeds, and livestock products.[1] In a world of free trade, countries would end up specializing in the production of goods for which they have comparative advantages, exchanging with other countries the portion of the goods that remains when domestic consumption is satisfied for goods in which they have a comparative disadvantage. Trade barriers are implemented to raise the price of foreign goods so that the domestic industry with higher relative costs of production is able to compete in its domestic market with firms located in countries having a comparative advantage in that good. It can be inferred from the data in Table 8.1 that the countries with the highest agricultural support levels do not have comparative advantages in the main agricultural commodities that are traded internationally. This is not surprising given that two of them are located close to the Arctic Circle and the other three are extremely mountainous. Because agriculture is a land-intensive industry (see Appendix 4.1), the relative scarcity of good agricultural land in these five countries suggests that they are high-cost agricultural producers. Policy reform that would lower the protection afforded to their farm industries could lead to very severe declines in their agricultural sectors although the gains to their taxpayers and consumers would outweigh these losses.

For countries that do have a comparative advantage in agricultural commodities as a result of abundant arable land among other factors, agricultural trade liberalization would lead to growth of their agricultural sectors. This is particularly true if all countries liberalize their agricultural trade regimes but it may also be true even if only the countries with a comparative advantage in agriculture do so. Such has been the experience of Australia and New Zealand, two countries with relatively extensive endowments of agricultural land, which dramatically reformed their agricultural policies in the 1980s. On the other hand, many of the countries that do not have a comparative advantage in agricultural goods have resisted changes to their policies because of non-economic concerns that they believe override the efficiency gains that would follow trade liberalization. Japanese and Korean officials argue that protecting their rice producers from foreign competition is essential for achieving food security in a world where wars, natural catastrophes, and political conflicts could cut off foreign supplies. In the next section of this chapter, Japanese and Korean agricultural policies are described and arguments about food security, multifunctionality, and other non-economic issues are addressed. This is

---

[1]   See Appendix 4.1 for a brief explanation of comparative advantage. For more detailed accounts, the reader is referred to any international trade textbook (e.g., Krugman and Obstfeld, 2000).

followed by an assessment of the Australian and New Zealand experiences with radical policy reform.

Japan and Korea

It has been noted on several occasions that Japanese farm policies rely heavily on trade barriers (market price support), particularly for its most important agricultural commodity, rice. The same can be said for Korea. Based on OECD data used in computing market price support in Japan and Korea, internal rice prices in 2007 were more than three times the world reference price and in 2000 they were six to seven times the world price. Although rice is the most protected commodity in these countries, there are many others that also receive relatively high levels of protection. Japanese beef prices were more than 38 percent higher than the world reference price in 2007, for example (OECD, 2008c). It is important to point out, however, that both Japan and Korea are major food importers that are highly dependent on world markets for much of their food supplies. With a population of about 128 million, Japan imported agricultural products worth $68.9 billion in 2007, an amount surpassed only by the value of agricultural imports by the United States (population over 300 million) and the EU (population almost 500 million). Korea imported agricultural goods worth $21.9 billion making it the seventh largest agricultural importer in the world in 2007 (WTO, 2008). Because Japan exports relatively few agricultural products ($7.6 billion in 2007), it is the world's largest net agricultural importer (with net imports defined as the value of agricultural imports minus the value of agricultural exports).

Many Japanese writers point to the high dependence on imported food in their country as justification for policies designed to assure self-sufficiency in rice, a staple food that occupies a very special place in Japanese households. Food self-sufficiency means that all of the food consumed in a country comes from that country's own production. For most countries, food security, defined as the availability of adequate food supplies from some combination of domestic production and imports, is a much more important objective than food self-sufficiency. Many analysts in Japan and Korea, however, see low and declining levels of food self-sufficiency as serious problems (Egaitsu, 1992; Yamaji and Ito, 1993; Kako, 2000; Honma, 2006). In the case of rice, the desire for self-sufficiency is bound up with broader perceptions of the significance of this food and the role that it plays in people's cultural and spiritual lives. Ohnuki-Tierney (2004) highlights Japanese traditions that draw on rice images to define what it means to be Japanese. She argues that people in Japan see rice as central to the foundation of Japanese civilization and as a symbol of beauty, peace, the human soul, and the divine. Moreover, foreign rice that would appear indistinguishable from Japanese rice to most observers is widely considered by Japanese consumers to be impure. The perception of rice as a cultural icon is common throughout Asia where most people see it as something other than just another commodity to be bought and sold at the most advantageous prices on global markets (Sombilla and Hossain, 2000).[2]

In a series of influential works written between 1938 and 1957, Karl Wittfogel put forth the idea that Asian civilizations had developed into authoritarian regimes because of the ecological setting that they confronted. These "hydraulic societies" relied on irrigated rice which required centralized agencies to manage the distribution and use of water resources. This need for centralized coordination gave rise to Wittfogel's "oriental despotism" (Wittfogel, 1981; see also Worster, 1985). Similar ecological arguments have been made to support the contention that irrigated rice cultivation gave rise to the institutions that govern Japan today (Imamura, Tsuboi and Odagiri; Yamaji and Ito, 1993). Imamura *et al.* argue that Japanese society is based on organizations that have their roots in the types of irrigation systems developed after the sixteenth century. To have access to water, farmers had to belong to organizations and this tendency to coordinate economic and social interaction through groups has been carried over into other aspects of Japanese life. In addition, the need for centralized control has meant that Japanese governments have a long history of involvement in the production and distribution of rice and other agricultural goods (Yamaji and Ito, 1993). The Liberal Democratic Party (LDP), which has dominated Japanese politics since its founding in 1955, has strong ties to rural areas which have often provided its margin of victory (Davis, 2003).

Japan and Korea share many common features. Both countries are mountainous with limited amounts of farmland. The average amount of arable land per farmer is less than 1 hectare in Korea and only 1.8 hectares in Japan in contrast to more than 22 hectares in France and Denmark and 60 hectares in the United States (Kim and Lee, 2006). Because of their geographic situation, it would be relatively easy for a hostile power to use a naval blockade to cut off foreign food supplies. Although Korea is located on a peninsula connected to the Asian mainland, access to the rest of the continent has been blocked since the 1950s by its relatively unfriendly neighbor to the north. Kako (2000) worries that Japan and Korea could experience food crises as a result of

---

[2]   The favored rice in Japan and Korea is high-quality japonica, a short-grained rice that tends to stick together after cooking. Long-grained indica rice is more widely grown than japonica although japonica varieties are cultivated fairly extensively in other parts of Asia, California, and Australia (FAO, no date).

military conflicts, political strife, economic blockades, or natural disasters. Many in Japan point to the 1973 U.S. embargo on soybean exports as an example of the unreliability of world food markets (Yoshioka, 1992; Kako, 2000).[3] The worldwide rice shortages and high food prices in 2008 have undoubtedly reinforced these perceptions. The sense that their countries are particularly vulnerable to unpredictable foreign events strengthens the desire to avoid becoming dependent on external sources for something as important and central to people's lives as rice.

Japan and Korea both undertook land reforms in the aftermath of the Second World War that resulted in numerous small farms. In Japan, these small farms have had to rely on off-farm income and there are a great many part-time farmers there while in Korea, most farmers work full time on their farms (Kim and Lee, 2006). Because they rely on farming for most of their household income, Korean farmers are poorer than their Japanese counterparts who have off-farm income to supplement their agricultural earnings. Honma (2006) reports that only about 13 percent of farm household income in Japan comes from farming activities while rural households in Korea obtain about two-thirds of their income from farming. Korean farm household income was only 73 percent of urban household income in 2002 while in Japan farm household income was 24 percent greater than average urban household income (Kim and Lee, 2006). As in Europe and the United States, the Japanese and Korean farm populations are aging with well over half of Japan's farmers over 60 years of age and 60 percent of Korean farmers over 50 (OECD, 1995; Korea. net). Most farmers in Japan and Korea grow at least some rice and Schuman (2005) documents similar demographic trends among rice farmers in the two countries.

Although Japanese and Korean rice policies have been particularly contentious in debates about international agricultural trade both within the WTO and in the context of bilateral trade relations with other countries, there have been conflicts over other agricultural goods as well. In 2007, support for rice farmers accounted for 36 percent of Japan's market price support and 30 percent of its PSE. For Korea, the corresponding figures were 26 percent of

---

[3]   The 1973 embargo on U.S. soybeans, soybean products, cottonseed, and cottonseed products was initiated by the Nixon administration because of shortages of high-protein meals used in livestock feed as a result of a decline in the amount of fish meal that was available (ERS, 1986). The United States also restricted grain exports in 1974 and 1975 when grain prices reached high levels at a time when the United States was experiencing the first effects of what would come to be known as stagflation. In 1980, the U.S. government responded to the Soviet Union's invasion of Afghanistan with trade sanctions that included a partial embargo on its growing exports of grain, oilseeds, and other agricultural products to the USSR (see ERS, 1986).

market price support and 24 percent of the PSE (OECD, 2008c). Other commodities that receive support in both countries include livestock products (beef, pork, poultry, milk, and eggs), other grains and oilseeds (wheat, barley, soybeans), and various fruits and vegetables. A significant conflict between Japan and the United States over Japanese policies on beef, citrus, and other food imports flared up in the 1970s. Japanese policies for these products were based on import quotas that limited the amounts of foreign goods that could be sold in Japan. In 1986, after prolonged discussions, the United States filed a complaint about quotas on a set of 12 commodities with the GATT. Beef and citrus products were not included in this initial filing which resulted in a 1987 judgment that most of the Japanese quotas on these items did not conform to GATT trade rules (Davis, 2003). In 1988, the United States filed another complaint with the GATT, this time aimed at Japanese quotas on beef and citrus imports. The Japanese government elected to negotiate a settlement to this dispute before the GATT panel issued its final ruling (Davis, 2003).

The elimination of the quotas reduced the level of protection significantly. Davis (2003) reports that Japanese beef imports grew 130 percent between 1988 and 1996 and imports of milk, tomato juice, and apple juice grew even more rapidly in the aftermath of the policy shift. Korea also restricted imports of a wide range of products through a system of import licenses until the late 1980s when many of these import quotas were phased out (ERS, 2008f). Both countries maintained de facto bans on rice imports until the adoption of the AA which stipulated that countries with high levels of protection would have to agree to some "minimum access" for the protected commodities. In Japan, the minimum access for rice was set at 4 percent of domestic consumption in 1995 rising to 8 percent by 2000 (Davis, 2003). Korea's Uruguay Round commitment on rice was a minimum access of 1 percent of consumption in the reference years of 1988 to 1990 with the expectation that this would increase to 4 percent by 2004 (ERS, 2008f). Japan had frequently imported rice from Korea and Taiwan before the Second World War and on two occasions during the post-war period (1984 and 1993), bad harvests forced the government to allow some rice to be imported (Meyerson, 2003). It took Korea somewhat longer to achieve rice self-sufficiency but aside from some emergency rice imports in 1980 as a result of poor harvests, Korea has been largely self-sufficient since the late 1970s (ERS, 2008f).

Tables 8.2 through 8.5 include OECD estimates of Japanese and Korean support. In both countries, market price support accounts for most of the PSE, ranging from 85 to almost 100 percent. The burden of agricultural policy in both Korea and Japan falls more heavily on consumers than taxpayers as shown at the bottom of Tables 8.2 and 8.4. GSSE are relatively modest in both countries accounting for only about 22 percent and 15 percent of the 2007

Table 8.2   Japanese agricultural support estimates, selected years (billions of current yen)

	1986	1995	2000	2005	2007
Value of production (farm gate)	**11,171**	**10,388**	**9,130**	**8,489**	**8,504**
Producer support estimate (PSE)	**7,726**	**6,841**	**5,804**	**4,908**	**4,149**
PSE/Value of production (%)	*65*	*62*	*59*	*54*	*45*
Market price support	6,973	6,228	5,169	4,338	3,533
Direct payments	753	613	635	570	616
General services support estimate (GSSE)	**1,164**	**2,314**	**1,451**	**1,044**	**1,187**
Research and development	41	83	78	93	93
Agricultural schools	31	29	26	12	38
Inspection services	8	10	8	10	10
Infrastructure	1,004	2,085	1,241	883	981
Marketing and promotion	23	27	29	24	21
Public stockholding	37	60	44	24	19
Miscellaneous	20	21	24	0	26
Consumer support estimate (CSE)	**−9,013**	**−8,778**	**−6,689**	**−5,725**	**−4,642**
Consumer transfers to producers	−6,706	−6,137	−5,168	−4,337	−3,532
Other transfers from consumers	−2,322	−2,664	−1,532	−1,396	−1,114
Taxpayer transfers to consumers	−14	26	6	4	2
Excess feed cost	29	−3	6	4	2
Total support estimate (TSE)	**8,877**	**9,182**	**7,261**	**5,956**	**5,338**
Transfers from consumers	9,028	8,801	6,701	5,733	4,646
Transfers from taxpayers	2,171	3,045	2,093	1,619	1,806
Budget revenues	−2,322	−2,664	−1,532	−1,396	−1,114

Source: OECD, 2008c.

total support estimates (TSE) for Japan and Korea, respectively. Recall that general services support for the United States made up 42 percent of the U.S. TSE in 2007 but accounted for less than 11 percent of the EU TSE in that year. In Japan, PSE has fallen since 1986 both in absolute terms (Table 8.3) and as a percentage of the value of farm income (Table 8.2). Korean support has increased since 1986 but appears to have leveled off since 2004 (Table 8.4).

Table 8.3   Japanese agricultural support estimates, 1986–2007 (billions of current yen)*

	TSE	PSE	PSE (MPS)	PSE (budget)	GSSE	CSE	MPS/PSE (%)
1986	8,877	7,726	6,965	761	1,164	−9,013	90.2
1990	7,578	6,190	5,534	656	1,361	−7,741	89.4
1995	9,182	6,841	6,228	619	2,314	−8,778	91.0
2000	7,261	5,804	5,169	635	1,451	−6,689	89.1
2001	6,816	5,376	4,722	654	1,433	−6,194	87.8
2002	6,931	5,511	4,862	649	1,414	−6,489	88.2
2003	6,904	5,462	4,819	643	1,438	−6,712	88.2
2004	6,352	5,191	4,611	580	1,156	−6,107	88.8
2005	5,956	4,908	4,338	570	1,044	−5,725	88.4
2006	5,547	4,566	4,163	403	979	−5,393	91.2
2007	5,338	4,149	3,533	616	1,187	−4,642	85.2

* TSE (total support estimate), PSE (producer support estimate), GSSE (general services support estimate), CSE (consumer support estimate). PSE is divided into market price support (MPS) which comes from consumers through higher prices resulting from trade barriers and commodity programs financed through the government budget (see Chapter 5). The last column shows the share of producer support resulting from trade barriers (MPS/PSE).
Source: OECD, 2008c.

It is worth pointing out that the Japanese PSE in 2007 amounted to $35 billion compared to net agricultural imports that year of $61.3 billion. For Korea, the PSE was over $25 billion which is larger than the value of Korea's net agricultural imports of $15.6 billion (imports of $21.9 billion minus exports of $6.3 billion; WTO, 2008).

The high levels of producer support in Japan and Korea are frequently justified as necessary to insure food security, with food security defined as self-sufficiency in some or all important food products. From this perspective increasing dependency on imported food is seen as a problem even if a particular nation is rich enough to be able to assure adequate food supplies through its own domestic production and trade (Egaitsu, 1992; Yamaji and Ito, 1993; Kako, 2000). Many analysts question the conflation of food security and food self-sufficiency (Wailes, Young and Cramer, 1993; Hayami, 2000; Honma, 2006). Food security in low-income countries may be threatened by supply interruptions due to political or military conflict, instability resulting from cyclical weather variations or broader shortages resulting from environmental degradation or increasing demand from rapidly growing middle-income countries. Many of these factors contributed to the 2008 rise in food prices.

Table 8.4   Korea agricultural support estimates, selected years (millions of current KRW)

	1986	1995	2000	2005	2007
Value of production (farm gate)	**12,660**	**25,855**	**31,829**	**35,995**	**37,396**
Producer support estimate (PSE)	**8,290**	**19,361**	**21,728**	**24,096**	**23,665**
PSE/Value of production (%)	*65*	*72*	*66*	*62*	*60*
Market price support	8,246	18,325	20,776	21,394	21,517
Direct payments	44	1,036	952	2,702	2.148
General services support estimate (GSSE)	**666**	**2,355**	**3,101**	**3,260**	**3,467**
Research and development	47	286	254	575	453
Agricultural schools	4	43	45	80	73
Inspection services	18	61	118	126	147
Infrastructure	314	1,595	2,162	1,839	1,822
Marketing and promotion	0	5	24	42	43
Public stockholding	283	364	497	599	929
Consumer support estimate (CSE)	**−8,287**	**−21,893**	**−22,678**	**−26,571**	**−29,219**
Consumer transfers to producers	−8,122	−18,317	−20,171	−21,394	−21,515
Other transfers from consumers	−221	−3,893	−2,609	−5,255	−7,812
Taxpayer transfers to consumers	55	317	102	79	109
Total support estimate (TSE)	**9,011**	**22,032**	**24,931**	**27,435**	**27,240**
Transfers from consumers	8,343	22,210	22,780	26,649	29,328
Transfers from taxpayers	890	3,715	4,760	6,041	5,725
Budget revenues	−221	−3,893	−2,610	−5,255	−7,812

Source: OECD, 2008c.

None of these dangers, however, appears to be a serious threat to food security in wealthy countries such as Japan and Korea. Hayami (2000) suggests that, to the extent that there is a potential for food shortages in these countries, the best policy would be to establish stable international relationships, food stocks and other protective measures not dependent on expensive subsidies to unproductive domestic agricultural enterprises. Food self-sufficiency is not necessary for food security and even countries with a comparative advantage in some agricultural goods find it economically beneficial to be able to import part of their food supplies.

Table 8.5   Korea agricultural support estimates, 1986–2007 (millions of current KRW)*

	TSE	PSE	PSE (MPS)	PSE (budget)	GSSE	CSE	MPS/ PSE (%)
1986	9,011	8,290	8,246	44	666	−8,287	99.5
1990	15,470	13,569	13,050	519	1,819	−13,582	96.2
1995	22,0392	19,361	18,325	1,036	2,355	−21,893	94.6
2000	24,931	21,728	20,776	952	3,101	−22,678	95.6
2001	23,895	20,453	19,216	1,237	3,313	−21,032	94.0
2002	25,357	21,747	20,249	1,498	3,498	−25,757	93.1
2003	24,585	20,492	18,737	1,755	3,793	−25,476	91.4
2004	26,697	23,445	21,901	1,544	3,155	−24,317	93.4
2005	27,435	24,096	21,394	2,702	3,260	−26,571	88.8
2006	27,359	24,064	21,746	2,318	3,200	−28,884	90.4
2007	27,240	23,665	21,517	2,148	3,467	−29,219	90.9

* TSE (total support estimate), PSE (producer support estimate), GSSE (general services support estimate), CSE (consumer support estimate). PSE is divided into market price support (MPS) which comes from consumers through higher prices resulting from trade barriers and commodity programs financed through the government budget (see Chapter 5). The last column shows the share of producer support resulting from trade barriers (MPS/PSE).
Source: OECD, 2008c.

Some analysts justify food self-sufficiency as a way to increase market stability. In fact, it is likely that world markets will exhibit greater price stability than would be the case in self-sufficient national markets. Weather-related supply disruptions occur frequently within a single country but almost never at the same time in all parts of the world. It appears that there has been greater market variability on Japanese rice markets than has occurred on the world market even though the world rice market is relatively thin[4] compared to the markets for other commodities (Wailes, Young and Cramer, 1993). Japanese rice production is also highly dependent on imported inputs, notably fertilizers, fuels, and other agricultural chemicals derived from petroleum products. Achieving self-sufficiency in rice has increased Japan's dependency on foreign countries for supplies of these inputs which, of course, could just

---

[4]   Thin markets are those in which a relatively small quantity is exchanged relative to the amounts produced and consumed. Such markets often experience great price variability because small changes in the amounts produced or consumed may have significant effects on the relatively small quantities traded.

as easily be cut off in a time of conflict as rice and other foodstuffs (Wailes, Young and Cramer, 1993). In addition, diversion of resources from other economic activities to relatively unproductive agricultural industries reduces overall economic growth. Stockbridge (2006) found that the effort to achieve food self-sufficiency in Korea slowed general economic growth and this negative impact became more pronounced over time. Beghin, Bureau and Park (2003) determined that Korean agricultural policy generates large economic losses with each won (in 2008, US$1.00 equaled about 975 won; 1 euro equaled 1,584 won) transferred to farmers costing consumers and taxpayers about 1.6 won.

In addition to food security, Korean and Japanese representatives often draw attention to other non-economic concerns as justification for their high levels of producer support. In international trade negotiations, for example, Korean delegates argue for inclusion of safeguards for small farms, the rural countryside, and rural economic viability (Lim, 2005). "Non-trade concerns," including environmental protection, rural development, poverty alleviation and food security among others, have become an important issue at the WTO where the negotiating framework for the Doha trade talks requires that they be taken into account (WTO, 2008e). Japanese and Korean negotiators have joined their counterparts from the EU and other agricultural protectionists (Norway and Switzerland) in arguing for the multifunctionality of agriculture. As noted previously, this concept draws attention to a set of positive externalities associated with agricultural production and that may include preventing environmental degradation, maintaining the rural landscape, and protecting rural communities. Some feel that coupled agricultural subsidies should be allowed as compensation to farmers for these positive contributions for which they are not currently remunerated.

The concept of multifunctionality is relatively new and has sometimes been used in different ways by different groups. In 2001, the OECD published a report attempting to reconcile the various senses of this expression and developing a framework for its analysis (OECD, 2001a). In this report and much subsequent work (see Vanzetti and Wynen, 2004), there are three elements that define the important properties of multifunctionality. The first is that the production of agricultural goods and the other goods (e.g., rural amenities) associated with agriculture is joint. There are many examples of joint products including leather and meat, wool and lamb, and soybean oil and meal (cake). In all of these examples, the production of one item necessarily gives rise to production of the other. In a similar manner, multifunctionality in agriculture means that non-agricultural goods produced jointly with agricultural commodities would disappear if the agricultural production were discontinued. The second characteristic described by the OECD is that there is some type of market failure associated with the non-agricultural output. In the case of the viability of rural communities, for example, the market failure is the absence of a market for such communities meaning that there is no price signal to indicate their value and to provide private sector agents with incentives to preserve them. The final issue related to multifunctionality concerns the need for public intervention to correct the market failure.

This framework implies that invoking multifunctionality as justification for agricultural subsidies would be inappropriate if production is not joint, there is no market failure, or if there are alternative solutions available from the private sector that make government intervention unnecessary. In defending the concept of multifunctionality, the Japanese Ministry of Agriculture, Forestry and Fisheries (MAFF) has suggested that paddy rice production protects land from flooding and erosion and helps to prevent landslides. But if floods, erosion, and landslides can be prevented through other means such as wetland or forest restoration, these amenities are not joint products with agricultural production and the justification for rice subsidies on the grounds of multifunctionality disappears. In cases where there is joint production and the market failure is a positive externality, there still remains a serious question about the valuation of the externality and the level of subsidization that would be appropriate. MAFF has suggested that agriculture helps to insure that rural communities remain viable and pleasant but the value of these attributes may be difficult to measure even if one agrees that the cessation of agricultural production would lead to their disappearance. Is it really necessary, for example, to raise the price of rice to four times the world price to insure that rural communities are able to thrive?

An honest accounting of the external effects of agricultural production would require taking both positive and negative externalities into account. Nitrate contamination of groundwater as a result of agricultural production is an example of a negative externality that has become a significant problem in the Tokyo region (Takashi *et al.*, 2006). In Japan, Korea and the EU, support for positive externalities is often coupled with subsidies to encourage farmers to discontinue practices that generate negative externalities (Bonnieux, Dupraz and Latouche, 2008). An alternative that might make more sense would be to count the value of the negative externalities against the value of the positive contributions, compensating producers for the good they do and fining them for the bad in line with the principle that the polluter should pay for damages inflicted on society. Of course, there are probably a great many uncompensated positive externalities generated by individuals in many walks of life and it is curious that agriculture is singled out for special consideration in this regard. Representatives of some developing countries have suggested that trade-distorting support based on non-trade concerns is actually a form of "special and differential treatment" for high-income countries (WTO, 2008e).[5]

One of the multifunctional attributes of agricultural production that is often mentioned by Japanese and Korean policy makers is food security. Food security, however, is not a joint product with agriculture as evidenced by city-states such as Singapore that have virtually no agricultural production but are food secure, nonetheless (see Vanzetti and Wynen, 2004). The discussions of non-trade concerns at the WTO seem mostly oriented toward providing justifications for the agricultural subsidies and protectionism that countries with a comparative disadvantage in agriculture would like to implement. According to Kang and Song (2004), even the modest policy reforms being discussed in the context of the Doha Development Round would be devastating for rice producers in Korea and Japan. Their analysis does show that agricultural policy reform would generate net economic benefits because gains to consumers and other economic agents would be greater than the losses to farmers. But, they argue, the political cost of such changes would be prohibitive. Given the high levels of protection afforded to Japanese and Korean agriculture, such results are not surprising.

Australia and New Zealand

Over the past 25 years or so, Australia and New Zealand have eliminated virtually all of their agricultural subsidies and today have the lowest support levels in the OECD. Although the adjustments brought about by changes in the agricultural policy environment included financial and economic difficulties for some individuals, the longer term effects were generally positive for consumers, taxpayers, and producers. Harris and Rae (2006) suggest that the reforms led to modifications that resulted in higher farm profits, increased agricultural productivity, and reductions in the income risk faced by farmers due to improved management and a more diverse portfolio of economic activities. Of course, it is likely that this favorable experience stems from the fact that Australia and New Zealand have comparative advantages in commodities that account for most of their agricultural output, such as dairy products, beef,

---

[5] Recall that WTO agreements include the concept of special and differential treatment for developing countries. This principle means that low-income countries are allowed longer implementation periods and/or less substantial reductions in trade barriers than is required of higher-income signatories. Honma (2006) notes that Korean representatives to the WTO asked that their country be treated as less developed during the first 10 years of any agreement reached to allow it to more easily make the transition to full agricultural liberalization.

lamb, wool, and wheat. The sheep and beef sectors accounted for 44 percent of New Zealand's agricultural production in 1984 as the reforms were launched and are still important farm industries today (Harris and Rae, 2006).

European explorers first made contact with these lands in the seventeenth century and by the nineteenth century the British had established colonies in both places. Australia was claimed for Great Britain in 1770 by Captain James Cook and initially used as a penal territory. Between 1825 and 1869, six colonies were set up there, joining together to form the independent Commonwealth of Australia in 1901 (Australian Government, 2008). In 1840, the Treaty of Waitangi, between the British and the indigenous Maori, established New Zealand as a British colony, a status that lasted until 1907 when it gained a degree of independence (INNZ, 2008). Both countries remain members of the Commonwealth and have historically had very close economic and political ties to the United Kingdom. These close relations meant open access to UK markets which absorbed the majority of Australian and New Zealand exports, including substantial agricultural exports. In 1940, the United Kingdom purchased 90 percent of New Zealand's total merchandise exports (Department of Statistics, New Zealand). In 1955, 37 percent of Australia's merchandise exports were shipped to the United Kingdom (Australian Bureau of Statistics).

Trade relations between the former colonies and the United Kingdom began to change significantly with the entry of the latter into the European Community (EC) in 1972. Table 8.6 displays data on these relations around that time. The United Kingdom generally purchased about 20 percent of Australia's agricultural exports prior to 1972 but by 1983 this proportion had fallen to about 1 percent. The decline in the share of New Zealand's agricultural exports shipped to the United Kingdom was somewhat slower falling from around 50 percent before 1972 to about 30 percent by the mid-1970s and to only 6 percent in 2006. A similar pattern holds for New Zealand's general merchandise exports, 36 percent of which were sold to the United Kingdom in 1970 compared with only about 5 percent in recent years. From another point of view, Australia and New Zealand together furnished almost 6 percent of total UK merchandise imports in 1967 but today provide less than 1 percent. Canada, another Commonwealth member with a comparative advantage in agricultural commodities and a substantial market for these goods in the United Kingdom, experienced a similar evolution in its agricultural trade relations. During the period 1945 to 1969, 29 percent of Canada's agricultural exports were shipped to the United Kingdom, 22 percent to the United States, and 49 percent to other countries. In the period 1975 to 1981, after the United Kingdom had joined the EC, the proportions were about 8 percent, 15 percent, and 77 percent, respectively (Agriculture Canada). As a result of the North American Free Trade Agreement (NAFTA), Canada today ships 48 percent of its agricultural

Table 8.6 Australian and New Zealand trade with the United Kingdom, various years

	Australian agricultural exports to UK[a] (%)	New Zealand agricultural exports to UK[b] (%)	Total New Zealand exports to UK[c] (%)	UK imports from New Zealand and Australia[d] (%)
1960			53.0	
1965	28.6			
1966	20.2			
1967	19.9	53.3		5.6
1968	20.4	55.9		5.2
1969		51.8		5.4
1970	19.9	47.4	36.0	5.1
1971	13.1			5.1
1972	16.4		30.5	4.7
1973			26.8	3.8
1974	3.8		20.6	2.4
1975	3.3	35.8	21.7	2.5
1976	1.9	30.1	18.9	2.3
1977		33.7	19.9	2.0
1980			14.0	
1983	1.3			
1985			9.0	
1989		6.3	7.0	1.0[e]
2006		6.3	4.9	0.8

[a] Australian exports of major agricultural commodities (cereal grains, dairy products, meat, sugar, fruits, and vegetables) to the United Kingdom as a percentage of total Australian exports of these commodities. *Year Book Australia*, Australian Bureau of Statistics, Canberra, various issues.

[b] Exports of major agricultural products (wool, beef, lamb, butter, and cheese) from New Zealand to the United Kingdom as a percentage of total New Zealand exports of these commodities. *New Zealand Official Yearbook*, Department of Statistics, Auckland, various dates.

[c] Total merchandise exports from New Zealand to the United Kingdom as a percentage of total New Zealand merchandise exports. *New Zealand Official Yearbook*, Department of Statistics, Auckland, various dates.

[d] UK merchandise imports from Australia and New Zealand as a percentage of total UK merchandise imports. *Annual Abstract of Statistics*, Government Statistics Service, Her Majesty's Stationery Office, London, various dates.

[e] 1991.

exports to the United States and Mexico and the share of the United Kingdom has fallen to 1 percent (Industry Canada, 2008).

The fact that the share of agricultural and merchandise trade between Australia and New Zealand and the United Kingdom has declined does not mean that Australia and New Zealand have had to get out of the business of exporting agricultural commodities. As UK trade with other members of the EC replaced trade with its Commonwealth partners, Australia and New Zealand began to develop new markets in Asia and North America. In 1955, Japan purchased only about 8 percent of Australia's merchandise exports compared to 37 percent shipped to the United Kingdom. In 1975, the figures were 28 percent to Japan and 5 percent to the United Kingdom. In 2006, Japan and China received 33 percent of Australia's merchandise exports compared to only 4 percent shipped to the United Kingdom. Agricultural exports have long made up a significant share of merchandise exports from both countries although that share has fallen substantially in Australia. In the 1960s, agriculture accounted for more than 60 percent of merchandise exports in both countries but by the 1980s, this share had fallen to 45 percent in Australia and in 2007 it was only 16 percent of total exports (OECD, 1987a; WTO, 2008). In New Zealand, the share of agriculture in total exports seems to have remained stable at just under 60 percent since the 1980s (OECD, 1987b; WTO, 2008).

Because of the importance of agricultural exports in both countries, their agricultural policies have traditionally targeted efficiency and competitiveness in agricultural production as well as income and price stability in the face of potential variability in world prices (OECD, 1987a, 1987b). Prior to the policy reforms of the 1970s and 1980s, the general economies and the agricultural sectors in the two countries were highly regulated. Anderson, Lloyd and MacLaren (2007) attribute Australia's slow economic growth following the Second World War to government regulations that favored manufacturing industries at the expense of export industries including agriculture. Scrimgeour and Pasour (1996) argue that New Zealand began pursuing protectionist strategies in the 1930s that eventually gave rise to highly distorted agricultural markets both for farm inputs and for agricultural commodities. They also point to trade barriers and other distortions in the manufacturing sectors of the New Zealand economy that reduced agricultural competitiveness.

Both countries made extensive use of commodity marketing boards to regulate the production and commercialization of farm outputs. Marketing boards are state-owned or state-sponsored enterprises with legal monopolies or monopsonies on the sale or purchase of agricultural commodities. Fleming (1999) suggests that marketing boards were established in the 1920s and 1930s in Australia and New Zealand as a way to reduce the instability of export earnings due to world price variations. In addition to their purchasing and distribution functions, marketing boards may provide marketing services such as commodity grading, research, or product promotion (OECD, 1987a). Marketing boards played an important role in many developing countries handling both agricultural imports and exports as we will see in the next chapter. In Australia and New Zealand, marketing boards for dairy products, wool, lamb, beef, and wheat generally controlled the marketing of these commodities both within the countries and on the world market. These state trading enterprises were also the conduit for carrying out government price policies by setting administrative prices which were enforced through the monopoly or monopsony power of the boards.

The Australian Wheat Board (AWB) can serve as an example of how marketing boards operated in Australia and New Zealand. Australia is a major wheat exporter although its share of world wheat exports fell to about 10 percent in 2006/7 below the shares of the United States (22 percent), Canada (17 percent), the EU (12 percent), and Argentina (11 percent) as a result of continuing drought. Over the period 2003/4 to 2005/6, the Australian share of world wheat exports was the same as Canada's at 14 percent surpassed only by the United States with 27 percent. Between 2000 and 2007, on average, 68 percent of the wheat produced in Australia was exported (author's calculations based on data from ERS, 2008a). Government intervention in Australia's wheat markets began during the First World War with state procurement of wheat at fixed prices (Cockfield and Botterill, 2007). From 1939, the AWB was given authority to purchase and market the entire wheat crop and this authority was made legally permanent in 1948 (McCorriston and MacLaren, 2007). Wheat was purchased at prices set by the AWB based on estimates of the costs of production and sold to domestic and foreign consumers with any profits realized from international sales held in a fund used to supplement producer prices in years when prices were low (Cockfield and Botterill, 2007). McCorriston and MacLaren (2007) argue that the original objectives of the AWB and the farm legislation that accompanied it were to increase farm incomes and reduce their variability.

Agricultural policy reform in Australia took place gradually. Beginning in the 1970s, the government began to modify the roles of the marketing boards, including the AWB, and to reduce state and national government influence on prices and trade. In 1989, domestic wheat marketing was privatized although the AWB retained control of exports. In 1999, the wheat board was made into a private corporation through transfer of ownership to growers and the final removal of the link between the AWB and government price-setting authority (AWB, 2008). The private corporation, AWB Limited, still controls all exports with the objective of maximizing returns to wheat growers and maximizing profits to holders of shares in AWB Limited that can be traded ("B class" shares). "A class" shares were given to growers and cannot be traded on the stock exchange (McCorriston and MacLaren, 2007). In 2006, the investigation into illegal payments to former Iraqi dictator, Saddam Hussein, in the context of the United Nations Oil-for-Food program implicated the AWB and this turn of events may herald the beginning of the end of its monopoly on Australian wheat exports (Cockfield and Botterill, 2007).

The structure of the Australian dairy marketing authorities prior to the reform effort was much more complex than that of the AWB. Separate dairy marketing boards were set up in each of the six Australian states to regulate the fluid milk markets, setting producer prices at levels above the equivalent world price and controlling trade among the different states (Edwards, 2003). Fluid milk is generally not traded internationally although there is extensive trade in less-perishable dairy products such as cheese, butter, and milk powder. Milk used in the manufacture of these products was segregated from the fluid milk markets and supported through price floors and export subsidies by the national government (Edwards, 2003). Dairy reforms in Australia were begun in 1986 with the introduction of a tax on both fluid and manufacturing milk levied on producers and used to finance an export subsidy on manufactured products (Edwards, 2003). Prior to these reforms there had been a significant reduction in the number of dairy farms, a process that continued in the following years. Harris and Rae (2006) report that the number of dairy farms in Australia fell 58 percent from more than 30,000 in 1974–5 to just under 13,000 in 1999–2000. Further market liberalization was undertaken during the 1990s and in 2000, price supports were ended and a national market for both fluid and manufacturing milk was established. To soften the blow of deregulation, the Australian government offered financial aid to dairy producers to assist in restructuring the industry (Harris and Rae, 2006).

Precipitated by an economic crisis in 1984, New Zealand's policy reforms were much more abrupt (Harris and Rae, 2006). Input subsidies and price supplements similar to the U.S. deficiency payments were eliminated as were some of the marketing boards although most exports continued to be controlled by statutory state agencies (Scrimgeour and Pasour, 1996). Today, only dairy and kiwi fruit exports are still regulated through the grant of statutory export rights to private firms (OECD, 2007a). As shown in Tables 8.7 and 8.8, the main support for New Zealand's agriculture is provided as general services in the form of expenditures for research, inspection services, and infrastructure. General service support is also significant in Australia although the Australian PSE in 2007 still accounts for the greatest part of the total support estimate (Tables 8.9 and 8.10). More than half of the 2007 Australian PSE is in the form of decoupled payments and there was no market price support in that year.

Table 8.7 New Zealand agricultural support estimates, selected years (millions of current NZ dollars)

	1986	*1995*	*2000*	*2005*	*2007*
Value of production (farm gate)	**6,322**	**9,215**	**13,682**	**13,766**	**15,683**
Producer support estimate					
(PSE)	**1,511**	**142**	**62**	**196**	**112**
PSE/Value of production (%)	*20*	*2*	*0*	*1*	*1*
Market price support	130	84	1	100	51
Direct payments	1,381	58	61	96	61
General services support					
estimate (GSSE)	**230**	**150**	**192**	**233**	**267**
Research and development	108	108	125	86	92
Agricultural schools	0	0	9	21	23
Inspection services	71	17	36	71	75
Infrastructure	51	23	21	55	78
Marketing and promotion	0	1	1	0	0
Consumer support estimate					
(CSE)	**−139**	**−75**	**−1**	**−99**	**−55**
Consumer transfers to producers	−130	−75	−1	−97	−50
Other transfers from consumers	−10	0	0	−1	−4
Taxpayer transfers to					
consumers	0	0	0	0	0
Total support estimate (TSE)	**1,741**	**292**	**254**	**430**	**379**
Transfers from consumers	139	75	1	99	55
Transfers from taxpayers	1,611	217	254	332	329
Budget revenues	−10	0	0	−1	−4

Source: OECD, 2008c.

As a result of these reforms, agricultural industries in both countries underwent substantial restructuring. Resources were reallocated from less competitive industries that had been protected in the past to industries with comparative advantages that were able to make better use of the resources. As the number of dairy farms in Australia declined, their average size increased, their owners diversified their sources of income, and improved production methods led to an increase of almost 50 percent in the average milk yield per cow (Harris and Rae, 2006). In New Zealand, overall agricultural productivity increased following the policy reforms and there were significant shifts in the relative size of the main agricultural industries as the beef and dairy industries expanded at the expense of sheep raising (Harris and Rae, 2006). Some of these changes can be seen in the figures in Table 8.11. Wool production and

Table 8.8   New Zealand agricultural support estimates, 1986–2007 (millions of current NZ dollars)*

	TSE	PSE	PSE (MPS)	PSE (budget)	GSSE	CSE	MPS/ PSE (%)
1986	1,741	1,511	130	1,381	230	−139	8.6
1990	293	159	64	95	133	−64	40.3
1995	292	142	84	58	150	−75	59.2
2000	254	62	1	61	192	−1	1.6
2001	277	114	42	72	163	−34	36.8
2002	257	60	10	50	197	−10	16.7
2003	334	125	72	53	209	−69	57.6
2004	339	119	53	66	220	−51	44.5
2005	430	196	100	96	233	−99	51.0
2006	413	148	84	64	265	−89	56.8
2007	379	112	51	61	267	−55	45.5

* TSE (total support estimate), PSE (producer support estimate), GSSE (general services support estimate), CSE (consumer support estimate). PSE is divided into market price support (MPS) which comes from consumers through higher prices resulting from trade barriers and commodity programs financed through the government budget (see Chapter 5). The last column shows the share of producer support resulting from trade barriers (MPS/PSE).
Source: OECD, 2008c.

exports declined in both countries although much of this decline was probably due to competition from synthetic fibers rather than changes in the support policies. Note that wool exports from Australia and New Zealand have made up a relatively constant share of declining world wool exports, 70 to 76 percent, over the past 36 years. In New Zealand, the reallocation of resources in favor of beef and dairy production meant that exports by these two industries expanded while both wool and sheep meat exports fell. In all of the other export industries, both production and exports have increased over the past 35 years, often quite dramatically.

McCorriston and MacLaren (2007) argue that the Australian policy reforms have not resulted in the complete deregulation of the wheat industry and, as a result, the policy changes have not increased the competitiveness of the Australian wheat industry nor have they led to broad social benefits. At the same time, it is important to recognize that in recent years, the severe drought in Australia has lowered production and exports of wheat and other crops such as sugar and rice. On the whole, most analysts seem to feel that the Australian and New Zealand policy reforms have been beneficial. Harris and Rae (2006)

Table 8.9 Australian agricultural support estimates, selected years (millions of current Australian dollars)

	1986	1995	2000	2005	2007
Value of production (farm gate)	**16,965**	**27,332**	**34,432**	**38,417**	**38,327**
Producer support estimate (PSE)	**1,870**	**1,693**	**1,564**	**1,802**	**2,238**
PSE/Value of production (%)	*11*	*6*	*4*	*4*	*6*
Market price support	1,146	613	8	87	0
Direct payments	724	1,080	1,556	1,715	2,238
General services support estimate (GSSE)	**358**	**355**	**742**	**1,000**	**1,069**
Research and development	136	173	328	590	579
Inspection services	76	50	67	133	141
Infrastructure	59	114	321	250	341
Marketing and promotion	53	4	11	9	9
Miscellaneous	34	14	15	17	0
Consumer support estimate (CSE)	**−540**	**−240**	**−216**	**−273**	**−248**
Consumer transfers to producers	−540	−240	−3	−46	0
Other transfers from consumers	0	0	0	0	−6
Taxpayer transfers to consumers	0	0	−213	−237	−242
Total support estimate (TSE)	**2,228**	**2,049**	**1,093**	**2,574**	**3,066**
Transfers from consumers	540	249	3	46	6
Transfers from taxpayers	1,688	1,800	2,090	2,528	3,065
Budget revenues	0	0	0	0	−6

Source: OECD, 2008c.

suggest that they forced some farmers to leave agriculture but those who weathered the initial difficulties were able to realize impressive productivity gains that resulted in increased profitability on the basis of production methods that were better for the environment because they required fewer chemical inputs and used less environmentally fragile land (see also Trebeck, 2002). Kalaitzandonakes (1994) shows that productivity growth in the New Zealand beef and sheep industries increased markedly once the protectionist policies in place prior to 1984 were removed. Scrimgeour and Pasour (1996) argue that hardships caused by the reforms in New Zealand were largely transitory with farm incomes recovering fairly rapidly after 1984.

Smith (2006) notes that the number of farms increased following the New Zealand reform with growing numbers of farms given over to new agricultural enterprises such as deer, ostrich and emu farming, cut flowers, fresh fruit, wine, and olives. Both countries can take advantage of their locations in the southern hemisphere to produce cut flowers and other fresh products not

Table 8.10   Australian agricultural support estimates, 1986–2007 (millions of current Australian dollars)*

	TSE	PSE	PSE (MPS)	PSE (budget)	GSSE	CSE	MPS/ PSE (%)
1986	2,228	1,870	*1,146*	*724*	358	−540	61.3
1990	2,475	2,077	*1,520*	*557*	398	−635	73.2
1995	2,049	1,693	*613*	*1,080*	355	−240	36.2
2000	2,093	1,564	*8*	*1,556*	742	−216	0.5
2001	2,411	1,843	*143*	*1,700*	780	−272	7.8
2002	3,976	3,330	*1,412*	*1,918*	859	−873	42.4
2003	2,472	1,777	*4*	*1,773*	913	−222	0.2
2004	2,160	1,560	*2*	*1,558*	823	−226	0.1
2005	2,574	1,802	*87*	*1,715*	1,000	−273	4.8
2006	2,756	2,000	*1*	*1,999*	993	−243	0.0
2007	3,066	2,238	*0*	*2,238*	1,069	−248	0.0

* TSE (total support estimate), PSE (producer support estimate), GSSE (general services support estimate), CSE (consumer support estimate). PSE is divided into market price support (MPS) which comes from consumers through higher prices resulting from trade barriers and commodity programs financed through the government budget (see Chapter 5). The last column shows the share of producer support resulting from trade barriers (MPS/PSE).
Source: OECD, 2008c.

available during the winter months in the northern hemisphere. Wine production in Australia and New Zealand has more than tripled since the late 1970s (FAOSTAT, http://faostat.fao.org/site/). Smith (2006) argues that many of the changes in New Zealand agriculture had begun prior to the reforms which mainly accelerated tendencies that were already underway. The restructuring of New Zealand's agriculture also put strains on the provision of such rural services as health care, banking, and postal services (Smith, 2006). The dramatic changes in agricultural policy in these two countries did disrupt social and economic patterns that had developed over long periods of time but the end result is agricultural sectors that are healthier, more profitable and, arguably, more sustainable than had been the case when they were subject to intense government intervention.

Conclusion

It should be noted that the agricultural reforms in Australia and New Zealand took place at the same time that broader economic reforms were being initiated

Table 8.11   Average production and exports of main commodities in Australia and New Zealand, 1970 to 2005/6* (1,000 metric tons)

	1970–9	1980–9	1990–9	2000–5/6	2000–5/6 1970–9 (Ratio)
Australia					
Wheat production	9,767	14,932	17,209	19,926	2.04
Wheat exports	7,609	12,432	11,529	14,990	1.97
Meat production	2,587	2,647	2,959	3,849	1.49
Beef/Veal exports	507	508	751	904	1.78
Sheep meat exports	171	136	225	278	1.63
Milk production	6,719	5,982	8,286	10,418	1.55
Butter exports	41	16	66	91	2.22
Cheese exports	35	61	114	217	6.20
Wool production	777	797	827	574	0.74
Wool exports	598	565	496	384	0.64
New Zealand					
Meat production	1,077	1,237	1,262	1,394	1.29
Beef/Veal exports	199	235	283	345	1.73
Sheep meat exports	412	470	357	355	0.86
Milk production	6,171	7,312	9,486	12,370	2.00
Butter exports	187	215	255	342	1.83
Cheese exports	78	85	160	252	3.23
Wool production	312	360	280	227	0.73
Wool exports	172	141	59	46	0.27
For reference: World wool exports	1,036	931	786	596	0.58

* Figures in the table are simple averages for each 10-year period from 1970 to 1999. The most recent data are for the period 2000 to 2005 for exports and 2000 to 2006 for production. The final column shows the ratio of the 2000–5/6 data to those for 1970–79.
Source: FAOSTAT.

and deregulation in other parts of the economy facilitated the transition to more market-oriented agricultural systems (Scrimgeour and Pasour, 1996; Anderson *et al.*, 2007). External trade relations were also liberalized as a result of the Uruguay Round Agreement on Agriculture and the formation in 1983 of the Australia New Zealand Closer Economic Relations Trade Agreement (ANZCERTA). The two countries are currently working toward the creation of a single economic market and each of them has also entered into a range of regional and bilateral free-trade agreements with other countries

(Australian Government, 2008a). Meanwhile, in Japan, Korea, the EU, the United States, and many other countries, efforts to liberalize international trade continue to be undermined by resistance to the kinds of changes in national agricultural sectors that would be occasioned by economic and agricultural policy reforms similar to those implemented in Australia and New Zealand.

Trebeck (2002) argues that national policy reforms are a more effective route to greater global market integration than the WTO process based on the exchange of concessions. Agricultural productivity increases invariably put pressure on the farm economy to move resources, including farmers, out of agriculture. According to Trebeck (2002), policy conflicts in the international arena stem from different views of how these adjustments should be distributed across countries and the rate at which they should be made. He believes that as long as countries fail to recognize the economic gains they will receive from policy reforms even when other countries do not alter their agricultural support systems, governments will continue to find ways to circumvent the rules adopted by the WTO leaving world agricultural markets seriously distorted. Because trade negotiations are conducted through offers to make economic sacrifices only if others make equally or, preferably, more severe sacrifices in return, the benefits of unilateral policy reform often remain unexamined. Trebeck hopes that the United States and the EU will use their economic and political influence to advance agricultural trade liberalization and domestic policy reforms that are in their own interests as well as those of the Cairns Group and other countries that depend heavily on agricultural exports.

Of course, Trebeck's vision of how global food and agricultural markets should be arranged is unappealing to many who feel that without extensive protection the world food system will end up dominated by large corporations motivated more by profit maximization than by good nutrition, environmental sustainability, and the flourishing of family farms. While it does appear that the farm industries that emerged from the reforms in Australia and New Zealand are healthier, more productive, and more profitable, it is not clear that similar results would be realized in countries like Japan or Korea should they elect to follow the path of their neighbors to the south. In any case, there appears to be little desire on the part of Japanese and Korean officials to test this proposition and the 2002 and 2008 farm bills in the United States suggest that there is no more appetite for fundamental policy changes there than there is in Japan or Korea. Conflicting visions of appropriate agricultural policy directions are as widespread and as deep in developing countries as they are in the OECD countries, as we shall see in the next chapter.

9

Agricultural Policy in Developing Countries: Cheap Food

Introduction

In response to rising food prices in 2008, the government of Argentina restricted beef exports and raised export taxes on wheat, maize, and soybeans (Barrionuevo, 2008). Taxes and other restrictions on exported goods have the effect of lowering domestic prices and, in the case of major exporting countries such as Argentina, contribute to higher world prices. Conventional explanations for the run-up in world food prices in 2008 included export restrictions initiated by important food exporters as well as supply decreases resulting from drought in Australia and demand increases caused by income growth in China and India and the increased use of agricultural commodities for biofuels. The Argentine export restrictions were implemented in an effort to slow inflation and, in particular, to prevent politically unpopular increases in food prices. Argentine farmers reacted strongly to these policies, staging strikes and blocking roads. The Argentine government was eventually forced to back down and rescind the tax increases although export taxes on Argentina's main agricultural commodity exports remain in effect (*The Economist*, July 24, 2008).

The Argentine government's response to rising world food prices was consistent with traditional patterns of government intervention in developing countries. Faced with threats of urban riots if food prices increase, these governments have often felt compelled to initiate measures that prevent such increases. In food-exporting developing countries, export taxes and other types of export restrictions have been common while in food-importing countries, import subsidies, overvalued exchange rates, food aid, and other measures have been used to accomplish the goal of keeping food cheap.

Cheap-food policies[1] have generated a great many inefficiencies in the economies of developing countries not the least of which is the lowering of producer prices. The strong reaction of the Argentine farmers stemmed in part from the feeling that they were being deprived of the opportunity to cash in on the favorable world prices at a time when they had every reason to expect a profitable marketing campaign (Barrionuevo, 2008). In general, low producer prices in developing countries, whether they result from cheap-food policies in the developing countries themselves or from the farm subsidies and other policies practiced by the governments of high-income countries, curb economic incentives to expand output because they reduce or eliminate the economic gains that would normally follow the adoption of technological innovations or expanded use of improved inputs.

In 1986, the World Bank devoted a significant part of it annual *World Development Report* to agriculture and the importance of agricultural policies, noting that:

> Developing countries clearly tend to tax agricultural commodities and thus encourage imports and discourage exports. The effect is often stronger … because of overvalued exchange rates. Industrial countries, in contrast, tend to support domestic production and thereby inhibit imports and encourage exports (World Bank, 1986).

The authors of the report suggested that these agricultural policies gave rise to food shortages in developing countries and food surpluses in high-income countries. In 2008, the World Bank again devoted most of its annual development report to agriculture arguing that in most developing countries agriculture still has a central role to play in stimulating broad economic growth

---

[1] Some agricultural writers in the United States consider U.S. agricultural policies to be cheap-food policies. The origin of this notion is the introduction of deficiency payments in 1972 (see Chapter 6). These payments guaranteed farmers a price for their output that is higher than the free-market equilibrium price. At this higher price, farmers increase the amounts marketed and the only way the market can clear is for the price paid by consumers to fall below the original equilibrium price. The deficiency payment is the difference between the guaranteed producer price and the depressed consumer price. Because the consumer price is lower than the original equilibrium price, some see this policy as part of a cheap-food strategy. I do not think that deficiency payments transform U.S. policies into cheap-food policies, at least not in the way that expression has been applied in developing countries. The goal of U.S. policy has always been to support farm incomes and any price-depressing effects are secondary to the main objective. In developing countries, however, the primary goal is to lower consumer prices so I think the modifier "cheap-food" applies more appropriately to policies in developing countries and will generally use it in this book only in that context.

and poverty reduction. The more recent report also identified several developing countries that have begun to make the transition from economies based primarily on agriculture to more diversified economies that include growing industrial sectors and increasing urbanization. Some of these countries have also begun to shift from the cheap-food policies common in developing countries to policies more often associated with high-income countries. In Brazil, for example, the OECD PSE was negative (representing a tax on agriculture) in the mid-1990s but has been positive since 2000 (OECD, 2008c).

The purpose of this chapter is to provide a profile of agricultural policy in developing countries and to sort out the evidence on the impacts of agricultural policies in both high-income and developing countries on consumers and producers in low-income countries. Most developing countries were colonies of various European powers at some point in their history. Many of the 141 countries that have joined the United Nations since its founding in 1945 gained their independence during the wave of decolonization following the Second World War. It is difficult to make broad generalizations about these countries because of their enormous diversity. Brazil, Russia, India and China, often referred to collectively as BRIC, occupy vast territories (together they cover about 30 percent of the land surface area of the planet) and contain 42 percent of world population (World Bank, 2008b). In contrast, the 43 countries belonging to the network of Small Island Developing States contain less than 1 percent of both world surface area and world total population (United Nations, 2003). Argentina, Brazil, Thailand and Indonesia are major agricultural exporters while Algeria, Egypt, Namibia, Mozambique, Bolivia and Haiti are highly dependent on food imports, purchasing between 30 and 62 percent of their cereal grain supplies on the world market (FAOSTAT, http://faostat.fao.org/site/). An overview of developing countries is presented in the next section followed by a discussion of the reasons cheap-food policies have been prominent in these countries with specific examples of how such policies have been implemented. The final section concerns the economic impact of both the cheap-food policies of the developing countries and the agricultural subsidies discussed in previous chapters on well-being in low-income countries.

The Developing World

About 84 percent of the world's population live in the developing countries of Europe, Asia, Africa, and Latin America but the total gross national income (GNI) for these countries amounts to only 26 percent of world income

Table 9.1   World population and income

	Population in millions, 2007	Annual population growth, 1975–2005** (%)	Annual population growth, 2005–15** (%)	Real GNI per capita (PPP$)*, 2006	Share of 2007 world population (%)	Share of 2007 world income (%)
Sub-Saharan Africa	800	2.8	2.3	2,032	12.1	1.6
Middle East/ North Africa	313	2.6	1.9	6,447	4.7	1.5
South Asia	1,520	2.1	1.5	3,444	23.0	2.7
East Asia & Pacific	1,914	1.3	0.7	6,821	28.9	8.2
Latin America & Caribbean	563	1.8	1.2	8,798	8.5	6.3
East Europe/ Central Asia	446	0.3	–0.2	9,662	6.7	5.8
All low & middle income	5,556	1.9	1.3	5,664	84.0	26.1
High income	1,056	0.6	0.5	34,701	16.0	73.9
World	6,612	1.6	1.1	10,218	100.0	100.0

* Per capita GNI (gross national income) in dollars adjusted for inflation and purchasing power.
** *Source*: UNDP, 2008.
Source: World Bank, 2008b.

(Table 9.1). In 2007, real per capita GNI in the United States was $46,040, almost 20 times the average of $2,337 for all low- and middle-income countries and about 80 times the average of $578 for the 53 countries (34 in Sub-Saharan Africa) the World Bank classifies as low income (World Bank, 2008b). The number of countries belonging to the United Nations reached 192 with the addition of Montenegro in 2006. The World Bank classifies 149 of these countries as low or middle income, 24 in East Asia and the Pacific, 26 in Europe and Central Asia, 29 in Latin America and the Caribbean, 14 in the Middle East and North Africa, 8 in South Asia, and 48 in Sub-Saharan Africa (World Bank, 2008e).

The World Bank country classification shown in Appendix 9.1 defines low-income countries as those with 2006 per capita GNI of $905 or less and divides the middle-income countries into lower middle-income (per capita GNI of $906 to $3,595) and upper middle-income ($3,596 to $11,115).

High-income countries are those with per capita GNI of $11,116 or more. The United Nations uses three broad categories including more developed regions (Europe, North America, and Japan); less developed regions in Africa, Asia, Latin America, and Caribbean and Pacific islands; and 50 least developed countries (see Appendix 9.1) mostly in Sub-Saharan Africa (United Nations, 2008). The UN has also established an office for three overlapping groups of countries (105 countries and territories in total): the least developed countries; landlocked developing countries; and small island developing states. The United Nations Development Program (UNDP) ranks 177 countries in terms of a human development index based on life expectancy at birth, educational attainment, and per capita income. These rankings are divided into high, medium, and low human development. The UN Food and Agriculture Organization maintains a list of 37 "Countries in Crisis Requiring External Assistance" (FAO, 2008a) and the World Food Program (WFP) identified 30 countries, 22 in Sub-Saharan Africa, considered "Highly Vulnerable to Increased Food Commodity and Fuel Prices" (WFP, 2008a). There is considerable overlap among these various classificatory systems. Most of the 48 countries in Sub-Saharan Africa, for example, are at the bottom of all rankings based on income or other measures of well-being.

Most people living in low-income countries face a variety of hardships including poverty, lack of economic opportunity, disease, educational deficiencies, social isolation, and political insecurity. Table 9.2 displays aggregate World Bank data on a number of economic and social indicators for various groups of countries. With about 12 percent of world population, the least-developed countries get less than 1 percent of world income while high-income countries with about 16 percent of world population take in more than three-quarters. The number of calories available per person per day is about 2,150 in the least-developed countries and 2,370 in low-income countries compared with 3,463 in high-income countries where, in addition, the amount of protein consumed is twice the amount available in the least developed countries (FAOSTAT, http://faostat.fao.org/site/). People in developing countries live shorter lives on average, consume less energy, have higher fertility and population growth rates, and have less access to health care than those in wealthier countries. Life expectancy at birth in Sub-Saharan Africa has fallen to less than 50 years (compared with 82 in Japan), partly as a result of the HIV/AIDS pandemic which has hit Sub-Saharan Africa particularly hard (with about 12 percent of world population, this region has 63 percent of total world HIV/AIDS cases), while infant mortality rates there are 20 times the levels found in Europe or North America (UNDP). Maternal mortality rates are 564 and 919 per 100,000 live births in South

Table 9.2   Selected economic and social statistics by country group, 2006*

Statistical indicator	Least developed	Low income***	Lower middle income	Upper middle income	High income
Share of world income (%)	0.8	2.6	9.8	11.0	75.8
Share of world population (%)	11.9	25.1	34.8	12.4	15.8
Per capita GNI (US$)	431	649	2,038	5,913	36,608
GDP growth (%)	7	8	9	6	3
Agriculture, value added (% of GDP)	27	20	12	6	2**
Industry, value added (% of GDP)	27	28	44	32	26**
Services, value added (% of GDP)	46	52	44	62	72**
Exports (% of GDP)	25	27	40	33	26**
Imports (% of GDP)	34	30	36	30	26**
Per capita energy use (kg of oil equivalent)**	312	486	1,216	2,248	5,498
Population (millions)	781	1,638	2,276	811	1,031
Population growth (%)	2	2	1	1	1
Life expectancy at birth	55	60	71	70	79
Under 5 mortality rate (per 1,000)	142	112	36	26	7
Fertility rate (births per woman)	5	3	2	2	2
Adolescent fertility rate (births per 1,000 women aged 15–19)	119	82	24	56	22
Immunization, measles (% of children 12–23 months)	74	69	90	94	93
Births attended by skilled staff (% of total births)	38	43	86	94	99

* See Appendix 9.1 for country lists.
** 2005.
*** Low-income countries not including the least-developed countries.
Source: World Development Indicators, World Bank, http://www.ddp-ext.worldbank.org/ext//DDPQQ/report.do?method=getMembers&userid=18queryId=135.

Asia and Sub-Saharan Africa respectively compared with 14 in the high-income countries (World Bank, 2008b). The good news in Table 9.2 is that economic growth is currently much higher in the low- and middle-income countries than in the high-income countries, offering some hope that the poor may eventually begin to catch up.

In many developing countries, agriculture remains the most important economic sector in terms of employment, contribution to GDP, and exports. Agricultural value added represents 20 percent of GDP in low-income countries and 27 percent in the least developed. In contrast, agriculture accounts for only about 2 percent of the economies of high-income countries which are now dominated by service industries. Some 44 to 45 percent of the labor forces in China, Thailand, and Indonesia are employed in agriculture and the proportion is even higher in Cambodia and Vietnam (60 percent), Uganda (69 percent), and Madagascar (78 percent). In Burkina Faso, Burundi, Cambodia, Eritrea, Ethiopia, Malawi, Nepal, Niger, Rwanda, Sri Lanka, and Uganda, more than 80 percent of the population live in rural areas. The value added in agriculture accounts for almost half of the GDP in Sierra Leone, Tanzania, the Democratic Republic of Congo, and Laos. In the Central African Republic, 55 percent of GDP is from agricultural value added (World Bank, 2008e). Agricultural exports account for more than 40 percent of total merchandise exports in Argentina, Côte d'Ivoire, Ghana, Kenya and Tanzania and more than 80 percent in Nicaragua and Paraguay (WTO, 2008).

The first time the *World Development Report* included a significant discussion of agriculture was in the 1982 issue which highlighted the tendency for employment and value added in agriculture to decline as development proceeds (see Table 9.2). But the authors of that report also noted that there were few countries in which broad economic growth was achieved without significant development of their agricultural sectors. More than a quarter century later, it is still the case that agriculture in many developing countries accounts for most of the employment, generates significant amounts of export revenue, constitutes an important source of government revenue, and has the potential for playing a key role in overall economic development. The authors of the 2008 *World Development Report* divide developing countries into three categories: those that are still predominantly agricultural; those that while still having significant agricultural sectors have begun the transition to more urbanized societies dependent on industrial manufacturing; and those that have completed the transition even though they cannot yet be identified as high income. Agriculture is the key sector for development in the agriculturally dependent countries but also has important roles to play in the others. The transitional countries are often characterized by income disparities between rural and urban areas which can only be reduced by further agricultural development. In the urbanized countries, reducing the environmental impact of agricultural production has taken on increased importance (World Bank, 2008e).

Beginning in the mid-1960s, India and a few other countries in South Asia experienced a dramatic increase in the domestic production of wheat and rice. Known as the Green Revolution, the technological innovations of this period led to higher yields and increased output. Wheat yields in India increased at an average annual rate of 3.5 percent between 1961 and 1986, a period during which population grew about 1.8 percent per year (FAOSTAT, http://faostat.fao.org/site/). The technological innovations of the Green Revolution involved high-yielding seed varieties developed at two international research centers, the International Maize and Wheat Improvement Center (known by its Spanish acronym, CIMMYT) located in Mexico and the International Rice Research Institute (IRRI) located in the Philippines. The new varieties were more responsive to fertilizer applications and irrigation than traditional varieties and were bred to include a gene for semi-dwarfism that resulted in sturdier plants less likely to fall over as a result of the heavier seed heads being produced.

Norman Borlaug, one of the principal scientific investigators behind the Green Revolution, was awarded the Nobel Peace prize in 1970 for his contribution to taming the age-old scourge of hunger and malnutrition (Nobel Foundation, 1970). Other international agricultural research centers have been established and today there are 15 institutions where research on various aspects of food production is carried out (CGIAR, 2008). The technological innovations generated by these centers and research institutions in both the developing and high-income countries have contributed significantly to increased agricultural productivity and rising per capita food supplies in developing countries. Developing countries in general have registered higher agricultural output growth than the high-income countries that were traditionally at the forefront of technological change in agriculture (World Bank, 2008e). Even in Sub-Saharan Africa, which has generally lagged other developing countries in growth and development, Fulginiti, Perrin and Yu (2004) find fairly robust growth in agricultural productivity, particularly since 1985. Unfortunately, funding for the international research centers has declined in recent years and less foreign aid is currently being allocated to agricultural projects. The authors of the 2008 *World Development Report* call for increased spending on agricultural research and renewed interest in agriculture as an engine for development pointing to the potential role it can play in reducing poverty and stimulating economic growth if it is placed at the center of the development agenda (World Bank, 2008e).

Of course, making agriculture a force for broad development may mean different things in different countries. In addition to differences in economic structure and income levels, some developing countries have comparative advantages in agricultural goods while others do not. Many of the poorest countries in the world depend on imports for their food security. The final agreement at the end of the Uruguay Round of trade negotiations included a commitment to provide assistance to developing countries that might experience financial difficulties as a result of the higher food prices that were expected to result from the AA. Least-developed countries as defined by the United Nations and a set of 19 net food-importing countries (see Appendix 9.1) were singled out for this special consideration. Konandreas and Sharma (2000) found that both of these groups would face higher food import bills as a result of the AA and called for full implementation of the protective measures in the final Uruguay Round agreement.

Diaz-Bonilla and Thomas (2003) question the use of these two lists, however, pointing out that some net food-importing countries are not really threatened by food insecurity while some net food-exporting countries may also be food-insecure. Using national data on food production, agricultural imports and exports, calorie and protein availability, and the non-agricultural population as a share of total population, they define 12 categories reflecting varying levels of food security. The authors group these clusters into three broader classifications referred to as "food-insecure" (77 countries), "food-neutral" (56 countries), and "food-secure" (47 countries). The list of food-insecure countries includes most of Sub-Saharan Africa plus Bangladesh, Cambodia, Laos, India, Pakistan, Vietnam, the Philippines, several small island states, and a few Central American and Central Asian countries. Diaz-Bonilla and Thomas (2003) argue that while the countries on the list of least-developed countries do merit special protection from rising food bills, many of the net food-importing countries are actually in the food-neutral and food-secure categories.

Choosing an appropriate classification system is important not only as a way to sort out the characteristics of the large set of countries making up the developing world and to identify which countries should receive special treatment in international agreements but also for empirical analysis of the impact of policy reforms on low-income countries. Most analyses of trade liberalization and policy reform group countries by geographic regions or levels of development as in the World Bank or similar classifications. Thompson, Smith and Elasri (2007) use the classification based on food security suggested by Diaz-Bonilla and Thomas. Some analysts work with smaller sets of countries that are taken to be representative of particular types of countries (Hertel *et al.*, 2006; Stockbridge, 2006; Ivanic and Martin, 2008). The appropriate analytical object depends in part on the purpose of the study being done but the wide range of model structures that have been employed can lead to results that either are or appear to be contradictory (*The Economist*, May 31, 2008). We will return to the question of assessing the impacts of policy changes after a review of the kinds of policies often implemented in developing countries as well as the reasons such policies have been chosen.

Agricultural Policy in Developing Countries

In 1979, Theodore W. Schultz and W. Arthur Lewis shared the Nobel prize in economics for their work on economic development (Lindbeck, 2001). Schultz, an agricultural economist, was recognized for his study of the impact of human capital investments on economic growth in low-income countries. He is also known for his observations that peasant farmers in developing countries make efficient use of the limited resources they have and that they do respond to economic incentives (Schultz, 1964). The idea that farmers in low-income countries are economically rational represented a departure from the conventional wisdom of the time which held that because peasant farmers produce for their own subsistence, they have no interest in market prices (Stevens and Jabara, 1988). If true, governments would have been able to pursue cheap-food policies without fear of perturbing traditional agricultural production because peasant farmers were not thought to take prices into account when making decisions about the allocation of their time and resources. The perception that peasant farmers did not respond to economic incentives supported the common bias against agriculture in the development strategies of many low-income countries where agriculture was taxed and urban consumers were subsidized. Today, most economists have accepted Schultz's characterization of traditional agriculture and recognize the importance of economic incentives in agricultural development.

Lewis was recognized for his work on economic growth in developing countries. Interestingly, one implication of Lewis's analysis was that in most low-income countries, the traditional agricultural sector has to be taxed to fuel overall development. Lewis's conceptual model drew on his sense of how development had unfolded in Europe. He suggested that economies in developing countries initially have large traditional sectors where most people are employed. The process of development then involves the transfer of labor from the traditional sector to a growing modern sector (Lewis, 1953). This transfer is facilitated by the fact that much of the labor in the traditional sector actually contributes very little to total output. In Chapter 2 (Appendix 2.1), we saw that firms maximize profits by hiring resources to the point where the value of their marginal product is equal to their cost. In Lewis's model, the marginal product of labor in the traditional agricultural sector approaches zero. Although the marginal contribution of labor is inconsequential, everyone shares equally in the total output. In other words, workers in the traditional sector receive their average product (total output divided by the number of workers) rather than their marginal product the value of which is close to zero.

If these conditions appropriately characterize developing countries in the early stages of development, labor can be withdrawn from the traditional sector without reducing its total output. The workers removed from the traditional sector can be employed in modern, capitalist enterprises at a wage slightly higher than the traditional wage. The higher wage gives workers an incentive to relocate and at that wage, the supply of labor to the modern sector is perfectly elastic. In other words, modern-sector employers can hire as much labor as they want without driving up wages. If the modern-sector capitalists reinvest their profits, their enterprises grow and they will need to hire additional workers. This process continues until all the surplus labor in the traditional sector has been withdrawn and put to work in the modern sector. At this stage, the two sectors must compete for workers but the country will have made the transition to a more modern economy. For many, the traditional sector in Lewis's model is the kind of agricultural system described by Schultz with its low levels of productivity, efficient use of limited resources, and subsistence production.

The basic assumption of the Lewis model, that the marginal product of labor is equal to zero, turns out to be empirically false (Norton, Alwang and Masters, 2006). Nevertheless, the model provides valuable insights. Suppose, for example, that the surplus-labor assumption is true and workers in traditional agriculture can be induced to move to the modern sector with a wage slightly higher than the average traditional wage. Once these workers have left for the modern sector, there will be fewer workers in the traditional sector although total output will not have changed (because the contribution of the workers who have left is zero). Unless some of the traditional output is transferred to the modern sector, workers in the traditional sector will simply increase consumption because the same amount of output is shared among the smaller number of workers who remain after some have moved to the modern sector. This means the traditional wage has increased and unless the modern-sector wage is also increased, the supply of labor to the modern sector would dry up. But if the modern-sector wage is raised, profits are reduced and there is less investment and less economic growth. The first implication of this analysis is that it will be necessary to tax the traditional sector so as to transfer agricultural goods to the modern sector and to keep the traditional wage from rising and cutting off the flow of labor to the modern sector.

Implicit in this model is the idea that workers who have moved to the modern sector will draw on the agricultural surplus that is being transferred out of the traditional sector for their food and other consumer goods. The problem is that the workers in the modern sector are now receiving slightly higher wages and are likely to want to increase their consumption.[2] But while the transfer of labor from the traditional sector has not led to a fall in total output, it has not led to an increase either and this means the supply of food to the modern sector is unchanged. The increase in demand means that modern-sector workers will bid up the price of food and this food-price inflation will erode the real modern-sector wage until the real wage differential between the traditional and modern sectors is eliminated, removing the incentive for surplus workers to move to the modern sector. This analysis thus leads to the conclusion that governments in low-income countries will have a strong interest in controlling food-price increases which, in fact, has been the case as noted previously.

The problem of potential food-price increases leads to what is probably the most important insight to be drawn from the Lewis model, that even with surplus labor, development will require an increase in the traditional agricultural output. In other words, traditional agriculture must become more productive to generate the additional food required by workers in the modern sector so that real wages do not fall as a result of food-price inflation. This places agricultural development at the center of the overall development process. It turns out that in addition to increased food production, agricultural output needs to expand to produce the exports needed for the country to be able to import capital and raw materials needed for the modern-sector production. Thus, traditional agriculture is called upon to provide the food, raw materials and exports as well as the labor that will drive modernization of the economy. And as the agricultural sector modernizes and becomes more productive, its contribution to national development can only be assured if at least part of the new agricultural surplus is transferred to the modern sector through some system of taxation. The development pattern described by

---

[2] In economic terms, the income elasticity of demand (the percentage change in quantities demanded given a one-percent increase in income) will be positive and may even be fairly large. For example, Seale, Regmi and Bernstein (2003; see also ERS, 2008e) estimated the income elasticity of demand for food in low-income countries to be 0.729 suggesting that a 10-percent increase in income would lead to an increase in food consumption of 7.29 percent. Changes in food consumption in high-income countries in response to income growth are likely to be much smaller. In the same study, the income elasticity of demand for food in the United States is estimated to be 0.103.

Lewis replicates pretty closely the experiences of both England and Japan where industrialization was driven by the shift of resources out of agricultural sectors that were themselves becoming more modern and productive (World Bank, 1986).

Much economic research on development has been done since Schultz and Lewis made their contributions and understanding of the role of agriculture in overall development as well as of the best approaches to transforming traditional agriculture has been greatly advanced. These advances have been bolstered by the accumulation of a large amount of empirical evidence about the process of development. It turns out that the implications of Lewis's model concerning agricultural taxation were often followed too enthusiastically by governments in less-developed countries. For these governments, of course, agricultural taxation and cheap-food policies were practical necessities given the economic structure of the countries they governed. Because the rural sectors in developing countries made up such large portions of the national economy, there was little choice but to look to agriculture for exportable goods, government finance, low-cost food, and natural resources. The problem, of course, has often been that the rate of taxation has been so high that agricultural modernization has been stymied. As noted above, the development process as described by Lewis depends critically on the transformation of traditional agriculture, a development goal that has generally not been pursued with sufficient vigor.

Most of the policies discussed in this book are targeted directly at food and agricultural markets. Of course, governments also pursue a wide range of policies designed to influence the performance of other economic sectors as well as of the economy as a whole. Macroeconomic policies on employment, interest rates, inflation and exchange rates, for example, are carried out to achieve broad economic goals and are generally not driven by the interests of a particular economic sector such as agriculture. But these policies do affect the various economic sectors that make up the national economy. Monetary policies influence interest rates, inflation and exchange rates and can have real effects on trade, production, and consumption. Earlier (Chapters 1 and 4), the financial problems many developing countries encountered in the 1980s were described and the structural adjustment programs (SAP) that were imposed as a remedy for these problems were discussed. The SAP required trade and macroeconomic policy reforms, including exchange rate devaluations and anti-inflationary policies among others.

The effect of overvalued exchange rates is to make imported goods cheaper while raising the price of the country's exports to foreigners. In food-importing countries faced with the risk of politically unpopular food-price increases, the temptation to allow exchange rates to become overvalued was hard to resist. In many of these countries, the currencies were not convertible[3] and the official exchange rate set by the treasury could be chosen arbitrarily. It was also a common practice for these countries to expand the money supply as a way to finance large government expenditures. With an open economy and floating exchange rates, the inflationary tendencies set in motion by such policies would have led to the natural depreciation of the currency. As long as governments were able to maintain fixed exchange rates, however, the currency could not depreciate becoming ever more overvalued. The problem with such policies, of course, is that they are unsustainable. Because the country's exportables are more expensive, there is likely to be a fall in exports at the same time that imports increase. The result will be the kind of trade and payments imbalances that led to the financial crises of the 1980s and 1990s.

Cheap-food policies based on overvalued exchange rates were often augmented by the food assistance programs of the high-income countries. Food aid is a form of export subsidy in that food produced in wealthy countries is donated or sold at prices below commercial rates to consumers in low-income countries. These programs have also been characterized as surplus-disposal programs through which the high-income countries are able to get rid of price-depressing excess production allowing them to maintain high prices for their producers but contributing to low prices for producers and consumers in the recipient countries. In addition to overvalued exchange rates and food aid from the high-income countries, some developing countries were able to subsidize commercial food imports to lower the prices faced by urban consumers. Until the 1990s, the Tunisian Office des Céréales (cereal board) handled the assembly of domestic cereal supplies as well as imports of durum (used to make pasta and couscous) and bread wheat, barley, maize and other feedstuffs (Newman *et al.*, 1989). For imported grain, the board would request bids from international grain traders accepting the offers with the lowest prices including those made on the basis of subsidized food aid. Both domestically produced and imported wheat were sold with subsidies from the government which aimed to maintain stable prices at uniform levels across the country

---

[3] Convertible currencies are traded internationally and can be exchanged for other convertible currencies or gold on foreign exchange markets. Currencies that are not convertible are not redeemable on foreign exchange markets and have no value outside the country that issues them. Some central banks restrict the convertibility of the currencies they issue in an effort to control the allocation of foreign exchange reserves among potential importers or because they believe exchange controls will protect the country from volatile financial movements. When non-convertible currencies are overvalued, it is not uncommon for parallel or black markets to be established. These markets are illegal but because they operate on the basis of the free exchange of currencies they may provide a more accurate measure of the true value of a currency than the official exchange rate posted in the country's banks.

(Newman *et al.*, 1989). The effect of these policies was to lower food prices for both urban consumers and rural producers. They were also very costly, draining financial resources from the government budget.

The bias against agriculture was often exacerbated by the import-substitution strategies commonly employed to encourage industrialization. Recall that import substitution is based on the use of trade barriers to prevent or reduce the importation of manufactured goods that would compete with domestic industries. The result is higher prices for these manufactured goods some of which are purchased by farm households. These households are doubly penalized as they receive lower prices for their output and pay higher prices for the goods they purchase from the market. On top of all these measures, traditional agricultural sectors have often been heavily taxed to support the government's need for revenue. Because the agricultural sectors of developing countries often include significant export industries, an easy way to extract resources from rural producers is to levy a tax on agricultural exports. If exports are handled by the private sector, the tax can be applied at the point of shipment and paid by the firms managing the exports. Not only do such taxes raise revenue for the government, they also lower consumer prices if the export commodities are also consumed internally. Historically, export taxes have been an important component of cheap-food policies in food-exporting countries such as Thailand or Argentina (World Bank, 1986).

In some countries, staple food crops are exported as well as consumed internally and export taxes or other restrictions can be used to lower the prices of these commodities. In addition to the staple crops, whether exported or not, farmers in many developing countries also produce cash crops that are sold almost exclusively for export. Bananas, coffee, tea, cocoa, and palm oil are examples of such crops. In 2003, only 16 percent of the bananas produced in Ecuador were consumed internally and an even smaller proportion, 6 percent, of the cocoa produced in Ghana was consumed within the country (FAOSTAT, http://faostat.fao.org/site/). An easy way to raise taxes from producers of these commodities is to establish marketing boards that are the sole legal purchaser and exporter of a particular crop or set of crops. These boards buy the commodity from domestic producers at a fixed price and sell it at a higher price on the world market. The revenue from these transactions is used to finance the operations of the marketing board as well as the general government budget. As noted in the previous chapter, marketing boards have also been set up to handle agricultural commodity exports in high-income countries such as Australia, New Zealand, and Canada.

In many developing countries, commodity marketing boards were initially established by the colonial power. This was the case for Ghana's Cocoa Marketing Board which was created in 1947, 10 years before Ghana gained its independence in 1957 (Ghana Cocoa Marketing Company, 2008). This board extracted very high tax revenues from cocoa producers throughout much of its history. In the 1980s, Ghanaian cocoa producers received only 30 to 40 percent of the world price for their cocoa. Low producer prices acted as a production disincentive and Ghana's share of the world cocoa market fell substantially, from 40 percent in the early 1960s to 18 percent in the early 1980s (World Bank, 1986). Part of the decline in world market share may have been due to the fact that Ghanaian producers had strong incentives to smuggle their cocoa across the borders to Côte d'Ivoire and Togo where it could be sold at higher prices and exported from those countries. Côte d'Ivoire and Togo both belong to the West African Economic and Monetary Union (UEMOA, see Chapter 1) which uses a common currency (the CFA franc) supported by France and the European Union while Ghana at that time had a non-convertible currency (the cedi) that was highly overvalued. Cocoa smuggled to these countries could be sold for the more stable CFA franc which could be exchanged on the black market for greater amounts of Ghanaian cedis than could be obtained at the official exchange rate. Alternatively, the CFA francs obtained through sale of the smuggled cocoa could be used to buy consumer goods that were not readily available in Ghana. These scarce goods fetched high prices when smuggled back into Ghana. The Ghanaian cocoa marketing system was partially privatized in 1992 but the marketing board retains a legal monopoly on the commercialization of the crop and the state continues to extract tax revenue from the sale of cocoa (Vigneri and Santos, 2007). The cedi has been convertible since 1990 when the exchange rate was allowed to float.

Although the primary goal of agricultural policy in most developing countries has been to lower urban food prices, governments in these countries have also wanted to increase agricultural output and food self-sufficiency. These objectives are difficult to realize as long as producer prices remain depressed. One way to mitigate the effects of cheap-food policies on agricultural output is to provide subsidies for agricultural inputs such as irrigation, fertilizer, and credit. According to the World Bank (1986), fertilizer subsidies of between 30 and 90 percent of the cost of the fertilizer were common in developing countries during the 1980s. The problem with input subsidies is that they are expensive and it has often been difficult to assemble sufficient supplies to meet the demand at the subsidized prices. The result is that the amounts available often have to be rationed by government agencies which are subject to political pressure to assure supplies to larger farmers with stronger connections to government officials (World Bank, 1986). In addition, input subsidies can lead to a wide range of distortions that encourage overuse of chemical inputs, inappropriate technologies, and diversion of scarce public resources from more effective uses (Norton, Alwang and Masters, 2006). To top it all off, it is not clear that these subsidies have the desired effect of encouraging greater output in the face of low producer prices.

The pursuit of food self-sufficiency can also lead to contradictory policies. Amid (2007) describes Iranian efforts to achieve self-sufficiency in wheat while at the same time subsidizing the price of bread for low-income consumers. The cheap-bread policies undermined the efforts to increase domestic wheat production and reduce reliance on imported wheat. I argued in the previous chapter that food security is a more sensible goal than food self-sufficiency in countries like Japan and Korea and the same is generally true for developing countries as well. Efforts to achieve food self-sufficiency in developing countries have sometimes been justified by noting that their agricultural sectors were distorted by colonial policies that encouraged the cultivation of cash crops for exportation at the expense of food crops for domestic consumption (Lynn, 2003). The export crop bias introduced by the colonial powers is alleged to have increased dependency on food imports which absorb large amounts of foreign exchange that could be used for other purposes. The desire to reduce import dependence often leads to the use of trade barriers designed to protect domestic producers of staple foods from foreign competition. One problem with this sort of strategy, of course, is that it raises consumer prices subverting efforts to maintain low food prices for urban consumers. Protectionism also introduces other inefficiencies particularly if the country actually has a comparative advantage in the export crop and a comparative disadvantage in the protected staple food crops.

Beginning in the 1980s, many of the policies used to tax agriculture and to insure cheap food for urban consumers were modified as part of the SAP policy reforms. As noted earlier, the World Bank, in its 2008 report, distinguishes between agriculturally dependent countries located primarily in Sub-Saharan Africa and countries that are either being transformed into more urban countries or have already completed the transition. The World Bank (2008e) estimates that net agricultural taxation was cut in half between the early 1980s and 2000–4 in a sample of 11 Sub-Saharan African countries taken to be representative of the countries classified as agriculturally dependent. In addition, export taxes in these countries were reduced from 46 percent in the earlier period to 19 percent after the turn of the century. Agricultural protectionism in countries pursuing the goal of food self-sufficiency has also been cut back, with the average tariff rate reduced from 14 to 10 percent between 1980–4 and 2000–4. In addition to changes in the policies directed exclusively at the agricultural sectors of these countries, macroeconomic policy reforms have resulted in currency devaluations and other reforms that have allowed favorable commodity prices to be transmitted to export crop producers in low-income countries (World Bank, 2008e).

Similar trends are found in the developing countries that are less dependent on agriculture. The World Bank places countries such as India, China, Indonesia, Vietnam, and Thailand in the category of countries undergoing the transition to urbanization while Brazil, Chile, Argentina, Mexico, Malaysia, South Africa, Turkey, the Russian Federation, and Ukraine are considered to be urbanized countries. In many of these countries, agricultural taxation has been replaced with agricultural protectionism. Table 9.3 displays data on agricultural support in 2005 in six urbanized developing countries for which the OECD computes support estimates. Brazil and China generally taxed agriculture in the early part of the 1990s but in recent years have begun to subsidize farmers and tax consumers. In South Africa, Turkey (a candidate for membership in the EU), Ukraine and Russia, farmers have been subsidized since the late 1980s (OECD, 2008c). In all six of these countries, the producer support estimate represents a fairly small percentage of farm income (percentage PSE), ranging from 6 to 21 percent (Table 9.3). The proportion of producer support stemming from trade barriers is relatively low in Brazil (28 percent) and China (34 percent). Turkey, the Russian Federation, and South Africa rely on trade barriers for most of their producer support, 62, 68, and 84 percent, respectively, while in Ukraine trade barriers account for 44 percent of producer support. OECD data on producer and consumer support in another urbanized country, Mexico (data not reported), indicate that there have been times when agriculture was taxed and consumers subsidized but since 1996, Mexican agricultural policy has emphasized producer support at the expense of consumers and taxpayers. At 14 percent, the Mexican percentage PSE in 2007 was similar to the support levels in the other six urbanized countries.

Orden *et al.* (2007) develop estimates of agricultural support in India, Indonesia, China, and Vietnam. For China, they find that government policies have been neutral, neither taxing nor subsidizing agriculture over the period 1995 to 2001. Indian policies have tended to offset international price movements with agricultural support increasing in years when world prices are low and declining as these prices rise. Overall, Orden *et al.* find that agricultural taxation in India declined during the 1990s with policies becoming mildly protectionist by 2002. They document a similar evolution from taxation to subsidization in Vietnam. In contrast, Indonesian policies have subsidized agriculture since 1990. Stockbridge (2006) explores the evolution of agricultural policies in six countries that have recently experienced relatively high rates of economic growth, Korea, Malaysia, Indonesia, Vietnam, Chile, and Botswana. His results for Indonesia and Vietnam are about the same as those obtained by Orden *et al.* (2007). Malaysia seems to have followed a pattern similar to that of Indonesia while Botswana pursued cheap-food policies with heavy producer subsidies financed from revenues earned from the sale of

Table 9.3 Agricultural support estimates, transitional countries, 2005 (millions of units of local currencies)*

	Brazil	China	S. Africa	Turkey**	Russia	Ukraine
Value of production (farm gate)	**170,966**	**3,292,420**	**71,816**	**75,150**	**1,210,507**	**91,429**
Producer support estimate (PSE)	**10,607**	**291,777**	**6,560**	**17,468**	**197,051**	**11,256**
PSE/Value of production (%)	*6*	*8*	*9*	*21*	*15*	*12*
Market price support	2,941	103,407	5,501	11,278	133,568	4,949
Direct payments	7,666	188,370	1,059	6,190	63,483	6,307
General services support estimate						
(GSSE)	**4,878**	**137,021**	**3,857**	**804**	**28,112**	**3,259**
Research and development	787	4,679	1,997	44	2,792	191
Agricultural schools	1,492	13,893	0	6	10,076	981
Inspection services	139	5,288	593	66	9,105	723
Infrastructure	2,088	59,417	832	8	2,844	971
Marketing and promotion	85	0	12	677	581	7
Public stockholding	227	53,746	0	0	268	431
Miscellaneous	59	0	423	10	2,444	85
Consumer support estimate (CSE)	**−3,507**	**−128,654**	**−5,503**	**−8,340**	**−128,556**	**−6,298**
Consumer transfers to producers	−5,799	−126,881	−4,750	−9,241	−117,813	−4,775
Other transfers from consumers	−562	−19,339	−753	517	2,066	−1,319
Taxpayer transfers to consumers	493	93	−533	0	0	0
Excess feed cost	2,361	17,473	0	384	−12,809	−204
Total support estimate (TSE)	**15,979**	**428,892**	**10,417**	**18,272**	**225,163**	**14,514**
Transfers from consumers	6,361	146,220	5,503	8,723	115,747	6,094
Transfers from taxpayers	10,180	302,011	5,667	9,031	107,350	9,739
Budget revenues	−562	−19,339	−753	517	2,066	−1,319

* On June 24, 2008, 1.00 Brazilian real = $US 0.624; 1.00 Chinese yuan renmibi = $US 0.146; 1.00 South African rand = $US 0.125; 1.00 Turkish new lira = $US 0.814; 1.00 Russian ruble = $US 0.042; 1.00 Ukrainian hryvnia = $US 0.211; and $US 1.00 = 0.642 euro.
** 2007.

Source: OECD, 2008c.

diamonds. Chile adopted liberal trade and agricultural policies in the 1970s eliminating agricultural taxation and allowing its producers to exploit the country's agricultural comparative advantage.

Recent economic policy reforms in developing countries have done much to improve their financial situation, lower trade barriers, and stimulate economic growth. As structural changes transform countries dependent on agriculture into more urbanized countries with growing industrial and service sectors, there is a tendency for agricultural taxation to be replaced by agricultural subsidization. In many developing countries there are elements of both taxation and support for agriculture. Considering the combined effects of these two policy orientations, the World Bank (2008e) concludes that net agricultural taxation has been substantially reduced over the past 30 years. The net taxation rate is estimated to have fallen from 28 percent to 10 percent in agriculturally dependent countries and from 15 percent to 4 percent in the countries undergoing the transition to urbanization. Urbanized countries have shifted from net taxation to net protection rates averaging 9 percent (World Bank, 2008e). It is important to note, however, that these aggregate results often mask considerable distortions in particular agricultural markets. In some cases, high rates of agricultural taxation for some commodities are balanced by subsidies for others making the estimates of net agricultural taxation somewhat misleading. These qualifications suggest that, although most developing countries have made good progress in implementing constructive policy reforms, there is more that could be done. In the next section, we review some of the studies that estimate the economic impact of potential agricultural and trade policy reforms by both low- and high-income countries.

The Impacts of Agricultural and Trade Policy Reforms

Empirical analysis of the impact of agricultural policies requires decisions about the specific policies to be considered as well as the sets of countries to be included. The policies studied may include only border measures such as import barriers, export subsidies, export taxes, and import subsidies applied to all merchandise trade or just to trade related to one or more economic sectors (e.g., agriculture). Some studies focus exclusively on domestic subsidies, such as direct payments to OECD farmers or food subsidies for low-income consumers. Others include both trade policies and domestic subsidies. Having identified the specific policies to be included in the analysis, it is also necessary to decide how the policies are to be modified. In some studies, for example, the impact of partial liberalization of the chosen policies is analyzed while others investigate the effects of eliminating the policies altogether. In addition to these decisions, it is necessary to choose the sets of countries that are presumed to be modifying their policies. In some cases, only the OECD countries are assumed to liberalize their agricultural or trade policies while others analyze the impact of policy changes in all countries or some other set of countries. The impacts of the chosen policy changes can be estimated for high- and low-income countries, net-food importing countries, or some other grouping. Finally, the models generate measures of the impacts of the chosen policy modifications on specific countries, regional aggregates, or country categories arranged by income level expressed in terms of various economic variables such as changes in GDP, prices, trade flows, and so on. Obviously, there are many combinations of these alternative assumptions making the range of analytical results quite large.

Most of the studies reviewed so far have focused on the impact of trade liberalization although several have also included predictions of the effects of eliminating domestic agricultural subsidies. The consensus appears to be that tariffs and other border measures cause more serious distortions of world markets than do direct payments and other domestic support policies. That understanding coupled with the ongoing WTO trade talks has resulted in extensive analysis of the potential impact of various degrees of agricultural trade liberalization in the context of the Doha Development Round (McCalla and Nash, 2007). The results of three such studies are shown in Table 9.4. The figures in the table are not strictly comparable as they involve estimates of different variables at different times. Of greater interest than the actual numbers is their relative size in the various policy reform scenarios. In all three studies, full trade liberalization leads to the greatest benefits for all groups of countries. Two of the studies show substantial gains to high-income countries if only the developing countries liberalize their agricultural trade policies although these latter countries do realize some gains. The same two studies found somewhat greater benefits to developing countries if only the high-income countries reform their policies. In contrast, the third study indicates that the developing countries would actually lose if only the high-income countries reform their policies. The authors' explanation for this is that policy reform in the high-income countries removes some special arrangements that had benefitted developing countries in the baseline predictions (Vanzetti and Sharma, 2007). That study also suggests that developing countries would gain substantially from their own trade policy reforms independently of any changes in the high-income countries.

In the study by van der Mensbrugge and Beghin (2004) described in Chapter 5 (see also van der Mensbrugge and Beghin, 2005), the effects of complete liberalization of all merchandise trade including agricultural trade policies and domestic subsidy policies were estimated to lead to an increase of $385

Table 9.4   Impacts of agricultural trade policy reform, selected studies

	Full policy reform in all countries	Policy reform in high-income only	Policy reform in developing countries only	Partial policy reform in all countries
1. Rosegrant and Meijer (2007). Net benefits in 2020, billions $US to:				
Developing countries	14.4	12.0	4.9	6.3
High-income countries	10.0	4.7	13.3	4.8
World	24.4	16.7	18.2	11.1
2. Vanzetti and Sharma (2007). Welfare changes, billions $US to:				
Least developed countries	0.7	−0.4	−0.2	0.8
Developing countries	5.3	−1.9	11.4	2.7
High-income countries	17.7	25.3	−1.1	15.2
World	23.7	23.0	10.0	18.7
3. Dimaranan, Hertel and Martin (2007). Welfare changes in billions of 1997 $US in:				
Developing countries	15.8	12.7	4.1	13.2
High-income countries	42.3	14.6	26.0	26.7
World	58.1	27.3	30.1	39.9

Source: McCalla and Nash, 2007.

billion in real world income in 2015 compared to baseline predictions based on a continuation of policies in place in 1997. Of this, about 69 percent of the change ($265 billion) is due to agricultural policy reform in both high-income and developing countries. If only the high-income countries implement agricultural policy reforms, the total income gains are only $102 billion and most of this ($92 billion) goes to the high-income countries themselves. As in other studies described earlier, the greatest gain from policy reforms for any given country usually comes from liberalizing its own trade and agricultural policies. In this study, developing countries realize income gains of $129 billion if they reform their agricultural policies at the same time that the high-income countries modify theirs but only $10 billion if only the high-income countries carry out the reforms. Huff *et al.* (2007) cite several other studies that report similar results with annual welfare gains of about $100 billion or more shared equally between developing and high-income countries assuming that all countries reform their agricultural policies.

The 2008 *World Development Report* draws on research done by Anderson, Martin and van der Mensbrugge who studied trade liberalization and domestic subsidy removal in all countries (see also Anderson *et al.*, 2006a, 2006b). Because domestic subsidies and export subsidies appear to account for very little of the market distortions, these studies actually focus primarily on trade liberalization finding that the full elimination of border measures for agriculture and other manufactured goods would lead to an annual increase in total real world income of $287 billion by 2015. More than 60 percent of this increase is due to agricultural liberalization and most of the gain accrues to high-income countries. In the case of developing countries, this study reports net gains in annual real income of about $85 billion made up of a loss of almost $30 billion as a result of higher prices to consumers counterbalanced by income gains to producers and exporters of about $115 billion. Although the estimated impacts of trade reform differ across the various analyses, they are generally of the same order of magnitude and lead to the same overall conclusions.

Even if the net gains to developing countries are positive, there is still concern that some low-income countries could experience serious economic stress from broad policy reforms as a result of the higher consumer prices. As noted in Chapter 5, most analyses show that policy reforms would lead to higher world market prices for agricultural commodities. Although there is some variation in the results of different analyses, the greatest price increases are predicted for cotton, sugar and dairy and some suggest that rice and oilseed prices would also rise substantially (see Table 5.4). Obviously, price increases do not benefit all developing countries equally. For those that are net food importers, for example, rising food prices can cause severe social disruption particularly if the increases are sudden and sizeable. Thompson, Smith and Elasri (2007) use two models to explore the impact of policy reforms on countries classified as food insecure or food neutral using the system suggested by Diaz-Bonilla and Thomas (2003) that was described earlier. One set of results shows that a continuation of the Uruguay Round provisions to lower export subsidies could result in a decline of 0.1 to 0.3 percent in the amounts of calories consumed in the food-insecure countries. Continued implementation of the UR market access provisions would have no effect on most food-insecure countries and no greater reduction in calories consumed than 0.1 percent in the countries where discernible effects could be identified. Overall, the first set of results indicates that further trade liberalization would have very little impact on access to food in low-income countries. Similar results are obtained from an analysis of an extension of the UR agricultural provisions to all countries and agricultural sectors based on a general equilibrium model. The results from this second analysis suggest that liberalization would actually improve food security slightly in food-insecure and food-neutral countries.

The worry that agricultural policy reforms will lead to higher world prices causing hardship for low-income consumers in developing countries often gives rise to a peculiar argument in favor of continued farm subsidies. Davies (2006), for example, suggests that price-depressing agricultural subsidies in the United States and European Union benefit poor food consumers in Africa. From this perspective, surpluses caused by farm subsidies are a useful way to reduce the extent of hunger and malnutrition in the world and their elimination would lead to an increase in poverty and hunger. Some recent working papers written by economists at the World Bank offer contradictory evidence on this question. Hertel *et al.* (2006) use predicted effects of trade liberalization on world prices along with household data from a set of 15 developing countries to assess the impact of such reforms on poverty in the selected countries. They find that agricultural trade policy reforms in high-income countries would lead to significant reductions in poverty in 13 of the 15 countries studied despite the higher food prices. The authors of this study argue that the only losers from agricultural trade liberalization by high-income countries would be wealthy farmers in the high-income countries themselves.

In contrast, Ivanic and Martin (2008) find that while the consequences of higher food prices vary considerably across a set of nine developing countries, the overall effect would appear to be a significant increase in poverty.[4] Because slightly different sets of developing countries are analyzed in these studies, the extent to which the overall conclusions are true for developing countries in general is not clear (see also *The Economist*, May 31, 2008). Although it seems likely that policy reform by the high-income countries will contribute to poverty reduction in some developing countries, it may well be the case that rising food prices threaten food security in other low-income countries, at least in the short run. But there are more direct ways to protect low-income consumers from rising food prices than to subsidize farmers in wealthy countries to induce them to produce surpluses that can be dumped on the world market to depress food prices. If the OECD countries shifted their spending on producer support ($268 billion in 2006) to poverty programs and direct assistance directed at the rural and urban poor in developing countries, the amount available would dwarf current official development assistance ($104 billion in 2006) and, assuming that effective programs could be designed, would almost certainly have a much greater impact on poverty in low-income countries than continued farm subsidies in the high-income countries.

---

[4]   Ivanic and Martin actually studied the impacts on poverty of the rapid food price increases in 2008 due to changes in the supply and demand conditions rather than price changes resulting from policy reform.

Of course, the primary objective of producer support in high-income countries is not to fight world hunger in any case but, rather, to assist their own farmers. And although farm subsidies that depress world prices may benefit low-income consumers, part of the reason that these individuals are vulnerable to food-price shocks in the first place is that historic cheap-food policies in developing countries slowed the growth of domestic agricultural production. From a longer-term perspective, increased investments in agricultural research, infrastructure, and agricultural development programs would lead to more productive farmers and greater food security even in the absence of food aid and price-depressing farm subsidies. Given that many of the people who are most food-insecure are farmers and that increased productivity is the main avenue for increasing incomes over time, such investments are likely to have a much more substantial effect on poverty reduction than a strategy based on maintaining current farm policies in high-income countries as a way to assist developing countries to sustain cheap-food policies.

Conclusion

Measuring the effects of agricultural and trade policies is not an exact science and the results reported throughout this book should be interpreted with caution. Nevertheless, there appear to be enough similarities in the empirical analyses to allow a few broad conclusions to be drawn with some confidence. Governments in both high-income and developing countries intervene in agricultural markets indirectly through trade barriers and directly through price supports, direct payments to producers, consumer subsidies, and so on. The distortions introduced by these policies may benefit certain groups but these benefits are substantially less than the costs imposed on other economic agents both within and outside the country implementing the policies. The net benefits of eliminating these distortions are thought to be fairly large and they are larger if all countries participate in the reforms rather than just a few. Most analysts seem to agree that the gains that developing countries would realize if only the high-income countries liberalized their trade and agricultural policies would be much smaller than the gains that could be had if the developing countries themselves elected to join in the policy reforms. There also seems to be agreement that policies that operate through trade barriers have greater impacts on world markets than do most domestic agricultural subsidies. This last conclusion may not hold for all commodities and there is some evidence that domestic policy reform is a necessary complement to trade liberalization (OECD, 2007b).

It might be thought that the analyses of agricultural policies reported in this and other chapters suggest that governments have no role to play in rural and agricultural development. In fact, there is much that governments in developing countries should be doing, perhaps with assistance from the governments of high-income countries, international organizations, and charitable groups. The authors of the World Bank report (2008e) argue that in addition to eliminating the policies that distort prices and give rise to inappropriate incentives, governments should provide needed public goods and correct pervasive market failures. Insufficient investment is currently being made in agricultural research and many developing countries lack key infrastructure including all-season roads, port and storage facilities, information systems, health and educational establishments, and much more. In addition, market failures caused by ambiguous property rights, corruption, and underdeveloped legal systems not only slow agricultural development but also lead to environmental degradation, deforestation, and inappropriate uses of the natural resource base.

Many developing countries have made great strides in shifting from conventional cheap-food policies to more development-oriented policies aimed at increasing productivity and establishing sustainable economic growth. In some cases, these changes have been imposed by outside forces in the form of structural adjustment programs not all of which have paid off as expected. The institutional settings in many developing countries and particularly those in Sub-Saharan Africa are often so deficient that any benefits of policy reform are captured by local elites and large, international firms while the poor find their lives made even more difficult. In such cases, the solution is to improve the country's institutions so that its citizens can all benefit from increases in economic growth and development. Because institutional development is often complicated, however, there may be good reasons to maintain some food subsidies to protect the very poor from serious deterioration of their living standards. Foreign aid, preferential trade agreements, and the special and differential treatment of developing countries at the WTO may have roles in helping developing countries create a safety net for people living on less than $2 a day.

Some upper middle-income countries have not only done away with their cheap-food policies, they have gone further and begun to subsidize farmers instead of taxing them. It is possible that the motivation for this shift is similar to the original rationale for farm subsidies in the high-income countries. The fact that farmers in the high-income countries often had lower incomes than those in other economic sectors provided some justification for policies that favored farmers at the expense of consumers and taxpayers. In many developing countries, including the upper middle-income, farmers make up a disproportionate share of the poor. While most of Brazil's producer support is in the form of subsidies for credit and insurance, other middle-income countries such as South Africa, China, Russia, and Turkey rely heavily on trade barriers (OECD, 2008c and Table 9.3). There is a danger that as countries raise their income levels, trade-distorting producer support will become institutionalized under the shield of special and differential treatment. The consequences of the resulting inefficiencies could be as serious as those brought about by the more conventional cheap-food policies.

Appendix 9.1: Country Lists

I. Least Developed Countries (UN classification, 50 countries):

Afghanistan	Guinea	Rwanda
Angola	Guinea-Bissau	Samoa
Bangladesh	Haiti	São Tomé and Príncipe
Benin	Kiribati	Senegal
Bhutan	Lao People's Dem. Rep.	Sierra Leone
Burkina Faso	Lesotho	Solomon Islands
Burundi	Liberia	Somalia
Cambodia	Madagascar	Sudan
Central African Rep.	Malawi	Timor-Leste
Chad	Maldives	Togo
Comoros	Mali	Tuvalu
Dem. Rep. of the Congo	Mauritania	Uganda
Djibouti	Mozambique	United Rep. of Tanzania
Equatorial Guinea	Myanmar	Vanuatu
Eritrea	Nepal	Yemen, Rep.
Ethiopia	Niger	Zambia
Gambia	Cape Verde	

II. Low-Income Countries (World Bank classification, 53 countries):

Afghanistan	India	Rwanda
Bangladesh	Kenya	São Tomé and Príncipe
Benin	Korea, Dem. Rep.	Senegal
Burkina Faso	Kyrgyz Rep.	Sierra Leone
Burundi	Lao People's Dem. Rep.	Solomon Islands
Cambodia	Liberia	Somalia
Central African Rep.	Madagascar	Sudan
Chad	Malawi	Tajikistan
Comoros	Mali	Tanzania
Côte d'Ivoire	Mauritania	Timor-Leste

Dem. Rep. of the Congo	Mongolia	Togo
Eritrea	Mozambique	Uganda
Ethiopia	Myanmar	Uzbekistan
The Gambia	Nepal	Vietnam
Ghana	Niger	Yemen, Rep.
Guinea	Nigeria	Zambia
Guinea-Bissau	Pakistan	Zimbabwe
Haiti	Papua New Guinea	

III. Lower-Middle-Income Countries (World Bank, 55 countries):

Albania	El Salvador	Namibia
Algeria	Fiji	Nicaragua
Angola	Georgia	Paraguay
Armenia	Guatemala	Peru
Azerbaijan	Guyana	Philippines
Belarus	Honduras	Samoa
Bhutan	Indonesia	Sri Lanka
Bolivia	Iran	Suriname
Bosnia and Herzegovina	Iraq	Swaziland
Cameroon	Jamaica	Syria
Cape Verde	Jordan	Thailand
China	Kiribati	Tonga
Colombia	Lesotho	Tunisia
Congo, Rep.	Macedonia	Turkmenistan
Cuba	Maldives	Ukraine
Djibouti	Marshall Islands	Vanuatu
Dominican Republic	Micronesia	West Bank and Gaza
Ecuador	Moldova	
Egypt	Morocco	

IV. Upper-Middle-Income Countries (World Bank, 41 countries):

American Samoa	Kazakhstan	Poland
Argentina	Latvia	Romania
Belize	Lebanon	Russian Federation
Botswana	Libya	Serbia
Brazil	Lithuania	Seychelles
Bulgaria	Malaysia	Slovak Republic
Chile	Mauritius	South Africa
Costa Rica	Mayotte	St. Kitts and Nevis
Croatia	Mexico	St. Lucia
Dominica	Montenegro	St. Vincent and Grenadines

Equatorial Guinea	Northern Mariana Isl.	Turkey
Gabon	Oman	Uruguay
Grenada	Palau	Venezuela
Hungary	Panama	

V. High-Income Countries (World Bank, 60 countries)

Andorra	France	Netherlands
Antigua	French Polynesia	Netherlands Antilles
Aruba	Germany	New Caledonia
Australia	Greece	New Zealand
Austria	Greenland	Norway
Bahamas	Guam	Portugal
Bahrain	Hong Kong, China	Puerto Rico
Barbados	Iceland	Qatar
Belgium	Ireland	San Marino
Bermuda	Isle of Man	Saudi Arabia
Brunei	Israel	Singapore
Canada	Italy	Slovenia
Cayman Islands	Japan	Spain
Channel Islands	Korea, Rep.	Sweden
Cyprus	Kuwait	Switzerland
Czech Republic	Liechtenstein	Trinidad and Tobago
Denmark	Luxembourg	United Arab Emirates
Estonia	Macao, China	United Kingdom
Faeroe Islands	Malta	United States
Finland	Monaco	Virgin Islands (U.S.)

VI. Net Food-Importing Countries (as recognized by the WTO, 19 countries):

Barbados	Honduras	Peru
Botswana	Jamaica	St. Lucia
Cuba	Kenya	Senegal
Côte d'Ivoire	Mauritius	Sri Lanka
Dominican Republic	Morocco	Trinidad and Tobago
Egypt	Pakistan	Tunisia
		Venezuela

VII. Small Island Developing States (United Nations):

14 Non-UN Members:

American Samoa	Cook Islands	New Caledonia
Anguilla	French Polynesia	Niue
Aruba	Guam	Puerto Rico

British Virgin Islands	Montserrat	U.S. Virgin Islands
Northern Marianas	Netherlands Antilles	

38 UN Members:

Antigua and Barbuda	Guyana	St. Vincent and
Bahamas	Haiti	Grenadines
Bahrain	Jamaica	São Tomé and Príncipe
Barbados	Kirbati	Samoa
Belize	Maldives	Seychelles
Cape Verde	Marshall Islands	Singapore
Comoros	Mauritius	Solomon Islands
Cuba	Federal States of Micronesia	Suriname
Dominica	Nauru	Timor-Leste
Dominican Republic	Palau	Tonga
Fiji	Papua New Guinea	Trinidad and Tobago
Grenada	St. Kitts and Nevis	Tuvalu
Guinea-Bissau	St. Lucia	Vanuatu

10

Conclusion: Whither Agricultural Policy?

In April 2008, the government of Korea agreed to re-open the country's market to imports of U.S. beef triggering massive demonstrations that lasted for several months (Sang-Hun, 2008). Beef imports from the United States had originally been suspended after the discovery in 2003 of a U.S. cow infected with bovine spongiform encephalopathy (BSE) also known as mad-cow disease. BSE is thought to be caused by proteins called prions that are transmitted through consumption of brain and nervous tissue from infected animals (CDC, 2008). The human version of this disease is known as variant (or "new variant") Creutzfeldt–Jakob disease (vCJD) which may be transmitted by beef products that contain tissue from cattle infected with BSE. There is no known cure for either BSE or vCJD both of which are horrifying afflictions that are invariably fatal. According to the Extended European Collaborative Study Group of CJD (NEUROCJD, 2008), there were a total of 208 cases of vCJD reported between 1996 and 2008 and 80 percent of these cases were in the United Kingdom, the country most seriously affected by the diseases. Only three cases of vCJD have been reported in the United States and all of these are thought to have been contracted while the individuals were living in other countries. A total of three cases of BSE have been documented in the United States where more than 30 million head of cattle are slaughtered each year (CDC, 2008). One source estimated that the risk of dying in an automobile accident in the United Kingdom is as much as 100,000 times greater than the risk of coming down with vCJD in that country (Bandolier, 2008). The CDC reported a risk estimate for the United Kingdom of one case of vCJD per 10 billion beef servings but noted that this estimate was little more than a guess.

The risk in Korea of contracting vCJD from imported U.S. beef is clearly incredibly small. Moreover, to the extent that there is any risk at all, the precautionary measures put in place by governments around the world following the initial outbreak of BSE have lowered that risk still further. The BSE epidemic in the United Kingdom was caused by the use of processed animal tissues in cattle feed. Once the connection between these practices and the outbreak of BSE was identified, livestock feed producers became much more careful in their use of animal byproducts in livestock feed rations. The U.S. government was initially reluctant to implement a serious program to test for BSE because of opposition from the beef industry and this contributed to skepticism about the safety of U.S. beef (Sang-Hun, 2008). Still, the reaction of the Korean demonstrators seems exaggerated given the extremely low risk associated with the sale of U.S. beef in Korea. The World Health Organization (WHO) attributed 5.4 million deaths in 2004 to world-wide tobacco use and predicted that tobacco-related mortality will rise to 8.3 million a year by 2030. In comparison, there have been less than 20 deaths per year on average between 1996 and mid-2008, none in Korea, as a result of vCJD and the incidence of this disease appears to be falling. Almost 30 percent of Korean adults smoke tobacco and the odds of dying from the effects of smoking or, for that matter, from injuries sustained while demonstrating against U.S. beef imports are probably millions of times greater than the odds of contracting vCJD from imported U.S. meat.

Why were the Korean demonstrators so anxious about their government's decision to allow U.S. beef to be imported? Some might argue that this is simply another example of human irrationality. The rational response to a risky situation is often thought to involve figuring out the expected value of alternative courses of action with expected value computed as the product of the probability that an event will occur and the payoff (or cost) if the event does, in fact, occur. Because contracting vCJD is so improbable, the expected value of this risk is very low compared to the expected value of the risk of dying from lung cancer as a result of smoking. This calculation does not work if the value of life (or the cost of death) is viewed as infinite, the most likely estimate that each individual would make concerning her own life, since infinity multiplied by any non-zero probability no matter how small is still infinity. It also turns out that there is a great deal of empirical evidence that few people actually deal with risk by thinking about probabilities and expected values. Although it is widely understood that the probability of being killed in an automobile accident is much higher than the probability of dying in an airplane crash, many individuals are much more worried about air travel than they are about driving long distances in their cars. One reason may be that people feel, perhaps incorrectly, that they are safer if they are the ones doing the driving rather than trusting their lives to some unknown pilot.

Drawing on work by behavioral economists and cognitive psychologists, Sunstein (2005) details a number of reasons people make poor judgments about risk, including a focus on worst cases, aversion to changes in the status quo, and biases resulting from the prominence in the news of dramatic events such as terrorist attacks or mad-cow disease. Because people often make mistakes in estimating the likelihood of good or bad events, Sunstein argues for attaching more weight to expert opinion than to broad public feelings in the design and implementation of public policy. Kahan *et al.* (2006) disagree suggesting that individuals evaluate risks in terms of their particular cultural values and that purging public decision making of these "irrationalities" would be profoundly undemocratic. In the case of the Korean demonstrations, those who agree with Sunstein might argue that because it is so unlikely that vCJD might be transmitted to Korean consumers of imported U.S. beef the demonstrators were simply irrational and should be ignored. Those on the other side might suggest that the demonstrators were expressing deeply held beliefs about the kind of society in which they wished to live and should be lauded for their democratic courage. This latter interpretation is consistent with some of the other aspects of the Korean episode. The Korean president was quite unpopular and widely felt to be too subservient to the United States, a country viewed by many Koreans as arrogant and domineering (Harden, 2008; Sang-Hun, 2008). According to most accounts, the popular uprising was actually about much more than just fear of mad-cow disease.

Nevertheless, the fact that a food product was the catalyst for the demonstrations is significant. In all societies, food is a central part of celebrations and observances related to such major rites of passage as birth, marriage and death as well as a daily necessity that is an important part of family interaction and social intercourse. Vegetarianism, fasting, and food taboos may reflect profound religious or ethical values. The cultural centrality of rice in Asia, European distaste for "unnatural," genetically modified foods, and efforts in the United States to promote local over imported food are all manifestations of deep feelings about food and its place in human life as well as reflections of other personal or social values. Although pejorative terms for farmers (hayseeds, hicks, bumpkins) are found in many societies, it is not uncommon for farmers to be viewed as having exceptional virtue that qualifies them for special consideration. Following the reasoning of Kahan *et al.* (2006), such feelings and beliefs about food and farming may reflect visions of the good life that favor tradition and local customs over technological progress and cosmopolitan globalization.

Of course, such preferences are not universally held. Around the world, there are many who see farming and food as businesses that are and should be subject to the logic of capitalism and the economic laws of supply and demand. From this perspective, the benefits of trade and globalization far outweigh any costs that might arise as a result of the changes they cause. Others may be less concerned with broad social meanings focusing rather on their particular interests as farmers or consumers. And, of course, there may be many other views concerning desirable food and agricultural systems. The lack of consensus on these questions often leads to political conflicts over the kinds of agricultural policies that should be implemented. These disputes play out in national settings influencing both domestic policies and international economic relations. As shown in Chapters 6 through 9, history and cultural factors condition the national value systems that frame the internal political debates and shape the positions defended by the parties to international negotiations.

Disagreement about the significance of food and farming is particularly acute in dealing with the rules and regulations related to international trade and the overall process of globalization even though food and agriculture are just one part of broader altercations about the way to structure national economies and their global interaction. Most of those who are uncomfortable with globalization seem to share a strong distaste for large corporations, the global organizations associated with trade and international finance (World Bank, IMF and WTO), and capitalism in general regardless of their more particular concerns which range from labor laws and environmental destruction to the rights of indigenous peoples and organic food (Engler, 2007). The Rainforest Action Network (RAN), for example, has launched a campaign aimed at multinational agribusiness firms that are charged with damaging the rainforest, exploiting poor workers, harming indigenous people, and ruining the livelihoods of traditional family farmers (RAN, 2008). It is likely that many of the Korean demonstrators identified with one or more of the groups associated with the broader anti-globalization movement.

Many who disagree with the tactics and arguments of the opponents of global capitalism may actually share some or all of their objectives. In this book, I have generally taken the position that trade and globalization can be beneficial to all parties if appropriate legal institutions, rules, and regulations are established. Agricultural policies are part of the institutional landscape and most of the results reported in this book seem to indicate that many of these policies reduce general well-being. The specific policy issue identified at the outset was the impact on developing countries of farm subsidies in the wealthy countries. The contention that has been examined is that these subsidies give farmers in wealthy countries incentives to expand output with the resulting surpluses diverted to world markets where they depress prices and contribute to poverty in low-income countries. Based on the quantitative and qualitative assessments reported in this book, this argument appears to be valid albeit with a number of qualifications that make the story much more complex.

An important initial task was to figure out what kinds of government interventions are being counted to arrive at the figure of a billion dollars a day.

As detailed in Chapter 5, the OECD total support estimate for all 30 countries belonging to that organization has frequently reached or approached that level. But that estimate includes not only direct payments to producers from government budgets but also consumer transfers to producers resulting from trade barriers, government support for agricultural research, rural infrastructure and other services, and government transfers to consumers. The total support estimate may include programs that do not have obvious causal links to the increased production that is thought to be depressing prices and lowering the incomes of poor farmers in developing countries. The U.S. food stamp program, for example, may increase demand and raise producer prices in the United States by small amounts but it is unlikely that this program has much impact on farm decisions about how much to produce. Some general support services such as publicly financed marketing and promotion may not be entirely neutral with respect to the farm prices that influence production decisions but, as in the case of the nutrition programs, the link between government-funded services and farm surpluses seems pretty weak.

The producer support estimate, on the other hand, may be a fairly good measure of the subsidies that influence producer decisions and lead to price-depressing surpluses. It includes the main types of support—trade barriers, export subsidies, and domestic support—that are under discussion by delegates to the WTO. Over the period 2000 to 2007, annual producer support in the OECD countries averaged about $254 billion or almost $700 million a day, reaching a maximum of $283 billion (about $775 million a day) in 2004 (OECD, 2008c). Producer support is provided by both consumers through the effects of trade barriers and taxpayers through government budgets. Of course, consumers and taxpayers are ultimately the same people but the distinction between these sources of support is useful in analyzing the impacts of agricultural policies. Most analysts find that trade barriers disrupt markets more severely than do direct government payments even when they are coupled. The proportion of producer support that is charged to consumers through the use of trade barriers varies from zero in Australia to over 90 percent in Korea. Largely as a result of policy changes in the EU, Australia and New Zealand, reliance on trade barriers as a way to support producer incomes in the OECD countries has declined from 72 percent of the producer support estimate in 1986–8 to 49 percent in 2007.

The economic reasons for government policy interventions developed in Chapter 2 include correcting market failures associated with imperfect competition, public goods, externalities, common pool resources, missing markets, and so on. Policies that target poverty and inequality may also be legitimate government interventions although some would argue that there is no economic justification for such public programs. Libertarians often oppose policies that are designed to redistribute income whether they are aimed at poverty and inequality or not. Nevertheless, most governments in high-income countries do implement poverty and safety-net programs and I think that they are right to do so. In fact, it is often impossible to design policies that actually address only a market failure without having any impact on income distribution. A second question that has been explored in this book is whether or not actual agricultural policies can be justified as efforts to correct market failures or to redistribute income in an effort to reduce poverty or economic hardship. Many of the farm subsidies included in the producer support estimates fail this economic test because they do not correct market failures and the income redistribution they bring about is often from middle-income taxpayers to well-to-do farmers rather than being directed at poverty reduction.

On the other hand, many of the services supporting agriculture have the characteristics of public goods or operate to correct information problems or other types of market failures and government subsidies for these services can be of broad social benefit. As noted on numerous occasions, some agricultural research is a public good and public financing for these activities has paid off handsomely. Publicly supported agricultural research has benefitted both developing and high-income countries through its contribution to increased productivity. More productive farmers realize higher incomes while consumers benefit from lower prices brought about by the greater abundance of food that is produced. In a similar manner, public support for agricultural schools can build human capital which carries with it broad social benefits. Other public services to agriculture such as inspection services, infrastructure, and public stockholding are not pure public goods because they are generally not non-rival. As noted in Chapter 2, non-rival goods can be consumed by two individuals at the same time and this is generally not the case for many of these services. Roads, for example, are subject to congestion if there are too many users while this is not the case for pure public goods such as national defense. Nevertheless, these types of services are often provided by governments and usually contribute significantly to general economic prosperity. In fact, such programs are often precisely what are needed in developing countries to facilitate the modernization of traditional agriculture and to establish the institutional framework needed for an effective market economy in rural areas.

On the surface, the final category of government-supported general services, marketing and promotion, does not appear to address a market failure. A small amount of spending in this category amounts to advertizing for private-sector goods paid for by taxpayers. The biggest item under marketing and promotion, however, is the portion of the U.S. food stamp program that is not included in the consumer support estimate. This spending accounted for 74 percent of

OECD marketing and promotion services in 2007. Other programs included in this category include foreign assistance, such as food aid, and information services. Food aid can benefit low-income consumers in developing countries if distributed appropriately although the requirement that the food be purchased in the donor country means that producers in that country receive part of the benefits of these programs. It is also true that food aid often causes economic harm to low-income producers in developing countries. Despite the problems with food aid, most of the spending for general services can be justified as providing public goods or as publicly supported efforts to overcome information problems and other externalities. In a similar manner, the part of the OECD consumer support estimate that represents consumer subsidies is made up almost entirely of transfers in the United States through food stamps and other domestic nutrition programs. In fact, U.S. nutrition programs account for more than half of the total OECD expenditures on general services support and taxpayer transfers to consumers. Because these programs generally target low-income consumers, they are part of the social safety net that can be justified on grounds of social justice and poverty reduction.

Subsidies included in the producer support estimates, however, seem less directly connected to market failures or poverty reduction. In Europe and North America, farm subsidies were often justified initially as efforts to help struggling farmers who were generally poorer than others. Some of the more urbanized developing countries (Brazil, Russia, and South Africa, for example) seem to be following the same pattern as they shift from taxing agriculture to subsidizing producers who may be poorer than those working in their growing industrial sectors. In Japan, the United States, and Western Europe, however, today's farm households generally realize incomes that are higher than the average levels for non-farm households so the argument for producer support based on their relative poverty no longer seems valid. Not all farmers in the OECD countries are rich, of course, and those who are struggling deserve financial support to the same extent as any other citizens in high-income countries who face economic hardships. It appears that a majority of the voters in Western democracies do not object to income redistribution as long as it is directed toward individuals who are truly in need. In some cases, there is also an expectation that such assistance will be temporary. If these perceptions truly reflect the preferences of democratic majorities in the high-income countries, farm subsidies that are permanent entitlements and that flow disproportionately to the non-poor would seem to be unjustified.

Another common rationale for agricultural subsidies in high-income countries is that agriculture is inherently risky because of its vulnerability to variations in the weather and other factors that may reduce the ability of farmers to completely control output, costs, and revenue. Some of the riskiness of agriculture has been reduced by technological innovations but as shown by the 2008 floods in the U.S. Midwest, widespread wildfires in Europe in the summer of 2007, and the severe Australian drought, farming is very clearly not a risk-free occupation. Ordinarily, economic agents are able to purchase insurance to manage the risks they face but there can be insurance market failures that may justify government intervention. Governments in many high-income countries do subsidize insurance for crop failures and other risks faced by farmers and many of the farm subsidies in Brazil also seem to be associated with insurance markets. Japan's crop insurance program is administered by the national government while programs in Canada and the EU are operated at the provincial or member-state level and Australia seems to leave insurance to the private sector.

There is some evidence that market failures such as moral hazard and adverse selection do affect crop insurance markets in the United States (Roberts, Key and O'Donoghue, 2006) and this is likely to be true in other countries as well. On the other hand, the U.S. crop insurance program has often served as a mechanism for subsidizing farmers beyond the level required to protect against crop or livestock failures and even when farmers are eligible for subsidized disaster insurance, U.S. politicians usually decide to make additional disaster payments available to them when there are widespread weather-related losses (Glauber, 2004). Skees (2001) claims that the level of subsidization in the U.S. crop insurance program is excessive and Babcock (2007) argues that program costs could be reduced significantly without compromising its risk protection. In this case, it appears that only part of the insurance subsidy is justified as a way to correct the insurance market failures.

In a broader sense, it could be argued that all agricultural subsidies are types of insurance in that they afford producers protection against whatever might put the farm enterprise in jeopardy. Programs that support agricultural incomes are sometimes referred to as farm safety nets. Income supports differ from typical insurance programs in that they are financed by taxpayers rather than by premiums paid for by the beneficiaries. Of course, farmers are not the only ones who face the risk of income fluctuations. All OECD countries have implemented public programs to insure against income loss due to unemployment and there are other safety-net programs available to both the farm and non-farm populations. In contrast to the income guarantees offered to farmers, these social safety nets generally have no occupational requirements and are usually triggered only in cases of real economic hardship. Farm income supports in most OECD countries increase if prices are low but farm households do not have to be experiencing economic difficulties to be eligible for payments. In fact, many farms that are quite profitable receive substantial government support.

Unless there is some other justification, it is not clear that many farmers in high-income countries either need or deserve the subsidies available to them. It is true that modern welfare states provide subsidies to all of their citizens including non-farmers who are not poor. In 2007, the U.S. federal budget included $365 billion for income security (the main programs for low-income Americans) less than half of the $750 billion in foregone government revenue (referred to as "tax expenditures") resulting from various income-tax deductions for middle- and upper-income taxpayers (U.S. Census Bureau, 2008). And, of course, much government intervention in high-income countries transfers tax revenue to wealthy individuals and powerful industries. Such special treatment for the non-poor is driven more by political considerations and campaign contributions than by concern for inefficiencies or economic justice and this is true whether one is considering subsidies for farm households with ample income or tax expenditures in favor of middle- and upper-income families.[1] While practical politics may encourage these types of subsidies, they do not appear to be required by economic or ethical considerations.

There is still the question of other market failures such as externalities and public goods that might justify subsidies to reduce inefficiencies in the agricultural sectors of high-income countries. Representatives of the EU, Japan, Korea, and other European countries often point to multifunctionality as an example of market failure in agriculture. As noted in several previous chapters, this concept is based on the assertion that farming generates positive externalities and valuable public goods for which farmers are not remunerated. The result is that they allocate too few resources to the activities that give rise to these benefits and agricultural subsidies can help to overcome this inefficient resource allocation.[2] It should be clear by now that I do not find this

---

[1] Economists often refer to lobbying by special-interest groups seeking beneficial economic treatment as "rent-seeking." Rent-seeking is the process of using productive resources to influence the government to distort economic conditions (e.g., to introduce a tariff on competing imports) so that they favor the rent-seeker. Such activity is doubly costly because firms and individuals use resources that could have been invested in productive activities to influence politicians to introduce economic distortions that generate their own social costs.

[2] In a sense, this is a second-best argument in favor of farm subsidies. The theory of the second best was referred to in footnote 9 of Chapter 4 concerning customs-union theory. In an economy that meets almost all the conditions for an economic optimum, it may turn out that welfare would be reduced if some market failures were eliminated while others were not. Suppose that an economy meets all the conditions identified in Chapter 2 except that there is a polluting monopoly. There are two market failures here: pollution is a negative externality and the monopoly violates the requirement of perfect competition. The first-best solution would be to eliminate both market failures which would unequivocally raise social welfare. But suppose that while the monopoly can be broken up into competitive firms, nothing can be

argument persuasive, mainly because it ignores the many negative externalities associated with agricultural production. In addition, such public goods as "rural amenities" are often hard to define and assessments of their value are highly subjective. Subsidies are also an inefficient way to correct multifunctional market failures if such failures exist at all. For these and other reasons enumerated in previous chapters, I believe that the concept of multifunctionality fails as a justification for farm subsidies.

This does not mean that there are no positive externalities associated with agricultural production. It turns out, however, that many such externalities can be handled through voluntary agreements among the interested parties as in the case of honey production and pollination services, for example. These externalities have been internalized with no government intervention other than the establishment of the law of contract and other standard market regulations that allow private markets to operate. On the other hand, the many negative externalities associated with agricultural production are rarely eliminated without government intervention. Governments in wealthy countries seem to favor paying farmers to control negative externalities rather than fining them for the harms caused by their use of chemical inputs, irrigation, and other farming practices. Conflicts over the use of surface and ground water are likely to intensify in coming years because of growing competition for a resource that may be becoming increasingly scarce as a result of climate change. The use of water resources is a classic case of a common pool externality that is unlikely to be managed effectively in the absence of some sort of legal or customary institutional arrangement. It should be emphasized that the social costs flowing from negative agricultural externalities and conflicts over resource use only become more acute as farm subsidies increase or agricultural commodity prices rise.

Evidence reported in previous chapters shows that many of the farm subsidies included in the OECD producer support estimates are sustained because of the political influence of farm groups and agribusiness rather than because

---

done about the pollution. Then it may not be beneficial to eliminate the monopoly because the pollution would be made worse by the increased production from the competitive firms (recall that monopolies restrict output to raise prices and profits). The monopoly is a market failure that mitigates the effects of the other market failure, pollution. In a sense, an argument for farm subsidies based on multifunctionality is a second-best argument: the distortions introduced by the subsidies lead to inefficiencies but without the subsidies there would be a greater inefficiency related to the under-supply of rural amenities (allegedly a public good), for example. The problem, as noted in the discussion of Japanese and Korean policies in Chapter 8, is that there really is no need for a second-best solution in these cases. The government could finance the public good directly by paying farmers to supply the rural amenities making subsidies tied to agricultural commodities unnecessary.

they correct market failures or distributive injustices. It is no doubt also true that cheap-food policies in developing countries were originally set up to benefit special interest groups although in this case the politically powerful were associated with urban consumers rather than farmers and agribusiness firms. In contrast to the high-income countries, developing countries are often subject to conditions imposed by international organizations and wealthy countries supplying foreign aid with the result that they may have carried out more substantial agricultural policy reform than has been done in wealthier countries. The governments of high-income countries do have the WTO to give them some cover in reforming their agricultural policies but so far most of the changes made have been fairly modest. Arguably, the EU has made the most dramatic policy changes with the 2003 reforms possibly because pressures from the AA have been accompanied by new exigencies associated with the recent enlargements. It is too soon to tell whether these reforms will be sustained and expanded but they do appear to mark a turning point in EU agricultural policy. Although the United States has traditionally been a champion of free agricultural trade, the 2002 and 2008 farm bills seem to reflect a somewhat more protectionist stance, possibly because the historic agricultural comparative advantage of the United States has begun to shift toward Brazil and other agricultural exporters.

Some of the many quantitative analyses of the impacts of agricultural subsidies have been discussed in previous chapters. In general, it appears that the net economic costs of all the policies that distort market prices, including those found in developing countries, may amount to as much as a few hundred billion dollars a year. For the most part, these costs are borne by consumers and taxpayers in high-income countries and agricultural producers in developing countries. The beneficiaries of the policies are farmers and agribusiness firms in high-income countries and consumers in developing countries. These generalizations about the distribution of the costs and benefits of farm subsidies oversimplify the situation quite a bit. Because the value of the farm subsidies in wealthy countries is incorporated into land prices, farmers who rent land may actually lose more from the subsidies than they gain. In addition, higher-income farmers get the lion's share of the subsidies, which are also frequently available only to producers of certain commodities. Thus, agricultural producers in high-income countries do not all benefit equally from these policies.

Some farmers in developing countries receive preferential access to markets in high-income countries although it is not always clear that their gains from these preferences outweigh the losses resulting from low world prices brought about by farm subsidies in the high-income countries. In any case, they would lose this advantage if there were broad agricultural policy reforms in the high-income countries. Cheap-food policies in developing countries have generally served as complements to the farm subsidies in wealthy countries, helping urban consumers at the expense of traditional farmers. More recently, some middle-income developing countries have begun to subsidize farmers through the imposition of trade barriers that raise consumer prices. Because of the complex structure of world food and agricultural systems, broad agricultural policy reforms could have highly variable impacts across different sets of countries. On the other hand, if, as seems likely, the total benefits of policy reform are greater than the total costs, it would be possible to compensate those who lose from the reforms, wherever they are located and whatever the cause of their losses, and still leave those who benefit better off. The obvious problem is that there are few mechanisms for clearly identifying individuals who would be harmed by the reform process and insuring that they are appropriately compensated.

Despite these complications, it is still the case that measured efforts to eliminate the trade-distorting policies in both developing and high-income countries would be advantageous. Such policy reforms, however, need to be accompanied by programs to reduce poverty and to establish an institutional framework, particularly in developing countries, that will insure that the economic gains are not completely captured by wealthy elites and large corporations. While there has been some policy reform in developing countries, there are still price-distorting policies that are very costly. In fact, increased agricultural protectionism seems to be highly correlated with income growth in the more prosperous developing countries. According to most studies, the benefits to developing countries of policy reforms only in the high-income countries would be far less than the benefits they would realize through changing their own policies as well. There is some disagreement about the magnitude of the effects of agricultural subsidies but virtually all studies seem to show that the greatest benefits of policy reform are realized by the countries carrying out the reforms themselves.

The experiences of Australia and New Zealand with substantial agricultural policy reform illustrate this latter point quite well. It is true that the reforms caused fairly severe adjustment pains, but the end result was healthier, more productive, more profitable, and more sustainable agricultural sectors. Of course, these countries have comparative advantages in their primary agricultural industries so the elimination of farm subsidies led to reallocation of resources from uncompetitive industries to agricultural enterprises that were able to employ them to increase output and income. In many other high-income countries, the elimination of farm subsidies would be far more disruptive although the net benefits of such reforms would still be positive. The fact that policy reform would be beneficial even in countries with uncompetitive agricultural sectors may not matter a great deal if, as suggested earlier, agricultural policies are primarily driven by political rather than economic considerations. In Japan and Korea, opening national markets to free rice imports would be opposed not only by the protected producers but also by rice consumers despite the fact that they would stand to gain a great deal from the lower prices.

Labeling foods to indicate their origin or production methods could circumvent the conflict between the economic advantages of open markets and the nationalistic preferences for protectionism. Suppose that Japan and Korea open their national rice markets to imports while requiring labeling to distinguish imported from domestic rice. If consumers truly feel that home-grown rice is sacred and superior to imported rice, they will want to purchase the domestic product even if it costs considerably more and they could, of course, afford to pay the higher prices because that is what they are paying now. Labels would allow them to exercise their preference without resorting to protectionist trade barriers. Likewise, consumers in the EU who do not wish to consume genetically modified foods would be able to select more expensive "natural" foods that are certified and labeled as free of GMOs. Of course, labeling and certification are not costless and many exporters object to such requirements on the grounds that they are de facto trade barriers. But if Japanese consumers wish to purchase only Japanese rice regardless of the price, should they not have that option? A basic premise of most economic analysis is that consumers are the best judges of their own interests and should be allowed to choose what they consume even if an outside observer might consider their choices to be foolish or misguided.

Governments sometimes approach the idea of labeling and certification from what appear to be hidden protectionist motives. U.S. livestock producers object to labels indicating that their products have been produced with hormones because they do not want consumers anywhere to think that there might be something wrong with their meat or dairy products. They would prefer that other countries simply accept them as safe and nutritious and the U.S. government has been willing to back this position in the course of trade disputes with the EU. Labeling has not been adopted to solve the U.S.–EU hormone conflict in part because of opposition in the EU. Allowing meat from animals treated with hormone supplements to enter the EU would undermine its original rationale for the hormone ban. To justify this policy, EU policy makers have argued that hormone-treated meat is potentially unsafe, a condition that would not be altered by the addition of a label.

Interestingly, the EU sees labeling as the preferred approach to GMOs. Some genetically modified food and livestock feed can be sold within the EU but must be labeled as such (European Commission, 2006). The U.S.

government and producer organizations have generally opposed labeling of GMOs and hormone-treated livestock products although the 2008 Farm Bill includes mandatory country-of-origin labeling for livestock products and certain fruits, vegetables and nuts (U.S. Congress, 2008). Country-of-origin labeling seems to represent an effort to discourage consumption of imports rather than a measure to enhance consumer choice by providing useful information. Anderson (2003) argues that differing policies on GMOs in the EU and United States can be explained by the differential impact of genetically modified crops on farm incomes in the two regions. Although labeling makes good economic sense, its supporters and opponents seems to be driven primarily by considerations of strategic political advantage.

Most of the quantitative analyses find that elimination of subsidies in the high-income countries would have relatively modest effects on world prices. For some commodities, however, the price-depressing effects of subsidies in the OECD countries may be more significant. Most analysts predict that dairy product prices, in particular, would increase a great deal if subsidies were eliminated. The main beneficiaries of such a change would be dairy producers in Australia and New Zealand rather than low-income farmers in developing countries. On the other hand, the gains to developing country producers could be much more substantial if cotton and sugar policies in the OECD countries were reformed. Several of the analyses find that policy reforms would cause the prices for these commodities to rise fairly substantially. Because many developing countries have comparative advantages in these crops, they would realize net welfare increases if they could expand their exports in response to more favorable world prices. It is likely that higher cotton prices would be particularly beneficial for African producers such as those in Benin or Mali, for example.

As noted earlier, food commodity prices increased very rapidly between 2005 and mid-2008 as a result of demand increases and supply shortfalls. The overall food-price increase of about 80 percent over that period is a weighted average of price indices for cereals, vegetable oils and protein meals, meat, seafood, sugar, bananas, and oranges (IMF, 2008). Some of these price indices rose a great deal while others fell or changed much less. The price indices for cotton, sugar, rice, and maize are plotted in Figure 10.1. All four indices moved together until 2005, after which the prices of maize and rice rose much more substantially. The index for rice reached about 410 in June 2008 compared with the base of 100 in 2000 representing a price increase of 310 percent. In contrast, the price indices for cotton and sugar rose by much less. Note that if the nominal prices used to construct these indices were adjusted for inflation, the resulting real price indices would decline for all four commodities at least until about 2006. As noted earlier, food and agricultural

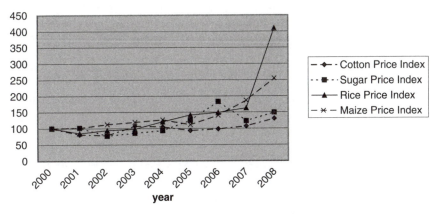

Figure 10.1 Selected world price indices, 2000 to mid-2008
Source: IMF, 2008.

commodity prices usually move together because of competition for land and other resources. Faced with rising maize prices, for example, farmers are likely to devote more of their land to maize and less to alternative crops such as cotton or other grains with the result that supplies of these crops decline, triggering price increases for them as well. In the case of sugar, increased demand for ethanol made from sugar cane should have added to the upward pressure on prices. Thus, one might have expected that both cotton and sugar prices would have increased substantially between 2000 and 2008 along with all the other rising agricultural commodity prices. In fact, they did increase but only by about 31 percent for cotton and 49 percent for sugar, much less than the price increases for grains, oilseeds, and other commodities.

One reason for the less impressive price increases for these commodities may have been the presence of cotton and sugar subsidies and trade barriers in the OECD countries. World sugar prices are influenced by agricultural policies in the EU and United States which sever the relationship between these enormous markets and the thinner world market. The IMF data show that sugar prices in the EU and United States were virtually constant between 2005 and mid-2008 while the free-market sugar price rose slightly. World cotton prices did not really start to increase until 2008. Between 2000 and 2002, cotton prices fell more than 20 percent as noted in Chapter 1. After two years of modestly higher nominal prices, they again fell in 2005 and 2006. By 2007, cotton prices were only 7 percent higher than in 2000 so most of the 31-percent increase noted above came after 2007.

The somewhat higher cotton prices arrived too late for large numbers of Indian cotton farmers. Indian agricultural policy reforms in the 1990s eliminated subsidies and guaranteed prices for cotton. To compete on the world market, many producers switched to genetically modified cotton varieties that are supposed to be resistant to the main insect pests that attack cotton. Unfortunately, these seeds have to be purchased each year and are expensive so many farmers turned to moneylenders to finance their crops. If the rains fail or other problems arise, they can wind up with unmanageable debt (Sengupta, 2006). Even if they are able to produce and sell cotton, the relatively stagnant cotton prices on the world market meant that their total incomes may have been insufficient to purchase adequate amounts of their staple foods, wheat and rice, the prices of which began to climb very rapidly in about 2006.

For many indebted farmers, suicide has seemed the best way out. Dolnick (2008) reports that some 160,000 Indian farmers have committed suicide since 1997, often by drinking the very pesticides that were purchased to increase their crop yields. Most of the farmers who have taken their lives have been cotton producers unable to compete with subsidized exports from the United States and other OECD countries. According to the IMF study cited earlier (IMF, 2004), the cost of producing cotton in India is higher than in many African and South American countries but still less than in the United States. Some analysts blame globalization and world trade for the epidemic of suicides among Indian farmers, arguing that structural adjustment programs, WTO trade agreements, and monopolistic multinational seed companies are the real culprits in this tragedy (Shiva, 2004). Shiva also points to the effect of U.S. cotton subsidies on the prices for which the Indian farmers can sell their crops as a cause of the epidemic of farmer suicides. I think that stagnant prices have probably been a more important factor in these misfortunes than the SAP, trade liberalization, or the introduction of genetically modified seeds. Average cotton yields in India increased by 71 percent between 1998–2000 and 2004–6 suggesting that the adoption of the new seeds had a positive impact on farm productivity. The opening of India's economy through trade liberalization and other economic reforms has been a key element in that country's recent impressive economic growth (see Ahluwalia, 2006).

Moreover, some of the difficulties experienced by Indian cotton farmers stem from Indian institutional arrangements related to the structure of credit and other domestic markets. Because the Indian financial system is not always well developed in rural areas, farmers have little or no access to reasonably priced loans. Rural moneylenders often charge exorbitant interest rates making it extremely hazardous for low-income farmers to take out loans.[3] These

---

[3] Credit market problems are not limited to India and other developing countries as shown by the sub-prime mortgage crisis in the United States as well as the continuing financial difficulties of many U.S. consumers who face very high interest charges on their expanding credit-card

circumstances were not imposed on India by the IMF and World Bank policy reforms nor do they result from the opening of markets to trade and multinational seed companies. Nevertheless, the extreme hardships encountered by some farmers at the same time that substantial economic reform has been undertaken make it more difficult to convince the skeptics that globalization and trade liberalization have played a positive role in Indian development. As suggested in the first chapter, agricultural subsidies often stand in the way of producers in developing countries taking full advantage of the opportunities provided by global markets. The danger is that national governments may return to the protectionist, anti-market policies of the past because the benefits of opening their economies to global forces are obscured by the policies of the wealthy countries, including those related to food and agriculture.

Despite the fact that agricultural subsidies in both high- and low-income countries actually make up only a very small part of the world economy, there are many good reasons to continue the laborious process of reducing and eliminating them. In particular, wealthy countries ought to be able to find ways to assist their vulnerable farmers without distributing lavish subsidies that flow disproportionately to farmers who are generally well off and that distort world market prices often to the detriment of poor farmers in developing countries. It is also clear, however, that just eliminating farm subsidies in wealthy countries will not bring prosperity to low-income farmers. In fact, many farmers who are net food purchasers and poor urban consumers in developing countries would find any further increase in food prices extremely burdensome. Governments in developing countries have much work to do in creating the institutional framework for a market economy, building needed infrastructure, and financing agricultural research, education and other public goods. Governments in wealthy countries can support such efforts through foreign aid, open trade policies that allow developing countries to exploit their comparative advantages, and agricultural policies that do not run counter to the very important task of developing the agricultural sectors in low-income countries.

The Korean demonstrations in opposition to U.S. beef imports are illustrative of the cultural and economic centrality of food and agriculture in both high-income and developing countries. Given the significance attached to food and farming, it is not surprising that the parties belonging to the WTO always encounter great difficulty in reaching agreement on measures to liberalize agricultural trade or that agriculture was the cause of the 2008 collapse of the Doha Round. National farm and food policies are always

debt. See Besley (1998) for a discussion of the problems of credit markets in developing countries and the role of governments in addressing these problems.

contentious and it seems clear that reforming these policies can only be a slow process. But some policy reform has been accomplished and given the sensitivity of the issues it may be unreasonable to expect more rapid change. Many developing countries have altered their cheap-food policies and some high-income countries have made substantial changes in both their methods and levels of producer support. Although economics is known as the "dismal science," most economists seem to have a positive view of the future and in that spirit I wish to end on a note of optimism: there may be much left to do in establishing sensible food and agricultural policies that solve actual problems and move the world toward a more just, equitable, and productive future but some progress has been made and it may not be overly quixotic to think that the world community will continue this process despite the collapse of the Doha Round trade talks and the apparently Sisyphean nature of the task.

References

Abdelnour, Rita and E. Wesley F. Peterson (March 14, 2007). "The WTO Decision on U.S. Cotton Policy," *Cornhusker Economics*, Department of Agricultural Economics, University of Nebraska-Lincoln.

Abel, Wilhelm, translated by Olive Ordish (1980). *Agricultural Fluctuations in Europe: From the Thirteenth to the Twentieth Centuries*. New York: St. Martin's Press.

About Business and Finance. "The History of Soaps and Detergents" website, http://inventors.about.com/library/inventors/blsoap.htm, last accessed June 14, 2006.

ADM. "A Leader in Agricultural Processing," Archer Daniels Midland Company, www.admworld.com, last accessed October 9, 2006.

Agriculture Canada (various dates). *Canada's Trade in Agricultural Products*, Ottawa.

Ahluwalia, Montek S. (2006). "India's Experience with Globalisation," *Australian Economic Review*, **39**(1): 1–13.

Akerlof, George (1970). "The Market for Lemons: Quality Uncertainty and the Market Mechanism," *Quarterly Journal of Economics*, **84**(3): 488–500.

Akrill, Robert (2000). *The Common Agricultural Policy*. Sheffield, England: Sheffield Academic Press.

Amid, Javad (2007). "The Dilemma of Cheap Food and Self-Sufficiency: The Case of Wheat in Iran," *Food Policy*, **32**(4): 537–52.

Anania, Giovanni, Colin A. Carter and Alex McCalla (1994). "Agricultural Policy Changes, GATT Negotiations, and the U.S.–E.C. Agricultural Trade Conflict," in *Agricultural Trade Conflicts and GATT*, edited by Giovanni Ananis, Colin A. Carter, and Alex McCalla. Boulder CO: Westview Press.

Anderson, Kym (2003). "Why Are US and EU Policies Toward GMOs So Different?" *AgBioForum*, **6**(3): 85–100.

Anderson, Kym, Peter Lloyd and Donald MacLaren (2007). "Distortions to Agricultural Incentives in Australia since World War II," *The Economic Record*, **83**(263): 461–82.

Anderson, Kym, Will Martin and Dominique van der Mensbrugghe (2006a). "Distortions to World Trade: Impacts on Agricultural Markets and Farm Incomes," *Review of Agricultural Economics*, **28**(2): 168–94.

Anderson, Kym, Will Martin and Dominique van der Mensbrugghe (2006b). "Impact of Global Trade and Subsidy Policies on Developing Country Trade," *Journal of World Trade*, **40**(5): 945–68.

Anderson, Kym, Will Martin and Ernesto Valenzuela (2006). "The Relative Importance of Global Agricultural Subsidies and Market Access," *World Trade Review*, **5**(3): 357–76.

Ansell, Christopher and David Vogel (2006). *What's the Beef? The Contested Governance of European Food Safety*. Cambridge, MA: MIT Press.

Australian Bureau of Statistics, *Year Book Australia*, Canberra, various issues and online at http://www.abs.gov.au/ausstats/abs@.nsf/mf/1301.0, last accessed on July 28, 2008.

Australian Government (2008). "European Discovery and Colonization of Australia," Culture and Recreation Portal, http://www.cultureandrecreation.gov.au/stories/category.htm#history, last accessed July 28, 2008.

Australian Government (2008a). "Australia New Zealand Closer Economic Agreement," http://www.austrade.gov.au/ANZCERTA/default.aspx, last accessed July 28, 2008.

AWB (2008). "About AWB," Australian Wheat Board, http://www.awb.com.au/aboutawb/corporate/history/, last accessed July 28, 2008.

Aziz, Nikhil (2007). "NAFTA is Killing the Tradition of Corn in Mexico," Grassroots International,http://www.grassrootsonline.org/news-publications/articles_op-eds/nafta-killing-tradition-corn-mexico, last accessed July 28, 2008.

Babcock, Bruce A. (2007). "How to Save Billions in Farm Spending," *Iowa Ag Review*, **13**(4): 4–7.

Babcock, Bruce A. and Chad E. Hart (2005). "Judging the Performance of the 2002 Farm Bill," *Iowa Ag Review*, **11**(2).

Baffes, John (2005). "The Cotton Problem," *World Bank Research Observer*, **20**(1): 109–44.

Bandolier (2008). "Risk," http://www.medecine.ox.ac.uk/bandolier/booth/booths/risk.html, last accessed July 28, 2008.

Barrett, Christopher B. and Daniel G. Maxwell (2005). *Food Aid after Fifty Years: Recasting its Role*. New York: Routledge.

Barrionuevo, Alexei (2008). "In Argentina's Grain Belt, Farmers Revolt over Taxes," *New York Times*, April 27.

Bascou, Pierre, Pierluigi Londero and Wolfgang Munch (2006). "Policy Reform and Adjustment in the European Union: Changes in the Common Agricultural Policy and Enlargement," in *Policy Reform and Adjustment in the Agricultural Sectors of Developed Countries*, edited by D. Blandford and B. Hill. Cambridge, MA: CAB International.

Bassett, Thomas J. (2001). *The Peasant Cotton Revolution in West Africa: Côte d'Ivoire, 1880–1995*. New York: Cambridge University Press.

Baumol, William J. and Alan S. Blinder (1991). *Economics: Principles and Policy* (fifth edition). New York: Harcourt Brace Jovanovich.

Beckerman, Stephen (1987). "Swidden in Amazonia and the Amazon Rim," in *Comparative Farming Systems*, edited by B. L. Turner II and S. B. Brush. New York: Guilford Press.

Beghin, John C. (2003). "The Cost of the U.S. Sugar Program," *Contemporary Economic Policy*, **21**(1): 106–16.

Beghin, John C. and Ataman Aksoy (2003). "Agricultural Trade and the Doha Round: Lessons from Commodity Studies," Center for Agricultural and Rural Development, Briefing Paper 03-BP 42, Iowa State University, Ames.

Beghin, John, Jean-Christophe Bureau and Sung Joon Park (2003). "Food Security and Agricultural Protection in South Korea," *American Journal of Agricultural Economics*, **85**(3): 618–32.

Beghin, John C. and David Roland-Horst (2002). "Global Agricultural Trade and the Doha Round: What are the Implications for North and South," Working Paper 02-WP308, Center for Agricultural and Rural Development, Iowa State University, Ames.

Berga, Alan (2007). "Farm Subsidies for the Rich," *Minneapolis-St. Paul StarTribune*, June 11.

Bernstein, Jason (1999). "The Euro and the Agricultural Sector," in *The European Union's Common Agricultural Policy: Pressures for Change*, Situation and Outlook Series, Economic Research Service, WRS-99-2.

Besley, Timothy J. (1998). "How do Market Failures Justify Interventions in Rural Credit Markets?" in *International Agricultural Development* (third edition), edited by Carl K. Eicher and John M. Staatz. Baltimore: Johns Hopkins University Press.

Bilal, Sanoussi (2000). "The Political Economy of Agricultural Policies and Negotiations," *Negotiating the Future of Agricultural Policies: Agricultural Trade and the Millennium WTO Round*, edited by Sanoussi Bilal and Pavlos Pezarus. Boston: Kluwer Law International.

Bill Moyers Journal (2008). "The Farm Bill Debate," broadcast on April 18, 2008 by the Public Broadcasting Service. See http://www.pbs.org/moyers/journal/04112008/profile2.html, last accessed July 28, 2008.

Blaug, Mark (1979). *Economic Theory in Retrospect* (third edition). New York: Cambridge University Press.

Bleitrach, Danielle (April 16, 2008). "Mieux vaut être une vache en Europe qu'un pauvre au Burkina Faso ou le véritable contexte des droits de l'être humain à la survie," *Alternatives International*, http://alternatives-international.net/article2005.html, last accessed November 19, 2008.

Boccanfuso, Dorothee and Luc Savard (2007). "Poverty and Inequality Impact Analysis Regarding Cotton Subsidies: A Mali-Based CGE Micro-accounting Approach," *Journal of African Economies*, **16**(4): 629–59.

Bonnieux, François, Pierre Dupraz and Karine Latouche (2008). "Experience with Agri-Environmental Schemes in EU and Non-EU Members," *Notre Europe*, available at http://www.notre-europe.eu/fileadmion/IMG/pdf/Bonnieux-EN.pdf, last accessed on July 22, 2008.

Boulding, Kenneth E. (1968). *The Organizational Revolution: A Study of the Ethics of Economic Organization*. Chicago: Quadrangle Press.

Bowers, D.E., W.D. Rasmussen and G.L. Baker (1984). "History of Agricultural Price-Support and Adjustment Programs, 1933–84," Agriculture Information Bulletin No. 485, Economic Research Service, USDA, Washington, DC.

Bradsher, Keith (2008). "An Oil Quandary: Costly Fuel, Costly Calories," *New York Times*, January 19.

Bradsher, Keith and Andrew Martin (2008). "Hoarding Nations Drive Food Costs Ever Higher," *New York Times*, June 30.

Braithwaite, John and Peter Drahos (2000). *Global Business Regulation*. New York: Cambridge University Press.

Brandow, G.E. (1977). "Policy for Commercial Agriculture 1945–71," in *A Survey of Agricultural Economics Literature, Volume 1*, edited by Lee R. Martin. Minneapolis: University of Minnesota Press.

Brasher, Philip (2007). "Strict Rules Accompany European Farm Payments," *Des Moines Register*, July 8.

Brault, Philippe, Guillaume Renaudineau and François Sicard (2005). *Le Principe de Subsidiarité*, Paris: La Documentation française.

Bread for the World (2007). "Senate Debate on Farm Bill Continues" Bread for the World & Bread for the World Institute, http://www.bread.org/take-action/take-action-farm-bill.html, last accessed July 18, 2008.

Brennan, Geoffrey (1996). "Economics" in *A Companion to Contemporary Political Philosophy*, edited by R. E. Goodin and P. Pettit. Cambridge, MA: Basil Blackwell.

Brenton, Paul and Takako Ikezuki (2005). "The Impact of Agricultural Trade Preferences with Particular Attention to the Least-Developed Countries," in *Global Agricultural Trade and the Developing Countries*, edited by Ataman Aksoy and John C. Beghin. Washington, DC: The World Bank.

Briggeman, Brian C., Allan Gray, Mitchell Morehart, Timothy Baker and Christine Wilson (2007). "A New U.S. Farm Household Typology: Implications for Agricultural Policy," *Review of Agricultural Economics*, **29**(4): 765–82.

Brouwer, F. and P. Lowe, editors (2000). *CAP Regimes and the European Countryside*. New York: CAB International Publishing.

Buchanan, James M. (1975). *The Limits of Liberty: Between Anarchy and Leviathan*. Chicago: University of Chicago Press.

Burfisher, Mary E. and Elizabeth A. Jones, editors (1998). *Regional Trade Agreements and U.S. Agriculture*, Agricultural Economics Report No. (AER771), Washington, DC: Economic Research Service, USDA.

Cahill, Carmel and Berkeley Hill (2006). "Policies Affecting Resource Adjustment in Agriculture in the European Union," in *Policy Reform and Adjustment in the Agricultural Sectors of Developed Countries*, edited by D. Blandford and B. Hill. Cambridge, MA: CAB International.

Carter, Jimmy (2007). "Subsidies' Harvest of Misery," *Washington Post*, December 12.

CDC (2008). "vCJD (Variant Creutzfeldt-Jakob Disease)," Centers for Disease Control and Prevention, U.S. Department of Health and Human Services, http://www.cdc.gov/ncidod/dvrd/vcjd/risk_travelers.htm, last accessed July 28, 2008.

Center for Rural Affairs (2007). "2007 Farm Bill Proposals" Walt Hill, Nebraska, http://www.cfra.org/policy/2007, last accessed July 28, 2008.

CGIAR (2006). "Water for Food, Water for Life: Insights from the Comprehensive Assessment of Water Management in Agriculture," report presented at World

Water Week in Stockholm, www.iwmi.cgiar.org/assessment/files_new/publications/Discussion%20Paper/InsightsBook_Stockholm2006.pdf, last accessed July 28, 2008.

CGIAR (2008). Consultative Group on International Agricultural Research, www.cgiar.org, last accessed July 28, 2008.

Cheung, S.N.S. (1973). "The Fable of the Bees: An Economic Investigation," *Journal of Law and Economics*, **16**: 11–33.

Choate, Pat (1993). "Jobs at Risk: Vulnerable U.S. Industries and Jobs under NAFTA—Analysis of the 48 Continental States," The Manufacturing Policy Project, Washington, DC.

Christison, Bill (2002). "Family Farmers Express Strong opposition to 2002 Farm Bill," *Motion Magazine*, June 8, http://www.inmotionmagazine.com/ra02/bcfb02.html, last accessed July 28, 2008.

CIA (Central Intelligence Agency, 2008). "The World Factbook," http://www.cia.gov/library/publications/the-world-factbook/index.html, last accessed July 28, 2008.

Clark, Gregory (2007). "The Long March of History: Farm Wages, Population, and Economic Growth, England 1209–1869," *Economic History Review*, **60**(1): 97–135.

Cleary, M.C. (1989). *Peasants, Politicians and Producers*. New York: Cambridge University Press.

CNN (2001). "Bananas a Touchy Subject Between Europe and the Americas," Cable News Network Business, http://www.cnn.com/SPECIALS/2000/yourbusiness/stories/trade.war/index.html, last accessed July 28, 2008.

Coase, Ronald H. (1960). "The Problem of Social Cost," *Journal of Law and Economics*, **3**: 1–44.

Cochrane, Willard W. (1979). *The Development of American Agriculture: A Historical Analysis*. Minneapolis: University of Minnesota Press.

Cochrane, Willard W. (2003). *The Curse of American Agricultural Abundance: A Sustainable Solution*. Lincoln, NE: University of Nebraska Press.

Cockfield, Geoff and Linda C. Botterill (2007). "From the Australian Wheat Board to AWB Limited: Collective Marketing and Privatization in Australia's Export Wheat Trade," *Public Policy*, **2**(1): 44–57.

Cohen, Sarah (2007). "Deceased Farmers Got USDA Payments," *Washington Post*, July 23, page 1, section A.

Comstock, Gary, editor (1987). *Is there a Moral Obligation to Save the Family Farm?* Ames, IA: Iowa State University Press.

Cordain, L., J.B. Miller, S.B. Eaton, N. Mann, S.H. Holt and J.D. Speth (2000). "Plant-Animal Subsistence Ratios and Macronutrient Energy Estimations in Worldwide Hunter-Gatherer Diets," *American Journal of Clinical Nutrition*, **7**(1): 682–92.

CRS (2007). "Comparison of the House and Senate 2007 Farm Bills," Congressional Research Service, Washington, DC.

Darwin, Charles (2003, originally 1859). *The Origin of Species*. New York: Signet Classic, New American Library.

DATA (2007). "The DATA Report 2007," http://www.data.org/pdfs/DATAREPORt2007.pdf, last accessed July 28, 2008.

Davies, Daniel (2006). "Africa Does Not Need More Expensive Food," *The Guardian*, http://www.guardian.co.uk/commentisfree/2006/jul/26/dumpingdumping, last accessed July 28, 2008.

Davis, Christina L. (2003). *Food Fights Over Free Trade: How International Institutions Promote Agricultural Trade Liberalization.* Princeton, NJ: Princeton University Press.

De Gorter, Harry and Johan Swinnen (2002). "Political Economy of Agricultural Policy," in *Handbook of Agricultural Economics, Volume 2B: Agricultural and Food Policy*, edited by Bruce Gardner and Gordon Rausser. New York: Elsevier.

de Janvry, Alain and Elisabeth Sadoulet (1995). "NAFTA and Mexico's Maize Producers," *World Development*, 23(8): 1349–62.

Del Ninno, Carlo, Paul A. Dorosh and Kalanidhi Subbarao (2007). "Food Aid, Domestic Policy and Food Security: Contrasting Experiences from South Asia and Sub-Saharan Africa," *Food Policy*, 32(4): 413–35.

Department of Labor (2006). "Trade Adjustment Assistance Reform Act of 2002," U.S. Department of Labor, http://www.doleta.gov/tradeact/2002act_index.cfm, last accessed July 28, 2008.

Department of Statistics (New Zealand), *New Zealand Official Yearbook,* Auckland, various dates.

de Rato, Rodrigo (2005). "Cotton Producing Countries Need Urgent Assistance," *Le Figaro*, www.imf.org/external/np/vc/2005/062405.htm, last accessed July 28, 2008.

Diakosavvas, Dimitris (2003). "The Uruguay Round Agreement on Agriculture in Practice: How Open are OECD Markets?" in *Agriculture, Trade, and the WTO*, edited by Merlinda D. Ingco. Washington DC: The World Bank.

Diamond, Jared (1999). *Guns, Germs and Steel: The Fates of Human Societies.* New York: W. W. Norton & Company.

Diaz-Bonilla, Eugenio and Marcelle Thomas (2003). "Trade Liberalization, World Trade Organization and Food Security," in *Agriculture, Trade and the WTO: Creating a Trading Environment for Development*, edited by Merlinda D. Ingco. Washington, DC: The World Bank.

Dimaranan, Betina V., Thomas W. Hertel and Will Martin (2007). "Potential Gains from Post-Uruguay Round Trade Policy Reform: Impacts on Developing Countries," in *Reforming Agricultural Trade for Developing Countries: Quantifying the Impact of Multilateral Trade Reform* (Volume II), edited by Alex F. McCalla and John Nash. Washington, DC: The World Bank.

Dimitri, Carolyn, Anne Effland and Neilson Conklin (2005). "The 20th Century Transformation of U.S. Agriculture and Farm Policy," Economic Information Bulletin Number 3, Economic Research Service, USDA, Washington, DC.

Division for Sustainable Development, United Nations (2002). "Johannesburg Declaration on Sustainable Development " at www.un.org/esa/sustdev/docu ments/WSSD_POI_PD/English/POI_PD.htm, last accessed on July 28, 2008.

Dixon, John, Aidan Gulliver and David Gibbon (2001). *Farming Systems and Poverty.* Rome: Food and Agriculture Organization of the United Nations, and Washington, DC: The World Bank.

Dobyns, Henry F. (1983). *Their Number Become Thinned: Native American Population Dynamics in Eastern North America.* Knoxville, University of Tennessee Press.

Dolnick, Sam (2008). "Overwhelming Debt Drives Indian Farmers to Suicide," *The Seattle Times*, May 13.

Dorel, Gérard (1987). "High-Tech Farming Systems in Champagne, France: Change in Response to Agribusiness and International Controls," in *Comparative Farming Systems*, edited by B. L. Turner II and S. B. Brush. New York: Guilford Press.

Dos Santos, Theotonio (1970). "The Structure of Dependence," *American Economic Review*, **60**(2): 231–6.

Dugger, Celia W. (2007). "Oxfam Suggests Benefit in Africa if U.S. Cuts Cotton Subsidies," *New York Times*, June 21.

Duplessis, Robert S. (1997). *Transitions to Capitalism in Early Modern Europe.* New York: Cambridge University Press.

Edwards, Geoff (2003). "The Story of Deregulation in the Dairy Industry," *Australian Journal of Agricultural Economics*, **47**(1): 75–98.

Effland, Anne B. (2000). "U.S. Farm Policy: The First 200 Years," *Agricultural Outlook, March 2000*. Washington, DC: Economic Research Service, USDA.

Egaitsu, Fumio (1992). "Japanese Agricultural Policy: Unfair and Unreasonable?" in *Agriculture and Trade in the Pacific Rim: Towards the Twenty-First Century*, edited by William T. Coyle, Dermot Hayes and Hiroshi Yamauchi. Boulder, CO: Westview Press.

Elbehri, Aziz, Johannes Umstaetter and David Kelch (2008). "The EU Sugar Policy Regime and Implications of Reform," Economic Research Report No. ERR-59, Economic Research Service, USDA, Washington, DC.

Energy Information Administration. "International Petroleum Monthly," Department of Energy, http://www.eia.doe.gov/ipm/supply.html, last accessed July 28, 2008.

Engler, Mark (2007). "Anti-Globalization Movement," *Encyclopedia of Activism and Social Justice*. Thousand Oaks, CA: Sage Publications.

Elobeid, Amani and John Beghin (2006). "Multilateral Trade and Agricultural Policy Reforms in Sugar Markets," *Journal of Agricultural Economics*, **57**(1): 23–48.

ERS (1986). "Embargoes, Surplus Disposal and U.S. Agriculture," Agricultural Economic Report 564, Economic Research Service, USDA, Washington, D.C.

ERS (2008a). "2002 Farm Bill," Economic Research Service, USDA, http://www.ers. usda.gov/Features/farmbill/titles/ titleIcommodities.htm, last accessed July 29, 2008.

ERS (2008b). "Common Agricultural Policy," Economic Research Service, USDA, http://www.ers.usda.gov/Briefing/EuropeanUnion/PolicyCommon.htm, last accessed July 29, 2008.

ERS (2008c). "EU Commitments in the Uruguay Round Agreement on Agriculture," Economic Research Service, USDA, http://www.ers.usda.gov/Briefing/European Union/Policy/Uruguay.htm, last accessed July 29, 2008.

ERS (2008d). "Feedgrain Database, Yearbook Tables," Economic Research Service, USDA, http://www.ers.usda.gov/Data/feedgrains/StandardReports/YBtable4.htm, last accessed July 29, 2008.

ERS (2008e). "International Food Consumption Patterns," Economic Research Service, USDA, http://www.ers.usda.gov/data/InternationalFoodDemand/, last accessed July 29, 2008.

ERS (2008f). "South Korea Briefing Room: Policy," Economic Research Service, USDA, http:www.ers.usda.gov/Briefing/SouthKorea/policy.htm, last accessed July 29, 2008.

ERS/FATUS. "Foreign Agricultural Trade of the US (FATUS)," Economic Research Service, USDA, www.ers.usda.gov/Data/FATUS/index.htm#summary, last accessed July 29, 2008.

Etter, Lauren and Greg Hitt (2008). "Bountiful Harvest: Farm Lobby Beats Back Assault on Subsidies," *Wall Street Journal*, March 27, page A1.

Eurobarometer (2006). "Europeans and Biotechnology in 2005: Patterns and Trends," European Commission, Directorate-General for Agriculture and Rural Development, http://ec.europa.eu/public_opinion/archives/ebs/ebs_244b_en.pdf, last accessed July 28, 2008.

Eurobarometer (2007). "Europeans, Agriculture and the Common Agricultural Policy," European Commission, Directorate-General for Agriculture and Rural Development, http://ec.europa.eu/public_opinion/archives/ebs/ebs_276_sum_en.pdf, last accessed July 28, 2008.

Europa (2008a). "European Union Institutions and Other Bodies," http://europa.eu/institutions/index_en.htm, last accessed July 28, 2008.

Europa (2008b). "Democratic Deficit," Europa Glossary, http://europa.eu/scadplus/glossary/democratic_deficit_en.htm, last accessed July 28, 2008.

European Commission (various dates). *The Agricultural Situation in the Community*, annual issues from 1972 to 1993, *The Agricultural Situation in the European Union*, annual issues from 1994 to 2000, and *Agriculture in the European Union—Statistical and Economic Information*, annual issues from 2001 to 2006, published by the European Commission, Brussels, Belgium. After 2000, the data were obtained online at http://ec.europa.eu/agriculture/publi/agrep/index_en.htm, last accessed July 28, 2008.

European Commission (2004). "The Common Agricultural Policy Explained," European Commission Directorate General for Agriculture, October.

European Commission (2006a). "Agriculture in the European Union—Statistical and Economic Information 2006," http://ec.europa.eu/agriculture/agrista/2006/table_en/index.htm, last accessed July 29, 2008.

European Commission (2006b). *EU Policy on Biotechnology*, EU Environment DG. Luxembourg: Office for Official Publications of the European Communities.

European Commission (2007). "Direct Payments," Agriculture and Rural Development, http://ec.europa.eu/agriculture/markets/sfp/index_en.htm, last accessed July 29, 2008.

European Commission (2008a). "EU Budget 2008," EU Financial Programming and Budget, http://ec.europa.eu/budget/library/publications/budget_in_fig/dep_eu_budg_2008_en.pdf, last accessed July 29, 2008.

European Commission (2008b). "CAP Reform—A Long-term Perspective for Sustainable Agriculture," Agriculture and Rural Development, http://ec.europa.eu/agriculture/capreform/index_en.htm, last accessed July 29, 2008.

European Commission (2008c). "Development- Geographical Partnerships," http://ec.europa.eu/development/geographicalgen_en.cfm, last accessed July 29, 2008.

EWG (Environmental Working Group). "Farm Subsidy Database," www.ewg.org/farm/index.php, last accessed July 28, 2008.

EWG (2007). "Big Ag's $100 Million Energy Subsidy," by Renee Sharp and Bill Walker, http://www.ewg.org/reports/powersubsidies, last accessed on July 28, 2008.

Fabiosa, J.F., J.C. Beghin, F. Dong, A. Elobeid, F.H. Fuller, H. Matthey, S. Tokgoz and E. Wailes (2005). "The Impact of the European Enlargement and Common Agricultural Policy Reforms on Agricultural Markets: Much Ado about Nothing?" Center for Agriculture and Rural Development Working Paper 05-wp 382, Iowa State University, Ames.

FAO (no date). "Rice Liberalization: Predicting Trade and Price Impacts," FAO Trade Policy Briefs No. 12, Food and Agriculture Organization, Rome.

FAO (2002). "World Food Summit: Five Years Later Reaffirms Pledge to Reduce Hunger," Food and Agriculture Organization, Rome, htttp://www.fao.org/WorldFoodSummit/english/index.html, last accessed July 29, 2008.

FAO (2004). *The State of Agricultural Commodity Markets 2004 (SOCO)*, Food and Agriculture Organization, Rome, www.fao.org/docrep/fao/007/y5419e/y5419e00.pdf, last accessed July 29, 2008.

FAO (2006). *The State of Food Insecurity in the World, 2006*, Food and Agriculture Organization, Rome.

FAO (2008a). "Countries in Crisis Requiring External Assistance," http://www.fao.org/docrep/010/ai465e/ai465e02.htm, last accessed July 29, 2008.

FAO (2008b). "Initiative on Soaring Food Prices Now Covers 54 Countries," Food and Agriculture Organization, Rome, http://www.fao.org/newsroom/en/news/2008/1000877/index.htm, last accessed on July 29, 2008.

FAO (2008c). "Policy Measures Taken by Governments to Reduce the Impact of Soaring Prices," Food and Agriculture Organization, Rome, http://www.fao.or/giews/english/policy/index.htm, last accessed July 29, 2008.

FAO (2008d). "Soaring Food Prices: Facts, Perspectives, Impacts and Actions Required," Rome: FAO High-Level Conference on World Food Security, http://www.fao.org/fileadmin/user_upload/foodclimate/HLCdocs/HLC08-inf-1-E.pdf, last accessed July 29, 2008.

FAOSTAT. Agricultural Statistical Database, Food and Agriculture Organization, Rome, http://faostat.fao.org/site/.

FAPRI (2002). "The Doha Round of the World Trade Organization: Assessing Further Liberalization of Agricultural Markets," Working Paper 02-WP 317, Food and Agricultural Policy Research Institute, Iowa State, Ames, November.

Federico, Giovanni (2005). *Feeding the World: An Economic History of Agriculture, 1800–2000*. Princeton, NJ: Princeton University Press.

Fennell, Rosemary (1979). *The Common Agricultural Policy of the European Community*. London: Granada.

Fennell, Rosemary (1997). *The Common Agricultural Policy: Continuity and Change*. New York: Oxford University Press.

Figini, Paolo and Enrico Santarelli (2006). "Openness, Economic Reforms, and Poverty: Globalization in Developing Countries," *Journal of Developing Areas*, **39**(2): 129–51.

Fleming, G.A. (1999). "Agricultural Support Policies in a Small Open Economy: New Zealand in the 1920s," *Economic History Review*, **52**(2): 334–54.

FNS (Food and Nutrition Service, 2007). "A Short History of the Food Stamp Program," Food and Nutrition Service, USDA, Washington, DC, http://www.fns. usda/fsp/rules/Legislation/history/2002.htm, last accessed July 28, 2008.

Fogel, Robert William (2004). *The Escape from Hunger and Premature Death, 1700–2100*. New York: Cambridge University Press.

Fuglie Keith, Nicole Ballenger, Kelly Day, Cassandra Klotz, Michael Ollinger, John Reilly, Utpal Vasavada and Jet Lee (1996). "Agricultural Research and Development: Public and Private Investments under Alternative Markets and Institutions," Agricultural Economics Report No. AER 735, Economic Research Service, USDA, Washington, DC.

Fuglie, Keith O. and Paul W. Heisey (September 2007). "Economic Returns to Public Agricultural Research," EB-10, U.S. Department of Agriculture, Economic Research Service, Washington, DC.

Fulginiti, Lilyan E., Richard K. Perrin and Bingxin YU (2004). "Institutions and Agricultural Productivity in Sub-Saharan Africa," *Agricultural Economics*, **31**: 169–80.

GAO (1982). "Market Structure and Pricing Efficiency of U.S. Grain Export System," General Accounting Office, http://archive.gao.gov/f0102/118679.pdf, last accessed July 28, 2008.

GAO (2000). *Supporting Sugar Prices has Increased Users' Costs While Benefitting Producers*. Washington, DC: Government Accountability Office.

Gardner, Bruce L. (1985). *U.S. Agricultural Policy: The 1985 Farm Legislation*. Washington, DC: American Enterprise Institute for Public Policy Research.

Gardner, Bruce L. (1992). "Changing Economic Perspectives on the Farm Problem," *Journal of Economic Literature*, **XXX**: 62–101.

Gardner, Bruce L. (2002). *American Agriculture in the Twentieth Century*. Cambridge, MA: Harvard University Press.

Gawande, Kishore and Bernard Hoekman (2006). "Lobbying and Agricultural Trade Policy in the United States," *International Organization*, **60**: 527–61.

Gelhar, Mark and William Coyle (2001). "Global Food Consumption and Impacts on Trade Patterns," in *Changing Structure of Global Food Consumption and Trade* edited by Anita Regmi, Agriculture and Trade Report WRS-01-1, Washington DC: USDA.

Ghana Cocoa Marketing Company (2008). "Our History," http:www.cocoamarketing. com/50th_anniversary.php, last accessed July 28, 2008.

Gillson, Ian, Colin Poulton, Kevin Balcombe and Sheila Page (May 2004). "Understanding the Impact of Cotton Subsidies on Developing Countries," Overseas Development Institute Working Paper, www.odi.org.uk/iedg/Projects/ cotton_report.pdf, last accessed July 28, 2008.

Gilpin, Robert (2000). *The Challenge of Global Capitalism*. Princeton, NJ: Princeton University Press.

Glaser, Lawrene K. (1986). *Provisions of the Food Security Act of 1985*, Agriculture Information Bulletin No. 498, Economic Research Service, USDA, Washington, DC.

Glauber, Joseph W. (2004). "Crop Insurance Reconsidered," *American Journal of Agricultural Economics*, **86**(5): 1179–95.

Godoy, Julio (April 25, 2008). "Europe: Subsidies Feeding Food Scarcity," *Inter Press Service*, http://ipsnews.net/news.asp?idnews=42123, last accessed July 28, 2008.

Goldberg, P. K. and G. Maggi (1999). "Protection for Sale: An Empirical Investigation," *American Economic Review*, **89**(5): 1135–55.

Government Printing Office (2008). *Budget of the United States Government, Historical Tables*, http://www.gpoaccess.gov/usbudget/fy09/pdf/hist.pdf, last accessed July 28, 2008.

Greer, Alan (2005). *Agricultural Policy in Europe*. New York: Manchester University Press.

Griffin, Keith and John Gurley (1985). "Radical Analyses of Imperialism, the Third World, and the Transition to Socialism: A Survey Article," *Journal of Economic Literature*, **23**: 1089–43.

Grossman, Gene M. and Elhanan Helpman (1994). "Protection for Sale," *American Economic Review*, **84**(4): 833–50.

Hallberg, M.C. (1992). *Policy for American Agriculture: Choices and Consequences*. Ames, Iowa: Iowa State University Press.

Harden, Blaine (2008). "Assurances from Rice Fail to Sway S. Koreans," *The Washington Post*, June 29.

Hardin, Garrett (1968). "The Tragedy of the Commons," *Science*, **162**: 1243–8.

Harris, David and Allan Rae (2006). "Agricultural Policy Reform and Adjustment in Australia and New Zealand," in *Policy Reform and Adjustment in the Agricultural Sectors of Developed Countries*, edited by D. Blandford and B. Hill. Cambridge, MA: CAB International.

Harris, Marvin (1974). *Cows, Pigs, Wars and Witches: The Riddles of Culture*. New York: Random House.

Harris, Simon, Alan Swinbank and Guy Wilkinson (1983). *The Food and Farm Policies of the European Community*. New York: John Wiley and Sons.

Hartman, Stephen (2007). "Antitrust Law," *West's Encyclopedia of American Law*, West's Legal Directory Law Information Center, http://iris.nyit.edu/ shartman/ mba0101/trust.htm, last accessed July 28, 2008.

Hassett, Kevin A. and Robert Shapiro (2003). "How Europe Sows Misery in Africa," *The Washington Post*, June 22.

Hayami, Yujiro (2000). "Food Security: Fallacy or Reality?" in *Food Security in Asia: Economics and Policies*. Northampton, MA: Edward Elgar.

Hayami, Yujiro and Vernon W. Ruttan (1985). *Agricultural Development: An International Perspective*. Baltimore: Johns Hopkins University Press.

Hayenga, Marvin and Robert Wisner (2000). "Cargill's Acquisition of Continental Grain's Grain Merchandising Business," *Review of Agricultural Economics*, **22**(1): 252–66.

Heilbroner, Robert L. (1953). *The Worldly Philosophers*. New York: Simon and Schuster.

Henning, Christian H.C.A. (2004). "The Role of Institutions in Agricultural Protectionism," in *Role of Institutions in Rural Policies and Agricultural Markets*, edited by Guido van Huylenbroeck, Wim Verbeke and Ludwig Lauwers. Ghent, Belgium: European Association of Agricultural Economists 80th Seminar.

Hertel, Thomas W., editor (1999). *Global Trade Analysis: Modeling and Applications*. New York: Cambridge University Press.

Hertel, Thomas W. and Maros Ivanic (2006). "Making the Doha Development Agenda More Poverty-Friendly: The Role of South-South Trade," *Review of Agricultural Economics*, **28**(3): 354–61.

Hertel, Thomas W., Roman Keeney, Maros Ivanic and L. Alan Winters (2006). "Distributional Effects of WTO Agricultural Reforms in Rich and Poor Countries," Policy Research Working Paper 4060, Washington, DC: The World Bank.

Hightower, Jim (1978). *Hard Tomatoes, Hard Times: A Report of the Agribusiness Accountability Project on the Failure of America's Land Grant College Complex*. Rochester, Vermont: Schenkman Books.

Hirschman, Albert O. (1977). *The Passions and the Interests*. Princeton, NJ: Princeton University Press.

Hirschman, Albert O. (1991). *The Rhetoric of Reaction*. Cambridge, MA: Belknap Press of Harvard University Press.

Hobbes, Thomas (1988/1651). *The Leviathan* (reprint). Buffalo, NY: Prometheus Books.

Hobsbawm, Eric (1989). *The Age of Empire:1875–1914*. New York: Vintage Press.

Hobsbawm, Eric (1994). *The Age of Extremes: A History of the World, 1914–1991*. New York: Pantheon Books.

Hoekman, Bernard and Michel Kostecki (1995). *The Political Economy of the World Trading System: From GATT to WTO*. Oxford: Oxford University Press.

Honma, Masayoshi (2006). "WTO Negotiations and Other Agricultural Trade Issues in Japan," *World Economy*, **29**(6): 697–714.

Hopcroft, Rosemary L. (1999). *Regions, Institutions, and Agrarian Change*. Ann Arbor: University of Michigan Press.

Hoppe, Robert A. and David E. Banker (2006). "Structure and Finances of U.S. Farms: 2005 Family Farm Report," Economic Information Bulletin No. 12, Economic Research Service, USDA, Washington, http://www.ers.usda.gov/Publications/EIB12/, last accessed July 28, 2008.

Hoppe, Robert A., D.E. Banker, P. Korb, E.J. O'Donoghue and J.M. MacDonald (2007a). "America's Diverse Family Farms, 2007 Edition," Economic Information Bulletin 26, Economic Research Service, USDA, Washington, http://www.ers.usda.gov/publications/eib26/eib26.pdf, last accessed July 28, 2008.

Hoppe, Robert A., Penni Korb, Erik O'Donoghue and David Banker (2007b). "Structure and Finances of U.S. Farms: Family Farm Report, 2007 Edition," Economic Information Bulletin, EIB 24, Economic Research Service, USDA, Washington, DC.

Huff, H. Bruce, Ekaterina Krivonos and Dominique van der Mensbrugghe (2007). "Review and Synthesis of Empirical Results of Studies of World Trade Organization Agricultural Trade Reform," in *Reforming Agricultural Trade for Developing Countries: Quantifying the Impact of Multilateral Trade Reform* (Volume II), edited by Alex F. McCalla and John Nash. Washington, DC: The World Bank.

Imamura, Naraomi, Nobuhiro Tsuboi and Tokumi Odagiri (1993). "Japanese Farm Structure: Trends and Projections," in *Japanese and American Agriculture*, edited by Luther Tweeten, Cynthia Dishon, Wen Chern, Naraomi Imamura and Masaru Morishima. Boulder, CO: Westview Press.

IMF (1996). *International Financial Statistics Yearbook*. Washington, DC: International Monetary Fund.

IMF (2004). "The Cotton Sector Reform in Benin and the Subsidies by Major Producing Countries," in *Benin: Selected Issues and Statistical Appendix*, IMF Country Report No. 04/370. Washington, DC: International Monetary Fund.

IMF (2006). *International Financial Statistics Yearbook*. Washington, DC: International Monetary Fund.

IMF (2008). "Indices of Primary Commodity Prices, 1998–2008," http://www.imf.org/external/np/res/commod/index.asp, last accessed July 28, 2008.

Industry Canada (2008). "Canadian Trade by Industry," Trade Data On Line, http://www.ic.gc.ca/sc_mrkti/tdst/tdo/tdo.php?lang=308&productType=NAICS, last accessed July 28, 2008.

Infoplease. "Benin," http://www.infoplease.com/ipa/A0107337.html, last accessed July 28, 2008.

Ingco, Merlinda D. and John Croome (2004). "Trade Agreements: Achievements and Issues Ahead," in *Agriculture and the WTO*, edited by Merlinda D. Ingco and John D. Nash. Washington DC: The World Bank and Oxford University Press.

INNZ (2008). "New Zealand History," INNZ Travel Office, http://www.innz.co.nz/about/ history.html, last accessed July 28, 2008.

International Herald Tribune (2007). "Banana Trade Dispute Returns to Fore," Associated Press, March 8.

Irwin, Douglas A. (1996). *Against the Tide: An Intellectual History of Free Trade.* Princeton, NJ: Princeton University Press.

Ivanic, Maros and Will Martin (2008). "Implications of Higher Global Food Prices for Poverty in Low-Income Countries," Policy Research Working Paper 4594, The World Bank, Washington, DC.

Johnson, Bruce (2008). "Nebraska Farmland Values and Cash rents Rise Sharply," *Cornhusker Economics*, Department of Agricultural Economics, University of Nebraska, Lincoln, Nebraska.

Jones, Ronald W. and J. Peter Neary (1984). "The Positive Theory of International Trade," *Handbook of International Economics*, Vol. 1, edited by Ronald W. Jones and Peter B. Kenen. New York: North-Holland.

Kahan, Dan M., Paul Slovic, Donald Braman and John Gastil (2006). "Fear of Democracy: A Cultural Evaluation of Sunstein on Risk," *Harvard Law Review*, **119**.

Kako, Toshiyuki (2000). "Economic Development and Food Security Issues in Japan and South Korea," in *Food Security in Asia*, edited by Wen S. Chern, Colin A. Carter and Shun-Yi Shei. Northampton, MA: Edward Elgar.

Kalaitzandonakes, Nicholas G. (1994). "Price Protecting and Productivity Growth," *American Journal of Agricultural Economics*, **76**: 722–32.

Kang, Soo and Yoocheul Song (2004). "Liberalization of the Agricultural Sector in Northeast Asia: The Effects of the Doha Development Agenda," *Asian Economic Papers*, **3**(2): 99–122.

Kay, Adrian (1998). *The Reform of the Common Agricultural Policy: The Case of the MacSharry Reforms*. New York: CABI Publishing.

Kelley, Hubert W. (1990). *Keeping the Land Alive*. Rome: Food and Agriculture Organization of the United Nations.

Key, Nigel and Michael J. Roberts (2007). "Commodity Payments, Farm Business Survival and Farm Size Growth," Economic Research Report No. ERR-51, Economic Research Service, USDA, Washington, DC.

Kim, Hanho and Yong-Kee Lee (2006). "Agricultural Policy Reform and Structural Adjustment in Korea and Japan," *Policy Reform and Adjustment in the Agricultural Sectors of Developed Countries*, edited by D. Blandford and B. Hill. Cambridge, MA: CAB International.

Koh, Lian Pin and David S. Wilcove (2008). "Is Oil Palm Agriculture Really Destroying Tropical Biodiversity?" *Conservation Letters*, **1**: 60–4.

Konandreas, Panos and Ramesh Sharma (2000). "Net Food-Importing Developing Countries: Role and Perspectives," in *Negotiating the Future of Agricultural Policies: Agricultural Trade and the Millennium WTO Round*, edited by Sanouussi Bilal and Pavlos Pezaros. Boston: Kluwer Law International.

Korea.net (2007). "Protecting Korean Farmers Key Goal of FTA Talks with China," Korea.net News, http://www.korea.net/news/news/newsView.asp?serial_no=20071029006, last accessed July 29, 2008.

Krauss, Clifford (2008). "Gas Prices Send Surge of Riders to Mass Transit," *New York Times*, May 10.

Krugman, Paul and Maurice Obstfeld (2000). *International Economics: Theory and Policy*. New York: Addison-Wesley.

Lak, Daniel (2007). "Feeding the World: Is International Food Aid Working?" Canadian Broadcasting Corporation News, May 3, http://www.cbc.ca/news/background/international-aid/food-aid.html, last accessed July 29, 2008.

Lal, Padma and Rita Rashmi (2005). "Potential Impacts of EU Sugar Reform on the Fiji Sugar Industry," *Pacific Economic Bulletin*, **20**(3): 18–42.

Lamy, Pascal (2008). "Director General Lamy Calls for 'Serious Reflection' on the Next Steps," http://www.wto.org/english/new_e/news08_e/meet08_chair_30jul08_e.htm, last accessed July 30, 2008.

Larsen, Clark S. (2003). "Animal Source Foods to Improve Micronutrient Nutrition and Human Function in Developing Countries," American Society for Nutritional Sciences, *Journal of Nutrition*, 133: 3893S–3897S.

Legg, Wilfrid (2003). "Agricultural Subsidies: Measurement and Use in Policy Evaluation," *Journal of Agricultural Economics*, **54**(2): 175–201.

Lenin, V. I. (1996, originally 1916). *Imperialism: the Highest Stage of Capitalism*. New York: Pluto Press.

Lewis, W. Arthur (1953). "Economic Development with Unlimited Supplies of Labor," *Manchester School of Economic and Social Studies*, **22**: 239–91.

Lim, Song-Soo (2005). "Korea's Approach to Non-Trade Concerns in the World Trade Organization," *International Journal of Agricultural Resources, Governance and Ecology*, **4**(3–4): 292–305.

Lindbeck, Assar (2001). "The Sveriges Riksbank Prize in Economic Sciences in Memory of Alfred Nobel 19692007," http://nobelprize.org/nobel_prizes/ economics/articles/lindbeck/ index.html, last accessed July 29, 2008.

Lopez, Rigoberto A. (2001). "Campaign Contributions and Agricultural Subsidies," *Economics and Politics*, **13**(3): 257–79.

Lucas, David (2003). "World Population Growth," http://adsri.anu.edu.au/pubs/BAPS/ BAPSChap3.pdf, last accessed July 29, 2008.

Lynn, Stuart R. (2003). *Economic Development: Theory and Practice for a Divided World*. Upper Saddle River, NJ: Prentice Hall.

Maddison, Angus (2001). *The World Economy: A Millennial Perspective*, OECD Development Center. Paris: Organization for Economic Cooperation and Development (OECD).

MAFF (2008). "What is Multifunctionality of Agriculture?" Ministry of Agriculture, Forestry and Fisheries (Japan), http://www.maff.go.jp/soshiki/kambou/joutai/ onepoint/public/ta_me.html, last accessed July 29, 2008.

Mahé, Louis and Terry Roe (1996): "Political Economy of 1992 CAP Reform," *American Journal of Agricultural Economics*, **78**(5): 1314–23.

Martin, Andrew (2008). "Fuel Choices, Food Crises and Finger-Pointing," *New York Times*, April 15.

Martin, Will and Kym Anderson (2006). "The Doha Agenda Negotiations on Agriculture: What Could they Deliver?" *American Journal of Agricultural Economics*, **88**(5): 1211–18.

McCalla, Alex F. and John Nash (2007). *Reforming Agricultural Trade for Developing Countries: Key Issues for a Pro-Development Outcome* (Volume I); *Quantifying the Impact of Multilateral Trade Reform* (Volume II). Washington, DC: The World Bank.

McCorriston, Steve and Donald MacLaren (2007). "Deregulation as (Welfare Reducing) Trade Reform: The Case of the Australian Wheat Board," *American Journal of Agricultural Economics*, **89**(3): 637–50.

McMillan, Della E. (1995). *Sahel Visions: Planned Settlement and River Blindness Control in Burkina Faso*. Tucson: University of Arizona Press.

Mesbah, Motamed, Kenneth A. Foster and Wallace E. Tyner (2008). "Applying Cointegration and Error Correction to Measure Trade Linkages: Maize Prices in the United States and Mexico," *Agricultural Economics*, **39**(1): 29–39.

Meyerson, Christopher C. (2003). *Domestic Politics and International Relations in US-Japan Trade Policymaking: The GATT Uruguay Round Agriculture Negotiations*. New York: Palgrave Macmillan.

Ministère de l'Agriculture et de la Peche (2006). "La Consommation Alimentaire," Bimagri HS no. 18, January, http://agreste.agriculture.gouv.fr/IMG/pdf/bima2008n18.pdf, last accessed July 19, 2008.

Minot, Nicholas and Lisa Daniels (2002). "Impact of Global Cotton Markets on Rural Poverty in Benin," paper presented at the Northeast Universities Development Consortium Conference Program, October, Williams College, Williamstown, Massachusetts.

Mittal, Anuradha (2002). "Giving Away the Farm: The 2002 Farm Bill," *Backgrounder*, Food First, Institute for Food and Development Policy, vol. 3.

Mohanty, Samarendu (1995). *United States–Canada Wheat Trade Dispute: Some Additional Evidence*, PhD Dissertation, University of Nebraska-Lincoln, Lincoln, Nebraska.

Molinari Institute (2006). "About Market Anarchism," http://praxeology.net/anarcres.htm, last accessed July 29, 2008.

Morgan, Dan (1979). *Merchants of Grain*. New York: The Viking Press.

Morgan, Dan, Gilbert M. Gaul and Sarah Cohen (2006). "Farm Program Pays $3.1 Billion to People Who Don't Farm," *The Washington Post*, July 2, page A01.

MSN Encarta (2007). "Native Americans of North America," Microsoft Encarta Online Encyclopedia 2007, http://encarta.msn.com/encyclopedia_761570777/Native_Americans_of_North_America.html, last accessed July 29, 2008.

NASS (National Agricultural Statistics Service, 2005). "Agricultural Prices: 2004 Summary," NASS, USDA, Washington, DC.

NASS (National Agricultural Statistics Service, 2007). "Agricultural Prices: 2006 Summary," NASS, USDA, Washington, DC.

NEUROCJD (2008). "Table 4: Variant Creutzfeldt-Jakob Disease, Current Data (June 2008)," http://www.eurocjd.ed.ac.uk/vcjdworldeuro.htm, last accessed July 22, 2008.

New Statesman (June 20, 2005). "Farm Subsidies that Starve the World," http://www.globalpolicy.org/socecon/hunger/economy/2005/0620farmsubsidies.htm, last accessed July 29, 2008.

New York Times (2003). "The Rigged Trade Game," Editorial, July 20.

New York Times (2004). "Those Illegal Farm Subsidies," Editorial, April 28.

New York Times (2008). "Man-Made Hunger," Editorial, July 6.

Newman, Mark D., James Ladd, Mongi Boughzala and Badr Ben Amar (1989). "A Plan of Action for Tunisia's Cereal Sector: First Phase Report," Agricultural Marketing Improvement Strategies Project, Abt Associates, Washington, DC.

Nobel Foundation (1970). "Norman Borlaug: The Nobel Peace Prize 1970," http://nobelprize.org/nobel_prizes/peace/laureates/1970/borlaug-bio.html, last accessed July 29, 2008.

Norton, George W., Jeffrey Alwang and William A. Masters (2006). *The Economics of Agricultural Development: World Food Systems and Resource Use*. New York: Routledge.

Nozick, Robert (1974). *Anarchy, State and Utopia*. New York: Basic Books.

NPP (National Priorities Project, 2008). "The War in Iraq Costs," http://nationalpri orities.org/costofwar_home, last accessed July 29, 2008.

NPP (National Priorities Project, 2008a). "World Military Spending, 2005," http:// nationalpriorities.org/world_military_spending, last accessed July 29, 2008.

OECD (1987a). *National Policies and Agricultural Trade: Australia*. Paris: Organization for Economic Cooperation and Development.

OECD (1987b). *National Policies and Agricultural Trade: New Zealand*. Paris: Organization for Economic Cooperation and Development.

OECD (1995). *Agricultural Policy Reform and Adjustment in Japan*. Paris: Organization for Economic Cooperation and Development.

OECD (2001a). *Multifunctionality: Toward an Analytical Framework*. Paris: Organization for Economic Cooperation and Development.

OECD (2001b). *The Uruguay Round Agreement on Agriculture: An Evaluation of its Implementation in OECD Countries*. Paris: Organization for Economic Cooperation and Development.

OECD (2003). "Agricultural Policies in OECD Countries: A Positive Reform Agenda," Policy Brief (June 2003), http://www.oecd.org/dataoecd/27/43/2955711.pdf, last accessed July 30, 2008.

OECD (2006a). *Agricultural Policies in OECD Countries: Monitoring and Evaluation 2006*. Paris: Organization for Economic Cooperation and Development.

OECD (2006b). "Decoupling Agricultural Support from Production," Policy Brief, November 2006, www.oecd.org/dataoecd/5/54/37726496.pdf, last accessed July 30, 2008.

OECD (2007a). *Agricultural Policies in OECD Countries: Monitoring and Evaluation 2007*. Paris: Organization for Economic Cooperation and Development.

OECD (2007b). "Agricultural Policy and Trade Reform: The Impact on World Commodity Markets," *OECD Agriculture and Food*, **2007**(4): 1–102.

OECD (2008a). "Aid Statistics, Donor Aid Charts," Development Aid Committee (DAC), http://www.oecd.org/countrylist/ 0,3349,en_2649_34447_1783495_1_ 1_1_1,00.html, last accessed July 30, 2008.

OECD (2008b). "Methodology for the Measurement of Support and Use in Policy Evaluation," http://www.oecd.org/dataoecd/36/47/1937457.pdf, last accessed July 30, 2008.

OECD (2008c). *Producer and Consumer Support Estimates, OECD Database 1986-2007*, http://www.oecd.org/document/59/ 0,3343,en_2649_33773_39551355_1_ 1_1_1,00.html, last accessed July 30, 2008.

Ohnuki-Tierney, Emiko (2004). "Rice as Self: Japanese Identities through Time," *Education about Asia*, **9**(3): 4–9.

O'Keefe, S. J. and R. Lavendar (1989). "The Plight of Modern Bushmen," *Lancet*, July 29: 255–8.

Olper, Alessandro (1998). "Political Economy Determinants of Agricultural Protection Levels in EU Member States: An Empirical Investigation," *European Review of Agricultural Economics*, **25**(4): 463–87.

Olson, Elizabeth (1999). "World Trade Group Picking Up the Pieces from Seattle," *New York Times*, December 13.

Olson, Mancur (1971). *The Logic of Collective Action: Public Goods and the Theory of Groups*. Cambridge, MA: Harvard University Press.

Orden, David (2003). "U.S. Agricultural Policy: the 2002 Farm Bill and WTO Doha Round Proposal," TMD Discussion Paper N. 109, International Food Policy Research Institute, Washington DC.

Orden, David, Fuzhi Cheng, Hoa Nguyen, Ulrike Grote, Marcelle Thomas, Kathleen Mullen and Dongsheng Sun (2007). "Agricultural Producer Support Estimates for Developing Countries: Measurement Issues and Evidence from India, Indonesia, China and Vietnam," IFPRI Research Report 152, International Food Policy Research Center, Washington, DC, September.

Oxfam International (2002). "Cultivating Poverty: The Impact of US Cotton Subsidies on Africa," www.oxfam.org.uk/resources/policy/trade/downloads/bp30_cotton. htm, last accessed July 30, 2008.

Oxfam International (2003). "Dumping Without Borders: How U.S. Agricultural Policies are Desrtroying the Livelihoods of Mexican Corn Farmers," Oxfam Briefing Paper No. 50, http://www.oxfam.org.uk/resources/policy/trade/down-loads/bp50_corn.pdf, last accessed July 30, 2008.

Oxfam International (2005). "Food Aid or Hidden Dumping? Separating the Wheat from the Chaff," OXFAM Briefing Paper 71, www.oxfam.org.uk/resources/policy/trade/downloads/bp71_food_aid.pdf, last accessed July 30, 2008.

Oxfam International (2006). "G8 Subsidies Contributing to WTO Crisis," Oxfam Press Release, http://www.oxfam.org/en/news/pressreleases2006/pr060711_wto, last accessed July 30, 2008.

Oxfam International (2008). "Make Trade Fair Campaign," www.oxfam.org.uk/get_involved/ campaign/make_trade_fair/, last accessed July 30, 2008

Oxford Economic Forecasting (2006). "Trade Liberalization and CAP Reform in the EU," *Economic Outlook*, **30**(1): 11–23.

Paarlberg, Robert (2008). "The Real Food Crisis," *The Chronicle of Higher Education*, Section B, June 27.

Paine, Thomas (1997, originally 1776). *Common Sense*. Dover Thrift Editions, Mineola, New York: Dover Publications.

Palm, Cheryl A., Stephen Vosti, Pedro Sanchez, and Polly Eriksen (2005). *Slash-and-Burn Agriculture: The Search for Alternatives*. New York: Columbia University Press.

Pan, Suwen, Samarendu Mohanty, Don Ethridge and Mohamadou Fadiga (January 2004). "The Impacts of U.S. Cotton Programs on World Markets: An Analysis of Brazilian and African WTO Petition," CER# 04-02, Cotton Economics Research Institute, Texas Tech University, Lubbock.

Parker, William B. (1924). *The Life and Public Services of Justin Smith Morrill*. New York: Houghton Mifflin.

Pasour, E.C. and R.R. Rucker (2005). *Plowshares and Pork Barrels: The Political Economy of Agriculture*. Oakland, CA: The Independent Institute.

Pearson, Jonathan (2007). "RPCVs: Urgent Action Alert on the Farm Bill!" National Peace Corps Association, Washington, DC.

Perrin, Richard K. (2008). "Ethanol and Food Prices—A Preliminary Assessment," Agricultural Economics Department, University of Nebraska-Lincoln, http:// digitalcommons.unl. edu/ageconfacpub/48, last accessed July 29, 2008.

Peterson, E. Wesley F. (2001). *The Political Economy of Agricultural, Natural Resource and Environmental Policy Analysis*. Ames, Iowa: Iowa State University Press.

Pokrivcak, Jan and Johan Swinnen (2003). "Decision-Making on the Common Agricultural Policy of the EU: The Influence of the European Commission," in *The Role of Institutions in Rural Policies and Agricultural Markets* edited by Guido van Huylenbroeck, Wim Verbeke and Ludwig Landers. Amsterdam: Elsevier.

Pollan, Michael (2006). *The Omnivore's Dilemma*. New York: Penguin.

Pollan, Michael (2007). "Weed it and Reap," Op-Ed Contribution, *New York Times*, November 4.

Preto, Ribeirao (2008). "Lean, Green and Not Mean," *The Economist*, June 28.

Pringle, Heather (1998). "The Slow Birth of Agriculture," *Science*, 282: 1446–53.

Rappaport, Roy A. (1979). "Ritual Regulation and Environmental Relations among a New Guinea People" in *Ecology, Meaning and Religion*. Berkeley, CA: North Atlantic Books.

RAN (May 23, 2008). "Rainforest Action Network Protests Bunge Shareholder Meeting," Press Release, Rainforest Action Network, http://ran.org/media_ center/news_article/?uid=4762, last accessed July 29, 2008.

Razi, Zvi (1986). Book Review of *The Control of Late Ancient and Medieval Population*, *American Historical Review*, **91**(2): 369–70.

Redclift, M.R., J.N. Lekakis and G.P. Zanias, editors (1999). *Agriculture and World Trade Liberalization: Socio-Environmental Perspectives on the Common Agricultural Policy*. New York: CAB International.

Reisner, Marc (2001). *Cadillac Desert*. New York: Pimlico.

Reuters, "Katrina Cost $40 bln–$55 bln, Consultant Group Says," Reuters News Agency,October6,http://today.reuters.com/business/newsarticle.aspx?type=ousiv&stor, last accessed October 27, 2005.

Robbins, Lionel (1932), *An Essay on the Nature and Significance of Economic Science*. London: Macmillan.

Roberts, Michael J., Nigel Key and Erik O'Donoghue (2006). "Estimating the Extent of Moral Hazard in Crop Insurance Using Administrative Data," *Review of Agricultural Economics*, **28**(3): 381–90.

Roemer, John E. (1988). *Free to Lose*. Cambridge, MA: Harvard University Press.

Ronen, Dov (1975). *Dahomey: Between Tradition and Modernity*. Ithaca, NY: Cornell University Press.

Rosegrant, Mark W. and Siet Meijer (2007). "Projecting the Effects of Agricultural Trade Liberalization on Trade, Prices and Economic Benefits," in *Reforming Agricultural Trade for Developing Countries: Quantifying the Impact of*

Multilateral Trade Reform (Volume II), edited by Alex F. McCalla and John Nash. Washington, DC: The World Bank.

Rosenthal, Elisabeth (2008). "Europe, Cutting Biofuel Subsidies, Redirects Aid to Stress Greenest Options," *New York Times*, January 22.

Runge, C. Ford, Benjamin Senauer, Philip Pardy and Mark Rosegrant (2003). *Ending Hunger in Our Lifetime: Food Security and Globalization*. Baltimore: Johns Hopkins University Press.

Sachs, Jeffrey D. (2005). *The End of Poverty: Economic Possibilities for Our Time*. New York: Penguin.

Samuelson, Paul A. (1954). "The Pure Theory of Public Expenditure," *Review of Economics and Statistics*, **36**(4): 387–9.

Samuelson, Robert J. (2006). "The Great Depression," in *The Concise Encyclopedia of Economics*, The Library of Economics and Liberty, http://www.econlib.org/library/Enc/Great Depression.html, last accessed July 29, 2008.

Sang-Hun, Choe (2008). "Korean Leader Considers Ways to Rework Government," *New York Times*, June 11.

Schmitz, Andrew, Troy G. Schmitz and Frederick Rossi (2006). "Agricultural Subsidies in Developed Countries: Impact on Global Welfare," *Review of Agricultural Economics*, **28**(3): 416–25.

Schultz, Theodore W. (1964). *Transforming Traditional Agriculture*. Chicago: University of Chicago Press.

Schuman, Michael (2005). "Of Rice and Men," *Time Magazine*, November 20, http://www.time.com/time/printout/0,8816,1132869,00.html, last accessed July 29, 2008.

Scrimgeour, F.G. and E.C. Pasour (1996). "A Public Choice Perspective on Agricultural Policy Reform: Implications of the New Zealand Experience," *American Journal of Agricultural Economics*, **78**: 257–67.

Seale, James, Anita Regmi and Jason Bernstein (2003). "International Evidence on Food Consumption Patterns," Technical Bulletin No. 1904, ERS/USDA, Washington, DC.

Sengupta, Somini (2006). "On India's Farms, a Plague of Suicide," *New York Times*, September 19.

Shepherd, Ben (2004). "The Impact of US Subsidies on the World Cotton Market: A Reassessment," Institut d'Etudes Politiques de Paris, Paris.

Shiva, Vandana (April 5, 2004). "The Suicide Economy of Corporate Globalization," http://www.countercurrents.org/glo-shiva050404.htm, last accessed July 22, 2008.

Skees, Jerry R. (2001). "The Bad Harvest: Crop Insurance Reform has become a Good Idea Gone Awry," *Regulation*, **24**(1): 16–21.

Slow Food (2008). "Slow Food International," http://www.slowfood.com, last accessed July 29, 2008.

Smith Adam (1776/1976). *An Inquiry into the Nature and Causes of the Wealth of Nations*. Reprint, Chicago: University of Chicago Press.

Smith, William (2006). "Agricultural Policies and Rural Development without Subsidies: New Zealand," *Coherence of Agricultural and Rural Development Policies*, OECD, Paris.

Sombilla, Mercedita A. and Mahabub Hossain (2000). "Rice and Food Security in Asia: A Long-Term Outlook," in *Food Security in Asia*, edited by Wen S. Chern, Colin A. Carter and Shun-Yi Shei. Northampton, MA: Edward Elgar.

Spiegel Online (2006). "EU Subsidies Fatten the Rich," Spiegel Online, May 26, http://www.spiegel.de/international/0,1518,druck-418216,00.html, last accessed July 29, 2008.

Stauffer, Nancy (2007). "MIT Ethanol Analysis Confirms Benefits of Biofuels," http://web. mit.edu/newsoffice/2007/ethanol.html, last accessed July 29, 2008.

Steenblik, Ronald (2007). "Biofuels—At What Cost?" Global Subsidies Initiative, International Institute for Sustainable Development, Geneva, http://www.global-subsidies.org/files/assets/oecdbiofuels.pdf, last accessed July 29, 2008.

Stevens, Robert D. and Cathy L. Jabara (1988). *Agricultural Development Principles*. Baltimore: Johns Hopkins University Press.

Stewart, Matthew (2006). *The Courtier and the Heretic: Leibniz, Spinoza, and the Fate of God in the Modern World*. New York: W.W. Norton.

Stiglitz, Joseph (1998). "The Private Uses of Public Interests: Incentives and Institutions," *Journal of Economic Perspectives*, **12**(2): 3–22.

Stiglitz, Joseph (2003). *Globalization and its Discontents*. New York: W.W. Norton.

Stockbridge, Michael (2006). "Agricultural Trade Policy in Developing Countries During Take-Off," Oxfam GB Research Report, http://oxfam.org/en/policy/stockbridge_trade_report/downloads, last accessed July 29, 2008.

Streitfeld, David (2005). "Hurricanes Show Shortcomings of Private Insurance," *Los Angeles Times*, October 6, http://news.cincypost.com/apps/pbcs.d11/article?AID=/20051006/BI, last accessed October 27, 2005.

Sumner, Daniel A. (2008). "Annex I: Effects of U.S. Upland Cotton Subsidies on Upland Cotton Prices and Quantities," http://aic.ucdavis.edu/research1/Sumner_WTO_Cotton.pdf, last accessed July 29, 2008.

Sumner, Daniel A. "Quantitative Simulation Analysis of the Impacts of U.S. Cotton Subsidies on Cotton Prices and Quantities," http://www.mre.gov.br/portugues/ministerio/sitios_ secretaria/cgc/analisequantitativa.pdf, last accessed July 29, 2008.

Sunstein, Cass R. (2005). *Laws of Fear: Beyond the Precautionary Principle*. New York: Cambridge University Press.

Takashi, Shingyoji, Otsuka Eiichi, Kaneko Fuminori and Matsumaru Tsuneo (2006). "Determining the Source of Nitrate Contamination Through Monitoring of Geochemistry and the Delta 15 N Value in Springs of the Shimousa Upland Area," *Bulletin of the Chiba Prefectural Agricultural Research Center*, **5**: 95–103.

Tangermann, Stefan (1994). "An Assessment of the Agreement on Agriculture," in *The New World Trading System: Readings*, papers presented at a workshop in Paris, April 1994, OECD Documents, Paris.

Tangermann, Stefan (2005). "Is the Concept of the Producer Support Estimate in Need of Revision?" *OECD Food, Agriculture and Fisheries Working Papers*, No. 1,

Paris: OECD Publishing, http://www.oecd.org/dataoecd/6/49/35091989.pdf, last accessed July 29, 2009.

Thakurta, Paranjoy Guha (July 27, 2006). "Rare Unity Against the West's Farm Subsidies," *Inter Press Service*, http://ipsnews.net/news.asp?idnews=34116, last accessed July 29, 2008

Thaler, Richard H. (1994). *The Winner's Curse: Paradoxes and Anomalies of Economic Life*. Princeton, NJ: Princeton University Press.

The Cairns Group (2008). http://www.cairnsgroup.org, last accessed July 29, 2008.

The Economist (May 20, 2006). "The Battle for Latin America's Soul," Leader.

The Economist (December 8, 2007). "The End of Cheap Food," Leader.

The Economist (May 31, 2008). "The Doha Dilemma," p. 82.

The Economist (July 24, 2008). "Et Tu Julio?" pp. 43–4.

The Economist (August 2, 2008). "So Near and Yet So Far," p. 14.

Thompson, Paul B. (1988). "The Philosophical Rationale for U.S. Agricultural Policy," in *U.S. Agriculture in a Global Setting*, edited by M. Ann Tutwiler. Washington, DC: National Center for Food and Agricultural Policy, Resources for the Future.

Thompson, Wyatt, Garry Smith and Armelle Elasri (2007). "The Medium-Term Impacts of Trade Liberalization in OECD Countries on the Food Security of Nonmember Economies," in *Reforming Agricultural Trade for Developing Countries, Volume 2*, edited by Alex F. McCalla and John Nash. Washington, DC: The World Bank.

Thu, Kendall M. and E. Paul Durrenberger, editors (1998). *Pigs, Profits and Rural Communities*. Albany, NY: State University of New York Press.

Timmons, Heather (2008). "Indians Find U.S. at Fault in Food Cost," *New York Times*, May 14.

Trabich, Leah (1997). "Native American Genocide Still Haunts United States," *An End to Intolerance*, Vol. 5 (June), Holocaust/Genocide Project, http://www.iearn.org/hgp/aeti/aeti-1997/native-americans.html, last accessed July 29, 2008.

Tracy, Michael (1989). *Government and Agriculture in Western Europe, 1880–1988*. New York: Harvester Wheatsheaf.

Trebeck, David (2002). "Must the Good Guys Always Lose?" *Policy*, **18**(2): 13–18.

Tutuola, Amos (1953). *The Palm-Wine Drinkard and his Dead Palm-Wine Tapster in the Dead's Town*. New York: Grove Press.

Tyson Foods. "About Tyson," http://www.tyson.com/Corporate/AboutTyson, last accessed July 29, 2008.

UEMOA. "Union économique et monétaire ouest-africaine," www.izf.net/IZF/FicheIdentite/ UEMOA.htm, last accessed on June 23, 2006.

Unctad (2008). "Marketing Boards," United Nations Committee on Trade and Development (Unctad), http://www.unctad.org/infocomm/anglais/cocoa/chain.htm#offices, last accessed July 29, 2008.

UNDP (2005). *Human Development Report 2005*. New York: United Nations Development Program.

UNDP (2008). *Human Development Report 2007/08*. New York: Palgrave Macmillan.

United Nations (2003). *World Statistics Pocketbook: Small Island Developing Countries*, Statistics Division, Department of Economic and Social Affairs, United Nations, New York.

United Nations (2008). "Definition of Major Areas and Regions," http://esa.un.org/migration/index.asp?panel=3, last accessed July 29, 2008.

U.S. Census Bureau (1975). *Historical Statistics of the United States, Colonial Times to 1970*. Washington, DC: U.S. Government Printing Office.

U.S. Census Bureau (2008). *The 2008 Statistical Abstract of the United States*. Washington, DC: U.S. Government Printing Office.

U.S. Congress (1862). "An Act Donating Public Lands to the Several States and Territories Which May Provide Colleges for the Benefit of Agriculture and Mechanic Arts." Washington, DC: U.S. Government Printing Office.

U.S. Congress (2008). "Food, Conservation, and Energy Act of 2008," House-Senate Conference Report, 110th Congress, Washington, DC.

USDA (2007). "USDA's 2007 Farm Bill Proposals," USDA Fact Sheet, Release No. 0019.07, Washington, DC.

USTR (2006). "United States—Continued Suspension of Obligations in the EC—Hormones Dispute: Comments of the United States on the Responses of Scientific Experts," Office of the U.S. Trade Representative (USTR), Washington, DC.

USTR (2008). "Trade Agreements," Office of the U.S. Trade Representative (USTR), Washington DC, http://www.ustr.gov/Trade_Agreements/Section_Index.html, last accessed July 29, 2008.

van der Mennsbrugghe, Dominique and John C. Beghin (2004). "Global Agricultural Liberalization: An In-Depth Assessment of What is at Stake," Working Paper 04-WP 370, Center for Agricultural and Rural Development, Iowa State University, http://www.card.iastate.edu/publications/DBS/PDFFiles/04wp370.pdf, last accessed July 29, 2008.

van der Mennsbrugghe, Dominique and John C. Beghin (2005). "Global Agricultural Reform: What is at Stake?" in *Global Agricultural Trade and Developing Countries,* edited by M. Aataman Aksoy and John C. Beghin. Washington, DC: The World Bank.

van der Mennsbrugghe, Dominique, John C. Beghin and Don Mitchell (2003). "Modeling Tariff Rate Quotas in a Global Context: The Case of Sugar Markets in OECD Countries," Working Paper 03-WP 343, Center for Agricultural and Rural Development, Iowa State University, http://www.card.iastate.edu/publications/DBS/PDFFiles/03wp343.pdf, last accessed July 29, 2008.

Vanzetti, David and Els Wynen (2004). "The 'Multifunctionality' of Agriculture and its Implications for Policy," in *Agriculture and the WTO*, edited by Merlinda D. Ingco and John D. Nash. Washington, DC: World Bank.

Vanzetti, David and Ramesh Sharma (2007). "Projecting the Effects of Agricultural Trade Liberalization on Developing Countries Using the ATPSM Partial Equilibrium Model," in *Reforming Agricultural Trade for Developing Countries: Quantifying the Impact of Multilateral Trade Reform* (Volume II), edited by Alex F. McCalla and John Nash. Washington, DC: The World Bank.

Vigneri, Marcella and Paul Santos (2007). "Ghana and the Cocoa Marketing Dilemma: What has Liberalization without Price Competition Achieved?" ODI Project Briefing No. 3. London: Overseas Development Institute.

Vlasic, Bill (2008). "As Gas Costs Soar, Buyers Flock to Small Cars," *New York Times*, May 2.

Vogel, David (1995). *Trading Up: Consumer and Environmental Regulation in a Global Economy*. Cambridge, MA: Harvard University Press.

Voigtländer, Nico and Hans-Joachim Voth (2007). "The Three Horsemen of Growth: Plague, War and Urbanization in Early Modern Europe," http://emlab.berkeley.edu/users/webfac/cromer/e211_f07/nico.pdf, last accessed July 29, 2008.

Wailes, Eric, Kenneth Young and Gail Cramer (1993). "Rice and Food Security in Japan: An American Perspective," in *Japanese and American Agriculture*, edited by Luther Tweeten, Cynthia Dishon, Wen Chern, Naraomi Imamura and Masaru Morishima. Boulder, CO: Westview Press.

Washington Post (2007). "The Fat of the Land: Whom to Help – Wealthy Cotton Farmers or Just About Everyone Else?" Editorial, June 24.

Washington Post (2008). "Farm Bill Update: Harvesting More Cash," April 10.

Weisdorf, Jacob L. (2003). "From Foraging to Farming: Explaining the Neolithic Revolution," Discussion Paper 03-41, Institute of Economics, University of Copenhagen.

Weisman, Steven R. (2007), "Bush and Democrats in Accord on Trade Deals," *New York Times*, May 11, http://www.nytimes.com/2007/05/11/business/11trade.html, last accessed July 29, 2008.

Westebbe, Richard (1994). "Structural Adjustment, Rent Seeking, and Liberalization in Benin," in *Economic Change and Political Liberalization in Sub-Saharan Africa*, edited by Jennifer A. Widner. Baltimore: Johns Hopkins University Press.

WFP (2008a). "An Analysis to Identify 30 Countries Highly Vulnerable to Increased Food Commodity and Fuel Prices," WFP Global Vulnerability Index. Rome: World Food Program, United Nations.

WFP (2008b). "WFP's Operational Requirements, Shortfalls and Priorities for 2008." Rome: World Food Program, United Nations.

White, Jr., Lynn (1962). *Medieval Technology and Social Change*. New York: Oxford University Press.

WHO (2008). *World Health Statistics 2008*. Geneva: World Health Organization, United Nations.

Widner, Jennifer A. (1994). "Introduction," in *Economic Change and Political Liberalization in Sub-Saharan Africa*, edited by Jennifer A. Widner. Baltimore: Johns Hopkins University Press.

Winters, L. Alan (2005). "The European Agricultural Trade Policies and Poverty," *European Review of Agricultural Economics*, **32**(3): 319–46.

Winters, L. Alan, Neil McCulloch and Andrew McKay (2004). "Trade Liberalization and Poverty: The Evidence So Far," *Journal of Economic Literature*, **42**(1): 72–115.

Wise, Timothy A. (2004). "The Paradox of Agricultural Subsidies: Measurement Issues, Agricultural Dumping, and Policy Reform," Global Development and Environment Institute Working Paper No. 04-02, Tufts University, Medford, MA.

Wittfogel, Karl (1981). *Oriental Despotism: A Comparative Study of Total Power.* New York: Vintage Books.

World Bank (1982). *World Development Report 1982.* New York: Oxford University Press.

World Bank (1986). *World Development Report 1986.* New York: Oxford University Press.

World Bank (1990). *World Tables, 1989–90 Edition.* Baltimore: Johns Hopkins University Press.

World Bank (2002). *Cotton Policy Brief,* www.worldbank.org/afr/cotton, last accessed July 30, 2008.

World Bank (2004). "Celebrating the Bretton Woods Institutions: The Founding Fathers," http://external.worldbankimflib.org/Bwf/60panel3.htm, last accessed July 30, 2008.

World Bank (2008a). *Country Brief: Guinea,* www.worldbank.org/WBSITE/EXTERNAL/COUNTRIES/AFRICA/GUINEAEXTN/0,menuPK:351805~pagePK:141132~piPK:1411907~theSitePK:351795,00.html, last accessed July 30, 2008.

World Bank (2008b). "Key Development Data and Statistics," http://www.worldbank.org/WBSITE/EXTERNAL/DATASTATISTICS/0,contentMDK:20535285~menuPK:1192694~pagePK:64133150~piPK:641331~theSitePK:239419,00.html, last accessed July 30, 2008.

World Bank (2008c). "Overview," PovertyNet, http://web.worldbank.org/WBSITE/EXTERNAL/TOPICS/EXTPOVERTY/0,contentMDK:20153855~menuPK:373757~pagePK:148956~piPK:216618~theSitePK:336992,00.html, last accessed July 30, 2008.

World Bank (2008d). "Rising Food Prices: Policy Options and World Bank Response," World Bank Information Note, http:siteresources.worldbank.org/NEWS/Resources/risingfoodprices_backgroundnote_apr08.pdf, last accessed July 30, 2008.

World Bank (2008e). *World Development Report 2008: Agriculture for Development.* Washington, DC: World Bank Publications.

World Public Opinion (2007). "U.S. Public at Odds with Government Policy on Farm Subsidies," http://www.worldpublicopinion.org/incl/printable_version.php?pnt=83, last accessed July 29, 2008.

World Socialist Party (2006). "The Market System Must Go!," http://www.worldsocialism.org/ spgb/pdf/go!.pdf, last accessed July 29, 2008.

Worster, Donald (1985). *Rivers of Empire.* New York: Pantheon Books.

WTO (1998). *Trade Policy Review, Republic of Benin, 1997.* Geneva: World Trade Organization.

WTO (2007). *International Trade Statistics 2007,* http://www.wto.org/english/res_e/statis_e/its2007_e/its07_toc_e.htm, last accessed July 30, 2008.

WTO (2008), *International Trade Statistics 2008.* http://www.wto.org/english/res_e/statis_e/its2008_e/its08_toc_e.htm, last accessed November 20, 2008.

WTO (2008a). "Agreement on Agriculture," in *A Summary of the Final Act of the Uruguay Round,* http://www.wto.org/english/docs_e/legal_e/ursum_e.htm#aAgreement, last accessed July 30, 2008.

WTO (2008b). "Cotton Initiative," www.wto.org/english/tratop_e/agric_e/negs_ bkgrnd20_cotton_ e.htm, last accessed July 30, 2008.

WTO (2008c). "Dispute Settlement: Dispute DS267, United States Subsidies on Upland Cotton," http://www.wto.org/English/tratop_e/dispu_e/cases_e/ds267_e. htm, last accessed July 30, 2008.

WTO (2008d). " European Communities—Measures Concerning Meat and Meat Products (Hormones)," http://www.wto.org/english/tratop_e/dispu_e/cases_e/ ds26_e.htm, last accessed July 30, 2008.

WTO (2008e). " 'Non-Trade' Concerns: Agriculture can Serve Many Purposes," Agriculture Negotiations Backgrounder, http://www.wto.org/english/tratop_e/ agric_e/negs_bkgrnd17_ agri_e.htm, last accessed July 30, 2008.

WTO (2008f). "Non-Trade Concerns and Multifunctionality," Agriculture Negotiations Backgrounder, http://www.wto.or/english/tratop_e/agric_e/negs_bkgrnd10_nontrade_ e.htm, last accessed July 30, 2008.

WTO (2008g). "Regional Trade Agreements," www.wto.org/english/tratop_e/region_e/ region_e.htm, last accessed July 30, 2008.

WTO (2008h). "Standards and Safety," in *Understanding the WTO: The Agreements*, http://www.wto.org/english/thewto_e/whatis_e/tif_e/agrm4_e.htm, last accessed July 30, 2008.

WTO (2008i). "Trade and Environment," http://www.wto.org/english/tratop_e/ envir_e/envir_e.htm, last accessed July 30, 2008.

WTO (2008j). "United States Continued Suspension of Obligations in EC—Hormones Dispute: Request for Consultations by the European Communities," http://www. wto.org/english/ tratop_e/dispu_e/cases_e/ds320_e.htm, last accessed July 30, 2008.

WTO (2008k). "Work on Special and Differential Provisions," http://www.wto.org/ english/ tratop_e/devel_e/dev_special_differential_provisions_e.htm, last accessed July 30, 2008.

Yamaji, Susumu and Shoichi Ito (1993). "The Political Economy of Rice in Japan," in *Japanese and American Agriculture*, edited by Luther Tweeten, Cynthia Dishon, Wen Chern, Naraomi Imamura and Masaru Morishima. Boulder, CO: Westview Press.

Yoshioka, Yutaka (1992). "Development of Agricultural Policy in Postwar Japan," in *Agriculture and Trade in the Pacific Rim: Towards the Twenty-First Century*, edited by William T. Coyle, Dermot Hayes and Hiroshi Yamauchi. Boulder, CO: Westview Press.

Zepp-LaRouche, Helga (May 16, 2008). "Instead of Wars of Starvation, Let Us Double Food Production!" *Executive Intelligence Report*, Washington, DC: Schiller Institute.

Index